THE SECURITY ARCHIPELAGO

Social Text books
Edited for the collective by Brent Edwards, Randy Martin,
Andrew Ross, and Ella Shohat

THE

SECURITY ARCHIPELAGO

Human-Security States, Sexuality Politics,

and the End of Neoliberalism

Paul Amar

Duke University Press   Durham and London   2013

© 2013 Duke University Press
All rights reserved
Printed in the United States of America on acid-free paper ∞
Designed by Courtney Leigh Baker
Typeset in Whitman and Trade Gothic by Tseng Information Systems, Inc.
Library of Congress Cataloging-in-Publication Data
Amar, Paul (Paul Edouard), 1968–
The security archipelago ; human-security states,
sexuality politics, and the end of neoliberalism / Paul Ama.
pages — (Social text books)
Includes bibliographical references and index.
ISBN 978-0-8223-5384-3 (cloth : alk. paper) —
ISBN 978-0-8223-5398-0 (pbk. : alk. paper)
1. Human security—Brazil—Rio de Janeiro. 2. Human
security—Egypt—Cairo. 3. Sex—Political aspects—
Brazil—Rio de Janeiro. 4. Sex—Political aspects—Egypt—
Cairo. 5. Neoliberalism. I. Title. II. Series: Social text books.
JC599.B72R53 2013
362.83′561096216—dc23
2013009709

Contents

Acknowledgments

The trip from my hometown — Middletown, Kentucky — to here has been an adventure. Since this is my first solo book, I will take this opportunity to look back and trace a broader timeline of influences and moments, and to recognize the debts I owe to a number of individuals who shaped this book's research questions and methods — and my professional development — along the way.

My intellectual journey began at Duke University, where I encountered bold new ways of knowing. There, I soaked up the lectures of Fredric Jameson, Ariel Dorfman, and Eve Sedgwick, and was generously advised in my first research projects by Jan Radway. I am forever indebted to miriam cooke for those years of 8:00 AM Arabic lessons, which illuminated new worlds of literature and gender theory, and that transformative summer study trip to Morocco. My undergraduate education also led me to Paris, where I pursued my training in anthropology at L'Université de Paris VII (Jussieu) and international relations and comparative politics at l'Institut d'Études Politiques, under the guidance of the late Rémy Leveau. I am so grateful to this master teacher.

After immersing myself in the Arab activist and artist community in Paris, I decided to use my savings to go off to Egypt to study acting and film directing at the Giza High Institute of Cinema. I adored Egypt's revolutionary socialist cinema of the 1960s, and its musicals of the 1940s. I moved into an apartment in al-Batniyya — the poorest (and funkiest) margin of the popular quarters of Cairo. Many thanks to Umm Hamoksha, the late Sheikh Mohammad 'Ersa, and especially Hussein Sayyid for welcoming me to adDarb alAhmar and integrating me into the community. After taking a few film classes and working on set with Amr Diab in the musical-comedy classic *Ice Cream fi Gleem*, I began working as a freelance journalist for the *Cairo Times*. The team at the *Times* helped me hone my investigative research skills.

I am so grateful to Khaled Fahmy, Gasser Abdel-Razek, Dina El Khawaga, and Sandrine Gamblin, whom I met early in this period in Egypt and whose conviction, political savvy, and vision inspired me to go on to graduate school. I began studying Arabic literature at the American University in Cairo (AUC), and am profoundly grateful to the Center for Arabic Studies Abroad program that enabled me to acquire fluency in Arabic and Egyptian colloquial. Those twelve months at AUC were a time to meet wonderful friends—Jillian Schwedler, Agniezska Paczynska, Carrie Johnson, Adrea Akel, Kouros Esmaili, Julia Elyachar, and the forever-young Anthony Shadid, who died at the height of his phenomenal journalistic career. During those years, I took a seminar class with Nawal Al-Saadawi, whose energy animated my initial research adventures. Khaled Fahmy passed me a copy of Timothy Mitchell's *Colonizing Egypt* on the beach at Basata in the Sinai. After devouring the book, I said, "If this is political science, then sign me up!" I set aside my fantasy of acting in Arabic musical cinema and turned my sights to New York City, where Mitchell had joined the faculty of New York University (NYU).

When I returned, later on, to Cairo for two years of dissertation research and writing, I was supported by the Fulbright Commission in Egypt and the Centre d'Études et de Documentation Économiques, Juridiques et Sociales. I would like to thank the Cairo University faculty of Economics and Political Science, and Professor Mustapha Kamel ElSayyid at the Center for Developing Country Studies, where I was affiliated during my research, for their hospitality and guidance. I am deeply grateful to Naz Modirzadeh, Amr Shalakani, Mona Abaza, Diane Singerman, Asef Bayat, and my inspiring friends Mozn Hassan and Amr Abdelrahman for their ideas as I entered the last phase of Egypt research for this book. And I want to convey a special degree of gratitude to Neil Hewison, at American University in Cairo Press, for being such an amazing friend, host, and confidant during my latter-stage research visits.

Between these trips to Cairo and later ones to Brazil, the essential framework for this book emerged during my time in New York City, where I earned a doctorate in politics and took classes across a variety of other disciplines at NYU. For much of this time I held a day job as an international projects specialist at the United Nations Development Programme (UNDP), first in the Central America division, then in the Programme of Assistance to the Palestinian People. I am grateful to UNDP, where many of my views about political-economic order, international relations, and the rise of the Global South were formed while working for El Salvador peace building and reconciliation projects there, and on the implementation of the Palestine-Israel Oslo Accords. I learned so much working under the bold leadership of un Secretary-General Boutros-Boutros Ghali and under the direct supervision of the generous and courageous Enrique Neuhauser, who was a former cabinet member of President Allende of Chile. I also had the privilege of working with Rick Hooper, who was later killed in the bombing of the un headquarters in Iraq.

In my role as a proper (or not so proper) graduate student, I stretched the New York inter-university consortium agreements to the limit as I took classes all over town. Through this exciting transcampus and trans-disciplinary education, I shaped the project that eventually evolved into this book. I am deeply grateful to the late Charles Tilly at Columbia University, who included me for three years in his Contentious Politics Seminar, where I presented early versions of several of this book's chapters. Professor Tilly read and made detailed comments on these drafts and shaped my notion of contending securitization logics and my concept of parastatal orderings. My political theory framework was also influenced by Chantal Mouffe, with whom I was able to study at the New School, and by Pasquale Pasquino and Partha Chatterjee, visiting professors in nyu's Department of Politics. Janet Abu-Lughod at the New School and Sharon Zukin from Brooklyn College gave me an intensive education in global-cities studies and urban sociological and political-economic analysis. And when I taught as a full-time lecturer in the Political Science Department of Hunter College of the City University of New York, I was grateful for the mentoring and friendship of the brilliant Brazilianist Michael Turner, and the guidance, fellowship, and inspiration of Rosalind Petchesky. I feel profound gratitude for my advisors and teachers at nyu at that time, especially George Yúdice, Andrew Ross, Christine Harrington, Samira Haj, Michael Gilsenan, and Wahneema Lubiano, and for Mark Ungar at Brooklyn College. My research was propelled by the energy, insights, brilliance, political vision, theory innovations, and overall fierceness of Lisa Duggan. And I cannot thank enough my principal dissertation advisor, Timothy Mitchell, who revolutionized the way political science grapples with power, the state, colonialism, and modernity. I am forever in his debt for his kind mentoring, good humor, and gentle critiques—and for all those letters of recommendation. The world that materializes in this book would have been invisible to me without the epistemological lenses that Mitchell developed.

As I expanded this project to encompass a transregional comparative study of security regimes in both the Middle East and Latin America, and to assess emergent global formations of governance, my research turned to Brazil, and to Rio de Janeiro. My pathway to Rio was laid out for me by my friends Marcelo Montes Penha and Micol Seigel, then at NYU, and Michael Turner at Hunter, and by a brief but pivotal meeting with the Brazilian political theorist, anthropologist, and revolutionary security-sector policy innovator Luiz Eduardo Soares. After I arrived in Rio, I enjoyed the support and advice of Celi Scalon and Carlos Hasenbalg, then at Instituto Universitário de Pesquisas do Rio de Janeiro; Heloisa Buarque de Hollanda and Carlos Messeder Perreira at Universidade Federal do Rio de Janeiro; Ignacio Cano and Sergio Carrara at Universidade do Estado do Rio de Janeiro; and my wonderful colleagues and collaborators Rosana Heringer, Osmundo Pinho, Joselina da Silva, Jacques D'Adesky, Monica Treviño, and Livio Sansone, then at the Center for Afro-Brazilian Studies (CEAB) and Cândido Mendes University. Remembering those Rio years, I want to send a shout-out to the diaspora of the Afro-Brazilian "Fábrica de Ideias" and the CEAB! I am also very grateful to the Center for Studies on Public Security and Citizenship (CESeC), and for the tireless, pathbreaking leadership of Silvia Ramos, Julita Lemgruber, Barbara Musumeci Soares, and Leonarda Musumeci in their work there on policing, gender, race, sexuality, citizenship, punishment, and political culture. Research for this book took on an added urgency and sophistication as I served as Fulbright Professor at the Universidade Federal Fluminense (UFF). At UFF, I was thankful for the opportunity to work with and learn from a spectacular group of ethnographers, political scientists, cultural studies specialists, and international relations scholars. These colleagues included Roberto Kant de Lima, Sonia Torres, Eduardo Gomes, Teotonio dos Santos, Maria Celina d'Araujo, and my good friend Paulo Gabriel da Rocha Pinto, with whom I founded and directed the Center for Middle East Studies at UFF.

In 2005, I moved to the beautiful University of California, Santa Barbara (UCSB), where I enjoyed efficient, friendly, and generous support for my research trips to complete this book from Barbara Walker, Katie Bamburg, and Alanna Matlick at the Institute of Social, Behavioral and Economic Research (ISBER). And I thank the Academic Senate and UC Regents for their research support, as well as the Interdisciplinary Humanities Center, Dean Melvin Oliver, and Associate Dean Leila Rupp, and my supportive departments, the Law and Society Program, and the Global and International Studies Program. I have also enjoyed the support of David Theo Goldberg's UC Humanities Research Institute. I also feel very grateful to have had the mentoring, guidance, and unwavering comradeship of my UCSB colleagues Hilal Elver, Kathleen Moore, Dwight

Reynolds, Nancy Gallagher, and Richard Falk, who have raised the bar for qualities of generosity and wisdom. Howard Winant, France Winddance Twine, and Mireille Miller-Young have been such good friends, soul mates, and intellectual companions at UCSB, and have shared countless good times and fantastic conversations, as we have worked together to advance the critical study of race, politics, globalization, and sexuality. Their friendships are more than dear. Eve Darian-Smith has been such a powerfully positive, insightful, and tirelessly supportive colleague and professional role model. And Lisa Hajjar has given me such constant encouragement, joy, ideas, and friendship; she is a miraculously committed builder of community among progressive scholars of the Middle East, and is the social and political soul of Santa Barbara. These colleagues made this long process fun and never let me mope or get discouraged. I am also grateful to my colleagues Giles Gunn, Rich Appelbaum, Mark Juergensmeyer, Jan Nederveen Pieterse, Alison Brysk, Esther Lezra, Nadege Clitandre, Marguerite Bouraad-Nash, Raymond Clémençon, Phil McCarty, and Aashish Mehta for their support and suggestions.

Draft chapters or papers representing key ideas and case studies for this book have been presented in five languages in a number of helpful contexts, and I am grateful for the intelligence, perceptiveness, and hard work colleagues have invested in reading and commenting on my work in all these fora. These include workshops at the American University of Beirut, the American University in Cairo, the Free University of Berlin, the British Academy, Kent Law School, Oxford University, George Mason University, Cornell University, University of São Paulo, Cairo University, Université Paris Diderot–Paris 7, the Federal University of Rio de Janeiro, the Fluminense Federal University, Cândido Mendes University, the Brazilian National Assembly of Social Sciences (ANPOCS), the Universities of California at Berkeley, San Diego, Los Angeles, and Davis, the University of Southern California, the International Political Science Association, the American Political Science Association, the International Studies Association, the Cultural Studies Association, the American Studies Association, the Law and Society Association, the Brazilian Studies Association, the Middle East Studies Association, the Social Science Research Council, the Ethnic Studies Association, and the European University Institute and Mediterranean Research Council Montecatini workshop.

Very special thanks to Jillian Schwedler and Laleh Khalili for their extremely helpful readings, friendship, and insights, and to Sadia Abbas and Omnia El Shakry for their hard work reading and elevating my chapters and ideas. Our collaborations and adventures are just beginning, sisters! In addition to many of those mentioned above, others who have provided detailed comments on papers that became chapters include Sonia Côrrea, Judith Halberstam, Lisa Duggan, Ella Shohat, Macarena Gómez-Barris, Gil Hochberg, Lisa Wedeen, Hind Mahmoud, Michael McCann, Mark Ungar, Nayan Shah, Ros Petchesky, Saba Mahmood, Vijay Prashad, Paola Bacchetta, Cynthia Enloe, Charles Hirschkind, Juliet Williams, John Chalcraft, Mozn Hassan, Amr Abdelrahman, David Lloyd, Caren Kaplan, and Sudipta Sen.

A much earlier version of chapter 4 appeared in the volume *Contested Histories in Public Space: Memory, Race, and Nation* (Duke University Press, 2009), edited by Daniel J. Walkowitz and Lisa Maya Knauer. An earlier version of chapter 5 appeared in the journal *Security Dialogue* 40, nos. 4–5 (August–October 2009). And an earlier version of chapter 6 appeared in the *International Feminist Journal of Politics* 13, no. 3 (September 2011). These essays have been significantly revised. I am greatly indebted to these editors and to anonymous peer reviewers for their suggestions, critiques, and guidance, which so enhanced the quality of this work.

I am full of thankfulness for the University of Bristol in the United Kingdom, which hosted me for a sabbatical in the Department of Politics and at the Global Insecurities Centre. There, colleagues such as Martin Gainsborough, Mark Duffield, Jutta Weldes, Paul Higate, Marsha Henry, Wendy Larner, and a dozen graduate students helped with every single chapter of this book in workshops with me, and encouraged my embrace of cutting-edge approaches to security studies, constructivist geopolitics, theories of the state and transnational governance, conflict and militarization studies, and feminist political theory. And how can I adequately thank Terrell Carver, who, at Bristol and forever after, offered mentoring, editing, networking, and advising—and an endless supply of brilliance, good humor, and friendship.

During this long process of multicontinental investigation, I have benefited from the diligent research talents of scholars whose efforts were truly remarkable. These include Kate Lyra, Mozn Hassan, Tess Popper, Katharina Lenner, Alaa al-Din Haddad, Jenna Gray-Hildenbrand, and Silvia Ferreira. Without their hard work, this kind of in-depth and cross-regional analysis would have been impossible to complete. And as for editing and formatting, I must give special thanks to Anitra Grisales, who worked so hard to make this volume's prose legible and its concepts intelligible. Jade Brooks at Duke University Press has been extraordinarily helpful and generous with me. And Duke University Press's editorial director, Ken Wis-soker, provided enthusiasm, patience, and support that kept me sane as I finalized this manuscript. His advice on framing the book and the introduction were invaluable. I also owe a great debt of gratitude to Ella Shohat, Randy Martin, and others at the *Social Text* collective for supporting this project for their book series from the early stages, and for encouraging me to keep moving onward and upward during this process.

Finally, I want to thank my unique and loving family. Thanks to Aunt Guriprana (née Suzanne Amar), who became a Hindu Vedanta nun in Calcutta and wrote me those mind-melting and soul-elevating letters as I was growing up, and to Aunt Rose, who during her adventures around Africa and the South Pacific sent me equally inspiring (if significantly less pious) letters—and the occasional stuffed crocodile that she shot dead. And thanks to Uncle Bud for his humor, stories, and ass-kicking. Thanks to my great-grandmothers Gigi, Lulie, and Mama Frix, who each lived about a century and conveyed oral world history to me through their stories of my ancestors on the prairies, in the Appalachians, in Pacific ports, down in speakeasies, and up on the high seas. Thanks to the unwavering, kind, warm support of my father, whose love has enabled me to journey so far without ever feeling alone. And thanks to my kind, hilarious, talented, and rock-steady brother, Jeremy, for being my good friend and confidant; my sister-in-law, Traci, a visionary designer and buddy; and Dakota, my six-year-old singing, dancing, chess-winning, karate-chopping, YouTube-dominating nephew, for his energy and love. Most of all, I send thanks and love to my deceased mother, Janice Faye. She was a beautiful, courageous, loving, creative, Irish-Cherokee girl born in Birmingham, Alabama, and raised in Chattanooga, Tennessee. She was a woman of drive, heart, dreams, and will. She loved to laugh out loud with true joy in quiet rooms, and to give standing ovations at concerts when everyone else remained seated. She was my best friend. This book is for you, Mom, "to the end of the numbers."

THE ARCHIPELAGO OF
NEW SECURITY-STATE UPRISINGS

Revolution in Egypt

On 11 February 2011, Egyptian president Hosni Mubarak resigned, his thirty-year rule terminated at last.[1] Vice President Omar Soleiman gave the news, his blinking countenance flickering on huge screens that hovered above Tahrir Square, his voice trembling with rage, disappointment, and resentment. The Supreme Council of the Armed Forces (SCAF), chaired by the defense minister, Field Marshal Hussein Tantawi, had announced the evening before that the military would be assuming control of the country "because it is the responsibility of the Armed Forces and our commitment to the protection of the people, their interests and safety. It is our prerogative to look to the safety of the nation and its citizens, and to protect the possessions and heritage of the great Egyptian people, and to endorse the people's rightful, legitimate demands" (El Naggar 2011). The council later added that "it [was calling] on the civilian police forces to recommit to their slogan 'the police serve the people.'"[2] Millions of youth, laborers, women, Islamist, and anti-police-brutality protesters who had occupied Cairo's Tahrir Square, as well as the town centers of Alexandria, Suez, Mahalla, and many other Egyptian cities, erupted in cheers that were echoed by a billion celebrants around the world who had been riveted by the courage, creativity, and paradigm-shattering tactics of Egypt's mass uprising (fig. intro.1).[3] Yousra Aboustait, a young female protester, said of her experiences in Tahrir Square, "[Women] feel like they can be around and involved without any fear of being bothered or abused. It is like they have finally been given the way to be an equal, effective and important part of society with no constraints or barriers" (O'Neill 2011).

For many at that moment, it seemed that along with Mubarak's resignation, a neoliberal national pact and a repressive global security con-

FIGURE INTRO.1. The mother of the police-brutality martyr Khaled Saeed celebrates in Tahrir Square on the day of Mubarak's resignation (11 February 2011). Photo credit: Al Masry Al Youm / Ramy Hammad (http://www.almasry-alyoum.com).

tract had been terminated. In their place, a contradictory coalition of military institutions, youth and labor movements, human-rights organizations, and resurgent religious political organizations were stepping forward to attempt to shape a fresh kind of democratic politics that would focus on humanizing the security state. As the Egyptian Sonia Farid wrote from Cairo, "Forget about wasting so much time and effort analyzing the layers of meaning of the word 'civil' and whether it was coined to be the antonym of 'army' or 'police' and examining the different takes on words like 'purging' or 'cleansing' or 'reforming.' How about using words as simple as 'human' or 'humane' or 'humanizing?'" (Farid 2011). Mubarak, his wife, and their sons had come to be identified with the most extreme forms of privatization, crony capitalism, and moral hypocrisy, as well as the most exclusionary and repressive forms of neoliberal market reform (Amar 2011b; Amar 2011c; Beinin 2011a; Hanieh 2011). Soleiman, Mubarak's intelligence chief, and Habib elAdly, his interior minister, had built massive security and policing apparatuses that worked for decades to block any resistance to US wars in the region; ensure the imposition of International Monetary Fund accords; engineer the selloff of factories and national patrimony to Asian and Western investors; and facilitate the deepening of Persian Gulf ideological and financial domination. But in the end, contradictions within the security state itself, the influence of the emergence of new Global South investors and power-brokers like China, Russia, Brazil, and Saudi Arabia (and rivalries between them), and the organizing efforts of Egypt's social movements, themselves, intersected in ways that brought down the Mubarak order and gave birth to a new order of governance that triangulated contradictory formations of moralizing religiosity, militarized humanitarianism, and labor collectivism. In this revolutionary context (and in this moment when a global balance of powers is shifting epochally), I raise a particular question: which transformations in security state logics, and the "humanity" of its subjects, caused the emergence of these new forms of political assertion? The answer, I propose, lies in the particular ways that humanity was reconceived and secured through new forms of sexualized and moralized governance that emerged in and circulated between zones of struggle in certain socially militarized and culturally generative polities of the Global South beginning in the 1980s.

During the events in Egypt in February 2011, the military council, once it assumed control of the transitional government, moved quickly to launch a campaign to "rescue the nation" from the very protesters that had exerted popular sovereignty there. The SCAF preserved the essence of Mubarak's Emergency Decree, reinvigorated the military court system to arrest and try civilians, and extended the repressive power of its class- and sexuality-driven logics of domination (El Naggar 2011). Many of those detained were young, male, working-class labor protesters whom the armed forces identified not as political dissenters with rights but as "thugs" (baltagiya) or "fags" (khawaliya) who defiled national dignity and its moral security and "insulted the army" (El Gundy 2011; Human Rights Watch 2011b). They detained women protesters and administered "virginity tests," hymen inspections that are of course forms of molestation or rape in themselves (Scott Long 2012), insisting that only pious single young women could speak as legitimate voices of the people, and that the army would exclude from politics the working-class "whores" whose public presence was an attack on national honor.[4] In August 2011 SCAF blocked the nomination of any female governors by arguing that the military could not guarantee protection of their security and dignity during this time of chaos (Mayton 2011) (fig. intro.2). Security in the revolution

FIGURE INTRO.2. Egyptian army arrests woman protester during a demonstration against the Supreme Council of the Armed Forces (16 December 2011). Photo credit: Al Masry Al Youm / Mohamed el-Shamy (http://www.almasry-alyoum.com).

became a form of sexualized and gendered sovereignty for SCAF, which acted to amplify the forms of class domination and moralistic repression that were the hallmarks of Mubarak's regime.

Acceptance of the armed forces' masculinist and class-phobic paternalism seemed to be the price for their cooperation in routing Mubarak. In exchange, the armed forces did keep several of their other promises. They ditched (at least for a few months) accords with the International Monetary Fund (IMF) and World Bank, reappropriated the assets of some of the most corrupt oligarchs, renationalized some large factories whose privatizations were most contested, and affirmed the newly independent labor federation. And after being pressed by months of brave objections and a second set of massive Tahrir protests in July 2011, the Supreme Council of the Armed Forces wheeled the former president Mubarak on a stretcher into civilian court and launched his trial on charges of "conspiring in the premeditated and attempted murder of protesters during the uprising, abusing power to amass wealth, and allowing below-market price gas sales to Israel."[5]

In many ways, Egypt's 2011 Revolution marked the crystallization of new types of emergent structural conditions and political-cultural for-

FIGURE INTRO.3. Billboards that proclaimed "The Army and the People Are One Hand" were mounted throughout Cairo as the Egyptian military struggled to cultivate a "human security" image for itself during the postrevolution transition (10 April 2012). Photo credit: Hesham Sallam.

mations. Granted, there is nothing new about massive, well-organized labor protests in Egypt or about the army participating in politics in that country. Indeed, when the Egyptian armed forces helped precipitate Mubarak's resignation and promised to protect and fulfill the new revolution, many observers were correct to suspect that they were moving to restore their hegemony over the state and the economy; SCAF's repressive moves between July 2011 and January 2012 confirmed these suspicions. But there was much that was quite new about this uprising within and around the apparatuses of Egypt's coercive security state, including the operation of a new grammar of power and legitimacy structuring the actions that the Egyptian armed forces deployed to secure the country and rescue its people from chaos (fig. intro.3). This time, the military's interventions were structured by a grammar of humanitarian protection or securitized humanization. In other words, the military had intervened in accordance with a particular Global South variant of humanitarian rescue doctrine. And this rescue doctrine continued to define modes of rule, with the volume of moralistic and religious rhetoric amplified, as the military ceded power to the Muslim Brotherhood leader Mohammad Morsy, who had eked out a narrow victory in the presidential elections of 16–17 June 2012.

This doctrine is realized through two processes: one is the forcible protection and moral rehabilitation of the citizenry, restoring dignity and "humanity" to certain communities marked by gender, sexuality, and culture and seen as menaced by "perversions of globalization"; another is the securing and policing of certain forms of space, labor, and heritage seen as anchors for counterhegemonic development models. As I will detail, a set of humanitarianizing security interventions circulating between governance laboratories in the Global South had come to define the state during the Mubarak period, providing a model for rule and a cultural language for a new kind of international order (Rabbani 2011; Tadros 2011). The norms and aims of this kind of military-humanitarian rule are not necessarily less coercive than the nationalist or socialist-leaning agenda that propelled military rule in the 1950s and 1960s in Egypt, but their operations and subjects are quite distinct. In the last three decades, neoliberal market legitimations and consumerist ideologies have gradually lost their power to prop up militarized forms of governance in rapidly changing regions of the Global South. Forms of humanized security discourse that generate particular sexual, class, and moral subjects have come to define political sovereignty and to articulate the grammars of dialectically unfolding and internally contradictory forms of power.

If the neoliberal state had orbited around one logic of subjectivity—the rational-liberal individual who was market-investor, consumer-chooser, and entrepreneur-innovator—by contrast, a new kind of governance that I term the human-security state emerged as a node of four intersecting logics of securitization: moralistic (rooted in culture and values based on evangelical Christian and Islamic piety discourses); juridical-personal (focused on rights, privatized property, and minority identity); workerist (orbiting around new or revived notions of collective and social security and postconsumer notions of participation and citizenship); and paramilitary (a masculinist, police-centered, territorially possessive logic of enforcement). These relatively autonomous four logics of securitization came together in what I call here a human-security governance regime. They all explicitly aimed to protect, rescue, and secure certain idealized forms of humanity identified with a particular family of sexuality, morality, and class subjects, and grounded in certain militarized territo-

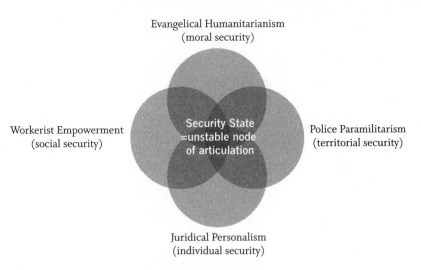

Evangelical Humanitarianism
(moral security)

Workerist Empowerment
(social security)

Security State
=unstable node
of articulation

Police Paramilitarism
(territorial security)

Juridical Personalism
(individual security)

FIGURE INTRO.4. Contending security logics since the 1990s. The governance formation I label the human-security state is a highly productive but unstable articulation of four relatively autonomous securitization modes, each one identified with a particular cluster of subjects and institutions.

ries and strategic infrastructures (figs. intro.4 and intro.5). It should be noted that armed humanitarian interventions deployed in international operations governed by humanitarian law, commonly known as the laws of war, do this as well (Esmeir 2012; Glasius 2008). But the distinct story of how humanized securitization became a contradictory complex of radically repressive and emancipatory tactics of rule in domestic, urban contexts within the Global South is one that follows a narrative that diverges from the Global North–centered tale of the unfolding of international law on the one hand, or the timeline of economic liberalization on the other.

The emergence of these forms of humanized securitization reflects forms of structural resonance between semiperipheral sites. Human-security governance was shaped by certain transnational forms of public-private partnership, NGO mobilization, and development expertise, which I group together in this book as "parastatal formations." These specific sites of experimentation that tested novel forms of securitization were linked together through intercontinental flows of security practices and protection discourses. In order to systematically weigh these structural parallels and trace these connections, I present a comparative and trans-regional analysis that brings together Egypt and Brazil.

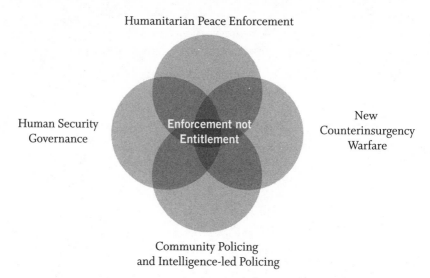

Humanitarian Peace Enforcement

Human Security
Governance

Enforcement not
Entitlement

New
Counterinsurgency
Warfare

Community Policing
and Intelligence-led Policing

FIGURE INTRO.5. The family of contemporary humanitarianized governmentalities, including Global South–originating human-security states.

"Revolution" in Brazil

While mass uprising continued in Tahrir Square in Cairo, on the other side of the world, in Rio de Janeiro, Brazil, a major upheaval in security-state rule was transpiring. On 14 February 2011, a seemingly incomprehensible alliance of armed forces and progressive social movements unleashed a new order that promised a "truly revolutionary" transformation of the security sector (Fiell 2011). The police reform leader Ignacio Cano proclaimed, "In a revolutionary shift, the aim is not to win the unwinnable 'war on drugs' any more, but to protect the population" (Cano 2011). These efforts focused on deploying a bold new humanitarian-intervention type approach to urban social control, to be carried out by a new, wholly repurposed police force, in conjunction, at first, with the national armed forces, whose joint aim was to finally arrest the trafficker-related violence that had besieged Brazil's public-housing projects and favelas for the last thirty years (fig. intro.6). In these marginalized zones, self-generated, unregistered communities hosted up to 30 percent of the urban population.

In the 1990s, Rio became infamous as one of the world's most spectacularly dystopian theaters of neoliberalism. The city was ravaged by racial and social inequality, besieged by police corruption and violence, and dominated by a culture of macho and brutal entrepreneurialism that the popular imagination spectacularly demonized (and eroticized) as an alli-

FIGURE INTRO.6. Representing the Brazilian military's occupation of favelas as a domestic "humanitarian intervention," a naval tank gunner in favela Complexo de Alemão wears a "friendly" blue cap that reads "Pacification Force" (8 September 2011). Photo credit: Michael Wolff.

ance between black trafficker commandos, white arms dealers, and transnational money launderers. But since the election of President Luiz Inácio Lula da Silva on 6 October 2002, leftist, labor, and community-based social movements in concert with a fractious political alliance of evangelical (Pentecostal Christian) groups, liberation theology-leaning Catholic activists, and secular-liberal human-rights organizations had been struggling to humanize and democratize the Brazilian security state.[6] In particular, they struggled with the militarized corruption and racialized brutality of the Militarized Police (Polícia Militar, PM) and the torture and corruption committed by the Civil Police (Polícia Civil, PC) (Human Rights Watch 2011a).[7] Between November 2010 and February 2011, social-movement leaders, Workers' Party officials, and their political allies in the Rio governor Sérgio Cabral's Democratic Movement Party of Brazil (PMDB) formed an alliance to carry out a bold plan. They would launch a vast wave of favela occupations spearheaded by new Police Pacification Units (UPPS) (fig. intro.7). In an article entitled "Notorious Rio de Janeiro Slum Taken Over by Brazilian Troops," the journalist Stuart Grudgings stated, "Under a so-called pacification program, Rio authorities are to follow up invasions by

FIGURE INTRO.7. The Police Pacification Units (UPPs) celebrate their one-year birthday. The UPPs serve as human-security enforcers and domestic peacekeepers in communities targeted for Olympic redevelopment (18 February 2012). Photo credit: Michael Wolff.

handing slums over to specially trained community police and providing services such as health centers and formal electricity and TV supply. The aim is to foster social inclusion and give the city's one million or more slum residents a bigger stake in Brazil's robust economy" (2011).

Established police forces could not be trusted to conform to the progressive government's humanized-security and social-empowerment projects in the favela shantytown communities; nor were the newly trained pacification brigades powerful enough to stand up to traffickers and rogue police militias. So the state government and its social-movement allies called on the national army to help stand up against corrupt police, vigilante militias, and trafficker organizations. The armed forces, the blood enemy of the political left in the days of the dictatorship (1964–85), stepped forward to offer their services to structure a new pact with the progressive social movements that now occupied positions of power in the Brazilian security state. In Brazil this was referred to as a "revolution in public security" (Kaleb 2011) and a "radically humanitarian" (Daniela Oliveira 2012) form of emancipatory occupation. On 26 January 2012, Brazil's minister of defense affirmed that "the military Peacekeeping Force in Rio de Janeiro constitutes the greatest Law and Order Enforcement operation ever realized by the Armed Forces, following the strictest constitutional principles and extended at the request of the entire Federation."[8] Of course, during the military coup of 1964, the armed forces called their putsch a "democratic revolution," too (Pereira 2005). But the military and police invasions of 2011 represented a distinct kind of militarized revolution—not against communism or terrorism, but explicitly in favor of human security.

"The cleaning up of degraded areas will help to improve human security . . . a symbol and result of the community's recent revival of pride and identity since pacification."[9] Enshrining this doctrine, in April 2011, the president (Chief Justice) of the Brazilian Supreme Court, Cezar Peluso, with the endorsement of President Dilma Rousseff and UN Secretary-General Ban Ki-Moon, announced a proposal to create a cutting-edge UN-affiliated University of Public Security and Social Development. This would be located in Brazil and based on that country's "pioneering human security concept . . . that involves not only the absence of internal violent conflict, but also [includes] fundamental rights, governance, access to health and education, etc." (Peluso 2011). This university and the UPP vision would eventually replace the figure of the corrupt, militarized, repressive police officer with a new kind of "public security manager . . . capable of working in the many areas of administration involved in the maintenance of public order [facilitating training and public partnerships with] private, community and non-government institutions" (Peluso 2011). The official government announcement proclaims, "This represents international recognition of the innovative Brazilian action taken against poverty (*Bolsa Família*) and violence (the implementation of the UPP in Rio de Janeiro, and also the Brazilian command of MINUSTAH [the United Nations Stabilization Mission] in Haiti). The establishment of a university of the UN in Brazil would represent a true 'export platform' of innovative measures formulated and implemented by Brazil" (Peluso 2011).

A new era for the politics of gender, security, and military politics had been inaugurated with the election of Dilma Rousseff as Brazil's first female president, on 31 October 2010. Rousseff, from 1967 to 1970, was associated with a group that engaged in armed action against the military dictatorship and allegedly kidnapped bankers for ransom to support anti-capitalist underground organizations. More recently, Rousseff led the successful campaign to assert popular sovereignty over and public ownership of Brazil's massive new oil discoveries (Brooks 2010; Leitão and Ferraz 2010; Winter and Nery 2010) (fig. intro.8). Brazil, which had long referred to itself as the "country of the future," had indeed finally become a beacon

FIGURE INTRO.8. Brazil's President Dilma Rousseff christens Petrobras oil platform 56 in southern Rio de Janeiro state (3 June 2011). Photo credit: Wilton Junior / Agencia Estado / AE (Agencia Estado via AP Images).

of hope for many in the Global South by blending dynamic capitalism with redistributive social justice and by presenting an appealing face for the counterhegemonic claims of emergent powers (Martins 2000).

Now at the helm of this rising superpower, President Rousseff did not hesitate to affirm the armed forces' new role as supporters of these domestically deployed humanitarian interventions and social pacification operations. Nevertheless, no one could say that she had become a pawn of the military apparatus. She dismissed some of the old-guard military officers (Flor 2011) and insisted on relaunching truth commissions into torture and disappearances during the 1964–85 dictatorship.[10] Perhaps to counter these efforts to marginalize them, Brazil's generals embraced their new role in domestic governance and internationalist humanitarianism with enthusiasm. The chief soldiers said their Rio pacification occupations drew on their recent experience leading the large UN blue-helmet mission in Haiti (which has been much critiqued within Port-au-Prince as a whitewashing of the anti-Aristide putsch). Since the 1990s, Brazil's armed forces had become quite proud of its international military-humanitarian roles, particularly in securing East Timor's independence, in encouraging peacebuilding in post-Saddam Iraq, and in promoting reconciliation and conflict resolution in Africa, as well as in taking charge of the UN peacekeeping mission in Haiti (Agência Estado 2010; Amar 2012b; Nieto 2012). On the home front, the uniformed Armed Forces had come to loathe Brazil's Militarized Police and to be threatened by the cops' corruption, brutality, and entrepreneurialism, just as the Egyptian military had come to hate Mubarak's police and central security forces. In both cases, the corrupt police had come to embody the chaos and deregulation of neoliberalism and had offended the notions of professionalism and institutional orderliness at the core of military norms. The Brazilian military had increasingly identified itself with national capital (often becoming the owner of development projects and settlements), participated in infrastructure projects, and remained loyal to developmentalist policy frameworks (Abraham 2009), and even, to some degree, backed the redistributive Workers' Party agenda. These new or renewed identifications had allowed it to distance itself from its 1970s role as the "hired guns of neoliberalism." And this change reflected a response by the military to the tectonic shifts within the nature of securitized governance pushed by South America's increasingly powerful and popular new Left governments that had swept to power since the late 1990s in what is sometimes referred to as the Pink Tide.

So in February 2011, the full power of the armed forces, along with a new military-humanitarian police operation, the Police Pacification Units, swept into the favela Complexo São Carlos in Rio de Janeiro (Daflon 2011) and then into Latin America's largest favela, Rocinha, in November 2011, as they had in Complexo do Alemão, Dona Marta, and many other communities in November and December of 2010 (Agência Brasil 2011b; Castillo 2010). And these military-humanitarian efforts then, by 2012, came to be paralleled by an evangelical-led campaign for *limpeza social*, for social purification and urban cleansing. As these events unfolded, leftist leaders in Brasilia as well as police, military, and municipal leaders in Rio increasingly entered into coalitions with evangelical political movements, whose "moral security" discourse legitimized, in part, the heavy-handed human-security interventions (Castrezana 2012). Of course, the participation of the military in restructuring the rule of the security-state in the poor shantytowns of Rio did not come without a price. And of course the UPP campaigns against police corruption and trafficker violence in Rio were never perceived worldwide as an emancipatory moment equivalent to the ouster of Mubarak and the uprising against the police state in Egypt. Nevertheless, the UPP project's claims, and its "revolutionary" human-security agenda, did resonate in certain ways with the Egyptian Revolution of 2011. Each country's fraught articulation of coercion forces, worker mobilizers, morality campaigners, and transnational humanitarians arose from what I argue are changes in security institutions, moral-cultural discourse, spatial formations, and human subjectivity that emerged in certain nodal sites of the Global South in the last three decades. These formations have a consistent character and political profile that I term the "human-security state."

The governance regime of this human-security state represents a new, wrenchingly productive formation born of the tense alliances between diverse, mass social movements (whether advocating moral piety, cultural security, workers' collective social security, or personal civil rights) and certain military institutions acting against authoritarian elites and "crony" factions of global capital and privatization. These articulations act roughly in favor of both national capital and a new kind of world order centered in the Global South. The new alliances and dynamics are queer or curious, indeed, when seen from the perspective of political analysts who assume military institutions are synonymous with authoritarian regimes, that the security state is the ontological opposite of civil society, or that all new forms of global governance only emanate in the Global North and then move southward.

Securing a New Humanity, Securing a New Global Ordering

Neoliberal market states today have been plunged into a dynamic period of collapse and reanimation. Security experts have struggled to respond to the crumbling legitimacy of neoliberalism's laissez-faire policies and financial infrastructures, as well as to the backlash against neoconservatism's wars on terror and disregard for human rights (Tabb 2003). Governments and activists have been scrambling to articulate new discourses and rationalize new logics of rule in order to reorganize forms of intensified intervention and regulatory governance. Late-twentieth-century *market-state logics*, in their neoliberal form, are struggling to survive the early-twenty-first-century era of financial crisis and geopolitical realignment (Pieterse 2011). But *security-state logics* are doing fine. Projects to extend international state-based and privatized forms of enforcement, control, and militarized intervention have endured waves of social resistance and human-rights opposition. And now these security states are prospering by focusing their efforts on rescuing sexuality and morality-identified subjects of humanity as well as cultivating militarized projects for securing cultural heritage and developmental infrastructure. Increasingly, self-identified progressive and conservative security doctrines intersect in their focus on the "humanization" (or, in these times, "humanitarianization") of military and police security apparatuses. Whereas the eras of the Cold War and the War on Terror emphasized that rights and security and even the rule of law must be traded away to enhance security, the relatively new paradigm of human security argues that by strengthening human rights, both states and societies can also enhance their safety (United Nations Development Programme 1994). Whereas modernization theory and neoliberalism insist that economic expansion requires political restrictions and repression, human security interweaves economic redistribution, political participation, and national development. As an explicit critique of earlier repressive security and development paradigms, human security doctrines promise to reconcile human rights and national security interests, rebalance humanitarianism and militarism, and expand the notion of politics to reintegrate social justice and economic development (United Nations Development Programme 1994). This links the aim of ensuring "freedom from want" to the prospect of "freedom from fear" (MacLean, Black, and Shaw 2006, 4).

But I claim that securitization projects' new targets — subjects that are portrayed as victimized by trafficking, prostituted by "cultures of globalization," sexually harassed by "street" forms of predatory masculinity, or "debauched" by liberal values — cannot be grasped if we recognize them merely as claimants in human-rights campaigns. Instead these subjects should be more accurately analyzed as human-security products emerging in particular gender, racial, and transnational forms in and around military and police operations and parastatal security projects. Evidence from case studies I present in this book will demonstrate that these new forms of identity and humanity have emerged not in the headquarters of the UN or in the humanitarian agencies of the Global North, but in a belt of the world that we used to call the semiperiphery. In this zone, particular military and police institutions of the state have clashed with and appropriated discourses from mass movements around morality, sexuality, and labor. And this mix of struggles and appropriations has decisively reshaped innovative forms of governance. The practices, norms, and institutional products of these struggles have then traveled across an archipelago, a metaphorical island chain, of what the private security industry calls "hotspots" — enclaves of panic and laboratories of control — the most hypervisible of which have emerged in Global South megacities like Cairo and Rio.

By zooming in on these hotspots, where structures of popular-class organizing, discourses of religio-moral populism, and prerogatives of military intervention in politics are strong, we can see how unique cultural processes and political alliances are generating new forms of rule in certain areas of the Global South. But to understand this process, we must develop new ways of thinking, researching, and analyzing the security state in the transnational context and in relation to the people it claims to protect. By examining in depth the pivotal, trend-setting cases of Brazil and Egypt, this book provides an alternative historical and theoretical framing of the rise and fall of neoliberalism and of the emergence of new humanitarian global security regimes in the Global South. I offer a new kind of political analysis of this current moment of transition in which neoliberalism is viciously redoubling its force in the United States and the Eurozone, but losing ground in the Global South. There, new regimes centered not on the market and consumerism but on axes of humanitarian militarism and "human-security democracy" are emerging. To be clear, these postneoliberal human-security regimes are not necessarily better than neoliberal ones, nor are they more consensus-based or less coercive. Ask anyone tortured or detained by the "humanitarian" military or "pious" Brotherhood government in Egypt or evicted from their homes by the stampedes of gentrification unleashed by the pacification police in Brazil. Through the case studies in this book I explore the distinctiveness of human-security governance by analyzing three sets of phenomena: (1) new political subjects that demonstrate the relative autonomy of human security from neoliberalism, (2) institutional roles and norms of military, humanitarian, and parastatal actors implementing new human-security models, and (3) the sexualizing and moralizing discourses of cultural rescue and trafficking prevention that human-security regimes use to justify their actions.

These sets of actors and discourses generate much of their power by targeting controversial sexualities. That is, they govern through moral politics not market policies. My mapping of the politics of sexuality in these sites draws on governmentality critiques, queer and feminist theories, and critical race studies approaches. I define sexuality politics by building on the models of Michel Foucault (2008) and Hazel Carby (1992), who have reconceptualized sexuality not as a set of orientations or minority identities, nor as a category of personal rights or reproductive health issues, but as a contradictory set of humanization dynamics and hypervisibilization processes. In other words, I conceive of sexuality politics in terms of security-sector struggles to discipline dangers and desires that mark the controlled boundary of the human. These uses of sexuality render overly visible certain race, class, and gendered bodies as sources of danger and desire, while rendering invisible the political nature of hierarchy and the identity of powerful agents. Thus, I use the expression "sexuality politics" in ways analogous to Stan Cohen's (1973) or Stuart Hall's (Hall and Jefferson 1976) use of the expression "moral panic politics," or Frantz Fanon's "phobogenic politics" (1988 [1952]), or Judith Halberstam's "technology of monsters" (1995). To be clear, I am not privileging the sphere of sexuality, and thereby implying that sexuality constitutes a more fluid or culturally animated realm than those of gender, race, or class. Each chapter of this book gives these latter formations their due. Gender, race, and class are thoroughly denaturalized and repoliticized here. In relation to these formations, I argue that in the universe of human security, sexuality is implicated in modes of governance that blend parahumanization (the creation of politically disabled "victim" subjects that must, essentially, be constantly protected or rescued by enforcement interventions regardless of their consent or will to be rescued), hypervisibilization (the spotlighting of certain identities and bodies as sources of radical insecurity and moral panic in ways that actually render invisible the real nature of power and social control), and securitization (the reconfiguration of political debates and claims around social justice, political participation, or resource distribution into technical assessments of danger, operations of enforcement, and targetings of risk populations).

These new forms of human-security power both depend on and struggle with new forms of organized labor, religionized morality campaigns, and mobilized popular-class communities. They struggle to police and redirect gender-identified and religion-infused social movements, and to capture entrepreneurial military and police organizations. By analyzing how these forms of power and subjects of rule emerged historically and traveled transregionally, I develop a new theory of how global hegemony is reconfigured and how new governance trends emerge, centering processes of moral-sexual subjectification and Global South securitization.

Rather than using the celebratory language of civil society or of the private sector to describe new governance actors in the security arena, I generate an intentionally ambivalent set of terms that all share the prefix *para*. Although I do highlight the constructive innovations of many bold NGOs and cutting-edge community organizations, I analyze these actors in the context of what I call *parastatal formations*. We understand that a *paramilitary* group is an armed band commissioned by state and elite actors to perform illegal acts of enforcement, coercion, and punishment, often acting as vigilantes preserving national security and protecting the impunity of those in power. When I use the term *parastatal*, I describe coalitions that can include government policymakers, NGOS, private-security agencies, morality campaigns, and property developers. I am not implying that these governance formations are secretly operating as paramilitary groups, of course. But by defining them as parastatal, I emphasize that they are performing the public functions of a state that has outsourced its functions into a parallel realm of reduced accountability and unregulated power. Sociolegal scholars Ruth Jamieson and Kieran McEvoy have called this process "state crime by proxy and juridical othering" (2005, 504).

In a similar vein, *parahumanization* refers to a notion of humanized security where rights-bearing subjects of the state become suspects under the control of privatized rescue industries. My use of *para-* represents my attempt to systematize the pervasive transnational vernacular use of terms like *shadow, shade, ghost, specter,* or *phantom,* which expressively capture the illiberal dimensions of security governance today. I use the term *parahuman* intentionally to estrange the reader, and in order to avoid the use of terms like *victim* or *suspect*, or the euphemism of "NGO client" or "aid recipient." Popular slang in Arabic and Portuguese has also resisted the language of neoliberalism that celebrates the role of NGOS and humanitarians by developing vernacular terms that speak of shadow states and parallel governance nodes where organized crime and vigilantes collaborate with state officials. "Shady" deals are struck between powerful corporations, drug traffickers, and warlords. "Phantom" developments are constructed by public-private partnerships, and then collapse when speculative bubbles burst. People feel they are haunted by increasing levels of enforcement and surveillance, followed by spies, "spooks," and "specters" of not-quite-visible control, intelligence, and judgment (Gordon 1996). Those in power also speak of shadows and phantoms. But when they use these terms they racialize and sexualize suspect populations, portraying them as linked to shadow powers and phantom menaces, seeing peoples of subordinate classes as inherently suspect. Many still see "racial mixture" as the source of security risk and cultural crisis, even as they celebrate the erotic and cultural power of these mixings. These racializing securitization discourses stimulate new waves of orientalist and tropicalist fantasy and panic. By developing an analytical framework around these *para-* terms, I attempt to articulate the insecurity people feel at the street level around parallel powers, paramilitary threats, shadows, phantoms, dark solidarities, and shady bodies.

Security in Revolution

In order to grapple with the recent revolutionary changes in Egypt and Brazil, the emergence of new security-state subjects of political humanity, and the rise of bold, new Global South models of governance and sovereignty, I draw on and speak to a set of complementary disciplines. These include international relations, comparative politics, political sociology, political anthropology, cultural studies, globalization studies, and urban political-economic geography. I bring these fields to bear on the emergent field of critical security studies, which is usually positioned at the intersection of constructivist international-relations theory and feminist peace studies. Today, critical approaches to the study of security are distinguished by two somewhat contradictory commitments: first, a healthy skepticism about risk, threat, and the politics of fear that accompany the identification of menaces to security (Weldes, Laffey, Gusterson, and Duvall 1999); and second, an interest in advocating a more enlightened security agenda that focuses on reducing state violence and develops non-coercive, nonrepressive interventions in response to threats (Peoples and Vaughan-Williams 2010; David Williams 2008). The interdisciplinary field sees security threats as constructed by imperialism, class domination, racism, and new discourses of control and dispossession, but then offers methods for humanizing and civilizing protective interventions. One can applaud the field for its interest in offering constructive alternatives and engaging policymakers, and for pushing beyond the moment of deconstruction. But does this reconstructive, humanizing gesture risk relegitimizing the politics of "securitization"? This problem derives from two gaps in the methodologies and units of analysis of critical security studies today: the tendency to ignore unique structures, intersections, and forms of agency generated in the Global South, and the gap that has emerged between the radical and liberal wings of the field.

In its commitment to seeing the objects of insecurity and threat as constructed, the radical wing of critical security studies has, quite correctly, refused to fetishize immigrants, urban margins, and cells of violence in the Global South as origins of violence. Instead, critical researchers on security states have turned their lens almost exclusively on imperialism, and on the unbound hypersovereignty of hegemonic military powers of the Global North. This literature interrogates how the economic structures, political cultures, and security complexes of hegemonic powers, particularly of the United States, have shaped domination through violent forms of racialization, control, dispossession, and neocolonialism. Meanwhile, the liberal wing of the field has maintained a critique of imperialism, but has engaged in fieldwork in the Global South rather than in the hegemonic North. This liberal scholarship tends to focus on demilitarizing and "civilizing" the more humanitarian alternatives to repressive approaches, promoting human rights, "gender mainstreaming," and working with NGOs and peacekeeping interventions. Both schools of scholarship, however, tend to see the states, peoples, and social formations in the Global South as external to the politics of security, as either projections of securitization processes or as victims of repression and war. Forms of structure and agency as well as autonomous political formations and alliances in the Global South matter little to critical security studies. Not wanting to blame the victim, the field blames the victimizer but still sees the people in the Global South, largely, as dependents or casualties.

I am interested in how we can deepen the impact of critical security studies scholarship, and develop more resonant political alternatives, by producing in-depth research on and in the Global South that takes its forms of structure, agency, and political formation seriously. To complement and reconfigure critical work on detention camps and war zones, we can add research on the urban hubs in the Global South that serve as security laboratories. To extend work on the most devastated zones of occupation, detention, and massacre, we can turn our attention to the "swing states" of the semiperiphery that leverage agency by alternating between collaborating with and mobilizing against hegemonic order.

Furthermore, to grab the electrified "third rail" of critical security studies, we need to appropriate the study of sexualized racialization and gendering away from the victimologists. Sexuality infuses and animates the essential logics of securitized domination, whether in the militarized masculinity of soldiers, cops, and patriarchal states, or in the identification of targets of enforcement and rescue, be they sexual minorities, trafficked children, war crimes victims, or "prostituted" women. But what can we learn by examining agencies in the Global South that deploy, mobilize, and reappropriate the troubled intersections where sexualized biopolitics (the governance of populations through medicine, health, and "protective" policing regimes) meet necropolitics (the exterminatory governance of populations through war, colonialism, and racism)? These intersection zones are often saturated with the erotic imaginaries and colonial legacies of tropicalism and orientalism that circulate globally, today, beyond the postcolonial regions of Latin America and the Middle East. In order to address these gaps in the literature and develop new methods and units of analysis, let us walk our way down, starting with theories of the security state and its subjects, and then deconstruct Eurocentric perspectives on human security that begin and end with the policymakers of the North.

The State of the Security State

Notions of the human-security state that structure my analysis are profoundly indebted to Charles Tilly's analysis of the role of war in state-making. War, for Tilly, is not an extraordinary time of mobilization or state of exception, but a regularly emerging space of contention and "opportunity" when populations mobilize demands for rights, and states struggle to constitute new political subjects and formations under extreme conditions of contradiction (Tilly 1985, 170–71). These conditions Tilly describes in terms of organized criminality and protectionist coloniality, rather than as "exceptionality," as Agamben (2005) would have it. In this way, Tilly claims that modern government emerged from the "protection-racket state," in which rights-claims remain haunted by legacies of coercion. This racket state stages fears and produces real dangers in order to generate public terror and insecurity. In effect, racketeers make you beg for rights and protection from the dangers produced by security formations themselves. Sidney Tarrow (2012) highlights the continued relevance of Tilly's insights in his analysis of the security state in the age of the War on Terror. Tarrow, drawing on Harold Lasswell's (1941) notion of a "garrison state," suggests that the boundarylessness of the War on Terror, the unpredictability of air attacks and terror attacks, and the globalization and totalization of surveillance and security industries may have changed the nature of war. War as a unique moment and opportunity to fight for rights might be ending, to be replaced by a continuous struggle against threats to rights and civil liberties. I would agree, and rephrase this to say that war as an exceptional time where states, seen in the liberal sense as limited by rights-claims, are replaced by a state not limited by rights but rather delimited by particular spatial practices of territorialization and embodiment. These securitization practices constitute clusters of visibilities around certain hotspots, an archipelago of heavily policed enclaves where logics of enforcement and entitlement are continuously denaturalized, subverted, and ferociously reenforced.

In Tarrow's and Lasswell's formulations, Tilly's "protection-racket state" thus begins to be characterized in ways that parallel how Michael McCann (1991; 2006) describes the legal or judicial state. McCann's work presents the legal state as a subjectifying or hegemonic set of institutions that continuously condition, limit, and set the terms for much of social protest and resistance, but also provide for moments of change, mechanisms of formalization, and outlets for social justice. In this case, this moment of change I identify is the emergence of the human-security state and attendant new subjects of politics in the Global South.

New Subjects of Humanitarian Politics

At the start of 2009, human security as a new hegemonic framework for militarized, interventionist governance was articulated forcefully by the French foreign minister, Bernard Kouchner (also the founder of Médécins sans Frontiers); the US secretary of state, Hillary Rodham Clinton; the leader of Canada's opposition, Michael Ignatieff; the new United Nations high commissioner of human rights, Navanethem Pillay; and others. In the reformist policy discussions of 2009, "hard power" (i.e., unilateral, preemptive, military-centered intervention) was delegitimized, but the alternative of "soft power" (aid and rescue missions, hearts-and-minds cultural intervention, and development assistance) also seemed inadequate. In this conversation, "smart power" (focusing on intelligence gathering, diplomacy, and combining enforcement and development interventions associated with Canadian and Norwegian foreign aid and intervention policies) rose to displace the logic of aggressive "preemptive war" advocated by the United States and Britain in the first years of the twenty-first century.

Components of this soft-and-smart power doctrine came to include a "family values"–intensive mission (consisting of sexual and gender-sensitive interventions), a free-market developmental program (favoring Global North and Western economies and focusing on urban creative economies, but anchored in the humanitarian pacification apparatuses in the state, not the private sector), and a victim-focused subject (legitimizing enforcement interventions). This new "soft-and-smart power" paradigm (Nye 2009) came to serve as the Global North's appropriated version of the human-security agenda. But was it significantly different from the governance practices of neoliberal or neoconservative regimes? Clinton, Ignatieff, and Kouchner supported the war in Iraq, accepted justifications for torture, and propelled the militarization and moral doctrine of new humanitarianism. So perhaps human security was just a new branding of these old doctrines in the Global North. In the United States, Hillary Rodham Clinton, who was widely acclaimed explicitly as the "human security champion" (Noor 2008), became the reference point for these new politics (Lee 2009). In the United States, the political vocabulary is impoverished; one can hardly imagine a serious conversation on television about either neoliberalism or socialism. But for the past two decades, in the rest of the world, the transformation of global governance and intervention architectures has been debated in the complex and ambivalent language of human security.

The literature on human security produced in the Global North can be grouped into three sets of conversations: one among humanitarian practitioners; another among feminist, antiracist political scientists and sociolegal analysts; and another among poststructuralist theorists of the state. Scholars working closely with humanitarian and UN agencies, development institutions, or aid organizations have traced the history of the concept back to the pre–Cold War era of the Nuremberg Trials (1945–46), which established limits on sovereign authority and launched the modern apparatus of humanitarian law and the prohibition of wars of aggression or acquisition. Some even trace human security back to the medieval period in Europe, when the legitimacy of a sovereign ruler was directly limited by a real or implied contract to provide protection not to the state but to the people (MacFarlane and Khong 2006, 58–60), or to the 1815 Congress of Vienna, where "states debated the notion of holding trials to punish the perpetrators of the slave trade" (Hampson et al. 2002, 64). Meanwhile, researchers focusing on the United Nations system trace the origin of human security to a much more recent period, the post–Cold War 1990s.

> [Then,] human security was influenced substantially by the work of Amartya Sen, an adviser to the World Bank and UN, and a consultant for the 1994 [Human Development Report], who in the 1990s designed a set of indicators that shifted the measurement of poverty away from household income to include a range of factors:

health, literacy, gender equity and respect for human rights. . . . Frustrated with statecentric readings of security, scholars such as Barry Buzan and the Copenhagen School critiqued the utility of national security in a world where national securities were becoming increasingly internationalized and where states could only logically achieve security through participation in their neighborhood "security community." (Battersby and Siracusa 2009, 4)

This set of critical international-relations scholars, analyzing international agencies and operations from close range, also were the first to see the Global North or Western biases of the concept, which by the 2000s, as David Chandler claims, was used to "divide the world" and suspend the sovereignty of states in the Global South "whose insecurity threatens the security of Western consumer society as the instabilities associated with conflict, poverty, and alienation threaten to spill over into and destabilize the West" (Roberts 2010, 19). In this light, this group of scholars began to focus on Western and imperialist motives behind the doctrine of human security, at least as it was appropriated by humanitarian-development operations in "failed states" (Duffield 2007), intelligence-based community-policing models (Sheptycki 2009), and in "hearts and minds"–oriented counterinsurgency operations (Foley 2008; Fox 2008; González 2010).

Although not always using the term *human security*, a group of critical feminist scholars in the fields of legal anthropology, political theory, and political science have developed a trenchant critique of the very same kinds of humanization at the intersection of the military, criminal-justice, and welfare apparatuses of the state. Kristin Bumiller (2008) has examined how state neoliberalism (in the United States) changed and grew even more powerful as it appropriated feminist movements that were demanding protection against sexual violence. Carol Harrington (2010) has critically analyzed the late-twentieth-century rise of gendered and medicalized peacekeeping operations and the "gender empowerment" missions of new kinds of international policing. Anna Marie Smith (2007) has explored the state's cooption of feminist discourses of family protection, human development, and marriage promotion in order to extend punitive and police-centered racial and class hierarchies. And Cynthia Enloe (2004; 2007) has been vigilant in tracing both globalizing military apparatuses and militarization doctrines' appropriation of feminist and gender-empowerment agendas, as well as the successful struggles to resist these appropriations and maintain the viability of radical alternatives.

Poststructuralist political theory, which I can touch on only very briefly here, has long been committed to the critique of humanism and humanization dynamics, particularly their imbrication with processes of state consolidation or repressive power. Of course, in *The Order of Things* (2002 [1966]), Michel Foucault proclaims the "end of man" or the end of humanism, and in later work illustrates the processes by which the modern human subject is generated by modes of surveillance, practices of discipline, and circuits of incitement, particularly at the intersection of state population protection (welfare) and population control (security) regimes. In his last work (which neatly foretells the emergence of human-security discourse in the international sphere and already provides a thorough critique of it), Foucault (2008) turns his attention away from explicitly punitive and repressive practices and toward the productivity and seemingly emancipatory "biopolitical" forms of rule that protect, cultivate, care for, and empower populations, markets, and territories, all through extending security apparatuses that he identified (in 1978) with neoliberal doctrines and practices. Recent work by Etienne Balibar (2003), Mara de Gennaro (2003), Jacques Lezra (2003), Athena Athanasiou (2003), and Samera Esmeir (2012) has extended this later work of Foucault, analyzing the technologies of humanness and forms of biopolitical rule in the context of new wars, racisms, and forms of humanitarian conflict and UN-sanctioned occupation. Coming from another angle, James Scott's *Seeing Like a State* (1998) focuses on the coloniality of modern humanitarian state practices, particularly during the high-modern period (mid-twentieth century) of utopian urban modernism, forced collectivization of agriculture, population relocation, and infrastructure extensions that caused mass displacements. Timothy Mitchell's *The Rule of Experts* (2002) explores the humanization and dehumanization of forms of capital, property, and development discourse in colonial and late-twentieth-century Egypt. He focuses particularly on how certain forms of technoscientific economic discourse deployed by the state mask the power and structured properties of elite power within the state, all while seeming to focus on the rehabilitation and rescue of the peasant or the poor. And most recently, a group of scholars, including Craig Calhoun (2010), Mariella Pandolfi (2010), Didier Fassin (2010), and Laurence McFalls (2010) have launched a conversation with Giorgio Agamben's work on states of emergency and with

Anne Orford and Mahmood Mamdani on the coloniality of humanitarian intervention. In this book, I complement and extend these conversations, while emphasizing and centering the role of actors, sites, and processes of the Global South.

What does a shift toward a Global South perspective offer? As I argue in this book, influential and globally circulating forms of humanized security governance did not emerge from UN conference rooms or US memos on "soft power" but were tested, deployed, hybridized, and disseminated within and between urban-security laboratories of the Global South. It is within these sites and circuits that particular variants of humanitarian subjects were configured and animated. Global South–originating human-security modalities and grammars have generated processes of sexualized infantilization and racialization that have blocked or dismantled entitlement-based "social security" models and extended enforcement-based "rescue or punish" securitization regimes that leftist as well as religious political movements then came to appropriate in contradictory ways. During the period discussed in this book, the matrix of human security was extended and naturalized in Cairo and Rio de Janeiro through cultural processes of militarization and subjectification, as well as through policing and urban-planning projects that produced and depended on reproducing key binaries: between economy (identified with global markets) and culture (identified with national tradition); between a particular kind of liberalism (for elite enclaves) and a technocratic form of militarized and moralistic populism (for the rest); and between the citizen (an ideal of security and propriety held just out of reach) and the securitized human or parahuman (targets of security operations and rescue missions deemed incapable of sovereignty over their selves).

As my findings demonstrate, human-security modes of governance extend their power through a particular set of interventions related to sexuality or embodied moralization. These include the identification and rescue of heritage culture by putting gender in its "traditional place" and rescuing the family from "perversions of globalization" in the cultural domain; by the arrest of sex traffickers accused not just of sexual violence and forced labor but also of trafficking in alien racial and sexual identities; and by the capture and control of predatory "thug" masculinities that are identified with the most menacing of global flows that threaten the urban social fabric and derail plans for the redevelopment of marginal areas. What the new doctrines of human security do not do is challenge the primacy of security discourse itself. When security logics come to serve as the articulating hub for governance and sociopolitical discourse, this process is called securitization. While striving to reconcile divergent modes of power, human security evacuates notions of security based on entitlement while extending enforcement prerogatives. Humanized security politics challenges individualistic and market-oriented neoliberal frameworks with moralistic, technocratic rescue doctrines, and substitutes the figures of creative entrepreneurs prospering in a flexible economy with that of rescued prostitutes, secured traffickers, and culturally redeemed communities that are disciplined and redeveloped through security operations and new policing technologies.

But these human-security logics are not invulnerable to resistance and change. In fact, they are intensely dynamic. Incommensurability between the components of securitized governance renders these processes contradictory and vulnerable to change from within as well as without. And this dynamic complexity reveals its uniqueness in the history, politics, and public cultures of Cairo and Rio de Janeiro. Forms of urban dissent and repression, contradictory trends in militarization and liberalization, and particular forms of transregional internationalist politics link these two megacities, and open up this human-security matrix to processes of change that can upset, reverse, or reimagine the prerogatives of the emergent human-security state. These were vividly demonstrated by the revolutionary transformations that swept Egypt and, to a lesser extent, Brazil in 2011 and 2012.

Comparative Frameworks and Global Questions

The analysis in this book compares similar processes that emerge in distinct contexts, presenting and testing evidence and arguments that demonstrate the novelty, uniqueness, and Global South origins of these new security-politics trends. Comparative analysis is justified by the fact that several structural factors and sociohistorical trends have positioned Egypt and Brazil in analogous locations. These correlative positions were recognized in the 1970s and 1980s by world-systems theory and its notion of the dynamic semiperiphery (Amin 1973; Arrighi 1985; Wallerstein 1976), but are largely ignored by contemporary globalization studies and "transition-to-democracy" studies. Those fields' focus on civil society and liberalization processes (markets and elections) has led to the marginalization of the phenomena that most capture the uniqueness of the semiperiphery.

Egypt and Brazil both have served as semiperipheral pivots of global capital and development discourse and as innovators for policing, detention, and security industries. Both countries act as world-scale tourism-sector pioneers that shape not just travel economies but also the postcolonial imagination of the moral and cultural character of "the global," all while relocalizing and rendering authentic the cultural realms identified with "religion." Both countries are oil and gas producers that geopolitically leverage these strategic fuel commodities. And both societies have been marked by regular involvement of the armed forces in politics and by extensive involvement of the police in shaping civic life and social identity. Further, in both Brazil and Egypt, military and police practices evolved in ways that reaffirm the coercive apparatuses as autonomous from the law and antagonistic to the elected political sphere. Moreover, the realm of the coercive apparatus is deeply fractured in both countries. Police resent and cast dispersions on the military, and vice versa. Also, in each case, colonial-era racialized and sexualized "knowledge/power" systems (orientalism in Egypt and tropicalism in Brazil) came to be appropriated by indigenous elites as modernist state-building ideologies. Then, from the 1950s through the early 1970s, international collaboration between Rio de Janeiro and Cairo expanded through cooperation in UN peacekeeping missions and decolonization efforts, and through public-intellectual exchanges around critical social theory (dependency theory, development theory, and urban modernist planning) (Amar 2012a; Prashad 2007).

In the 1970s, both Rio and Cairo served as pioneering test sites for neoliberalization, deployed in each site by a military junta. Then, in the 1980s, national militaries in both countries turned away from soldiering and government and toward infrastructure development. During this period, while armed forces became infrastructure entrepreneurs, police became paramilitarized and entrepreneurial in distinct ways. Police redirected themselves toward internal threats and untethered themselves from the supervision of either the military or the law. With this, the police stepped in to fill the "soldiering void" left by the civilianization of military activities, and "law enforcement" became the primary protagonist of securitization and militarization in the domestic context.

Also, the global-city status of both Rio de Janeiro and Cairo facilitates comparative analysis. Cairo remains the capital and sociopolitical laboratory of Egypt. In Brazil, the political capital moved from Rio de Janeiro to Brasilia in 1960 (Richard J. Williams 2005), with power gradually shifting between the cities over twenty years. But Rio has remained Brazil's window to the world, serving as a continental and global laboratory for security and development technologies, NGO and participatory governance innovation, and for spectacular world-scale carnivals, political summits, and sporting events, including the megascale 2014 World Cup and 2016 Olympic Games.

In the 1990s, landmark United Nations summits—in Rio in 1992 and in Cairo in 1994—opened space for both globalizing cities, and their home countries, to serve as global security innovators and to promote NGO-centered transnationalism (Schechter 2001). These pioneering meetings became laboratories for democratization and securitization of global governance. In these settings, two versions of human-security governance, one NGO-based and another based in repressive policing, clashed. And sometimes they merged, as entitlement and enforcement models of human security and human development transformed, particularly around subjects of sexuality rights, cultural rescue, and humanitarian intervention. Beginning in 2011, both Brazil and Egypt became theaters for humanitarian interventions by national armed forces within the domestic context, as armies were deployed to implement new forms of populist and national-capital-focused development projects and humanitarian rescue operations.

This contentious process of forging human-security governance proceeded through three phases. In the early 1990s, Rio and Cairo pioneered "cultural-rescue" models of human-security governance. Both cities separated economic globalization from cultural nationalism and isolated consumer spaces from heritage zones through security operations and redevelopment plans that came to orbit around the control of "perverse" sex tourism. Then, in the subsequent period, 2000–2009, Rio and Cairo pioneered "anti-human-trafficking" models of human-security governance, arresting sex traffickers and rescuing prostitutes. And by the second decade of the twenty-first century, a third phase had begun, in which the transregional circulation of parastatal formations and human-security governance logics brought the elites, NGOs, police, military, and humanitarian apparatuses of the two nations, as well as the other emergent powers of the Global South, into increasingly intensive interaction.

In this book I present these three phases of evolution and these sets of contradictory alliances and transregional flows through a series of case studies. These include two transregional analyses of diplomatic, NGO, and parastatal flows between the two countries in the security sector; two comparative case-study chapters focusing on issues of moralistic urban-security planning, embodied or racialized moralization, and gendered cultural rescue; and two comparative case-study chapters focusing on issues of police militarization and sexualized antitrafficking and antiharassment campaigns.

Mapping the *Security Archipelago*

This book is organized to provide an alternative political history of neoliberalism and to map out the politics and culture of what I describe as the human-security state. Though the chapters are ordered chronologically, the phenomena analyzed in each one inform and resonate with those in other chapters. For example, the rise of sexualized "antitrafficking" politics in the 2000s in Brazil and Egypt does not erase and, in fact, deeply depends on the logic of "cultural-rescue" politics that dominated the previous phase of the emergent human-security state in the 1990s. The rise of transregional cooperation between South America and the Middle East in the 2000s does not supersede forms of UN internationalism and globalist humanitarianism that peaked in the 1990s, but depends on it. The return of mass labor organization and populist politics in the 2000s challenges but also articulates with the liberalism and legal personalism that defined neoliberal-era opposition politics beginning in the 1980s. And the return of armed forces to domestic security and politics in the 2010s does not erase the legacy of the standoffs between police entrepreneurialism and human-rights legalism that dominated the 1980s, but entails a dialectical response to it.

RESTAGING NEOLIBERAL HISTORY AND THEORY

The first step in articulating a new political theory of securitization is to identify the transregional and structural causes behind the political rise of human-security governance in the geopolitical belt that we used to call the semiperiphery. Thus, I begin chapter 1 by addressing key gaps in the political study of the post–Cold War world order. What role did Global South policing and military security organizations play in the rise of new doctrines of UN internationalism and global civil society? Rather than analyzing United Nations humanitarian policies as instruments emerging from either the Security Council or from benevolent nonprofit foundations from the North, I take a bottom-up, Global South–centered approach. In this vein, I take seriously the host cities and social contexts that enveloped the UN's two most democratic and contentious summit events:

the Rio Earth Summit of 1992 and the Cairo Population and Development Conference of 1994. I identify the mechanisms that generated contention between police, religious, NGO, and military actors. I also assess the transformative impact of cultural, racial, and gender and sexuality social movements in and around these summits. I show how new forms of policing and security appropriated some of the language and logic of the more democratic and humanizing practices of global policymaking tested at these mega-events, planting the seeds of the human-security state.

In chapter 2, I provide an in-depth study of certain pioneer projects that tested new forms of sexualized securitization in these two global cities between the 1980s and 2000. Rather than provide a conventional political analysis of the rise of liberal NGOs and identity movements around security reform or human rights, I trace the rise of new kinds of illiberal urban-security planning schemes and policing practices and how they confronted antinationalist expressions identified as queer. Particular cases include the policing of militant forms of resistance by *travesti* prostitutes and the arresting of men for being "gay" debauchers and for advocating transnational erotic conviviality in Cairo. These confrontations between new security industries and forms of transnationally identified queer resistance generated new subjects of sexual rescue and emancipation around which this new brand of sovereignty and species of coercive governmentality coalesced. I refer to these coalitions of transnational investors, police and security consultants, and global-city redevelopers as "parastatal formations" in order to avoid the overgeneralizations and normative implications offered by the neoliberal terms "private sector" and "civil society." I draw on new readings of Michel Foucault (2008) as well as of Timothy Mitchell (1991b; 2002). I also build on political theory derived from studies of the privatization of the state in southern Africa and the Caribbean, and on subaltern and coloniality-conscious queer theory. Through these lenses, I develop a new approach to the state by examining how these parastatals securitized the spaces and subjects in Cairo and Rio through sexuality. With this, I help lay the foundation for a Global South–centered, transregional frame for the study of global security politics.

PLANNING AND CULTURE

In chapters 3 and 4, I build on the analysis of the politics and culture of human security laid out in chapters 1 and 2 by profiling the social and institutional causes behind the rise of cultural-rescue projects. With this, I map the forms of spatial segregation produced by morality policing missions that aim to protect authenticity and gendered normativity. These projects, which target heritage, are central to the prerogative of the emergent human-security state. In these chapters, I analyze, in this context, the rise of what I call infranationalism—a kind of politics that naturalizes and depoliticizes social, moral, and cultural binaries by building gendered, class, and moral control discourses into the grids, services, roads, and built infrastructural forms of these globalizing cities. This politics has the reactionary effect of hardening newly invented traditions and neoconservative values and pieties, but it can also have the radicalizing effect of generating new forms of national capital and new claims to territory by newly securitized agents.

In chapter 3, I analyze the remarkable overlaps between forms of purist religious militancy and the "cultural-rescue" regimes of human-security urban planning that emerged in the 1990s. Between 1994 and 1996, an Egyptian urbanist in Cairo worked in the quake-damaged but historically rich popular quarters of the city. There, he undertook social science fieldwork on how to recenter the human needs of the urban poor in the priorities of UN and Egyptian government projects. He was studying for a master's in urban engineering at Germany's Technical University of Hamburg and hoped to get a job at the United Nations as an expert on cultural preservation (McDermott 2002). In his thesis, he developed a detailed plan to promote humanized security and modernization, in Cairo, Aleppo, and other "Islamic cities," that represented the urban poor not as empowered subjects of participatory government, but as objects of a technocratically administered cultural-security project. This project would ignite economic development by restoring natural cultural balances and governing the perverting power of the global by resegregating women from men, purging working-class people from the sexualized tourism and consumer sectors, and removing "out of place" structures, especially certain kinds of high-rise towers. This urban planner's technocratic urban visions as they appeared in his thesis made no reference to Islamic jurisprudence, Shari'a, or Hadith doctrines, or to any militant ideology. In this Egyptian planner's vision, the curving alleyways and cul-de-sacs of Cairo and Aleppo were to be the protected zones for women, sensualized and sexualized—and "humanized"—by a cultural-security regime that would maintain them as centers for the reproduction of Islamic values and authenticity, while men would leave the meandering alleys for the straight city and its office towers. Rejected in his applications for United Nations jobs, this man, Mohamed Atta, eventually left for Afghanistan (Brook 2009).

His next contact with urban transformation was when he led the 9/11 attack on the World Trade Center towers in New York.

In chapter 3, I also contrast Atta's urban cultural-security plans for Cairo with those of local community groups and nonpurist popular religious expressions. These campaigns developed participatory practices and produced public signs and representations that "desecuritized" and deessentialized the politics of culture in Islamic Cairo. These forms of popular religiosity and public imaginaries went against the grain of both UN heritage-development and state tourism-marketing visions, while also rejecting Atta's obsessive concern with securing gender distinctions and class hierarchies through segregating spaces and protecting historical buildings.

In chapter 4, I take the reader to the scene of another "September 11th." That is, I explore the causes behind the massive prison uprisings and police strike that were intentionally launched in Rio de Janeiro to coincide with the one-year anniversary of the New York attacks. I extend the analysis of cultural-rescue urbanism and its radicalized gender, race, and sexuality doctrines. In Rio, the label "terrorist" is applied to many groups who take far less drastic action than Mohamed Atta did. As described by João Vargas, several favelas have attempted to establish their own security systems, in efforts to save themselves from the ravages of violence, impunity, and intimidation that they face at the hands of both Militarized Police and drug cartels. When the elected neighborhood council of a majority Afro-Brazilian community set up security cameras and monitoring equipment, the city responded with swift repression. In a city where middle-class condominiums, public spaces, and white neighborhoods have surveillance cameras and private security forces everywhere, one would think that installing more closed-circuit systems would be completely unnewsworthy. But when a black favela did it, and the targets of surveillance included corrupt policemen and government-linked militias, then the cameras were identified as a "terrorist threat" to public security (Vargas 2006). I analyze how international institutions and the regional government of Rio developed cultural-security projects that repolarized and forcibly retraditionalized gender and race in the favelas by marrying old tropicalist imaginaries of plantation blackness to the wealth of modern samba tourism. I also examine how community groups and progressive state officials who have an alternative view of security, culture, and gender become sexualized as dangerous or perverse. In sum, my discussion of urban planning and human security in chapters 3 and 4 follows the development of projects that deploy infrastructure in ways that naturalize and separate new racialized and gendered identifications.

POLICING AND SECURITIZED LABOR

Whereas in chapters 3 and 4 I trace the planning doctrines and politically situate the authenticist and segregationist impulses of new human-security regimes, in chapters 5 and 6 I move on to examine a slightly later period (2006–11) during which sex trafficking, sexual harassment, and concern with predatory masculinities came to dominate globalizing human-security discourse and policing priorities. In these deployments, a logic of subjectification I identify as parahumanism begins to emerge. In chapter 5, I provide an in-depth analysis of Rio de Janeiro's massive police, moral, and globally linked humanitarian campaigns against sex trafficking, first launched in 2006. This included the local media's favorite, Operation Princess, a set of police raids and televised awareness campaigns focusing on "sex trafficker" brothels. These operations were first deployed in Rio de Janeiro's touristic Copacabana Beach district and invoked the image of Princess Isabel, the monarch who finally abolished chattel slavery in Brazil in 1888 (and was then immediately deposed by furious white coffee planters). The campaign also referred to the iconic contemporary "princess" image of the generic virginal young girl, represented as embodying the honor of a nation, menaced by global forces that threatened to abduct, pervert, prostitute, and traffic her. Haunted by the legacy of the Candelária massacre (when police killed a group of homeless children in 1993), and thus hoping to change its image as a state that murders children and promotes prostitution and sex tourism, Brazil began a series of social-purity campaigns that combined the efforts of international organizations, transnational feminist social movements, evangelical Christian church organizations, the provincial Militarized Police, and the Federal Police. Programs like Operation Princess aimed to promote a new humanized security agenda. That agenda was to reform the corrupt and megaviolent Militarized Police by restoring their early-twentieth-century role of vice cops so that they would see themselves as moral guardians of society's gendered honor and sociocultural integrity. Operation Princess was meant to promote Brazil as a "human-security superpower" on the world stage, in ways that would not threaten the value agendas of its new Middle Eastern geopolitical partners or the US Administration of President George W. Bush.

At about the same time in Cairo, between 2003 and 2010, internationalist feminist campaigns advocated antiharassment projects that demonized working-class youth masculinities as well as "disreputable" public femininities in an attempt to intensify the policing of the city and to discipline public sociability. Through a politics of respectability and by allying itself with repressive police and security authorities, this internationally linked feminist antiharassment campaign demobilized class-based movements for democratic change. By contrast, inventive, alternative Egyptian feminist organizations adapted UN gender doctrines and legal mechanisms to their own purposes, mobilizing mass campaigns that critiqued frameworks of police protection and social respectability. They cultivated forms of assertive female agency that came to occupy center stage during the Egyptian Revolution of January and February 2011. By contrasting these distinct forms of global-local feminist organizing, I reveal in chapter 6 the queering power of new metaphors of masculinity, class struggle, and global female insecurity.

In chapters 5 and 6, I aim to shed light on how the politics of arresting human trafficking and stopping sexual predation became models or test laboratories for globalizing human-security governance, developed in the urban context of the Global South. The antitrafficking model and its anti-sex-harassment variants are powerful because their logic of sexualized securitization attacks forms of globalization and seems to challenge neoliberal insecurities. It adopts the stance of the nationalist antimarket vigilante, revives the ethical language of abolitionism and the Progressive Era, and blends uncomfortably with renewed discourses of socialism, workerism, and Third Worldism. This framework is based on tactics of extending enforcement and moral tutelage into the population, whose members are seen as suspects and as victims to be rescued and detained, regardless of their consent.

Analysis of these globalizing anti-trafficking campaigns in the urban theater allow us to identify some trends in humanized security as they continue to shift from peacekeeping models (based on notions of consent by all parties, the impartiality of the intervener, and the "conflict defusing" aims of the operation) (Tsagourias 2006) to a *peace enforcement* or "policekeeping" model. In this framing, consent is replaced by coercion, impartiality by moral righteousness. And conflict-resolution organizations are replaced by a rescue industry that detains and criminalizes both victims and victimizers, often without bothering to distinguish between the two. The conventional Eurocentric analyses of the origins of humanitarian intervention that emphasize the Red Cross, evangelical abolitionism, Florence Nightingale, and the Geneva conventions neglect an alternative set of histories and locations. The new sexualized security models of the contemporary anti-sex-trafficking era, tested in and deployed from the Global South, portray themselves as reconciling the humanitarian legacies of feminized and moralized humanitarian abolitionism with the muscular, masculinized anticolonialism of militarized peacekeeping.

The sexual securitization model represents both the "top-down" movement of international humanitarianism toward an enforcement model, as well as the "bottom-up" movement of urban law enforcement and national armed forces toward an internationalist humanitarian model. Local city police forces, which used to see themselves as controlling local forms of deviance and criminality, are increasingly seeing themselves as part of a global network of security industries, engaged in morally charged, heavily armed humanitarian campaigns that target the criminalizing perversions of globalization as they capture local spaces and populations. By shedding light on these shifts, I detail in chapters 5 and 6 the processes of political subjectification that the enforcement of human-security interventions produces.

END OF NEOLIBERALISM?

In the conclusion of this book, which ties in with my discussions of humanitarian subjectification and parastatal formations in chapters 5 and 6, I reanalyze these processes in the context of the changes wrought in and around the Great Recession, or the global financial crisis that began in 2008. I bring the reader back to the big issues—the possible end of Global North hegemony and the disintegration of the neoliberal logics of global governance that undergirded it. I wrap up the arguments I elaborated in the earlier chapters while also clarifying what I mean by the "end of neoliberalism" and the cultural politics of state transformation in the current context. I review the literature on the end of neoliberalism, particularly coming out of the contemporary Left in Latin America, as well as new work on authoritarian and military populism, which sees an alternative to neoliberalism coming, more probably, from the right wing. I end with a proposal for reframing the study of sexuality, militarization, social movements, and the state in the Global South in light of the end of neoliberalism.

The end of neoliberalism here does not herald the end of a period in history or the crisis of a mode of production. Rather, the end of neoliberalism signals a radical shift in perspectives. This shift can include a transition from mapping the globalization of investment markets and consumer subjects to apprehending newly animated bodies of mobilized morality and militarized populism. Or it could mean moving from totalizing the spread of North-centered financial globalisms to tracing the circuits of transmission of policy innovations and worker assertions between Global South sites. In the conclusion, I also suggest that we can see a new global balance of power emerging more clearly if we turn from framing reality in the technical language of economics to instead utilize concepts and lenses that can make some sense of the violent, contradictory, and dynamic logics of securitization and sexualization. Such processes, unfolding in accordance with contradictory human-security logics, created subjects of new mass uprisings and patterns of insurrection and intervention. They are propelling a new Global South–centered balance of world power into the twenty-first century.

1

MOORING A NEW GLOBAL ORDER BETWEEN
CAIRO AND RIO DE JANEIRO
World Summits and Human-Security Laboratories

Through which processes and in which kinds of sites can a new global model of governance emerge from the Global South? In the first decade of the 2000s, a new body of scholarship explored the governance innovations of leftist and populist regimes that had emerged since the late 1990s in South America. And more recently, a flurry of new analyses have weighed the causes and consequences of popular uprisings, in addition to new political assertions of military forces, mass movements, and religious political organizations in the Middle East during the so-called Arab Spring. But these studies, on the whole, have considered these shifts to be area-specific phenomena, that is, as local or regional revolts against "the global" rather than as manifestations of a new "global" overtaking the old. Global North–based observers have tended to discount or ignore the possibility that common structural positioning or sociohistorical links unite South America and the Middle East, tying together these two sets of political shifts. Rare acknowledgments of linkages between these regions have taken the form of caricatures, like that of Brazil's Lula meeting with the Arab League's Moussa, or queering representations of Lula's or Hugo Chavez's "romance" with Iran's Ahmadinejad (fig. 1.1). But do these curious encounters between the Middle East and South America have no historical context? Are these connections and convergences nothing but sideshows to a new balance-of-power drama that is largely scripted between Washington and Beijing?

In the first decade of the twenty-first century, examinations of shifts in world order and of the possible decline of Euro-American hegemony (for example, Halper 2010; Huang 2010) have tended to focus on China

FIGURE 1.1. Brazil's President Lula and Iran's President Ahmadinejad as a South-South romance of counterhegemony. Artist credit: Toni D'Agostinho.

and the challenges posed to the Washington Consensus by what has come to be termed the Beijing Consensus. Beijing's model is defined as one that rejects the "roll-back the state" doctrine of neoliberal restructuring and instead advocates expansive state spending, public coordination of industrial planning, and a nationally orchestrated promotion of investment, resource extraction, and market expansion campaigns abroad. Analyses of other emerging world powers, India and Russia in particular, have tended to measure these countries' degrees of resemblance to or divergence from the Beijing Consensus (Ferdinand 2007; Humphrey and Messner 2009; Lukin 2009; Sinha and Dorschner 2010). And after the Global North financial crisis of 2008, it was consistently argued that the statist China model became even more appealing for these large states (Abad 2010, 46–47). But beyond the three powers of Russia, India, and China, do the regions of the Global South that some used to call the semiperiphery play any role in constituting new global-scale orderings? And what role do questions of security, sexuality, and the constitution of new subjects of "humanity" play in shaping the substance of emergent global orderings?

In this chapter I identify processes and types of sites, and recover certain transregional political histories of social struggle, in order to begin to build an alternative analysis that substitutes the current United States-versus-China lens with one that takes seriously the generative nature of linkages between what once was referred to as "semiperipheral" powers, in this case between the Middle East and South America. To begin to build a Global South–centered history of both neoliberalism and post-neoliberal orders, I replace the Sinocentric notion of the Beijing Consensus with a distinct and more broadly applicable heuristic device, that of the human-security state. This optic highlights structural resemblances, political-historical linkages, and circulating cultural identities formed around certain "humanized" security or military-humanitarian practices in Egypt and Brazil. In order to locate the origins of these human-security subjects and practices, I identify political processes, meetings and networks, and flows of norms and discourse that have shaped their articulation. Here I present findings on forms of urban-security operations, NGO cultural- and sexual-rights campaigns, and militarized repressive and humanitarian interventions as they came together in the contexts of UN world conferences and transregional diplomatic summits hosted in Rio and Cairo. I argue that the contentions around these events helped to catalyze human-security regimes in regards to specific subjects of entitlement and enforcement that I label "parahuman." These are *parahuman* since they are configured as constantly requiring the *para*—the supplement or prosthesis—of rescue intervention. They need rescuing, police discipline, cultural protection, and extraordinary military intervention; this human subject of governmentality is supposed to be necessarily securitized, always-already disabled or insecure, a victim needing parallel, emergency, paralegal, or extralegal protective action or recue intervention in order to assume the provisional status of citizen.

In this chapter, I also identify the spatial context and cultural mechanisms by which emerging parahuman subjects and human-security enforcement regimes were transferred from a particular local context in the Global South to the general, international-policy context of the UN system via the landmark spaces of world summits and securitized urban clashes in the 1990s. I will highlight patterns of actors, alliances, and mobilizations of transnational sexualized and racialized identities that converged in new ways around the staging of these world-scale events. I argue that these new movements and subjects of politics gradually reframed the meaning of new bilateral agreements and partnerships between South America and the Middle East in the 2000s. Rather than choosing between a global-scale method, such as an international-relations analysis of United Nations–level meetings, or a local-scale ethnographic or political-sociological account of transnationally linked networks and movements in the Global South, I mix both perspectives. Weaving together the global and local, the international-diplomatic and transnational-urban, I draw a new kind of map of relationships and identify transregional subjects whose significance will become more apparent in the chapters that follow.

I begin with an examination of emerging security regimes, participatory mechanisms, and humanization doctrines around the United Nations Conference on Environment and Development (UNCED, better known as the "Earth Summit" in English or "Eco '92" in Portuguese) in Rio de Janeiro in 1992 and the UN Conference on Population and Development (which, due to the nature of the debates, virtually became the "World Sexuality Summit") in Cairo in 1994. Here, UN world conferences reveal themselves as nodal moments in time and space, where specific Brazil- and Egypt-based human-security practices "jumped scale" from the urban, Global South to the international level, shaping the terms and imaginaries of post–Cold War internationalism and beginning to sow the seeds of alternatives to neoliberalism. I then turn to the recent set of "South America–Arab States" (ASPA) summits between 2003 and 2009, and the Progressive States Summit and G-20 meeting of 2009, highlighting how these events articulated a new transregional family of racialized, sexualized, and moralized subjects that populated the emerging global order of human-security governmentality.

The studies presented here aim to build on discussions in transnational studies and global cities literatures that examine "mega-events" such as Olympic Games (Chalkly and Essex 1999; Surborg, Wynsberghe, and Wyly 2008), World Cup tournaments (Cornelissen 2008), World Expos (Lecardane and Zhuo 2003–4), and large international summits. UN conferences and social forums serve not just to create a new marketing image for a city or country (Gold and Gold 2008), and not just to make money or stimulate development for an "urban regime" coalition (Lauria 1997; Stone 2005), but as powerful and intensely productive envelopes of time and space that generate new governance, security, repression, participation, mobility, and migration norms and patterns (Doel and Hubbard 2002; Giulianotti and Klauser 2010; Harvey 1989; Michael Peter Smith 2001). At these mega-events, power struggles unfold and processes are concretized in real spaces that provide privileged access to technical experts, policymakers, security agencies, and the media, but usually very limited access to civil society, or they are notoriously lacking in participatory or accountability mechanisms. These high-status nodal events end up marking some practices, discourses, and identities as "global." They launch certain policies, practices, and networks into transnational circulation, where they assume world status and can then officially challenge predominant frameworks of order. These events also deploy police and planning practices that brand other spaces, social worlds, and cultural practices as "local," to be either captured and commodified to serve as symbolic markings of authenticity and difference, or detained and marginalized since they "pervert" these arrangements or are "out of place" in the cartography of newly defined local-global binaries.

From Summits to Streets

With the 1992 Earth Summit in Rio de Janeiro and the 1994 Cairo Conference on Population and Development, the international system ventured out from its diplomatic chambers in New York and Geneva onto the streets of major cities in the Global South. As argued by Sonia Corrêa, Rosalind P. Petchesky, and Richard Parker, "Since 1985, and with more intensity after 1990, the effects of the Washington Consensus were systematically criticized and civil society groups mounted demonstrations against the World Bank, IMF, and, later on, the World Trade Organization (WTO) and the Group of 7 (after 1994, the Group of 8) wherever these institutions held their high-level meetings. Concurrently, the UN adopted a deliberate strategy to encourage the engagement of civil society in policymaking processes, in particular in a series of international conferences on its development agenda, known as the UN cycle of social conferences" (2008, 17).

In these UN world conferences, and in the NGO meetings and street protests that surrounded them, the international community and local social movements came together with the aim of generating a new planetary model for participatory global governance and new processes for transregional policymaking. As Michael Shechter has argued, the Rio summit of 1992 marked the debut on the world stage of a kind of NGO internationalism, wherein Global South NGOs pushed their northern counterparts to take "relatively radical positions on issues related to [the negotiations in] Brazil. . . . Another innovation of note connected to the Rio conference—this time at the counter conference—was to a so-called alternative treaties project [through which] NGOs can better cooperate with one another at how to shape relations with other social sectors such as the youth and women's movements" (2001, 195–97). Essentially, these UN world conferences' political aims were to extend democracy and untangle the contradictions of liberalization, particularly around issues of the environment, sexuality, gender, and rights, and, in the case of Brazil, to openly commemorate the dismantling of military-authoritarian rule and the end of the Cold War. In the unfolding of these events, we can identify transformations in international security politics as they came to intersect with three varieties of "local state" enforcement practices, in particular, the militarization of urban public security, the humanitarianization of military interventions within domestic contexts, and the moralistic hypervisibilization of sexuality in the metaphors and logics of security.

The 1992 Earth Summit was explicitly concerned with articulating a new policy agenda for issues of biodiversity, sustainable development, and climate change (Schechter 2001, 3–7; Strong 1993). But issues of public security, cultural autonomy, and state militarization made at least as many headlines as those of climate change or biodiversity conservation. The street-level struggles occurring on the margins of the formal meetings between heads of state became the lead stories and often not only stole the show, but also redirected the policy discourses of the conference (William R. Long 1992b). This was the first major UN summit to host a parallel conference or "counter summit," the Global Forum (Parson, Haas, and Levy 1992), with official consultative status. This forum included more than fifteen thousand participants representing NGOs from around the world, operating as a self-declared Planetary Peoples' Assembly (Van Rooy 1997, 94–95).[1] The Global Forum demanded a democratization of international security and development institutions (Hochstetler and Keck 2007, chap. 3). In the Global Forum, issues of sexuality, culture, and policing often overwhelmed the original set of ecological issues (Parker, Petchesky, and Sember 2007, preface, chap. 2).

In the years immediately preceding 1992, international media representations tended to portray urban Brazil as a post–Cold War vision of both paradise and hell, with Rio providing spectacular displays of both the best of cosmopolitan progressivism and the worst of vigilante-supplemented

FIGURE 1.2. Brazilian military guards at the Riocentro conference center during the Earth Summit in Rio de Janeiro (2 June 1992). Photo credit: AP Photo / Ricardo Mazalan.

authoritarianism. The practices through which the Brazilian police, the military, and civil administration secured and governed the spaces of the Rio Earth Summit brought to light the contradictions of neoliberal market states and began the fraught process of fusing movements to democratize world governance with campaigns to extend police and militarily deployed humanitarian interventions. On the eve of the UN conference, massive, coordinated Militarized Police and federal armed forces operations swept through the city, cleaning its streets for the arrival of the NGOs and heads of state (Arias 2006, 15). This security and pacification operation deployed more armed forces troops and tanks — backing up and overseeing the operations of the Federal Police and Militarized Police — than had the military coup in 1964 (fig. 1.2). The *LA Times* reported that "[the Federal Police chief Romeu Tuma] said more than 1,000 federal police are working on summit security, and, according to press reports, 35,000 uniformed police and army troops are assisting" (Long 1992a). Assault vehicles and troop brigades moved through the city to cordon off the slum neighborhoods, keeping much of the black population incarcerated in their homes, unable to arrive at their jobs or access services. Brutal and often deadly tactics were used to clean the city of thousands of homeless "street children" and families without shelter, and to eradicate the presence of transsexuals and prostitutes from the face of the city. The "iron fist" policing profile of the UN summits highlighted the paradox of liberalization and globalization: the fact that the militarization of urban governance and the targeting of sexualized and racialized groups by militarized policing practices had intensified, not diminished, as political liberalization proceeded after the end of the military dictatorship (Ungar 2002, 48–55). The treatment of certain racialized and sexualized populations as suspect groups or enforcement targets had become normalized within processes of neoliberalization and democratization in Brazil (Amar 2005; Paixão 2005). Meanwhile, the Global Forum for NGOs provided a spectacle of democracy, social movement, and participation. In this context, two sets of issues rose to prominence in the forum: sexual rights and cultural autonomy. These issues also animated a transnational social movement to democratize global governance that took the form of what could be called an "entitlement model."

In 1988, Brazil approved a new constitution that deemed health care "the right of everyone and a state duty" (Vianna and Carrara 2007, 37). The struggle of social movements to end the military dictatorship in Brazil in the mid-1980s coincided with the arrival of the AIDS epidemic in the country. The emergence of powerful and innovative HIV/AIDS advocacy organizations in Rio de Janeiro, such as the Associação Brasileira Interdisciplinar de AIDS (ABIA), and in São Paulo meant that the struggle against dictatorship and for human rights in Brazil became entwined with the campaign for access to both universal health care and sexual rights (Nunn 2008). Between 1990 and 1992, strong civil-society mobilizations, favorable court decisions, and responsive ministries of the state came together to reformulate policymaking and governance processes (Nunn 2008). The creation in 1992 of a national program for STDS and AIDS, which integrated government and civil-society participation, became a model that inspired an array of movements for more progressive, participatory, protective forms of state and parastatal power—an important precursor to human-security governance replicated in other spheres of the Brazilian state and then taken up worldwide (Biehl 2004). In 1992, Brazilian sexuality-rights and public-health advocates pushed the World Bank to launch a large, innovative loan program called "AIDS One" for Brazil, serving as a landmark in the bank's attempt to humanize its profile. The idea that Brazil was morphing from a squalid dictatorship to a humanized, democratic power through movements for sexual health and rights transfixed the media and charmed many participants in the Earth

FIGURE 1.3. Representatives of indigenous groups from Mato Grosso and Amazonia, Brazil, demonstrate at the NGO Global Forum during the Rio Earth Summit (4 June 1992). Photo credit: AP Photo / Diego Giudice.

Summit. Global health policy advocates proclaimed that "the main policy debates and gains in the domain of sexuality—including those related to women's rights and HIV/AIDS—have played out in the intersections between national and global policy arenas. . . . The strategic relevance of the UN in this new cycle is not surprising given the history and mandate of the organization" (Corrêa, Petchesky, and Parker 2008, 18, 27).

The other major non-ecological campaigns that propelled the Earth Summit's move toward democratization and the humanitarianization of Global South security governance were movements for cultural rescue (Alicia R. Ramos 1998) and for protection of endangered traditions and heritage. Ascending to the UN level at about the same time as sexual-rights doctrine, a new wave of cultural-autonomy movements demanded the humanization of the security state, focusing on entitlement and self-determination (Warren and Jackson 2003; Yúdice 2003), not on enforcement or police-based "protective" notions of security. During the 1992 forum, movements for cultural autonomy were led by indigenous peoples' representatives who insisted that issues of biodiversity and climate management must not be used to introduce more police penetration or securitize indigenous peoples' cultures and settlements (fig. 1.3). They demanded that the cultural traditions and political autonomy of indigenous peoples not be folded into new forms of commodification and corporate governance by biotech corporations, or absorbed under the sovereignty of ecological conservation agencies of the state. Cultural-rescue doctrine promoted the role of NGOs and relied on the language of rights and anti-discrimination, mobilizing international financial and humanitarian aid institutions to conform to the communities' own priorities and cultural agendas. In the early 1990s these two movement framings—sexual rights and cultural rescue—were seen as siblings and allies, two versions of the same struggle for entitlement and empowerment. Together, they aimed to democratize authoritarian states, appropriate securitized state power, and eradicate the international "structural adjustment" agenda that they identified not just as neoliberal but as colonial. Cultural-rescue and sexual-rights models of humanized securitization in the early 1990s phase centered on modes of entitlement to indigenous land, cultural traditions, public-health resources, AIDS drugs, and participatory state processes. But another human-security model that rejected the politics of entitlement and instead centered on enforcement would soon assimilate and recode these movements for humanized security.

With the passage of less than two short years, from 1992 to 1994, these two tendencies, sexual rights and cultural autonomy, once two aspects of the same set of social-justice and entitlement claims, would start to become polarized antagonists, naturalized opposites in a binary regime (Afshari 1994). Displacing critical conversations around entitlement, the struggle to reconcile liberalization with empowerment became forcibly misrecognized as a struggle between naturalized and dehistoricized poles: modernity versus authenticity, economy versus culture, modernity versus traditionalism, queer visibilities versus family values. And this newly re-signified array of binaries, which crystallized around 1993, during a particular crisis of neoliberalism and global governance, was then projected back in time, as if these new binaries were age-old terms of civilizational struggle between West and East, secular liberalism versus religiosity and traditional morality.

As this shift progressed, humanitarian internationalists and anti-imperialist nationalists eventually joined forces, naturalizing enforcement and protection, rather than entitlement and empowerment, as the inevitable humanization logics of global security. The language of security became infused with constant references to "states of emergency" and extreme sexual violence: the rape of indigenous peoples and the natural world, the prostitution of cultures and peoples, the perversion of tradition, and the spread of sexually transmitted diseases and sex trafficking networks.

Quake and Massacre

Between the close of the Rio summit and the opening of the Cairo summit in 1994, two violent episodes—a massive earthquake in Cairo and a massacre of children in Rio—accelerated the evolution of militarized and securitized humanitarian interventions within global police cultures. The location and operation of these catastrophic events facilitated the transfer of local policing practices to the global scale. This period also witnessed the surge of an assertive missionary brand of neoconservative internationalism and the articulation of a coalition that linked US Mormons and Evangelicals, the Vatican and Opus Dei, Latin American Pentecostals, and the Organization of the Islamic Conference (Bernstein 2007; Corrêa, Petchesky, and Parker 2008, chap. 3). This newly crystallized and transnational network came to represent itself as the voice of religion, culture, and the family, and to adopt the mantle of the "real antiglobalization movement," appropriating and undercutting the ethical force of the Left and youth-centered antineoliberalism movements. This religiomoral bloc made its debut and became assertive during the transitional period of 1992–94. These forms of moralistic internationalism emerged in parallel with newly invigorated forms of "antivice" vigilantism among enforcement operations in the local context.

On 23 July 1993, Rio de Janeiro's Militarized Police attacked a group of homeless children sleeping against the walls of Candelária Church, a historic Catholic cathedral at the epicenter of Rio's rapidly gentrifying business district (Agência Brasil 2011a). The church had been providing food, shelter, education, and religious counseling to the homeless. Police saw these children as embodying the sexual threat of predatory forms of globalization that had been "perversely integrated" into global flows, jeopardizing the city's reputation and spreading the perversions of prostitution, organized crime, and drug trafficking (Inciardi and Surratt 1998; Silva 1994, 6–8; Zaluar 2004). Late that night, police vehicles encircled seventy sleeping children huddled against the cathedral and sprayed automatic gunfire into the crowd. At the time, eight children were killed and dozens more were maimed (Rochester 2008) (fig. 1.4). An additional thirty-nine children from this same group were killed by police or gangs in later con-

FIGURE 1.4. People look at a victim of the Candelária Massacre in Rio de Janeiro (23 July 1993). Photo credit: AP Photo / Morialdo Aravjo / AJB.

frontations. Fifty officers were implicated in the massacre, but only one was convicted. The occupation of streets and public spaces by heavily armored police and military forces that preceded the Earth Summit, and the Candelária Massacre that followed it, cast a shadow over and significantly reframed the spectacle of democratization and humanitarian solidarity that the international conference was supposed to project.

As attention shifted from Rio to Cairo for preparations of a subsequent UN world conference, conflicts between transnationally linked progressive NGOs, security agencies, and religiously identified social movements intensified. These tensions were brought to the surface as the Egyptian groups associated with these networks and agencies struggled to respond to a massive earthquake that struck the Egyptian capital on 12 October 1992.[2] The quake devastated large areas of this Arab-African megacity, killing more than five hundred people and destroying more than two thousand homes. Tens of thousands of other homes and entire working-class districts were damaged. The state declared whole blocks of working-class housing to be unsafe and ordered evictions (Sadek 1999). The quake also shook Egypt's political order. The disaster revealed that the economically "liberalized" but politically shuttered Egyptian police state—by then in the eleventh year of what would become President Mubarak's thirty-year term—had already lost all capacity to respond to the human needs of its population (Degg 1993). In the aftermath of the quake, displaced city-dwellers challenged the state ministries to come to their aid. Facing state paralysis and disregard, the population turned to Islamic social movements and charitable foundations, which stepped into the gap and provided social and humanitarian services (fig. 1.5). These organizations gained the gratitude (and demanded, in exchange, the political allegiance) of local populations, to the extent that the state moved to prohibit international funding of such charity organizations after the quake (Carapico 2002). Many locals and international observers assumed that the collapse of apartment buildings in Cairo would have an effect similar to the destruction of the Berlin Wall, that civil society would soon burst the bonds of authoritarianism in Egypt and overthrow Mubarak's regime (Walsh 2003).

The United Nations International Conference on Population and Development (the Cairo Summit), was held 5–13 September 1994, while the city was still rebuilding from the quake. Like the Rio Earth Summit that preceded it, the Cairo Summit became a sprawling urban spectacle of confrontation between cosmopolitan democratization (the global gathering of NGOs) and new globalizing forms of police deployment and secu-

FIGURE 1.5. On the eve of Egyptian elections, an "Islam Is the Solution" sign hangs on tents provided by Islamic charity organizations to aid victims of the Cairo earthquake (14 October 1992). Photo credit: AP Photo / Santiago Lyon.

rity discourse. The urban-security and humanitarian cultural implications of this summit, in the context of the quake responses, opened up a series of questions that went beyond the debate regarding the official UN agenda. Although the UN agenda centered not on environmental issues but on population control and reproductive health, the broader struggles around the Cairo conference reproduced and extended many of the same dynamics on display in Rio and pushed similar shifts in emergent humanized security and development doctrine. The Cairo Summit also featured a large NGO Forum, with representatives from seventeen hundred organizations attending (McIntosh and Finkle 1995). In Rio, but even more explicitly in Cairo, the democratization of the international order was now beginning to explicitly evolve from a "development" or "liberalization" phase to one in which "security" became the nodal framework for debating international aid interventions and multilateral action. As this transition unfolded, norms and policy prescriptions were articulated increasingly not as questions of entitlement versus enforcement, but as a sexualized struggle between rights and culture, transposed onto the poles of West versus East.

Inside the Cairo NGO Forum, progressive feminist groups, family-planning advocates, AIDS organizations, and sexual-rights activists demanded a thorough overhaul of the repressive "population control" regime. In the aftermath of the quake, and providing services through the evangelizing framework of Islamic charity, NGOS on the streets of Cairo were focusing less on individual and personal rights and more on family rights. This shift in focus was meant to stabilize community norms and traditional gender roles against the assault of what they identified as the threats of sexualization, alienation, and sexual violence, and against the "perversion" of traditional values in general (Petchesky 2003, 36–38). In official chambers, the heads of state squared off over the sexuality dimensions of the evolving formation of parahuman subjects and the human-security model. The product of the conference, the 1994 Cairo Programme of Action, did succeed in breaking new ground, enshrining for the first time the language of sexual rights in a formal international agreement. The program contained "a definition of 'sexual health' requiring that 'people are able to have a satisfying and safe sex life' as well as the right to decide 'if, when, and how often' to reproduce . . . and define[d] the purpose of sexual health as 'the enhancement of life and personal relations, and not merely counseling and care related to reproduction and sexually transmitted diseases. . . . And, most controversially, [the Programme of Action] include[d] references to 'family forms' in the plural in place of the more conservative singular ('the family') preferred by the Vatican and some Islamic countries" (Corrêa, Petchesky, and Parker 2008, 169).

But these important changes reflected a fleeting achievement. Subsequently, Cairo-based Islamic NGOS and the global "family values" coalition of actors marked the international policy agreement, and the UN forums that had generated it, as sexually and culturally deviant or threatening. They represented the UN sexual rights and cultural autonomy consensus as a threat to the security of the family and national culture. Islamic feminists in Egypt, along with lobbyists from the Holy See who became increasingly active in UN forums at this time, referred to the notion that sexuality is a realm of citizen rights and pleasures as a "lesbian epistemology," a direct threat to regional cultural security and moral authenticity (Heba Raouf Ezzat 2002; Vatican 2004). The common origins and once-shared entitlement logic that united both sexual rights and cultural-autonomy campaigns—embodied in the agenda shared by both AIDS activists and indigenous rights groups at the Rio Earth Summit in 1992—started to fracture and become unimaginable after the Cairo Summit in 1994. The challenge of adapting neoliberal governmentality to a project for cosmopolitan democratization became reframed as a set of sex and culture wars — between liberal moderns versus religious traditionalists, Westerners versus Easterners. As these terms evolved, policy debates increasingly portrayed these binaries as natural and eternal, displacing and suppressing the very recent origins of this shift in securitization and humanization regimes.

By the time that President Clinton and First Lady Hillary Rodham Clinton visited Cairo, on 26 October 1994, the conference had become a laboratory for testing policies that would "protect culture" by policing sexuality. Egyptian state agencies did this by cynically appropriating the moral banner of the Islamic charity organizations that had provided a model of humanitarian aid and governance in the wake of the 1992 quake. The Egyptian state and the actors in the transnational "family values" coalition appropriated the Islamist mission by evacuating these campaigns of their political challenge and reducing them to moralistic claims and gendered cultural-security control operations. The preservation and protection of gendered culture would open a road to development that could reconcile two "opposed" logics: profit and patrimony. It could tap into the booming tourist industry, which depends on authentic cultural difference, all while rescuing those forms of national culture and identity that sexual-rights politics were threatening. Stopping sex tourism and other "perversions of globalization" became the themes of this cultural-security phase of Rio-Cairo internationalism.

By the time the UN World Conference on Women convened in Beijing, in September 1995, these polarized positions on gender, sexuality, and culture had already become hardened. Movements for cosmopolitan democracy and the humanization of neoliberalism began to be framed as enforcement missions of rescue, not as projects of redistribution or re-entitlement. In the wake of the Tiananmen Square Massacre of 1989, Beijing did not allow the city to become a staging ground for enactments of planetary democracy or vibrant countersummits of transnational civil society, as in Rio and Cairo. Partly because of this, after Beijing, organizers of the Global NGO Forums split off and began to organize the World Social Forum movement, explicitly defined as a space for articulating an "epistemology of the south" (de Sousa Santos 2003, 237). It was only with the World Conference against Racism in Durban, South Africa (1–8 September 2001), that the UN, heads of state, and a broad array of social movements and NGOs came together once again in a tumultuous summit to deepen world democracy and to ask the toughest questions about humanization, dehumanization, race, sex, war, and colonialism.[3] But this fresh start for the process of debating the global-governance project that was by this time officially termed "human security" was immediately derailed— three days after the Durban conference closed, the World Trade Center in New York was attacked.

Linking South America and the Middle East

The US invasion of Iraq, launched less than two years after the September 11 attacks, provoked a surge of resistance to US hegemony among rising powers in the Global South. Consequently, a series of bilateral megasummits began to highlight and then formalize the intensification of transnational links between the Middle East and South America. This wave of transregionalism, explicitly projected as a counterweight to US military and commercial hegemony, picked up on the energy of record-setting, global mass protests against the war in Iraq that had erupted in the cities of Brazil, Egypt, and throughout the world in 2003, and channeled by the first World Social Forums held in Porto Allegre, Brazil, starting in 2001. In December 2003, President Lula traveled to Cairo to meet with the Arab League and its Egyptian secretary-general, Amr Moussa (fig. 1.6). Brazil then became the first new member, with observer status, of the Arab League in ten years (Dina Ezzat 2003), revealing the league's enthusiasm for Brazil's role in articulating a new global balance of power. Brazil had spent four decades flirting with the Non-Aligned Movement (NAM) and Bandung alliances, but had never officially joined (Braveboy-Wagner 2003). At long last Brazil had decided to formalize its Global South affinities by joining, perhaps rather oddly, not the NAM, but the Arab League.

Covering the meeting in the local press, Egypt's *Al-Ahram* newspaper gave prominence to Lula's call "for 'a new way to do politics,' both among Southern countries and between the South and North, that merits careful consideration from the Arab officials with whom he met. According to the Brazilian president, there is a need for a new approach towards inter-South political coordination. This approach should include the representation of the South in the UN Security Council 'to make sure that the UN works in a democratic way,' as well as adjusting the present imbalance of political power that, if left unchecked, could further endanger the interests of developing countries" (Ezzat 2003).

Following President Lula's visits with Arab heads of state in the Middle East and a bilateral meeting of foreign ministers in Rio de Janeiro in 2003,

FIGURE 1.6. The Egyptian Amr Moussa, then secretary-general of the Arab League, shakes hands with President Lula of Brazil during the signing of the Brasilia Declaration, founding the trade and diplomatic bloc ASPA (América do Sul-Países Árabes) (9 May 2005). Photo credit: AP Photo / Silvia Izquierdo.

Brazil hosted the first Summit of South American–Arab Countries (known by its Portuguese acronym, ASPA, for América do Sul-Países Árabes) in the capital Brasilia on 10 May 2005 (Baher 2009). This historic gathering produced the Brasilia Declaration, which formalized a transregional alliance between the two blocs. The principal aim of ASPA was, as Celso Amorim stated,

> the reciprocal rediscovery of two regions that shared historical affinities with a vast potential still to realize. In the past, the human roots between the two regions were narrowed by flows of Arab migration toward South America and particularly Brazil . . . and more recently, by South American migrants that made the reverse trip and began new lives in the countries of the Middle East. The countries of both regions live the daily search for economic development with social justice, value international law and multilateralism, [and] defend a multipolar world and a more cooperative

international system. This summit aspires to bridge the human distance between the two regions . . . stimulating the creation of new partnerships in the search for world solidarity. (2005, x–xi)

On 31 March 2009, after a month of preparations in Cairo, the second ASPA summit was hosted in Doha, Qatar.

In the four years between the gatherings in Rio and Brasilia and the Cairo-based preparations for ASPA II in 2009, commercial exchanges between South America and the states of the Arab League increased from 8 to 21 billion US dollars. In the aftermath of the US invasion of Iraq in 2003 and the massive Global North–centered financial breakdown of 2008, this summit process came to elaborate a new post-US-dominated global ordering, centered on a novel set of transregional principles, blending new patterns of development, culturally sensitive governance, and humanized security. These principles expanded well beyond issues of trade and reflected "a strong political will to strengthen South-South cooperation . . . representing a gradual political and economic shift from traditional European and US political influence and dependence on their markets" (Baher 2009). Through this diplomatic process, South America and the Arab world promised to share nuclear technology, enhance police cooperation, coordinate votes at the UN, facilitate cultural exchange, build joint libraries, collaborate to eliminate human trafficking and forced prostitution, and protect cultural heritage (ASPA 2005). South America and the Arab world hammered out areas of consensus to supplant the delegitimized Washington Consensus of neoliberalism and the failed wars of neoconservatism by mobilizing a counterhegemonic project that was distinct from the rising ambitions of China and Russia. This ASPA consensus consisted of specific notions of shared cultural heritage, national sovereignty, commercial-financial policy, and human security.

According to the official Brasilia Declaration signed by all ASPA leaders on 11 May 2005, the bloc reaffirmed the "growing importance of culture as a bridge between peoples and as an economic activity to promote development and mutual cooperation . . . [and agreed] to the necessity . . . of establishing a large-scale project for the protection of human heritage and to spread a culture of peace" ("Brasilia Declaration" 2005, chap. 3). Cultural-sovereignty enforcement and a humanitarian doctrine of cultural rescue or emergency protection thrived in a renewed spirit of nationalism, and, moreover, of nationalization. This spirit represented in part a backlash against the US invasion of Iraq and US support for coup attempts in Venezuela. In this context, ASPA proclaimed a demand for "full compliance with and respect for the principles of sovereignty and territorial integrity of States . . . and the preeminent right of States to their natural resources and the sovereign rights of peoples to dispose of such resources in their best interests." And ASPA asserted "the right of states and peoples to resist foreign occupation in accordance with the principles of international legality" ("Brasilia Declaration" 2005, chaps. 1 and 2). In terms of commercial and financial policy, ASPA's declaration embodied a geoeconomic critique of neoliberalism from within, advocating not the dismantling of the World Trade Organization, but the "elimination of present distortions in the multilateral trading system, particularly in agriculture, which prevent developing countries from benefiting from their comparative advantages" ("Brasilia Declaration" 2005, chap. 2). Several years before the financial crisis of 2008, the declaration expressed "concern for the volatility of international financial markets" and demanded "instruments for the prevention and management of financial crises . . . to ensure the sustainability of financial flows and to guarantee a more prominent role for developing countries within the decision-making process of multilateral financial organizations . . . [and to] stress in particular the need for the multilateral financial institutions to recognize that public expenditures in the social field and infrastructure should be treated as investments and not as public indebtedness" ("Brasilia Declaration" 2005, chaps. 6 and 7). Security concerns united the goal of a "nuclear free Middle East" (chap. 2) with the human-security demand to "urge the mobilization of larger sources of funding for scientific and humanitarian cooperation to combat the AIDS epidemic" (chap. 12).

But what kind of invigorated humanity would provide the vital force for this new human-security-based, sovereignty-bolstering, nationalism-infused, South-South partnership? The diplomats offered joint proposals for boosting transregional solidarities to create a hub of a new world order composed of lateral alliances between summit host cities and assertive governments in the Global South.

Miscegenations and Transnations

By the time of the 2009 ASPA summit and other global meetings that immediately followed, the new global human-security order deriving from this Rio-to-Cairo process played out as a theater of seductions and couplings. The metaphors and historical narratives of South-South contact that infused these meetings explicitly referenced not just economic partnership but cultural miscegenation, not merely "cultural dialogue" or hybridity but an eroticized "mixed-race" union that would give birth to a new counterhegemonic race of humanity by mating Arab and South American cultures—and their notions of humanized security. These intersecting orientalist and tropicalist metaphors animated not just the media coverage but also the official diplomatic pronouncements of the summits. Orientalism and tropicalism have been analyzed in the United States and Europe as forms of colonial cultural power and as disciplines of racialized and sexualized knowledge/power, but much less work has been done on the role that orientalism and tropicalism have played when appropriated by nationalist, state-building, modernizing, and counterhegemonic projects in the postcolonial world.

Lucia Newman, the Peruvian-born Latin American editor of *Al-Jazeera News*, opened her coverage of the 2009 ASPA summit with an invocation of lost love and a barely disguised narrative of "rediscovery" resonant with mixed-race eroticism:

> The Moors invaded and conquered much of the Iberian Peninsula in 711 AD. By the time they were driven out of Granada in 1492, the Arabs had left an indelible racial and cultural imprint. Both the Spanish and Portuguese languages have a marked Arabic influence. Yet when the Spanish and Portuguese crossed the Atlantic to conquer America, the close connection with the Arab world was somehow lost as the new colonies fought to establish their own identities. More than five centuries later, the arrival of South American heads of state in Doha, Qatar, to attend a presidential summit with Arab leaders is a conscious effort on each side to rediscover the other and forge a relationship that is seen as long overdue. (ASPA 2009)

The racialized and sexualized subjects that haunted this new South-South alliance helped to generate the appeal and legitimacy of these new frameworks for security and commitments of mutual support. At the 2009 meeting, Arab states promised collectively to support the induction of Brazil as a permanent member of the UN Security Council (a bold choice, passing over fellow Islamic claimants like Pakistan and Indonesia) (ASPA 2009). Brazil, in turn, promised the kind of economic aid that is too "national-security sensitive" for most other countries to contemplate. For example, it offered to provide nuclear technology and perhaps enriched uranium (for making electricity, not bombs) to the Middle East region, particularly Egypt, and sold airplanes and technologies for fighting desertification and preserving water resources (ASPA 2010). And during the twenty-two-day Israeli attack on Gaza in December 2008, Brazil led a chorus of condemnation of Israeli humanitarian violations. It portrayed Israeli violence as "disproportionate," comparable to attacking "someone holding matches with a bomb," and declared itself in solidarity with the Palestinian people.[4] Each region pledged to the other to generate a new notion of security that would reduce financial and geopolitical dependency on the United States and Europe, and that would foster improved human welfare, dignity, and sovereignty through South-South cooperation. Lula, then president of Brazil and the "most influential world leader," clarified the counterhegemonic aim.[5] In an interview with *Al-Jazeera*, he stated: "It is imperative for the countries of South America to establish a real understanding with the nations of the Middle East, with the Arab world, so that we can establish not just a commercial relationship, but a political and cultural relationship, so that we can be free of the ties and decisions of the so-called rich countries" (Newman 2009).

The Summit of South American–Arab Countries of March 2009 was squeezed between two other landmark meetings that captured a fleeting moment when social-democratic and Keynesian responses to the 2008 financial crisis were still dominating conversations, before the remarkable return in the United States and the Eurozone of hard-line neoliberal austerity politics. The initial, more social-democratic-oriented response to the financial crisis culminated in the Progressive Governance Summit, hosted by Chilean President Michelle Bachelet (of the Socialist Party) in Viña del Mar, Chile, on 27–28 March 2008, and the G-20 summit in London, hosted by the UK prime minister, Gordon Brown (of the Labour Party), in London on 1–2 April 2009. At the Progressive Governance conference, South America's social-democratic governments presented themselves as a confident bloc whose relative social and economic stability during the global crisis allowed it to promote a new world order, asserting the need for financial regulation and social investment. Just as the Progressive Movement in the United States and worldwide in the 1920s and 1930s developed social security and welfare policies to stave off threats from fascism and monopoly capitalists, on the one hand, and antiracist, anticolonial, and communist resistance on the other, this progressive summit (which included more than one president who had been jailed and tortured by right-wing regimes in the past) proposed itself explicitly as the

FIGURE 1.7. Lula proclaimed that the world financial crisis of 2008 was caused by "white, blue-eyed bankers." In this cartoon, he fixes the problem superficially by applying brown contact lenses. Artist credit: Amarildo Luis Leite Lima.

reasonable, humanitarian, feminist, social-democracy-identified middle ground that could scold and manage the bankers of the North as well as keep in check the new revolutionary alternatives presented by Venezuela and Bolivia.

But at least one leader of the surging Global South was not willing to accept the implicit white, Eurocentric pretensions of those who had caused (and those who were proposing to resolve) the financial crisis. Soon after the Progressive Governance Summit, in a meeting with Gordon Brown on the eve of the 2009 G-20 summit in London, President Lula lashed out that "white, blue-eyed bankers" had caused the financial crisis and dumped their problems on the brown-skinned world (Hinsliff 2009) (fig. 1.7). In the US press, this statement was read as an amusing, confusing proclamation of "reverse racism" by a man who is seen in Europe and the United States as white.[6] But through the lens of the tropicalist imagination, this expression embodies the logic of what Alexandra Isfahani-Hammond calls "white negritude" (2008).

These discourses problematizing the whiteness of global hegemony and "rediscovering" the "racial and cultural imprint" of past Moorish and "brown" transnationalisms seemed to revive the 1920s Progressive

Era imaginary of tropicalist modernism (Skidmore 1983), transplanting it into a new global context. Brazilian tropicalism, as articulated in the Brazilian national imagination by the work of Gilberto Freyre (1963), reconfigured nineteenth-century race sciences and married them to orientalist notions of the sexual and military prowess of the Moor (Burke and Pallares-Burke 2008). Since the 1930s, Brazilian tropicalist modernism, including the doctrine of racial democracy, has been woven into the fabric of national identity (Hanchard 1998). Whereas the dominant scientific paradigm from the mid-nineteenth century through the early twentieth maintained the race-science claim that blacks and whites were essentially different—the former passionate and physical, the latter rational and mental—tropicalism saw miscegenation as the solution to the "problems" of essentialized racial difference. Accordingly, each racial essence longs for the other. On its own, each race would be incapable of full modernity. Domestically, this usually played out as a narrative in which black needed white in order to conceive modernity; but displaced into the geopolitical realm, the formula became a narrative of the white Brazilian needing the brown or black Moor. Thus, erotic contact between the races and the resulting progeny—the "mixed-race" Moor (on the global scale) or the mulatta (on the national scale)—served as central metaphors for a new kind of modernity that was more powerful than exclusionary and hierarchical projects of either European race sciences or North American segregationism (Isfahani-Hammond 2013). In the tropicalist imagination, Moorish Granada (stripped of its actual histories of inquisition and ethnic cleansing) and the coffee plantations of northeast Brazil (stripped of the realities of enslavement and rape) become utopias of sensual mixing between races and models for counterhegemonic modernity (Aidi 2003a; Isfahani-Hammond 2008). Drawing on the symbolic allure of the Moor, Osmar Chohfi, the Brazilian chief-of-cabinet for external relations for Lula's predecessor Fernando Enrique Cardoso, opened a conference that laid the groundwork for ASPA with a vision: "The first centuries of our national formation—ethno-racial and cultural—as well underlined by Gilberto Freyre, reveals the mark of Moorish influence in various dimensions: in values and customs of the patriarchal family; in architecture with internal courtyards and fountains . . . ; in the hygiene of baths and the light and ventilation of spaces; in techniques of irrigation; and, in a very special way, in the very physiognomy of so many Brazilians" (Chohfi 2000, 10). But haunting the conjuring of the new Moorish transnational imaginary was another figure of globalizing sexuality: the "gay international."

Before the 2005 Summit of South American–Arab Countries in Rio de Janeiro, Brazil sponsored a petition at the United Nations Human Rights Commission, in 2003 and 2004, to ban discrimination based on sexual orientation (Girard 2007, 340–42). Brazil's sexual-orientation resolution was part of a series of efforts in several spheres of the UN at the time to underline the country's uniqueness as a modern, tolerant "human-security superpower" representing a cutting-edge force for sexual, racial, and Global South empowerment. Brazil aimed to declare its globality and modernity by moving ahead of countries—like Sweden and Canada, in particular—that felt they had "ownership" of the sexuality issue (Girard 2007, 341). The Brazilian resolution stated "that human rights and fundamental freedoms are the birthright of all human beings, that the universal nature of these rights and freedoms is beyond question, and that the enjoyment of such rights and freedoms should not be hindered in any way on the grounds of sexual orientation" (Girard 2007, 341). Pakistan, Saudi Arabia, and the Holy See, along with the US administration of George W. Bush, came together to lead the mobilization against the resolution. And then, decisively, the Arab states warned they would break off the plans for the ASPA summit and for transregional integration if Brazil did not drop its sponsorship of the nondiscrimination bill. Brazil did drop the resolution, and the summit proceeded (Girard 2007, 348; Redding 2006, 487–90). In this context, the linking of Brazil to the Middle East and the fashioning of a Global South–based alternative model of governance and notion of "humanity" meant the temporary jettisoning of an essential dimension of Brazil's emergent global human-security identity: the enforcement of sexuality rights and the protection of sexual minorities (Pazello 2005, 159). For the moment, the new "Moorist transnational" had conquered the "gay international."

Conclusion

Clyde Woods (2007) and Jan Nederveen Pieterse (2004, 54–59) have argued that University of Chicago economists in the 1970s invented what would be called neoliberalism by rebranding as economic theory what were actually police practices and racial attitudes that had aimed in the 1960s to reimpose "Dixie Capitalism" or "Plantation Capitalism" and roll back the gains of the civil-rights movement in the US South as well as turn back anticolonial liberation movements in the Global South. Elite economists stripped this racial sociopolitical doctrine of its history, its violence on bodies and cultures, and its social agendas, purifying it as a high-status, neoclassical economics reformulation. Substituting a repressive racial-security and recolonial project with an expert economics model, Washington's IMF and World Bank then globalized the masked political-racial project. The critics of this doctrine eventually termed it neoliberalism and its supporters called it the Washington Consensus, but both terms reinforce its status as a North-originating technical expertise and suppress its historical-political antecedents in the Global South, in the US South, and in Eastern Europe (Bockman 2011). Inspired by perspectives that revive the southern and eastern origins of North-identified governance models, but diverging from these analyses to some degree in my trajectory, I have argued that human-security governance did not emerge preformed as a doctrine designed by humanitarian technocrats and progressive economists at the UN in the Global North. Instead, I have proposed, the structural dynamics and forms of struggle within and between particularly contested, high-visibility sites in the semiperiphery, those with access to UN and transnational parastatal policymaking elites and processes, generated the antecedents of the human-security regime before it emerged as a technical-assistance and humanitarian agenda in the Global North.

Parahuman subjects and logics of securitized governance emerged from the intersection of three processes: the militarization of urban social-control operations; the NGOization of transnational civil society and its adoption of humanitarian enforcement doctrines; and the designation, by transnational actors and UN agencies, of certain racialized, moralized, and sexualized problems as requiring new kinds of intervention. This regime of practices emerged in Global South hotspots, then transferred to global human-development policy experts and UN institutions via particular encounters and in concrete contexts. As illustrated here, transfers happened in real places, where mechanisms of securitization and modes of resistance that had been developed in the struggles around military rule and civil-society militancy in Egypt and Brazil in the 1970s and 1980s "jumped scale" to the UN level. By the year 2000, these mechanisms and policies would be cleaned up, severed from their history, and reestablished as Global North expertise and as a UN-invented or Canadian/Scandinavian-generated human-security doctrine for technical and humanitarian assistance. But these histories of struggle and capacities for subversion and resistance would continue to foment innovation and insurrection in these key sites of the Global South.

2

POLICING THE PERVERSIONS OF
GLOBALIZATION IN RIO DE JANEIRO AND CAIRO
Emerging Parastatal Security Regimes
Confront Queer Globalisms

In a dilapidated cabaret in the Lapa zone of Rio de Janeiro, a group of *travesti* prostitutes gathered in October 1999 to formally sue the Brazilian government for the right to repudiate their own citizenship (Barbi 1999, 51).[1] Since 1987, this group, Associação das Travestis e Liberados (ASTRAL), had been demanding that the state protect them and their rights as laborers in the legal field of sex work.[2] In the 1980s, white neo-Nazi gangs began to mobilize in Brazil's cities, performing ritualized acts of homophobic and racist violence (Carrara and Vianna 2006; Ferreira 2003). Gang members had taken it on themselves to promote social purity, mutilating or executing prostitutes, especially travestis (Pessoa 2000). Rather than protect the sex workers from this terrorism, Rio's Militarized Police (Polícia Militar, PM) blamed the victims. The PM harassed and extorted sex workers and developed new antigang and public-space protection policies that ignored the fact that prostitution is legal in Brazil. In response, travestis mobilized for empowerment, recognition, and autonomous control of their territories and markets, and for sovereignty over their gender identity, demanding the right to choose by which gender the state would identify them on official documents. But the Brazilian state spurned them; instead it rounded them up, identified them unilaterally, and registered them as "marginals" in police files, a practice that amounted to stigmatizing their citizenship and officially disabling their social-status aspirations.[3] To make matters worse, a campaign to cleanse the city center for tourism redevelopment had labeled these internationally mobile sex workers literally as "perversions of globalization," sex traffickers, threats to the nation, and blights on Rio's image.

In the 1980s and 1990s, the city of Rio de Janeiro moved aggressively to appropriate New York City's "quality of life" program and "broken windows policing" programs (Herbert and Brown 2006, 771–73), which had prioritized the eradication of sex work in the cleaning up of Times Square. Rio reconfigured these policies and inserted them into its own autonomous social logics and political dynamics of securitization. These imported projects and alien US legal instruments put prostitutes in the same category as gangs that occupied streets and put at risk national security as well as the economic sectors dependent on the attractiveness of the nation's image. These "quality of life" sweeps through Rio's public spaces were referred to as the *blitz* of Rio.[4] They began in 1986, escalated when Rio's police and national military united to clear the city for the 1992 UN Earth Summit, and continued through the 1990s. Major police raids and roundups of transsexual prostitutes included Operation Shame, Operation Dragnet, Operation Sodom, and the infamous Operation Come Here Dollbaby.[5]

Facing this declaration of war by racist gangs, Militarized Police, and the new Municipal Police, and receiving little sympathy from the state or civil-rights movements, the ASTRAL activists gathered in the Lapa district of Rio to repudiate their national identity and citizenship. Since they felt they had been denied those rights and dignities as citizens, their leader, Jovana Baby, declared that they "should be exempt from the duties and obligations of citizenship," including the registration of name and gender, the requirement to vote in elections, and the payment of taxes (Barbi 1999, 51). These border-crossing sex-worker activists destroyed their documents of Brazilian national identity and appealed to the international community to affirm their status as world citizens. They demanded a different kind of state, one that extended beyond the frame of identity administration and patrimony protection. The ASTRAL activists were explicitly not demanding more protection from police or more intervention by the state, nor the passage of a hate crimes law that could, as Dean Spade has argued, increase the state's "resources and punishment capacity. . . . By naming the system as the answer to the significant problem of violence against trans people, we participate in the logic that the criminal punishment system produces safety despite the fact that the evidence suggests that it primarily produces violence" (Spade 2009, 358–59). Instead, with this action ASTRAL demanded a new kind of recognition. They insisted that the state be held accountable for the murder of travestis, and that travestis claim a global scale of recognition and agency. This protest aimed to end the forms of punitive hypervisibility that travestis had been facing.[6]

The Archipelago of Perversion

From the formal sites of policymaking analyzed in chapter 1, I now move toward an archipelago of sites that the global security industry refers to as "hotspots" or criminogenic, high-risk zones. Three mechanisms of securitization—sexuality discourses, policing practices, and street-level labor structures—animated the gradual emergence of the human-security practices that began crystallizing in Rio and Cairo in the 1990s and 2000s. Although these modes of securitization eventually distinguished themselves explicitly from neoliberal paradigms, I assess the degree to which they were historically embedded and relatively dependent on political-economic structures, investment patterns, and forms of labor discipline that are conventionally identified with the neoliberal policy agenda of the 1980s and 1990s.

During the last two decades of the twentieth century, certain global cities in the south experienced a realignment of imagined relationships between sex, nation, and modernity. A significant transnational shift occurred during this period in the practices of policing sexual identities and redeveloping districts associated with sex workers and working-class queer communities. These changes in policing cultures and labor-control regimes harmonized previously dissonant social-control models, challenging the precarious spaces in which sexually stigmatized communities staked claims to rights, public resources, and space. Two historically, culturally, and politically distinct global cities, Rio de Janeiro and Cairo, experienced a similar fusion of paramilitarization processes and humanitarian rescue-type interventions as urban-planning projects became reconfigured and regendered in an effort to arrest what policymakers in both cities explicitly referred to as "the perversions of globalization."

From the perspective of sex workers and certain hypervisibilized working-class or mixed-class communities identified by police as queer or perverse in Rio de Janeiro and Cairo, some of the most threatening elements from each of these cities' distinct policing models were fused into a new border-crossing paradigm. In the context of this emergent regime, which mixed securitization of sexuality and urban "quality of life" policing in both Rio and Cairo, certain stigmatized sexual publics were targeted as both the cultural enemies of the modernizing nation, and as economic liabilities for globalizing development. This agenda put the spotlight on certain subjects and rendered them responsible for urban insecurities associated with globalization, while deemphasizing or creating immunity for other powerful groups and processes. Nevertheless, the contradictions within this policing and planning paradigm, which I identify as a particular kind of human-security model, created breaches and opportunities for the revival of both local and transnational alternatives drawn from socialist, modernist, and populist pasts. In these openings, targeted groups were able to launch subversive protest action and articulate alternative visions of the global.

In order to reframe the transnational urban history of neoliberalism and how these two sites were positioned within it, I begin with the period of "structural adjustment" in the 1980s and 1990s. During this time, new sets of security-sector actors that I define as "parastatal"—international organizations, public-private development partnerships, corporate security consultants, and transnational social movements—engaged with the local state's policing and planning agencies to articulate new security and policing interventions around sexuality within and between both cities. These parastatal groups shared certain securitization logics, but in each site they territorialized and politicized such projects distinctly. But these political-economic changes and security logics need to be situated within even longer timelines of police and social militarization and urban planning. To do this, I look back to the high-modernist period of military dictatorships and authoritarian populism between the 1960s and 1980s, during which time both Egypt and Brazil were ruled by military governments that strove to fuse national security aims with economic development, often by deploying wrenching, totalizing urban-planning and social-cleansing projects. I then look beyond the period of the height of neoliberalism toward the emergence of parastatal forms of policing and planning in the first decade of the twenty-first century (2003–8), when both neoliberal economic doctrine and neoconservative liberalism faced challenges on international and local scales. At that point, figures of cultural authenticity and moralizing sexual regulation supplanted markets and terrorists as the primary subjects of a new order of security interventions and social controls. Through these processes, Rio and Cairo served as productive laboratories and originators of a new international architecture of human-security governance.

Recent sociological and anthropological work on neoliberal states reveals the contradictions and dilemmas that can arise when we employ neoliberalism's own conceptual tools to examine neoliberalism itself (Bayart, Ellis, and Hibou 1999; Hibou 2004; Mamdani 1996; Rigakos 2002). Do we use neoliberal concepts—where the state is portrayed as a monolithic actor operating "above" or outside a market that operates on its own terms—to explain the origin and deployment of security practices and politics? Building on scholarship emerging from work on parastatals in southern Africa, Andean South America, and the Caribbean that has developed new vocabularies for talking about privatized formations that provide public governance (Kingston and Spears 2004; Samah 2007; Stanley 1996; Tangri 2000), I identify new forms of agency not as "civil society" or as "private sector" (and thus in a realm of impunity, free of public claims or state responsibilities), but as what I label "parastatal formations." Although their nature and function are public—and they should be publicly accountable and controlled—these institutions have been sold, transferred, or contracted to social actors operating in a nonstate realm of deregulation or, in the case of aggressive police actions and urban-clearance projects that explicitly express antagonism to rights regimes and judicial authority, in a space of paralegality or counterlegality. These parastatals claim impunity as they perform the enforcement work and cultural labor that powerful elites hesitate to realize through the state itself, which still is, at least formally, identified with commitments to legality, transparency, and participation. Unfortunately, the governance roles of these parastatal formations have been obscured by methodologies that depend on a monolithic notion of the state's will, or the market's hand, or civil-society norms, while giving less attention to transnational technoprofessional groupings such as police trainers, humanitarian institutions, and urban-planning experts. In this discussion, I draw on the work in critical development studies, including that of Timothy Mitchell on the forms of subjects and spaces of power generated by technoprofessional planning and economics expertise (2002), and on the social forces and structural conditions that binary state-versus-society perspectives mask (1991b). I also draw on political anthropology and queer studies models that examine the politics of sexuality of development projects promoted by international financial institutions, as well as state-based market-making schemes in the Global South (Ara Wilson 2004; Bedford 2009; Boellstorff 2005); and I draw on critical work on urban modernism and neoliberal geography in these two countries (Bayat 2009; Caldeira 2000; Denis 2006; Ghannam 2002; Holston 1989), and critical tourism studies that trace processes of subject creation in the context of postcoloniality, race, and sexuality (Figari 2007; Gregory 2001; Pinho 2010; Wynn 2007).

As a transnational and comparative analysis, this chapter synthesizes two cases that represent radical difference in the past and convergence in the present. For most of the latter half of the twentieth century, Rio and Cairo grappled with the role of sexualized urban public space in different ways. Rio struggled to reconcile its traditional positive valuation of spaces of erotic conviviality—the city's and the nation's idealization of racial and class mingling—with a program for economic modernization that targeted spaces of sexualized mingling as locations of disorder and backwardness.[7] During this same period, the poles of culture and economy were reversed in postcolonial Egypt. In the sphere of culture, sexualized intermingling between nations and classes was characterized by metaphors of colonialism as rape of culture and penetration of the nation, rather than by terms which would portray sexual public spheres as fonts of conviviality and diversity, sources of more complex or vibrant forms of national identity. However, in the economic sphere, urban intermingling between peoples of different national origins was more consistently identified positively, seen as providing resources for modernization and progress, in the forms of tourism revenue and socialization opportunities.

From the 1950s to the 1970s, Cairo served as the capital for revolutionary Arab nationalism, a movement that mobilized populist movements for anticolonial cultural and political-economic sovereignty, and, in the 1980s, turned to focus increasingly on aspects of religiomoral distinction, expressing little interest in any politically productive role for cross-class or "interracial" intermingling. But these nationalist tendencies were, during this period, checked by the fact that one of Cairo's principal pillars of economic modernization and globalization has been tourism, an industry that claims to value transnational conviviality and often explicitly promotes and profits from sexualized cross-class and cross-national contact. Thus, in Rio stigmatized sexual publics have had some claim on the positive identities of *cultural* nationalism, but have been marked as impediments to some forms of economic renewal and urban globalization, whereas in Egypt sexualized publics have had some claim to grudging acceptance of their role in promoting *economic* globalization and modernization in consumer spaces through tourism, but have been perceived by many to threaten the nation as agents of cultural impurity and colonial penetration.

Through the analysis of these intersecting, though contradictory, securitization processes, I provide in the rest of this chapter an alternative, grounded history of the peak period of neoliberalization, first in Rio, then in Cairo, in order to reveal the common structural factors behind the policing and hypervisibilization of certain sites of sex commerce and erotic conviviality. These sites emerged as laboratories for new development models and an emergent set of parastatal subjects that articulate new expressions of transnational power. The contradictory actions and discourses unleashed by these parastatal formations generated creative forms of queer resistance.

Securitizing "Queer Globalism" in Cairo

In May 2001, eighteen months after the travesti uprising in Rio de Janeiro, Cairo served as the battleground for a set of parallel struggles that revealed a rescripting of the politics of security, national identity, and citizenship. Police and press identified a particular set of queer subjects with globalism, hypervisibilizing them in a wave of moral panic. This new kind of targeting occurred along some of the same lines as Operation Come Here Dollbaby in Rio, although with crucial distinctions. In the years leading up to 2001, Egypt's security forces and Vice Police (Shurtat al-Adab) had been intensifying their surveillance of female and male prostitution, and sexual contact between men. For many unemployed young men and women, spurned by the restructured state and cruising for opportunities, the selling of sex to elite Egyptians and tourists represented one of the only remaining access routes to hard currency, as the economic crisis had intensified since the East Asian financial collapse of 1997.[8] Between 1997 and 2000, press discourse (monitored during this period by the state and often dictated by the executive branch) began to generate a sex panic in which the virtual (online) and real spaces of globalization became identified with perversion, or the queering of the nation. In a move widely regarded as an attempt to divert attention from the economic crisis of globalization and the perceived moral degeneracy of Egypt's authoritarian regime, police and the official press generated a series of headlines featuring news of arrests of men who used the Internet to arrange rendezvous in Cairo (Pratt 2007). The press also gave prominence to reports of police raids in chic hotel lounges, where the mixing of hustlers, foreigners, and wealthy Egyptians supposedly led to degeneracy, cultural anomie, and murder.

Press and police painted a thirty-one-year-old Egyptian teacher of English, Sherif Hassan Farahat, as the face of this perverse shadow-world of globalization (Aql 2001). He and his family had a history of opposing President Mubarak's regime, and Farahat had published a few utopian statements on the Internet about global citizenship. His notion of globalism mixed Eastern and Western elements, articulating a language of sexual liberation and gay pride by citing erotic Persian devotional Sufi verse. Farahat explicitly disidentified with trends in Egypt, since the Sadat years, to frame Egyptian nationalism in the language of Islamic moralism versus "Westoxified" liberalism or East-versus-West "culture wars." For Farahat, sufism, cosmopolitan conviviality, and queer desire came together in an indigenous Egyptian formula that challenged moralistic securitization and narrow nationalism. A prominent state cultural magazine reported on a manifesto attributed to Farahat:

> The author wants to create a historical and humanistic link for homosexual perverts and their actions. . . . They refer to some points that exist in all religions that deny the existence of national borders as well as [blur the difference between] the revealed religions. They say that homosexuals do not believe in any nationality except the "Queer Nation," to which they belong exclusively. They do not admit the existence of borders and boundaries between the peoples of the earth . . . and they look forward to a near future in which everybody is queer and a citizen of the Nation. (Kamal 2001)

As evidence of the treason of Farahat and his "organization," the newspaper and its State Security informants noted that the group promoted the idea of ritual baths in the Dead Sea as a way for peoples of Islam, Judaism, and Christianity to meet on shared sacred ground. Since Egyptian participants would have to travel through Israel to visit the Dead Sea, the journalist presumed that Farahat's vision must be funded and scripted by Israeli Zionists and their American allies. Another Egyptian newspaper was thus able to reduce the manifesto's ideology to "Become a Pervert to Please Uncle Sam!" (cited in Schneider 2001).

Building momentum for campaigns that demonized sexuality, the Egyptian police gradually increased the frequency of raids on nightclubs and sites of female prostitution frequented by Egyptian elites and Arabs from the Persian Gulf, particularly along Giza's Pyramids Road, which had served for two generations as the west-end red-light district of Greater Cairo (Sha'iira, Magheeb, and Abu Zeid 1996). In the wake of these raids, protection rackets squeezed harder and extortion intensified. For female prostitutes, the raids made life more difficult and violent, but they were not hypervisibilized in the way that queer men were. Women sex workers' profiles remained low because the police and press identified the women as passive victims of poverty rather than as territories of East-versus-West, local-versus-global culture wars. Women prostitutes were represented as caught up in distinct East-versus-*East*, intra-Muslim conflicts driven by the corruption of Persian Gulf Arab oil wealth and the temptations of new forms of Arab-region-specific consumer lifestyles (see Wynn 2007).

By contrast to the older frameworks deployed around the female prostitute, during this period, the "male homosexual" became socially and criminologically identified for the first time in Egypt as a distinct social category, as a criminogenic community, and as a collective object of policing. Before this, men arrested for having sex with men or for public homoeroticism would more likely have been charged with non-same-sex-specific practices like solicitation or debauchery, then released within twenty-four hours after paying a fee or bribe. But the legal and discursive frameworks imposed on the detainees from the Queen Boat catalyzed a shift toward intensified categories of repression and subjectivation. The state and its media identified homosexuals as a new kind of high-risk group with a dangerous security profile. They were perceived for the first time as a globally propelled but locally cultivated Egyptian-Arab identity category. And worse, from the perspective of the police state, they responded not by offering bribes but by claiming citizenship and rights.[9] In Egypt the Arabic forensic psychological term *deviant* and the Arabic legal and police terms *debaucherer* and *blasphemer* marked the terms of this identity grouping (Katherine M. Franke 2002, 19–20). In this context, the state and police inserted the emergent homosexual figure into the category of national security threat at the intersection of two opposed forms of legal identification. On the one hand, international human-rights groups certified these men as rights-bearing members of international civil society, and, on the other, national security and parastatal policing organs classified them as members of quasi-terrorist transnational organizations.

On 11 May 2001, Egyptian security forces raided the Queen Boat, a woman-owned riverboat nightclub moored on the Nile between Cairo's most elegant five-star hotels. Not at all a marginal or underground site, the Queen Boat—named after the wife of the last king of Egypt—was a visible tourist venue floating at the epicenter of Cairo's business, hospitality, and casino zone. For years, local magazines and the general club-going public referred openly to the Queen Boat as one of several places in the area that hosted a campy, mostly male crowd. During the raid, all Egyptian men in the club were arrested, while women and foreign men were spared, although vice cops and press reports noted the foreigners' presence as proof of the club's perverse cosmopolitanism and of the young men's treasonous interest in mingling with "foreign elements" (Scott Long 2004).

The fifty-two arrested Egyptians were not detained by the Vice Police, a corrupt force that the nightlife world and Cairo's sexual minorities knew well and could manage through bribing. Typically, Vice Police would have rounded up the men, charged them as prostitutes for indecency, held them in jail for one night of humiliation and extortion, and then released them. Instead, the "Cairo 52" were transferred to the authority of State Security (King and Ray 2000). The security police bypassed the judicial system and transferred the group to Tora prison, where terrorist suspects and political detainees are incarcerated and tortured. Rather than being charged in civil courts for the misdemeanor of indecency, the Cairo 52 were remanded to the charge of extraconstitutional security tribunals, where appeals were never permitted and rights for the accused were strictly limited (Pratt 2007, 131). Thus it was in the context of antiterrorist campaigns and paralegal institutions in twenty-first-century Egypt that homosexuality-as-minority-identity first became a nationally hypervisible, politically urgent, and state-securitized identity.

The police in Egypt at that time identified and codified same-sex erotic conviviality as a security threat that violated not the laws of nature, nor the laws of the state, but the emergency counterterrorism decrees that evolved in Egypt after President Sadat's assassination in 1981. The "deviant/debaucherer" men were prosecuted under the same charges—terrorist blasphemy—used against the militant Jama'a Islamiyya for "exploiting religion to promote extreme ideas to create strife and belittling revealed religions" (Bahgat 2001; Scott Long 2004). Because they self-identified with sexualized global citizenship and frequented cosmopolitan city spaces deemed discordant with a moralistic national image, the Cairo 52 had unwittingly come to occupy the position of terrorists. Following this raid, and the emergence of this new security-profile-as-sexual-identity, Egyptian security police prioritized the campaigns and launched a "gay blitz" of the country that lasted for months, entering similar kinds of social spaces and rounding up individuals in cities up and down the Nile.[10] Such new forms of militarized policing and securitized targeting of this "cosmopolitan networks of debauchers" in Egypt like the targeting of "globalizing travesti gangs" in Rio demonstrate that the violence against sexualized subjects became most acute around particular urban spaces identified with the cultural and economic contradictions of globalization. Only at these junctions and within this matrix of parastatal power relations did violence take place with such intensity and propinquity.

Originally written as an analysis of the Queen Boat raids in Egypt, and global responses to it, Joseph Massad's article "Re-orienting Desire: The Gay International and the Arab World" (also included as a chapter in his book *Desiring Arabs* [2007]), lays out a critique of the discourses and practices of self-identified gay or LGBT European, American, and Arab-American human-rights groups. He accuses them of reactivating colonial legacies and imposing imported identity frameworks: "Indeed, as members of the Gay International, this minority is one of the main poles of the campaign to incite discourse on homosexuality in the Arab world . . . [where] the very ontology of gayness is instituted in a discourse that could have only two reactions to the claims of universal gayness: support them or oppose them without ever questioning the epistemological underpinnings. . . . The Gay International's fight is therefore not an epistemological one but rather a simple political struggle where the world is divided between the supporters and opponents of gay rights" (Massad 2002, 373–74).

Massad's approach, like that of Egypt's State Security institutions themselves, hypervisibilizes Arab-American and Western gay websites and movements, framing them as possessing a form of agentive power that merges with that of neocolonial globalization itself. He represents the "Gay International" as a form of globally menacing queer masculinity in ways that parallel the hypervisibilizing representations of travesti global gangs. Massad portrays the gay NGOs as "infiltrating," "penetrating," and "inciting" the embodied identities of the nations of the Arab world. It is certain that in the period analyzed by Massad (the mid- to late 1990s) many of these groups did draw heavily on a universalistic, liberal language of human rights. And these groups reinforced simplistic notions of discrimination that ended in calls for Western moral and even military interference to protect victims and enforce a global notion of law.

But what Massad's analysis ignores is the agency of transnational security cultures as well as the parastatal control formations of the Global South, which were certainly materially more influential in constructing spaces, security models, and subjects in these semiperipheral contexts than these gay websites were. These formations had acted, since at least the 1980s, to generate these "globalizing sexuality" subjects as their others. These securitization logics and the parastatal formations behind them highlighted "queer globalization," precisely to trigger particular patterns of misrecognition that justified intensified policing of society during times of forced economic marginalization. Shielded by these misrecognition dynamics, police states in the Global South, as well as their partners in the transnational security and redevelopment agencies, avoided responsibility and obscured their own agency and "epistemological underpinnings." To this end, they securitized populations by identifying them as "hotspots" or "risk categories" linked to globalizing perversions or queer internationalisms. As reported by Scott Long in the Human Rights Watch report *In a Time of Torture* (2004), it was the Egyptian police and security apparatus, not gay human-rights organizations, that mobilized precisely to incite discourse around globalizing "gay" terminologies and identities. As Long reported, the head of the Cairo Vice Squad repeatedly asked those arrested in the Queen Boat incident if they knew what the English word *gay* meant. The officer inspected them to see if they were wearing foreign-made, colored underwear or imported clothes (Human Rights Watch 2004). If the detained man was wearing such clothes and could pronounce the foreign term *gay*, then he was booked as a debaucherer, charged with blasphemy, and paraded in the media as a pervert. Interestingly, the hallmarks of neoliberal consumer literacy—having proficiency in English, wearing imported clothes, and participating in global consumer trends (skills avidly promoted by the state and elites as they embraced foreign investment and neoliberal development models)—were identified as evidence of queerness when deployed in certain ways, and in certain "vulgar cosmopolitan" spaces of the city. Evolving practices of policing and planning, much more than liberal ideological campaigns or identity categories of Western human-rights groups, had acted to identify this particular subset of global consumer practices with a new kind of human—alien, threatening, and perverse. This had the effect of disciplining resistance to and displacing accountability for the violence of neoliberalism. And this effect served the security prerogatives of these emerging governance apparatuses of the Global South.

The kind of account I offer here, as opposed to Massad's focus on transnational NGOs, brings the securitization of the Queen Boat drama into the same frame as the Egyptian police campaign against sexual contact and rock music communities on the Internet in Egypt (Bahgat 2004) and the intensified policing of unmarried couples strolling along the banks of the Nile and in the cosmopolitan consumer spaces of shopping malls. These kinds of policing campaigns had immediately preceded the Queen

Boat case and can be tied together as a set of operations aimed at turning spaces and technologies identified with "globalization" into territories occupied in order to extend police logics of moralization, enforcement, surveillance, and punishment.

Indeed, to avoid being targeted by securitization processes that would label them a fifth column for perverse globalization agendas or neocolonial Western plots, most Egyptian human-rights organizations refused to defend those rounded up in this Gay Blitz. They considered the actions of the accused either irrelevant to questions of human rights, seeing the same-sex underground as a foreign affront to the nation and its values, or as a forum for prostitution and public indecency: "Excuse me, this is prostitution, not human rights. . . . Certain organizations want to impose their personal views . . . including perversion, on us! . . . We cannot consider the case of a 'perverts' organization a human rights cause. . . . [Human rights] organizations, which deal with freedoms, should not defend prostitution. . . . They do not understand the different nature of the Arab and Islamic societies governed by religion" (Hilmi 2001). Certain nationalist human-rights NGOs in Egypt reproduced the Old Left prejudices against the rights of women and homosexuals, identifying them with superfluous consumption, waste, luxury, and indulgence. If real men and their politics were the meat and potatoes of the nation, sexual dissidents were like soft drinks. According to the Egyptian human-rights activist Naged Al Boraei, "To come in and talk about gays and lesbians, it is nice, but it's not the major issue. It's like I am starving and you ask me what kind of cola I want. Well, I want to eat first. Then we can talk about cola! It's a luxury to talk about gay rights in Egypt" (cited in Azimi 2006).

Not all human-rights groups in Egypt spurned the Cairo 52 case. Exceptions included Gasser Abdel Razeq and his team from the Hisham Mubarak Legal Aid organization, who defended several of the accused; Hania Mufti of Human Rights Watch; and Hossam Bahgat of the Egyptian Organization for Human Rights (EOHR) (Bahgat was dismissed when the EOHR panicked and decided to distance itself from the case). Even the president of the Lawyers Syndicate in Egypt defended one of the Cairo 52. So there were important actors in Egypt who resisted (and, not coincidentally, these brave dissident human-rights lawyers became some of the most prominent activists in the revolution in 2011), but the overall trend during this slightly earlier period was one of nationalist rallying against "perverts."

The power of the emerging repressive sexual-security paradigm that drove the 2001 Queen Boat raid cowed most other human-rights and social-justice organizations. Social groupings that were criminalized via sexuality were presented as the primary victims as well as the perpetrators of what this new transnational, interurban, sex-and-culture policing paradigm identified as "the perversions of globalization." As this security regime unfolded, working-class female sex workers were targeted as *hyperpassive agents*, duped, victimized, and trafficked across borders; they had to be rescued, contained, and localized, even if they asserted themselves as free-willing or did not identify as sex workers.[11] Queer men— whether identified as sex workers (similar to the case of travestis in Rio, who are usually self-identified during this period as male, although cross-dressed) or as a "perverse" sexual minority (as in the alleged gay men newly criminalized in Egypt)—were targeted as *hyperaggressive agents*, despised traitors who menaced national integrity, invaded or infected the country, and trafficked in practices that police categorized as threats to national security and framed in a new discourse of sexual terrorism.

In order to continue to develop an alternative transregional and structuralist account of the emergence of new sexualized policing and planning regimes, and to get beyond the framing of sexuality politics as East versus West, imported versus authentic, it may be useful to recover the social history of urban modernism during the military-authoritarian period that preceded the neoliberal periods in both Egypt and Brazil. Some of the crucial patterns established and forms of political processes forged at this time tend to be neglected by critical scholars, who often jump from the colonial era to the neoliberal period, skipping the crucial eras of national decolonization and social militarization. Both countries during this phase were deeply transformed by ideologies and projects of Third Worldism, military rule, and high modernism. To address this historical gap, in the next section I highlight the military, police, and urban-administrative changes that occurred during the revolutionary military-developmentalist or Third Worldist decades that followed the 1952 overthrow of the British empire-aligned king in Egypt and the 1930 overthrow of the semicolonial, oligarchical "plantation republic" in Brazil. These social histories remain alive and relevant in the urban-transnational zones of sexualized conviviality and "globalizing perversions" that remain hotspots or hypervisible human-security laboratories today. The parastatal formations at work in these spaces unite transnational urban-redevelopment experts with local businesses seeking to upgrade the class and racial profile of lucrative tourism and consumer zones.

Military-Modernist Period: Rio's Lapa

From the 1920s through the 1940s, the Lapa district of Rio de Janeiro served as a zone of symbolically productive and socially notorious encounters between classes and races and between bohemian erudition and vulgar popular culture. In Lapa, culture explorers and sex tourists "voyaged between social classes, races, religions, and landscapes of Brazil, discovering new dense resources for creativity. . . . The bohemian generation of Lapa [was] immersed in the parallel, marginal, abandoned urban universe of Rio, the federal capital of the Old Republic, true face of the social and cultural reality of Brazil" (Gardel 1996, 69).

Before it was "rediscovered" by developers in the 1990s, Lapa moved from bohemian notoriety to blighted neglect, and became a target for urban-cleansing operations. Between the 1940s and the 1960s, government "urban renewal" slum-clearance efforts and the subsidized development of southern beach zones for the wealthy evacuated Rio's downtown areas and reduced the diversity and vitality of its street cultures and nightlife (Vaz and Silviera 1999, 52). Successive waves of police raids and demolitions eliminated many brothels and cabaret spaces. Lapa's location at the cusp between the central business district and the coastal commuter beltways made it attractive for occupation and redevelopment by a variety of urban actors. By the 1970s and 1980s, *rodoviarismo* (highwayism) replaced centralized, concentrated urban-development models that had once brought classes, races, and urban functions together downtown. Highways, automobile tunnels, and subway routes were carved through the old mixed neighborhoods. Nevertheless, laborers and professionals never ceased streaming into central Rio to work. And wherever commuter money flowed, so did mobile sex workers. Whether male, female, or travestis, sex workers responded to the changes in policing, settling, and commuting by establishing roadside territories, positioning themselves to attract the cash of passing consumers driving in and out of the business district. Lapa and its environs represented a historic gateway plaza to downtown, at the crossroads of commuters, tourists, and executives coming in from the elite areas of the Zona Sul (the beach areas of Copacabana, Ipanema, etc.). Offices and businesses closed at night, leaving a commercial and spatial vacuum on the sidewalks, which these street-side sex workers then reoccupied with their own goods.

The Rio municipal government, composed of an alliance of public and corporate partnerships promoting globalization and an explicitly neoliberal development model, also worked to stimulate and benefit from the consumer spending of those same commuters. With the decentralization of urban-development funding, there was also a "municipalization" of national identity, as cities drew on their own urban heritages, each competing to serve as the primary representative of the nation, its gateway to the globe, and as a magnet for tourism and foreign investment. In this context the globalizing city did not organize a local identity that stood opposed to national and global orders, but, in competition with other municipalities, strived to restore the urban-local as the most authentic, "classy," productive, and secure bridge between the nation and the globe. Heritage development, from the perspective of public-private development initiatives, provided one of these crucial bridges: "Heritage preservation as well as education and health is a problem of the masses, and should be treated as such. . . . Heritage preservation is the principal means by which municipalities secure their cultural identity. To recognize, valorize, and protect the cultural references of different regions, cities, and communities is the daily task to which municipalities are dedicated" (Falcão 1991, 17–19).

The year 1978 marked the turning point between an age of federally driven urban renewal and rodoviarismo, and a new era of municipalized, private-sector-driven redevelopment of the city center as a tourism/heritage/business center. Rio Mayor Israel Klabin initiated the Cultural Corridor project in a few of the city center's most historic plazas (Mesentier 1992, 129–33). By 1987, with the passing of municipal law 1139/87, the area of Lapa had been fully integrated into the preservation map, which covered more than ten thousand buildings and the greater part of the urban nucleus. The project linked the preservation of what was left of Rio's baroque colonial and nineteenth-century beaux-arts architecture to a public-private collaborative effort to redevelop downtown as a center for private domestic and foreign investment, as a corporate headquarters, and "as an instrument to intensify the use of space in the central area to strengthen activities linked to culture, leisure, and tourism" (Mesentier 1992, 131).

There was a queer similarity between the touristic heritage project of the government and the seduction economy of the sex workers in Lapa: both sought to lure executive commuters to stop their cars, pull over, and consume the new diversions of the city center. Both sets of entrepreneurs competed for essentially the same clients, but each possessed radically different levels of legitimacy and degrees of sovereign domain to occupy city space. In the area of Lapa, these two strategies for luring consumers— heritage and hooking—collided. Community, resident, and popular cultural groups seeking to resurrect the collective memory of bohemian, mixed-use Lapa played a pivotal role. If they joined with the executives, integrated the "quality of life" paradigm, and supported the eviction of prostitutes, then their own claim to space would be undercut, as they would be the next targets of heritage speculators wanting to narrow the use of urban space and what qualifies as the proper use of culture and built form (Mesentier 1992, 141). Neobohemian, identitarian, and community groups in Lapa realized the key role that the demonization of sex workers played in the speculative development of heritage spaces and the city center as a whole. Lapa's groups also realized that their identity as the embodiment of the old Lapa that had helped produce Brazil's samba civilization and its positive class-race integrated reputation could not be substituted by an image based exclusively on museumized baroque and nineteenth-century façades. Basically, Rio's securitized and stigmatized sexual publics knew that the city would lose its competitive uniqueness and global attractiveness without its sexy people and convivial spaces.

Beginning in the 1990s, Lapa's bohemian identity as a zone of encounter was squeezed into the matrix of a new project that sought to clean up the identity and functionality of urban public space and promote a new sanitized, "executive" international image of Brazil. In the mid-1990s, reurbanization plans demolished the adjacent cultural and sex-worker community, the Mangue. On the cleared land where the red-light district and women's residential quarter flourished (Moraes 1996), the municipal government erected the glass and steel towers of the city's new administrative offices and planning bureau. The Mangue had survived the era of military dictatorship and economic crisis, but not democratization and Rio's decision to market itself as a respectable global city. Fortunately, in Lapa developers and the municipal administration rejected urban-renewal plans to bulldoze much of the quarter and instead advocated a new preservationist agenda whereby social and architectural pollution was to be cleared from the area, while development would focus on restoring built heritage. Yet travesti and other "traditional" occupants of these public spaces needed them more than ever, because territories where they could claim legitimacy and recognition, and access safety as well as economic opportunity, were growing more scarce (Ornat 2008, 50).

The collision between vernacular and executive uses of heritage spaces did not lead to the definitive eviction of sex workers, nor to a failure or cancellation of the heritage project, nor even to a delineation of fixed borders, hierarchies, or claims to territory. In fact, the internal frontiers were produced and seduced in flux. Heritage developers, sex workers, and consumer populations continued to coexist in unusual dynamism, despite the interrelated but autonomous efforts of police, skinheads, and corporate elites to clear the area and drive out the prostitutes.

This dynamism and the plural usage of space persisted because of the reappropriation of the spaces of Lapa not just by sex workers and prostitution-rights activists, but by other clusters of actors, too: social clubs associated with the black civil-rights movement, Afro-Brazilian cultural groups, a circus troupe, black lesbian *barraca* (outdoor café) owners, and white gay male party promoters. Although usually hesitant to identify with the interests of sex workers, particularly transsexuals, these diverse identity groupings came together to mobilize around an alternative form of cosmopolitan and patriotic Brazilian sexual and cultural citizenship. This literal form of intersectional politics stalled police and planners' attempts to implement security and upgrading projects in the area. But despite the mobilization of popular and cultural groups, and despite the visibility and persistent attractiveness of Rio's vernacular models of conviviality, the gentrification and "social-purity" dynamics of heritage-based city-center development increased their influence.

Securitizing "Erotic Democracy," Producing "Executive" Citizens

Throughout the twentieth century the promotion of Brazil as a utopia of sensuality, racial mixing, and progress had attracted both labor migrants and tourists. But in the late 1990s, a new coalition of parastatal interest groups channeled tourism dollars away from the spectacles of Carnaval, beach, sex, and soccer (Furlough 1998, 251). A new, respectability-obsessed, revanchist vision of Rio's proper touristic and national identity emerged, and it looked down with shame on the Lapa-and-Carnaval early-twentieth-century utopian project of populist cultural nationalism that had aimed for racial mixing and a uniquely sensualized modernity. The globally self-conscious elites of Rio, increasingly in dialogue with Pentecostal-Evangelical Christian groups, had begun to see Brazil's tropical, sensualist image as fake, dirty, and vulgar. They thought it perverted and prostituted the nation in the global economy. Tito Ryff, Rio's municipal secretary of planning in the mid-1990s, expressed his disgust after passing by the Plataforma, a mulatta showgirls Carnaval theater: "I always get a feeling of discomfort when I pass at night by the Plataforma in

Leblon and see the enormity of busses bringing tourists to attend a samba show that is a mimicry of popular culture. We should be able to redirect this interest to show some of the tourists . . . the historical-cultural patrimony of the city of Rio de Janeiro."[12]

Upgrading the class identity and "quality of life" for tourism became a priority for Brazil in the 1990s, and it could only be enacted with the leadership and agency of urban planning and the security sector. This upgrading effort was implemented with a priority on "sexual profiling" of those judged to be the wrong class of tourists and urban street-entrepreneurs. As stated by Caio de Carvalho, president of Brazil's private-sector-oriented Tourism Authority, "We want to change the profile of the tourists who come to Brazil and those who travel inside. We want those with a better buying power, who bring the family. . . . This change in mentality will attract a new quality of tourism, a tourism that is not just leisure, and much less, a perversion of leisure."[13]

In the late 1990s, tourism and municipal officials in Rio de Janeiro, in coordination with the national government, launched a wide-ranging attack on sex tourism in Brazil, and Rio in particular. As the press reported, "It is open season for hunting sex tourists. . . . Embratur [Brazilian Tourist Board], which until the start of the 1990s exploited the image of the sensuality of the Brazilian woman to sell the country overseas, will launch a counter-offensive, involving travel agencies, hotels, restaurants, and taxis" (Trinidade 1997a). Although its particular legal objective was the investigation and conviction of juvenile-prostitute traffickers, the effort was marked by an aggressive media and poster campaign demonizing sex tourism in general. Orwellian posters arrayed throughout public spaces proclaimed in English, "Beware! Brazil is watching you!" (Trinidade 1997a).

This media demonization of Brazilian prostitutes at home was flanked by a dramatic series of exposés targeting Brazilian sex workers traveling abroad as labor migrants. While the government campaigned against sex tourists, the media ran major reportages profiling local women who had emigrated for work and ended up enslaved for sex, ensnared by so-called folkloric cultural-exchange groups and promised English lessons abroad (Couri 1993), or seduced by entities masquerading as European immigrant-welfare agencies (Homem 1996; Gilberto Nascimento 1996). However, the representations of passivity and victimization for migrant sex workers did not carry over to the coverage of "male" travesti prostitutes. Travestis usually identify strongly as men. According to Don Kulick,

There is a strong consensus among travestis [at least, until the 1990s] that any travesti who claims to be a women is mentally disturbed. A travesti is not a woman and can never be a woman, they tell one another, because God created them male. As individuals, they are free to embellish and augment what God has given them, but their sex cannot be changed. . . . Public uncertainty about the precise nature (and hence, the precise boundaries) of travesti identity also generates a space of ambiguity that travestis can use to their advantage. If travesti identity remains fuzzy, it becomes possible to suggest that the identity, or at least key dimensions of the identity, are not specific to travestis, but are, instead, shared by others who do not self-identify as travestis. (1997, 224, 577)

However, as they were securitized by the press and police, migrant travestis were represented very distinctly as *men* whose queerness lay, perhaps surprisingly, not in effeminacy but in their attributed hypermasculinity—as endowed with enhanced, violent, global-scale agency. They were portrayed as aggressive, threatening members of militant transnational gangs that were violently invading foreign and national public spaces. In the late 1990s, the Rio press depicted with relish the wars between Brazilian prostitutes and the police in Rome and Paris (Bógus and Bassanezi 1998, 68–69). Journalists sought out and quoted the bold travestis. This hypervisibilizing coverage alternated between representing sex workers as terrifying collectives that embarrassed the country abroad and as heroes fighting against the rise of neofascism in Europe and in Brazil (Japiassu 1980; Louzeiro 1993; Netto 1986). In both cases, the travestis were described as possessing exaggerated agency and a daring sense of self-direction—as gladiators, terrorists, or revolutionaries—whereas women sex workers were depicted by the press, as well as by local anti-trafficking activists, as passive, economically dependent objects of the global sex-slave trade.

Parallel to these state and media campaigns to gentrify tourism, another form of gentrification occurred: the colonization of the sex labor market by the white middle classes of Rio. During the 1980s and 1990s, the buying power of the white middle classes eroded in Brazil as stable industrial jobs in both private and public industrial sectors were eliminated. During this period, some young members of the white middle classes began to engage in prostitution to halt their gradual slide down the social hierarchy and to maintain their presence in consumer society and in elite urban spaces. This phenomenon became so widespread that white middle-class sex workers began to push black, transsexual, and working-class prostitutes out of the safer and more lucrative pleasure zones. Meanwhile, as police and gang violence intensified in working-class sex-work areas, police left five-star clubs and more polished massage parlors untouched, or the cops absorbed them into protection rackets that guarded these clubs' exclusivity (Springer de Freitas 1984, 35). In these choice locations, red-light workers were replaced by white middle-class prostitutes who drew on their education, technology, and the anonymity and discretion afforded by whiteness in order to avoid the visibility that the darker-skinned street prostitutes could not escape:

> The classic figures of pimps, madams, and gigolos are turning
> into dinosaurs, in an extinction process caused by "girls" learning
> how to organize themselves and discover the advantages of self-
> management. The [girls themselves] are also changing. They are not
> necessarily poor women, condemned to live in the ghetto where
> paid sex is the only way of life. Today, a growing number of pros-
> titutes are regular folks closer to us than we imagine. She could
> be that discreet neighbor, a colleague at university, or that pretty
> young cashier. This new version of ladies of the night wants to
> maintain anonymity. In order to keep up, they have entered the age
> of technology, using and abusing cell phones and pagers. . . . Public
> space and street corners are ceding to other environments, gener-
> ally closed . . . to protect from urban violence. Activities are being
> dislocated more and more from the street to . . . discreet points of
> encounter. (Trinidade 1997b)

Working on the street in the mixed-class, mixed-race areas became increasingly dangerous for both clients and prostitutes. The streets around Lapa were contested territories where risk of abuse or theft by clients was high, as was exposure to violent harassment and police extortion. Prostitution was and is legal in Brazil, so sex work is not prohibited in Rio, but the penal code does criminalize "inducing someone into prostitution" (article 227), "opening a house of prostitution" (article 229), and "pimping or profiting from prostitution" (article 230).[14] In addition to enforcing these codes, in the late 1990s Rio's police imported from the United States highly militarized and legally controversial practices of collective tracking and profiling developed to control street gangs. In the event of a reported theft targeting a john or a foreign tourist, police would round up a whole community of transsexual and male prostitutes and register the individuals as members of a gang, regardless of proof of involvement in any particular crime. In the event of a reported case of forced prostitution or sex trafficking across borders, police rounded up women prostitutes to "rescue" them, but also to register them with a photo and fingerprint. This form of profiling and collective punishment tended to worsen working conditions and relations of exploitation within the sex sector, and it permanently categorized the registered individuals as a threat to public safety.

Rio's working-class prostitutes, exposed in public space on the streets, were caught between two relatively autonomous police forces, the Militarized Police and the Municipal Guards. The zone of Lapa is located where Militarized Police domains (racialized slums, principal highways) overlapped with Municipal Guard territories (business areas, tourist clubs, street-vendor zones), and where campaigns for upgrading heritage preservation overlapped with campaigns to root out sex trafficking and sex tourism. Thus, an urban nexus of seemingly abnormal violence and marginality became a site for fusing agendas modeled by policing and planning elites.

From Militarized Modernism to Neoliberalism
on Cairo's Pyramids Road

From the 1970s through the 1990s, Pyramids Road and the Nile Waterfront in Greater Cairo provided the stage for security crises and redevelopment efforts that displayed certain similarities to those in Rio de Janeiro's Lapa. Cairo's sex-worker zones served as borderlands where vernacular sexual cultures came into contact with international five-star tourism, where highway commuters encountered street-vendor economies, and where different modes of consuming and identifying public space collided. Pyramids Road and the Nile waterfront in the center of Cairo also provided a stage on which to enact postcolonial and nationalist tensions that were stirred up by the mingling of pleasure seekers from the wealthy Persian Gulf, tourists from the West, and nightlife consumers from among the local Cairene elite (Wynn 2007). For the most part, these three consumer groups remained somewhat segregated by space and time. Arabs from the Persian Gulf emirates and monarchies occupied hotels, theaters, and casinos in the summer; Westerners visited monuments and beaches in the winter; and Cairenes frequented malls and discos year round. But Pyramids Road and the Nile waterfront attracted attention from all of these groups in any season. Additionally, these particular spaces remained accessible and open to working-class Cairenes looking to become a part of the scene, and whose erotic labor was necessary to the attraction and profitability of the spaces.

Pyramids Road, the most notorious nightlife strip in Cairo during this period, had long functioned as a corridor linking the epicenter of downtown Cairo to the historic Sphinx and Pyramids Plateau of Giza. In the early 1900s, with the damming of the Nile and the draining of wetlands, the river's banks were settled and eventually became the site for office towers, hotels, apartment buildings, and government ministries. Subsequently, Giza, the province that covered the west bank of the Nile, became fully integrated as the "left bank" of Greater Cairo. In the 1980s, planning agencies and plans for subways and highways began to map the Nile as the metropolitan region's central axis rather than its western limit.

Pyramids Road was initially constructed in 1867 by Khedive Ismail, initiating the development of Giza and the Nile's west bank as an elite bucolic zone for country villas and as a base for tourism excursions to the Plateau of the Great Pyramids. The road became a nightlife zone only after a series of nationalist riots drove clubs and cabarets out of the city center, on the eastern bank of the Nile (Sha'iira, Magheeb, and Zeid 1996). At the end of the Second World War, when Britain reneged on its promise to fully decolonize Egypt, nationalist protesters led by the Muslim Brothers targeted nightclubs and cabarets in the Emadeddin and Tawfiqiyya areas of downtown Cairo, which they saw as nests of impurity and promiscuous mingling between Egyptians and British, foreigners and Muslims, men and women. This nationalist social-purity campaign led to the temporary prohibition of belly dancing and to the criminalization of prostitution in 1949 (Dunne 1996). Until then, the large cabaret sector or urban tourism sector in Cairo had been one of the few places where Egyptian women had established economic and social dominance. The nationalist scapegoating of the pleasure sector drove nightclubs and much of Egyptian women's wealth, talent, and entrepreneurship to Giza, to the urban margins of Pyramids Road.

In the early 1950s, religious nationalists (the Muslim Brothers, the bourgeois Wafdist nationalists, and the communists) combined forces and generated another attack on cabaret culture, focusing on Egypt's King Farouk as a puppet of the British, whose illegitimacy was reinforced by his supposed effeminacy and his preference for frequenting nightclubs downtown and on Pyramids Road (Sha'iira, Magheeb, and Zeid 1996). The attack forced Badi'a Masabni, the queen of Cairo's vaudeville and cabaret underground, to flee (van Nieuwkerk 1995, 48). Her successor, Kuka 'Abdu, led the next wave of nightclub transfers across the Nile to Pyramids Road. As Nasser's revolution occupied and transformed downtown, this area of Giza became an enclave where Egypt's cabaret culture and many women club owners came to reestablish a foothold. In the 1970s, this zone once again became a primary, hypervisible space where Egypt played out its anxieties about global integration or colonization. When the Palestinian-Egyptian superstar belly dancer Nagwa Fouad performed for Henry Kissinger and President Sadat at a Pyramids Road casino, the nationalist press characterized the event as a symbol of how Egypt and the Arab nation was prostituting itself to Israel and the United States. Nevertheless, the red-light zone continued to develop (Sami 1998). In 1977, and then in 1986, popular uprisings against Open Door liberalization and reconciliation with the United States and Israel (and simultaneous police riots against reforms) targeted nightclubs along Pyramids Road.[15] These protests were reminiscent of the sex-phobic nationalist violence in the 1940s and 1950s that targeted the downtown cabaret zones. In the words of the Al-Azhar sheikh Abdel-Maqsoud Al-Askar, "These establishments conflict with our moral values and principles and contradict the constitution, which says that Islamic Shari'a is the official source of state legislation. . . . They say the presence of these nightclubs is necessary to stimulate tourism and attract male and female visitors, even if they are naked! They say we need their dollars, and francs, and shekels. But our ethical values must govern our economic demands, not the other way around" (Al-Askar 1986).

But dollars, francs, and shekels were not much in circulation along Pyramids Road in this period; dinars and riyals were more common. Arabs from the Persian Gulf petroleum monarchies, and the Egyptian elites themselves, have always been more likely to visit these clubs than have Westerners (Wynn 2007, 4, 25). But the gaps between the rich and poor, men and women, and the Persian Gulf and the Nile continued to be represented as moral strife between West and East in the red-light zone (Amar 1998a). These representations of the Pyramids Road sex-worker zone as a Western neocolony, despite Egyptian (female) ownership of key establishments and majority-Arab patronage, reflect a discourse of "inverted orientalism." The binary of native tradition versus Western decadence continued to effectively obscure the importance of other forms of national, gendered, class, and transnational power and domination.[16]

During the 1970s, Persian Gulf Arabs with their new supply of wealth began frequenting Cairo as nightlife tourists. Bars, belly dancing clubs, brothels, and down-market discos sprung up along Pyramids Road to cater to this set, as well as to the Egyptian *nouveau riches* that emerged in the Sadat "Open Door" years. These establishments displaced the older country clubs and elegant casinos that had characterized the zone in the 1940s and 1950s. To resolve what were portrayed as cultural, moral, and spatial conflicts between cabaret cultures and the presumed family values of the resident population, the Giza Governorate, after the first set of riots in 1977, resolved to bulldoze all cabarets and bars,[17] replace them with low-cost housing units (Al-Diib 1986), and relocate the nightclubs to a new pleasure zone for tourists that Sadat planned to build around the Great Pyramids. UNESCO and international tourism organizations mobilized to protest this plan and succeeded in stalling it, fearing the obscuring of the desert vista and the cheapening of the "human heritage" of the Great Pyramids Plateau by relocating the cabarets and casinos to the immediate vicinity of the monuments. So, the clubs continued to operate until the 1986 police uprising, which destroyed a dozen cabarets and put the matter back at the top of the agenda of urban planners and nationalists.

In 1986, the Giza city council drafted a plan to domesticate the area as a residential zone by relocating all nightclubs to the desert far beyond the vista of the Pyramids Plateau (Abou Hawaar 1986; Ibrahim 1986). Belly dancers and cabaret workers on Pyramids Road protested, arguing that the distance could hurt business and put women in a precarious no-man's land, exposed and unprotected.[18] The National Ministry of Tourism took the side of the cabarets, deeming their continued operations necessary to sustain Egypt's crucial tourism revenues. In 1988, the tourism ministry said clubs could remain on Pyramids Road if they upgraded their image (Abdel-Hadi 1986). Establishments promptly dropped the title "cabaret" and renamed themselves "theaters" without changing their functions or clientele.[19]

In 1992, Adel Hussein proclaimed in the Islamist-leaning paper *Al-Shaab* that it was *haram*, or religiously impermissible, for Egypt to promote the kind of tourism that Pyramids Road offered. He declared that economic dependence on sexual and entertainment tourism was a corruption and perversion of the nation. The press declared, "The morals of Egyptians hang in the balance" (Saadiq 1993). In the 1990s, some militant groups took up this type of argument as a call to arms and attacked tourists rather than the clubs themselves. Pyramids Road continued to symbolize and serve as a battleground for the cultural and development crisis of Cairo and of the Arab world in general. The boulevard became a zone of confrontation between images of nostalgic elegance and contemporary overdevelopment, of elite decadence and the marginalized urban classes, and between dissonant cultural milieus: the international heritage of pharaonic tombs, the urban temptations of nightlife, and the rumblings of resurgent religious nationalism. All the while, tourist buses had no choice but to pass down the embattled road in order to take visitors to the Pyramids Plateau.[20]

Like the Pyramids Road area in Giza, the Nile riverbank in the city center has also served as an urban corridor for contact and conflict around norms of development, the reputation of the nation, and social-class polarization. In the early twentieth century, the British occupiers had restricted public access to the waterfront. But during the era of the 1952 Revolution, taking back the waterfront for the people became a national priority. The state nationalized embassy properties and private villas along the Nile's edge to build an open boardwalk, the pedestrian Corniche, and large riverboats and houseboats were allowed to moor permanently on both sides of the waterway. These boats cultivated a bohemian culture of radical reading groups, artists' colonies, and nightclubs where class, gender, and sexual norms were to some extent suspended.

In the 1970s, five-star tourist hotels and luxury residential towers constructed by new petroleum and entrepreneurial wealth began to encroach on this zone of cultural and popular-class liberation. The Nile Hilton, Ramses Hilton, New Shepherd's Hotel, The Meridian, the Cairo Marriot, and eventually the Cairo World Trade Center created a modern skyline for Cairo along the Nile and increased the social dynamism of the waterfront, where Gulf Arab and Western hotel guests, Egyptian elites, houseboat bohemians, and the popular classes on the Corniche converged. As an extension of the kind of intermingling that characterized Pyramids Road or Rio's Lapa, the Cairo waterfront had been represented, alternately, as the heart of a cosmopolitan open city where classes and nations could meet in a beautiful landscape of celebration, and as a high-risk space that threatened the security of the boundaries of social categories, gender and religious norms, and national independence.

Thus, in 2001, with the raid on the Queen Boat, moored on the waterfront at the Cairo Marriot, Egypt's security forces began acting aggressively against this more convivial, cosmopolitan model of public space in Cairo. Their actions represented an intensification of efforts to shut down the more fluid, multiple uses of the waterfront. Since 1998, wealthy residents had forced the closure of popular parks; the Vice Police had closed down "low-class" discos; the governorate had revoked houseboat mooring permits; and the Tourist Police had increased their presence around hotels to assure guests exclusive access to the waterfront. Presenting an exposé on rising rates of violent crime and sex crime in the city, the popular magazine *Sabah al-Khayr* in 1998 featured a cover illustration of a working-class couple courting on the Nile Corniche. As indicated by the magazine, the Nile waterfront, as a space of liberal intermingling, courtship, and play, had become the picture and metaphorical cause of the "breakdown of the family" and the "negative image of women in the eye of men" (Al-Zeitouni 1998). The Nile waterfront, where the police arrest of the alleged "gay terrorists" and "debauchers" took place, and Pyramids Road had become key sites of intermingling, which the police, press, and development elites in Cairo viewed as the cause of violence, a threat to economic development through tourism, and, most urgently, a threat to national culture that is embodied most essentially in gender norms. In order to examine what caused the spaces of Pyramids Road and the Nile waterfront to be targeted as a menace to cultural and economic security, it is necessary to trace the rise of new policing practices and urban social-control policies that have targeted these areas where classes and nations meet in a convivial, eroticized environment. Resegregating classes and nations had become a priority for Cairo's police and development community, which sought to reconcile this strict social-control project with the seemingly contradictory aim of increasing tourist visits and enjoyment.

For the European and North American tourist population, Cairo has represented, for the most part, merely a gateway to the pharaonic monuments of Giza and Luxor. However, for the elites of the Persian Gulf, the Levant, and sub-Saharan Africa, Cairo is their Rio de Janeiro—a place to consume music, soccer, cabaret, theater, and sex. Almost unnoticed by urban pleasure seekers from the West, Cairo is a lavish nightlife capital during July and August, when its population swells with tourists from the Middle East region. Aware of this market, in the late 1990s Cairo's governor launched a plan to address the problem of sex tourism by shifting investment in and the global marketing of Cairo's Islamic cultural heritage, its business and professional conference venues, and family-style attractions like shopping, cinema, and theater. Developing tourism while rooting out its vulgarizing cultural and moral effects centered on policing sex trafficking and banishing eroticized contact between classes and nation-alities (Amar 1998b, 8).

From Parastatal Formations to International Accords

As traced in the preceding discussion, human-security practices and parahuman subjects of militarized rescue or containment emerged in the locally contested and transnationally circulated policing and urban-planning practices of the 1980s and 1990s in these hotspots of the Global South. Subsequently, governance operations that fixated on producing binary regimes of sexuality and culture were formalized and internation-alized through a series of world conferences that brought international humanitarian movements, police and security agencies, and private-sector tourism promoters together with the governments of these devel-oping states. In October 1995, the World Tourism Organization, a UN Eco-nomic and Social Council-affiliated body, held a humanitarian summit in Cairo, where government tourism ministers and officials from 120 coun-tries, together with private-sector transnationals and municipal leaders, met to draft the Declaration on the Prevention of Sex Tourism, which condemned the practice as "exploitative and subversive to the basic aims of tourism." They initiated a three-pronged action plan that "(1) urges gov-ernments to enact measures against organized sex tourism; (2) asks the travel trade to strengthen professional codes of conduct and educate staff about the negative consequences of sex tourism; and (3) encourages the media and the traveling public to promote awareness of the problems of sex tourism, especially child prostitution and AIDS."[21]

Fulfilling the organization's prescription for spreading awareness about sex tourism via the media, a press-generated scandal erupted in Cairo's newspapers around the trafficking of young Egyptian women into hotels for Gulf Arab tourists and the marketing of young Egyptian men to "rich" middle-aged British women tourists (Kempadoo 1999). In referring to the latter practice, the Cairo media reported that sex trafficking had reached the heart of the Islamic world:

> Sexual trafficking has become one of the most profitable commer-cial sectors in the world . . . reaching the heart of the Islamic world
> . . . principally through the means of tourism and the modern tech-nology of the Internet[, in this case] drawing the women of Europe to visit Luxor and Aswan in order to enjoy sex with Upper Egyptian

sons of Pharaohs who possess extraordinary sexual powers superior to those of any other race, even to those of the *mulattos* celebrated by biological science . . . and therefore threatening our Arab and Islamic societies and our great values and making impure all that is holy and authentic.[22]

Despite very distinct social histories of racial formation and nationalist sexualization, both Brazil and Egypt articulated, during this period of moral panic, a common agenda of shame felt in response to the touristic marketing of "mulatto" hypersexuality, along with an expressed need to preserve authentic holy monuments, and generated a respectable, desexualized image of cultural-national authenticity. It is indicative of the transnational articulation of the policing of sex tourism that it is only in this context of sex panic around tourism that this Brazilian-style racial-science discourse problematizing "mulatto" hypersexuality has surfaced in contemporary Egypt.[23]

Controlling sexual *consumer migration* (sex tourism) was linked or collapsed with the issue of controlling the perverting effect of sexual *labor migration* ("trafficking in women"). Indeed, both processes were represented by police and press discourse as essentially linked. Again, gender mattered. Young men who traveled abroad to marry older, wealthier European women, or to live as companions of male tourists, were not represented as enslaved or in sexual bondage, nor as trafficked slaves. On the contrary, the media consistently identified young women as victims, as raw flesh rather than as subjects: "Nightmare! Disaster! Scandal! The flesh of our daughters has been dumped into the market. . . . The bait is ready, the fishhook bitten and the victim is innocent and raw" (Naasif 1994).

Traveling abroad to work in prostitution was portrayed never as a matter of choice for the "victims" but as the coercion of the young woman and the nation, forced by the inequalities of economic globalization and Western-originating criminal smuggling organizations. As one detained woman stated, "I was going there, I swear to God, to work in a folkloric belly dancing troupe as they told me, when I arrived I found they had reserved us a room in a five-star hotel and a number of men were waiting for us, I felt afraid and confused" (Fouad 1993; Naasif 1994). Faced with the fact that at least five thousand young women travel abroad each year to work as prostitutes, the Egyptian anti-trafficking activist Hassan al-Alfi asks, "How can we protect these girls and our nation's reputation?" (Naasif 1994).

For anti-trafficking activists and nationalists in Egypt, defending the country's reputation involved selective border controls that policed working-class women's sexuality and mobility under the assumption that a mobile, working-class woman was sexually deviant or prostituted until proven otherwise. The Cairo Vice Police thus monitored and interrogated the body, history, and home life of any working-class or lower-middle-class woman who wanted to cross the border and work abroad. During the late 1990s, the press and government in Cairo pressured the Vice Police to investigate all suspicious (i.e., non-elite) women seeking passports and to generate moral and sexual profiles of each one to determine the probability of their going abroad to engage in sex work. As mainstream tourism developers in Egypt sought to double the number of visitors each year, the press and police criminalized and restricted the mobility of women within the touristic parts of the city where they might encounter Gulf Arabs or Westerners, or at airports and borders where young women might migrate out of the country and defame the nation abroad by engaging in sex work (Rafa'at 2000).[24] This articulation—maximizing touristic consumer mobility and minimizing female labor mobility—was explicitly theorized as a way to make tourism development more profitable while minimizing its destabilizing effects on religious identity and on the purity of gender orders and class hierarchies.

In the late 1990s, international tourism conferences promoting hybrids of humanitarianism and development played key roles in reaching transnational consensus, particularly around the issue of reconciling global economic development and local cultural preservation. A new emphasis on policing illicit sexuality was instrumental to defining tourism's new humanitarian or human-security mission, focusing on apprehending transnational flows of sex predators and supplying troops for the "culture wars" around globalization, rather than engaging directly with questions of the tourism industry's role in promoting economic inequality, deploying repressive policing regimes, and heightening social vulnerability to global market fluctuations. One of the main international promoters of this sexual-security project was the World Travel and Tourism Council (WTTC), a transnational coalition of private companies. The WTTC advocated the "Millennium Vision," a seemingly contradictory policy mix that promoted the eradication of all economic barriers between countries, while preserving and even increasing protective cultural barriers.

By the late 1990s, tourism was to be the strategically crucial sector, fusing the pursuit of cultural localism with economic globalism, particularly through the control of "vulgar" forms of sexuality. The public sector—local states and police forces, as well as international institutions—needed to assume responsibility for making sure that urban tourist cities faced the sexual nature of the problem and took the necessary steps to reconcile economic integration with cultural preservation. Keeping the liberalized global economy from infecting the sanctity of local culture implied a mix of architectural and environmental heritage preservation linked to local value preservation, both implemented through sexual policing. In 1996, world tourism leaders gathered in Bali, Indonesia, to outline "the responsibility of local governments and parliaments for ensuring that tourism plays a positive role in protecting the environment and enhancing local cultures. . . . In this context, all forms of organized sex tourism, especially the sexual exploitation of children, must be banned and fought."[25] Appropriately, in the same year, the World Tourism Organization and UNESCO signed an accord to promote cultural preservation and heritage tourism as a development model. The World Tourism Organization and Pope John Paul II produced a joint video statement underlining the new urgency of sex tourism as a disease inseparable from AIDS: "Sex tourism not only violates human rights, it contributes to the spread of AIDS, degrades the social fabric of host countries, and tarnishes the image of the tourism sector worldwide."[26]

By shifting the focus onto forms of illicit sexual contact among working-class urbanites, and by formally adopting cultural rescue and heritage preservation as their aims, tourism industry leaders, in dialogue with Rio's and Cairo's business leaders, worked out a formula for advocating unlimited economic liberalization and dependence on the tourism sector as the only comparative advantage and employment generator. With the focus on tourism as a policing regime for cultural preservation and as an agent that rescued and defended developing nations and their vulnerable populations, attention was drawn away from more critical perspectives that saw development elites as exploiters, speculators, and colonizers. Anxieties about risk and security, in the context of increasing dependence on the highly volatile and image-driven tourism economy, were displaced into a national security war to save cultural values and public space from the menace of sexual deviancy.

Conclusion

The structural, historical, and political discourse analyses here have identified emergent patterns of policing and planning in the context of municipal struggles over cultural identity, economic modernization, and the regulation of sexualized public spaces. We have seen how the labor and consumer agency of sex workers and queer communities, in certain highly visible spaces and urban corridors, were securitized and hypervisibilized. Increasingly, during this period in both Cairo and Rio, sexually problematized agents were represented, if "female" and working class, as dangerously hyperpassive and vulnerable to foreign exploitation, or if "male" (travesti transnational "gangs" or the Queen Boat's queer globalist "traitors"), as hyperaggressive threats to the nation and its values, and they were targeted in new ways by these parastatal formations and their urban-security and -development models. Class and race relations among labor and consumers in red-light zones shifted as both working-class prostitutes and "low-class" visitors were increasingly denied access to public space while "executive" visitors were preferred.

We have also seen how planning officials in both cities came to focus on developing architectural heritage, five-star hotels, and shopping venues in order to attract wealthy executive consumers and investors and elite family-oriented tourists. These patrons were presumed to spend more money in formal businesses and on products and services offered by elite-owned franchises, and to consume the city visually, at a distance, rather than through sociocultural participation or eroticized, informal contact through which money could enter working-class communities directly, without corporate intermediation. This shift justified the clearing away of spaces of contact between classes and nations that were associated with a more disorderly form of urban conviviality and eroticized tourism; these spaces were represented as a pathogen that infected the city and nation with sex and violence. Finally, we have seen how fractured policing organizations in Rio and Cairo became increasingly militaristic in their targeting of sex workers and queer socialities in these spaces. They adopted an increasingly homogeneous vision of who was menacing urban modernization and national values and who thus deserved to be forcibly rescued and put back in their place. This new policing and planning model offered a transnationally consistent agenda for how to deal with threats to national culture and global development.

But also, this comparative and transregional analysis of struggles and histories in Rio and Cairo has aimed to demonstrate that in the military-modernist period and the subsequent neoliberal period in Rio, sexualized public communities were able to make cultural claims on public spaces identified with national heritage; in Cairo, sexually criminalized communities were able to make economic claims as attractions for tourism development. During this time, urban development and policing elites in both Cairo and Rio increasingly allied themselves with a newly emergent global-development paradigm that combined the cultural preservation of the nation with its economic integration into globalization. This paradigm was most clearly articulated in the policy agendas of public-private partnerships for tourism development, city image-marketing, and urban heritage preservation, which became the strategic fulcrums of broad strategies for parastatal governance as a whole.

As I describe them here, human-security policing strategies that circulated transnationally emerged late in the neoliberal period. Paradoxically, these self-identified "antiglobalization" security doctrines were articulated by transnationally linked parastatals, consisting of public-private partnerships and development coalitions linked to global investor flows and international tourism markets. Yet they posed themselves as cultural-sexual protectors of the local; that is, they claimed to rescue local difference from global forces of homogenization through the militarized policing of illicit sexualities and the spatial eradication of their public presence. This form of sexual-security politics naturalized the separation of culture from economy. *Culture* became associated with local scale, national(ist) values, tradition, and a monolithic view of the family and gender roles; *economy*, meanwhile, became associated with global scale, elite consumers and investors, market values, and a monolithic view of the need to restructure. This global project thus provincialized the local, in some registers and symbolic orders, in order to facilitate particular global economic and institutional arrangements.[27]

Policing sexuality, clearing spaces of conviviality, and remaking the city for elite heritage and shopping venues was constructed as the necessary and essential axis for stabilizing this marriage of essentialist culturalism with economic fundamentalism. Any space that destabilized or rearticulated the relationship between culture and economy, global and local, became marked as perverse and increasingly targeted for militarized repression. This sexualizing security paradigm generated a politics of identification that served important displacement functions, spotlighting some while obscuring the true agency of elites and parastatal security networks. Hyperpassive women ("prostituted" and "enslaved" by sex tourism) and hyperaggressive men (travesti "gladiators" in Rio, "gay traitors" in Cairo) were held accountable for the socioeconomic and cultural crises of these globalizing cities. Paradoxically, because of their assumed status as actors that perform beyond the normal range of respectable agency, and because they were associated with outside threats to both culture and economy, these actors were given exaggerated responsibility, while they were also deprived of recognition within categories of worker or citizen. At the same time, certain transnational consumer elites and influential parastatal actors were granted virtual global citizen rights in these nation-states and remained above accountability. Empowered by the new sexual-security paradigm, this bloc of parastatal formations pursued polarizing development and restructuring projects while avoiding visibility. In this context, nonelite communities striving to revive their social commitments to conviviality, erotic commerce, and popular cosmopolitanism faced new roadblocks to staking claims and occupying territories. But queer publics were not deterred. They responded by blazing new trails toward recognition, as well as challenging securitization dynamics by invoking utopic transnationalisms and reviving nationalisms centered on eroticized conviviality. These queer challenges would persist, and would eventually help to bring to crisis the repressive apparatus of new human-security regimes.

$\boxed{3}$

MUHAMMAD ATTA'S URBANISM

Rescuing Islam, Saving Humanity,
and Securing Gender's Proper Place in Cairo

As an architect raised and educated in an Oriental-Islamic city I have a personal obligation towards and a professional interest in those cities. Although I grew up in Cairo, I only "discovered" the old city of Cairo [for myself] at the age of 16. In spite of decay and change of use, I came across many things in the old city that I had subconsciously been longing for in the metropolis of Cairo. . . . In my academic studies, I had learned more about Gothic styles than Mamluk, and dealt with Frank Lloya Right [*sic*] more than Hassan Fathy. I feel that little can be done for the old cities through architecture by itself. I hope that urban planning will provide a chance for me to make a real difference. —**Muhammad El-Amir Atta (1999)**, two years before the September 11 attacks, during which he piloted American Airlines Flight 11 into the north tower of the World Trade Center

In preceding chapters, I have identified blocs of actors and subjects of contention behind logics of securitization that emerged between the 1970s and 1990s. During this period, particular sites in the Global South came to serve as human-security laboratories, fashioning cultures of control and practices of governance. These innovative security norms and practices transferred between regions or jumped to the international scale when taken up at United Nations meetings or absorbed by transnational parastatal development and security networks. These processes of security globalization depended on the fact that these sites served as privileged locations where UN international conferences, UNESCO meetings, global police networks, and the world tourism industry came together to negotiate and formalize a new generation of humanized or humanitarian models for security and development. Through this series of encounters and struggles, distinct blocs of actors (parastatal partnerships, semiprivatized state planning and security agencies, morality crusades and missionary campaigns, and liberal, workerist, and identitarian social movements) clashed around issues of power and redistribution. In this context, I traced how these disparate sets of actors eventually came to forge some degree of tactical consensus around modalities for rescuing or protecting "local culture" from the "global economy." This fragile consensus for human-security interventionism reshaped internationalized policing agendas and married them to urban-planning models reconceived as rescue operations. These security interventions justified themselves as extraordinary humanitarian interventions or cultural-rescue missions, concentrating attention on certain communities identified with public sexuality and with cultural or racial mixing. Spaces and peoples were configured as high risk but also as high value when disciplined properly through tourism and enforcement projects that identified "humanity" with certain kinds of family values and consumer practices. Nevertheless, the groups targeted by police and urban planners, in the spaces that preoccupied international diplomats and tourists, did not accept being reduced to scapegoats or test subjects for experimental security regimes. Instead, they organized resistance and generated bold campaigns aiming to turn these humanization logics inside out, challenging the binaries of the global-local and the moral-perverse. What I identify as the "human-security state" thus emerged not merely as a form of repressive sovereignty, but as a *state of contention and violently creative upheaval*, riddled with productive contradictions and opportunities.

My overall aim in the first section of this book was to generate a *securitization of humanity* narrative, offered as an alternative to the dominant *liberalization of markets* narrative. This critical securitization perspective centers a set of processes and subjects distinct from those of the critique of neoliberalism, centered on the subjects of liberalism, competitive marketization, and economic individualism. Like the critique of neoliberalism, the analytical narrative of securitization is also attentive to political economy, but it gives analytical priority to the productivity of subjects of morality, gender, sexuality, race, policing, and space-making in the Global South. The liberalization narrative (or the critique of neoliberalism) tends to identify those subjects with questions of marginalization or victimization, and so reifies their peripheral or exotic position with respect to power. I continue this recentering process in the chapters to follow. Instead of shuttling back and forth between the Middle East and Latin America, I concentrate on one location at a time in order to provide in-depth accounts from below of culture-intensive and morality-infused security regimes in these two globalizing cities. Drawing on two years of fieldwork in each of the two cities, I present findings from case studies that reveal the specific dynamism of emergent human-security models. These are never seamlessly consistent or overwhelmingly deterministic. Specific blocs of agents and contradictory securitization logics intersect in each security laboratory and around each set of subjects of rescue and protection. This complexity provides opportunities for subversion and appropriation at particular breaches and junctures that I identify.

I now turn to an analysis of the actors and factors that came together to constitute a project whose mission was to rescue and develop the historical assets of Cairo's Islamic architecture and the "heritage of humanity" they are said to embody. This rescue-and-redevelopment project was forged at the crux of the most urgent security dilemmas of the day: the marginalization of the frustrated poor by economic restructuring and state privatization; the eruption of "jihadist" militant groups and their targeting of tourist sites and financial institutions; and the radical intensification of "cultural-security politics" or "culture wars" in Egypt, driven on the one hand by state-provoked moral panics and on the other by the rapid growth of populist, transnationally funded, "puritan" movements, "originalist" preaching communities, and charity organizations known as Salafis or al-salafiyya.[1] Through this process, new populist, moralistic, and religiously conservative (but politically novel) forms of human-security governance emerged from the linking of "cultural rescue" to the marketing of "Islamic heritage." These security models combined contradictory gender, class, and development prerogatives that resonated with innovative forms of religious militancy. But they also reflected modern urbanism's gendered, sexualized, and moralistic response to governance crises within neoliberalism.

In the global public imagination and certainly in geopolitics scholarship, the era between 2001 and 2011—starting with the attacks on the World Trade Center and ending with the Arab Spring and the start of the US withdrawal from Iraq and Afghanistan—is portrayed as an exceptional time of unprecedented repressive emergency declarations, illegal wars, and extralegal acts of detention and repression. In this context, I explore the "9/11 decade" and some of its most notorious terrorist agents and incidents, but underline continuities and complexities, rather than sudden breaks and logics of exceptions. Here I move the lens of analysis away from Guantanamo detentions and US neoconservatism to the streets of Cairo's working-class quarters. This is not a hackneyed attempt to "take the pulse of the Arab Street" or to reveal that "Muslims are practical, peace-loving people, too." Instead, I reintegrate the events of the 9/11 decade with the struggles over development and security governance of the 1990s, as well as with the era of global uprisings, Salafi mobilizations, and militarized human-security enforcements that "suddenly" took center stage after the Arab Spring events and subsequent elections of 2011.[2]

Starting in the 1990s, in the core of Egypt's capital city, a thriving, densely populated (now mostly working-class) community known as Islamic Cairo or Fatimid Cairo became the nexus of new projects of heritage restoration, cultural moralization, and population management. Urban planners and historians refer to the area as Islamic Cairo or Fatimid Cairo because of its remarkable concentration of intact Islamic architecture dating back to between the tenth century and the nineteenth. Islamic Cairo also hosts the seat of Sunni Islamic learning and jurisprudence, al-Azhar University and the Grand Mosque, as well as several major sites for devotion and pilgrimage valued by Sufi orders, Shi'a visitors, Isma'ili pilgrims, and cultural tourists of all denominations. Its own residents, and the maps of the municipality, refer to these districts as al-Darb al-Ahmar, Husayniyya, and Suq al-Silah. This historic quarter once served as a walled administrative, commercial, political, and religious center, first as the seat of the Fatimid Empire (969–1171 AD). Later it was ruled by Salah al-Din (Saladin) and the Ayyubids (1171–1250 AD), and then the Mamluks (1250–1571 AD). The area also served as the seat of the modernizing rule of Mehmet Ali Pasha (Muhammad 'Ali) (1805–49 AD). At the end of the nineteenth century, Khedive Ismail moved the center of the city to the west, to the newly constructed Belle Epoque–era districts along the banks of the Nile (Abu-Lughod 1971, 98–105). Thus abandoned by government ministries and by its wealthier residents, Islamic Cairo came to be occupied by popular classes and their workshops; but the neighborhoods certainly did not lose their vitality. By the 1990s, Islamic Cairo had reemerged as a center of thriving, informal-sector manufacturing and subcontracting activities, all while remaining a treasure-trove of medieval Islamic architecture. Islamic Cairo became an arena of class conflict over globalization, a battlefield for wars over human patrimony and religious culture, and a test site for new globalizing security agendas attached to cultural authenticity and monumental heritage.

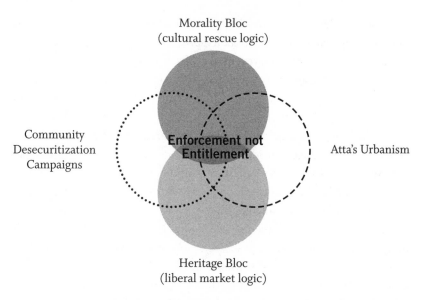

Morality Bloc
(cultural rescue logic)

Community
Desecuritization
Campaigns

Enforcement not
Entitlement

Atta's Urbanism

Heritage Bloc
(liberal market logic)

FIGURE 3.1. Rescuing Islamic Cairo: contentious logics of humanized securitization. Contradictions within the state, between logics of moral security and heritage marketing, open a rift, occupied both by Atta's radical plans for gender and cultural security and by less essentialist "desecuritizing" community mobilizations.

Rescuing "Humanity" from People?

Initial security-and-development paradigms fashioned around Islamic Cairo aimed to produce economic rent for the state and profits for well-connected tourism-sector investors. During the ten-year period I analyze here, roughly from 1995–2005, cultural-security and heritage-development projects aimed to construct the material infrastructure for new forms of gendered national culture, class hierarchy, and sexual morality, and to embed these identities and patterns in the fabric of city space being transformed by globalization. The implementation of these plans exacerbated the contradiction between two sets of actors that I term the *heritage bloc* and the *morality bloc*, each driven by its own logic of securitization (fig. 3.1). The heritage bloc brought together actors including the Ministry of Culture, the Cairo governor, UN agencies such as UNDP and UNESCO, US aid institutions, powerful regional contracting businesses, and export-oriented national-business interests to champion tourism as a central development objective and national (cultural) security aim. This heritage bloc tended to identify "humanity" with the built forms of monuments and historic architecture, and with those consumers and visitors who would appreciate and not degrade them. It argued that to protect the patrimony of humanity, preserve cultural value in the market, and generate economic revenue, locals needed to be cleared from the vicinity. This set of agents pursued two kinds of protection: the safeguarding of monuments from the pollution brought by the working classes and their dirty and noisy workshops, and the rescuing of consumer-class Egyptians and foreign tourists from purported harassment by thuggish residents. As this heritage bloc identified working-class community members with trash, environmental degradation, and pollution, it justified the deployment of a kind of emergency regime that revoked housing rights and shuttered local production collectives.

By contrast, the morality bloc was a populist grouping identified with religious authorities and other movements committed to overseeing doctrinal orthodoxy and social orthopraxy. This bloc of actors consisted of al-Azhar Mosque and University (the center of Sunni Islamic jurisprudence, moral guidance, and cultural censorship), populist political groupings that focused on morality politics rather than social-justice issues, and nationalistic intellectuals and journalists. Just as the heritage bloc tended to abstract the notion of "humanity," identifying it with the built forms of the old city, the morality bloc tended to abstract the notion of "the people," projecting it into an ideal image of the proper Islamic family under pious tutelage. Meanwhile, both blocs demonized the actually existing people of Islamic Cairo as an embarrassing assemblage of degradations and perversions. Nevertheless, the morality bloc appeared, at first glance, to be more empowering of community actors than the monument restorers were. These religious authorities and nationalist intellectuals claimed to stand with "the people" against the moral threat and cultural pollution of "the market" as borne by globalization and touristic commodification. The moral populists were preoccupied with rescuing authentic local culture by eliminating spaces of contact between locals and internationals, men and women, and orthodox religion and syncretistic vernacular spirituality. These separations ended up consistently reconfiguring local populations as impure, degraded, and incapable of self-government. This morality coalition targeted local residents with forms of humanized securitization that aimed to control and manage the community's economic diversity, its gender and class ordering, and its cultural expressions. Though their aims were different, there was a degree of overlap between the heritage and morality logics. Both coalitions designated heritage buildings and cultural values, rather than resident populations, as the privileged "human" objects of security intervention. But these two logics diverged sharply around the role of the market, the urban presence of modernist or "Western" built forms, and the circulation of gender, class, and nationality within these spaces.

In the 1990s, those interested in marketing Islamic Cairo's human heritage and urban patrimony spoke as rather orthodox neoliberals, insisting that "tourism is the locomotive of growth . . . with superior multiplier effects" (Sakr 1999). According to the Egyptian government's own statistics, the country had one of the highest levels of dependence on tourism of any in the world (Kamel 1997). In the 1990s, tourism contributed 11 percent of Egypt's GDP and provided at least 14.5 percent of all employment. In Islamic Cairo, where tourist-attracting monuments are concentrated, the dependency of the local labor force on tourism was even greater. To promote the development of tourism in Islamic Cairo, the Egyptian government endorsed a plan by the United Nations Development Programme (United Nations Development Programme 1997) that presented pre-restoration Islamic Cairo's mixed-use character as a space of social conflicts, confusing hybrids, and high risks. Its maps portrayed Islamic Cairo as a confounded *space* that had to be captured, purified, and controlled as a *time*. With this discourse, the actors clustered in the heritage bloc articulated an agenda that focused on the homogenization and localization of space based on theme coherence. They would rescue and restore a particular interpretation of medieval architecture, while Egypt's cultural contemporaneity and social complexity would be cleansed from view. The goal was to define historical authenticity through visual contemplation, not social interaction.

This practice of consuming Cairo as a visual tableau or living museum of the most alluring and exotic of Eastern customs dates back at least to the 1830s and 1840s, when the British artist, translator, and orientalist Edward William Lane produced immensely popular representations of the landscape of Islamic Cairo as he gathered paintings of architecture, composed voluminous descriptions of manners and customs, and retranslated the "Arabian Nights Entertainments" (a.k.a. *The Thousand and One Nights*) for a broad European public (Gregory 2005, 69–73). Rather than draw on oral traditional versions of the Arabian Nights, or on the hybrid original Persian, Indian, and Arab-language sources, Lane selected from a version composed in Egypt that situated the "1001" tales exclusively in Cairo.

Furthermore, Lane substituted his own voice as authoritative ethnographer and tour guide in place of the figure of Scheherazade, the Persian woman storyteller who in the original tales wove narratives each night to spare herself from execution. As analyzed by the geographer Derek Gregory, this particular staging or "narrativization" of Cairo proved fundamental not just to shaping the spatial practices of the global tourism industry, arguably founded with Thomas Cooke's tours in Egypt and North Africa during this era, but also to the popularization of orientalism. Any visitor could accrue the cultural power of orientalism and experience its potency and pleasure by learning how to consume exotic landscapes by visually identifying built forms, customs, and cultural types that the visitor had already encountered in an authoritative text such as Lane's (rather than enjoying one's journey as, for example, an open-ended social engagement with actual residents). "Islamic Cairo," seen as the narrativized inscription or living theater of the Arabian Nights, became, perhaps, the first and has remained one of the most vivid of the staging sites of this intersection of tourism and orientalism. In the early twentieth century, many of these same ethnologized narratives of Cairo were rearticulated in the context of urban sociology's theory of the Islamic City. This theory interpolated the reality of Islam mainly as an urban-spatial phenomenon, comprehensible not through an analysis of social structures or a semiotic analysis of cultural discourses, but as a mapping of the placement of mosques and shrines and a typification of popular practices arrayed around them (Janet Abu-Lughod 1987, 156–58). In these ways, both transnational tourism and social science intersected around investments in what Nezar AlSayyad, Irene Bierman, and Nasser Rabbat call the "medievalization of Cairo" (2005, 2–3).

This narrativization of medievalized Cairo animated the (re)launch in 1995 of projects to restore Islamic Cairo as an exhibition of authentic, "original" heritage and to enable its successful reintegration into the world tourism system. Egyptian consultants for UNDP insisted, "The architecture of the zone should echo its original urban character and its original cultural identity. . . . Public spaces should be redesigned, equipped, and managed not in function of their use, but in function of their national traditional character" (Abou al-Futuh 1998, 49). This overall project of staging or thematization aimed to transform the most densely populated working-class manufacturing and residential community in Egypt into an open-air museum, a model of the country's tourism-centered security-and-development model. At the center of this cluster of heritage-project

advocates stood President Mubarak and the military-bureaucratic apparatus of the state (fig. 3.2). After Mubarak's regime had cut social welfare,
shuttered subsidized cooperatives, and ended public-education projects
in working-class neighborhoods during the late 1980s and early 1990s,
the Fatimid Cairo heritage plan rose "to the top of the President's list of
priorities" (alHussein 1998).

At the center of the heritage bloc, Mubarak's minister of culture, Farouk
Hosni, worked to coordinate planners, public-private contracting firms,
and international agencies with the goal of increasing Islamic Cairo's prestige, exclusivity, and rent-generating capacity. His role was to portion up
the space, drawing lines between those urban zones to be managed by
the technical experts of international organizations (UNESCO and UNDP),
while other areas would be controlled by transnational private-sector developers (hotel chains and charter companies), and still others would be
run by foundations like Agha Khan, Ford, and globally linked national
businesses (restoration specialists, infrastructure contractors, and Egyptian Armed Forces–controlled building companies). Another key actor,
the Cairo governor—a military general appointed by President Mubarak
via the minister of the interior—was granted exceptional policing and
eviction powers as the executive coordinator and overseer of all planning
and development projects in his region. As detailed in the 1994 Law of
Local Administration, the governor was responsible for two kinds of security: food and physical structures. "Food security" is concerned with assuring the distribution of basic staples to residents of the governorate in
order to limit or prevent bread riots and student protests. Likewise, "spatial security," the protection of housing, offices, infrastructure, and development projects—and the eviction of those who stand in the way—is also
linked to controlling opposition to economic development (Daniszewski
1998) (fig. 3.3).

Contrary to what one may expect, the Cairo governor's duties were
not to police terrorism, drug trafficking, street crime, or vice. Instead,
his job was described primarily as protecting buildings and clearing protesters and squatters from public spaces. By securing Islamic Cairo for
tourism development, Governor Abdel Rahim Shehata emphasized, "We
think we have a treasure in Cairo. We think that treasure can generate
income. . . . We have to search for that treasure as soon as possible" (Daniszewski 1998). In the zone of Islamic Cairo, the governor assumed the
power to unilaterally abrogate the rental contracts of area residents and
small-scale manufacturers ('Aqaari 1998; Seif Al-Nasr 1998). He also dis-

القاهرة الإسلامية

على قائمة اهتمامات
الرئيس

FIGURE 3.2. President Mubarak puts the rescue of Islamic Cairo "at the top of his priorities" (April 1997). Source: *Metr Murabba' Magazine*, Cairo, 1997.

FIGURE 3.3. Metal workshop, targeted for removal from Islamic Cairo (May 1997).
Photo credit: Paul Amar.

banded state-organized production collectives, rent-control protections, and local representative councils, thus liquidating the last vestiges of what Diane Singerman calls Egypt's "social contract state" (1995, 244–45).

The heritage bloc of state security entrepreneurs also included the General Organization for Physical Planning for Greater Cairo (GOPP). The GOPP's technical discourse tended to describe residents and laborers in the manufacturing sector as monstrous hybrids of pollution, noisy traffic, and dirty workshops. Meanwhile, old buildings were the real citizens, anthropomorphized as the "heritage of humanity" that required extraordinary rescue-and-protect interventions. GOPP reports technically rendered locals and their labor-intensive industrial productions as blights that threatened the value of heritage for tourist consumption: "This zone is subjected to social, environmental, traffic, and pollution problems; it lacks services, and its buildings are unhealthy for the most part. Its patrimony deserves preservation. . . . These projects aim to highlight the value of the urban environment; . . . preserve heritage and raise the value of historic buildings; and relocate noisy and polluting industries toward desert zones" (Edward 1998, 41). Thus, heritage redevelopment favored the needs of international tourists while marginalizing the interests of resident shopkeepers and labor. The polluting businesses that were removed included lemon, onion, and garlic markets, along with aluminum, plastic, and furniture workshops—the key flavors and materials of affordable, sustainable daily life.[3] When Governor Shehata abruptly canceled most stores' long-term leases in 1998, shop owners found themselves categorized as squatters. Along with the stock of informal housing, and housing that had been reclassified overnight as illicit and informal, the workshops were targeted for forced clearance or relocation to distant locations, inaccessible to consumers and suppliers.

In the United Nations Development Program's 1997 report, Egyptian development consultants elaborated an inverted modernization theory wherein commercial development and tall office towers were identified as evidence of urban decline. The consultants proposed the area be redeveloped in order to "restore" its fundamental cultural identity (Abou al-Futuh 1998). They described the modern industrial-manufacturing activities of contemporary Cairenes as threats to cultural security and sustainable development because they supposedly did not respect the valuable architecture that constituted the fundamental fabric of this ecosystem. As a prominent redevelopment specialist stated, "The great majority of shopkeepers in the area of historic Cairo do not have sufficient environmental consciousness. . . . The continuous drop in living standards and income for the past fifty years has had negative effects on the neighboring environment. . . . These people do not have the resources to protect the area's environment, much less to be attractive for tourists coming to the area" ('Ali 1998).

According to the plans of the governor and international agencies, resident activities and workshops that did not directly interfere with monuments or tourist pedestrian corridors were to be nocturnalized. That is to say, vehicle traffic was blocked from the main historic concourses of the area, except between 10 PM and 6 AM. During the day, boys, not vehicles, would carry deliveries, machinery, and supplies through the quarter. Apparently, the view of children carrying heavy loads on their backs was considered an appropriate part of the new medieval-heritage landscape, but mini-pickup trucks were not.

Two maps produced by UNDP in cooperation with the Government of Egypt and UNESCO consultants revealed the geography of cultural rescue and the binary segregation of culture from economy. In the first map (map 3.1) we see the diverse landscape of social and economic production in Islamic Cairo as it appeared in the late 1990s, where spheres of

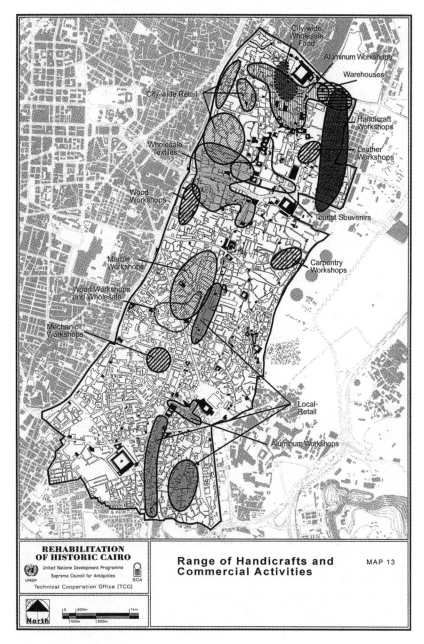

MAP 3.1. The dense landscape of multiple social, cultural, and economic uses in Islamic Cairo, before the launch of heritage projects. Source: United Nations Development Programme, et al., 1997.

manufacturing, crafts, subcontracting, and mechanics, as well as historical, religious, and community institutions overlapped and interacted in a vital, productive, complex social geometry. The second map (map 3.2) depicts the projected future for Islamic Cairo. A gray corridor carves culture from economy, evacuating modern industries and working-class populations in order to create an open-air museum for monument tourism. By 2005, about 50 percent of this plan had been successfully completed on the ground. Before, there had been a diverse, productive, efficient space of popular activities. After, there would be museums, security corridors, and isolated working-class community enclaves.

THE MORALITY BLOC

At the heart of Islamic Cairo, one monument of Fatimid architecture stood firm against the plans of those in the heritage domain. Al-Azhar University, the preeminent world center for Sunni Muslim scholarship and jurisprudence, had served as the rallying point for allied movements that engaged the contradictions of the powerful project of the heritage protection advocates. Al-Azhar University's allies included the Ministry of Al-Awqaf (Islamic charitable endowments, which traditionally maintain mosques and Islamic monuments), pious Muslim investors primarily from Saudi Arabia and South Asia, as well as other notable pilgrims and donors. This bloc stood against touristification of Islamic Cairo and remained suspicious of Western investment, which it perceived as a cultural, social, and moral threat. Although purist and moralist in character, religious critiques mobilized by al-Azhar did not stem from Salafi mobilizations. In fact, al-Azhar religious scholars are mostly products of Sufi orders that stand staunchly opposed to the Salafi movement and to Saudi-originating Wahhabi jurisprudence and preaching. Nevertheless, al-Azhar's increasing identification with the politics of morality and censorship did reflect attempts to beat the increasingly popular Salafiya at their own game (figs. 3.4 and 3.5).

By the 1990s, the state had confirmed al-Azhar as the moral and cultural guardian of the Egyptian people (and much of the broader Sunni Muslim population). In this role, it acted as official censor of Egyptian culture (films, literature, television serials, websites); delineated personal, gender, sexual, and family jurisprudence; and controlled curriculum in schools and universities. Tamir Moustafa (2000) argues that in the 1990s, al-Azhar increased its role in governance because of, rather than in spite of, Mubarak's struggle against Islamic and particularly Salafi radicalism.

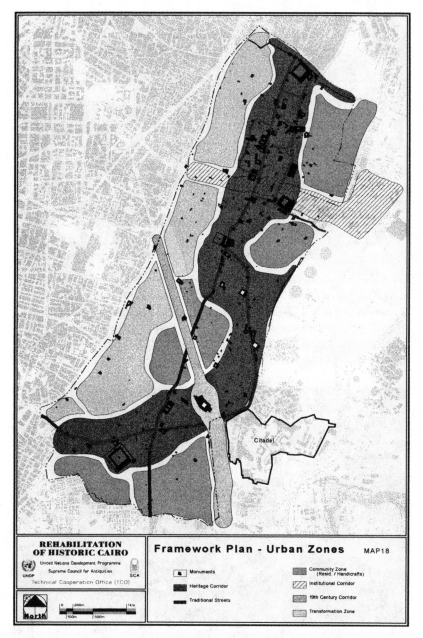

REHABILITATION OF HISTORIC CAIRO

United Nations Development Programme
Supreme Council for Antiquities
UNDP   SCA
Technical Cooperation Office (TCO)

North   0 100m 200m 500m   1km

Framework Plan - Urban Zones   MAP18

Monuments   Community Zone
                             (Resid. / Handicrafts)
Heritage Corridor   Institutional Corridor
Traditional Streets   19th Century Corridor
                             Transformation Zone

Citadel

MAP 3.2. Projected segregation of uses and populations around the "heritage corridor" (in dark gray) after project implementation. The economic and social uses of space are no longer indicated. Source: United Nations Development Programme, et al., 1997.

FIGURE 3.4. The demonstration "Millionein Hussein" (Two Million March). Sufi guild members mass in the historic square between al-Azhar's Grand Mosque and the Mosque of Imam Hussein in Cairo to protest the rise of Salafi militancy that specifically targeted Sufi shrines and practices. This moment marked the political awakening of normally apolitical Sufi organizations (29 March 2011). Photo credit: Al Masry Al Youm (http://www.almasry-alyoum.com).

FIGURE 3.5. The Grand Mufti of Egypt, Ali Gomaa (a prominent Sufi Sheikh), speaks against anti-Christian sectarianism and Salafist intolerance at the first World (Political) Conference of Sufism, held at al-Azhar in Cairo (25 September 2011). Photo credit: Al Masry Al Youm (http://www.almasry-alyoum.com).

Mubarak's government became increasingly dependent on al-Azhar for cultural and religious legitimization in the face of the rising popularity and influence not of "terrorist" groups but of preachers, anticorruption crusaders, and charity benefactors. Salafi groups had established increasing moral and civic authority at the grassroots level, buoyed by remittances from workers in the Gulf as well as by direct aid from pious Saudi royals (Jonathan Brown 2011, 4). Seeking to be more pious than the Salafi Islamists by deploying classphobic and gender-segregating forms of moralism, the coalition of political elites around al-Azhar came to perform many crucial state functions in the realm of public culture and the law, while maintaining the university's authenticity as a seemingly extrapolitical legitimizing force, a symbolically autonomous institution, even though it was embedded in Mubarak's apparatus of repression.

In the late 1990s, the morality bloc escalated its cultural and moral-security-centered campaign against its rival, the heritage bloc, and its global-tourism-oriented preservation program. This began with a cycle of debates about the restoration of the al-Azhar Grand Mosque, itself. In 1998, heritage restorers closed off the mosque and carried out preservation activities without inviting participation from the resident religious scholars. Furthermore, shoddy work aiming to clean the Grand Mosque's carved gateway (constructed in 973 AD) apparently scraped off many of the original Quranic inscriptions. Al-Azhar University saw the monument's restoration by international agencies for the benefit of foreign tourists as a form of theft. From this perspective, tourism marketing was not the savior of sacred heritage, but an apostasy of globalization. The journal al-Wafd railed against the plan: "The Americanization of Islamic Antiquities! A Suspicious American Project to Convert Islamic Monuments into Restaurants and Nightclubs! . . . The essence of the project is to convert Islamic monuments into modern distortions in the context of a new world order of 'globalization' that we can see materializing. USAID has selected to renovate and modify for reuse five monuments . . . with the aim of penetrating the inside of Egyptian society and wiping out its Islamic character, even its architectural heritage" (Mataawi 1998).

The morality bloc saw the strategy of repurposing religious buildings and monuments to generate revenue as an "Americanization" model, synonymous with alienating, violent, and ungodly forms of globalization. Muhammad al-Kahlawi, professor of Islamic architecture, asked, "Why does it always have to be *Islamic* monuments that get turned into restaurants, hotels, pizza joints, and ice-cream stands? Why do the Americans need to turn them into investment projects? Why does this happen only to Islamic monuments and not pharaonic or Coptic [Christian] monuments?" (Mataawi 1998). Gendered and sexualized metaphors of penetration, perversion, and prostitution were consistent themes in this discourse targeting Americanization and globalization. These discourses evoked the Egyptian nation as a woman's body whose rape was both the essence of violence and the justification for masculinist vendettas of counterviolence against the United States and those Middle East authorities associated with it. In October 1998, al-Musafir Khana, a medieval mansion in Islamic Cairo, caught fire during reconstruction work and was burned beyond rescue. Outraged critics declared, "Our Islamic heritage is the victim of the carelessness of the experts" (Yaseen 1998). Leveraging the crisis produced by the blaze and by the damages to al-Azhar and the critique of "perverse American-style" projects at Saladin's Citadel, the populists mobilized (Amar 1998c).

These groups, in alliance with donors and pilgrimage organizations from the Persian Gulf, encouraged police suppression of popular spiritual festivals, particularly Sufi mawlids (mawālid), Islamic popular festivals that celebrate the birthdays of members of the Prophet's family and other local historic Islamic spiritual leaders or quasi-saints. Sufi spirituality is not the kind of religiosity favored by Gulf donors or their allies in the morality bloc, so mawlids became increasingly policed and demonized as irreligious sensuality or misrepresented as Shi'i (Shiite) aberration. This trend reflected a return of the reformist discourses that characterized the early twentieth century in Egypt, when mawlids were marked as sites of sexual licentiousness, accused of being staged only for either foreign tourists or vulgar peasants, and thus representing false or prostituted superstitions (de Jong 1999, 312–13). In the early twentieth century, preaching and writings by Wahhabi or Salafi scholars that targeted Sufism, such as those of al-Azhar shaykh Mahmud Khattab al-Subki in 1913, faced strong push-back from the majority of al-Azhar scholars (de Jong 1999, 315). Later, in 1953, the leader of the Muslim Brothers, Hasan Ismail al-Hudaybi, proposed the total prohibition of Sufi orders; but the then revolutionary Military Council and the Arab Socialist Union (the governing party in the 1960s) moved against the Brothers and began to protect the Sufi orders and cultivate their collective life as a counterweight to the Islamists (de Jong 1999, 319–20).

By the late 1990s, four decades of state appropriation and corporatist administration of Sufi orders had weakened their independence, vitality, and legitimacy as sites of popular mobilization. The Salafi critique of Sufism returned with a vengeance. One victim of this resurgent critique was the mosque and faith community around Fatima al-Nabawiyya in al-Batniyya in Islamic Cairo. This popular shrine anchored a vital mawlid festival that was particularly important to working-class and peasant women from across Egypt who came to participate in *zikr*.[4] In 1999, the mosque was razed (Fayza Hassan 1999) and replaced by a towering, wholly new "faux-Mamluk" mosque. This mosque, funded by Saudi investors as an act of piety, was purged of local social use and expunged of any marks of Sufi or vernacular spirituality. Similarly, in 1999, the Sufi *zawiya* of Abdel Rahman was also closed. It was soon reopened as a museum, deconsecrated as a shrine for popular religiosity.[5] Also in 1999, women's spiritualist dance and music gatherings, called *zars*, became increasingly policed, again because popular spirituality was seen as an aberration to the program of the morality bloc. The optic of the morality bloc identified the people of the quarter as victims who must be secured and rescued from moral and cultural contamination by vulgar, "perverse," popular religiosity, seen as intersecting with the "prostituting" impact of globalization (figs. 3.6, 3.7, and 3.8).

Alternative Assertions

In the breach that opened up between the heritage bloc and the morality bloc, between the market- and tourism-centered project and the moral-purification campaign, two radically distinct alternatives materialized. First, working-class community groups within the popular quarters of Islamic Cairo mobilized a set of nonviolent campaigns to push for a more inclusive and participatory security-and-development process. Second, an alternative urban-management plan offered a vision that would design a set of technical interventions and designate an elite group of morally and professionally qualified families that would reconcile the global profit-making potential of the heritage-rescue plans with the morality bloc's desire to restore the purity of local working-class cultures and their "natural" norms of gender and family. This latter plan was the vision that 9/11 hijacker Muhammad Atta articulated in his urban-planning master's thesis of 1999.

To elaborate on these alternatives, I draw on my ethnographic fieldwork and interviews (the first round were conducted in 1997–98, with follow-up interviews conducted in 2004 and 2008). Before this period, I

FIGURE 3.6. Sheikhat Anhar, leader of Zar spiritualist gatherings in al-Darb al-Ahmar (Islamic Cairo), was attacked by Salafis and charged by Vice Police with witchcraft in 1997. Photo credit: Paul Amar.

FIGURE 3.7. Women chanting zikr at the mawlid of Fatima al-Nabawiyya (1992).
Photo credit: Paul Amar.

FIGURE 3.8. A miniature drag king: gender-bending during the mawlid of Fatima al-Nabawiyya, in adDarb alAhmar (1992). Photo credit: Paul Amar.

had established my networks while living for two years (1990–92) among vendors and working-class organizers in al-Batniyya, at the center of the most densely populated quarter of this district of Islamic Cairo, before the area was struck by the major 1992 earthquake, and then transformed by monument-restoration projects that commenced in 1995. I also offer a first look at the master's thesis of Muhammad El-Amir Atta, which was recovered thanks to the helpful cooperation of his former academic advisor, Professor Dittmar Machule at Germany's Technical University of Hamburg. Interview-based findings from social movements and solidarity committees in Islamic Cairo help to highlight the specificities of Atta's urbanism and underline the contrast between his plans and contrasting ones generated by working-class communities in the affected areas. These groups rejected the paternalism, moralism, and violence of militant agendas; they articulated grassroots, non-nationalist alternatives to the "humanism" of the heritage bloc and to the cultural-political narrowness of the "populism" of the morality bloc.

Both of these alternatives—the community coalition's and Atta's—were mobilized in the context of heightened state interventions and insurgent attacks that shook Egypt during the mid-1990s. In October 1995, General Security forces came to remove a squatter settlement located at the historic northern gate to the medieval city walls of Cairo.[6] On the designated day, families of workers and street vendors awoke to an invasion they had long dreaded. The job of the uniformed force was to clean up the medieval fortifications of the old city, removing Cairene communities that had gradually, over the centuries, built settlements along the walls. At the northern edge of Islamic Cairo, Saladin had built fortified curtains of stone to protect against Crusaders. But by the 1990s, the old walls had become a front in a distinctly modern battle: to open the city to Western tourism and remove the blight inflicted on Cairo by its own popular classes. Bulldozers approached the wall to execute plans drawn up by a broad urban redevelopment alliance of police and planners; state ministries for security, tourism, and culture; the municipal authorities for infrastructure and environment; and international development agencies including UNESCO, UNDP, USAID, and teams from France, Italy, and Germany. As the bulldozers razed cement-block and shack houses, residents hastily rounded up personal possessions and the police hustled the community off the site. The demolition action came as no surprise to these residents who had struggled for months to save their homes.

Present that day were several local and international urban-planning

FIGURE 3.9. Muhammad Atta, with his sister, before leaving Egypt for Germany in 1998. Photo credit: Norbert Schiller / Getty Images.

officials who were monitoring the scene and supervising the development of the wall and its heritage zone. Among them was one Egyptian engineer who was studying the restoration of the old city wall as part of his urban-planning training for a German university. The young man was pursuing a degree in urban redevelopment and heritage preservation in Hamburg, Germany. He was passionate about rescuing the ancient monuments, but furious about the refusal of international agencies to give him a job or award him a contract to work on the project. His German colleagues report that around the time of the squatter clearance, his level of frustration and disgust rose sharply, and he returned to Hamburg with a new, intense level of motivation. This man was Muhammad Atta (fig. 3.9). As the *New York Times* reported: "The project, [Atta] came to believe, involved little more than knocking down a poor neighborhood to improve the view for tourists. 'It really made him angry,' recalled Ralph Bodenstein, one of two German students in the program. 'He said it was a completely absurd way to develop the city, to make a Disneyworld out of it.'"[7]

Two years later, by the fall of 1997, residents of the old quarter of Islamic Cairo were still dealing with the threat of slum clearance and shop evictions by police and planning authorities. The effects of redevelopment interventions, housing evictions, and police harassment were compounded by a crisis that struck on 17 November 1997, when the al-Jamaʿa al-Islamiyya (the militant "Islamic Grouping") murdered fifty-eight visitors who were exploring the tomb of the woman pharaoh Hatshepsut in the Theban Necropolis across from Luxor in the south of Egypt. The attack was slow and gory. The al-Jamaʿa al-Islamiyya militants raped and disemboweled the European women among the group of tourists and shot the men in symbolic retaliation for foreign penetration and the emasculation of Islam. Three hours passed before Egyptian State Security officers finally arrived to drag out a few survivors from among the corpses.[8]

In the wake of the attack, President Mubarak demanded the West take action to enhance bilateral security cooperation and to sever financial flows to militant groups. He insisted, "If the world community had cooperated in combating terrorism, this would not have happened. . . . The terrorists who make the plans and provide the financing live in Europe and Afghanistan" (Khalil 1997). Many in Egypt responded with horror at the scale and spectacle of the Luxor Massacre. "Everyone feels like death. It's a grim life for us," said one Egyptian proprietor of a touristic shop (Khalil 1997). Jobs vanished as the country's largest employer, the tourism industry, collapsed overnight. Before the attack, tourism flows had approached a record 4.5 million visits for 1997, bringing in billions of dollars and offering far more jobs and opportunities than any other sector of private, public, or micro enterprise (Awad 1998, 5). After the attack, tourism sector receipts dropped to near zero for several months.

It seemed that as the tourism economy evaporated, so did the impetus for respecting human rights. State security forces set new restrictions on student groups and religious organizations, and intensified surveillance and counterterrorism efforts. President Mubarak launched a massive overhaul of the security apparatus and brought in US policing and security advisors to train rapid-strike forces.[9] The opposition press protested what it saw as the president's opportunism, suggesting he leveraged the attack to justify placing foreign advisors within the national security apparatus. The liberal daily al-Ahrar reported: "Security Specialists Are Foreign Made" and "Intellectuals Prefer 'Importation' of Experts from Abroad." A dissenting police general insisted, "This is an invitation to return to colonialism once again."[10]

Community "Desecuritization" Movement

In this context, shopkeepers and community associations in Islamic Cairo mobilized after the 1997 Luxor Massacre to develop a grassroots movement that explicitly rejected violence, of both the state and antistate varieties. The residents of the quarter cobbled together a movement, based in al-Darb al-Ahmar, the workshop hub of Islamic Cairo, whose Arabic title translates as the Darb al-Ahmar Committee for National Consciousness, or CNC. Interestingly, they gave their movement a different name in English, the True Egyptian People.[11]

Its organizing committee was composed of individuals whom state police had previously profiled and frequently arrested as dissidents. The movement grouped together prominent local members of the Muslim Brotherhood, disgruntled secular Nasserist socialists, traditional tent-maker craftsmen, computer-programming specialists from tourism companies, informal-sector tourism guides, and women that ran Islamic social-welfare charities and community savings associations in the quarter. The goals of the CNC were twofold. First, they aimed to convince and reassure the state and the international community that Islamic Cairo was not a perpetrator of terrorism, but was a collective victim of state violence and an agent of transnational solidarity (fig. 3.10). The community-based CNC also articulated empathy and delineated spaces of affinity with the foreign targets of violence themselves. The committee identified against both the market fundamentalism of the heritage-protection advocates and the moral purism of the populists. In particular, they worked to advocate a collective basis for Egyptian patriotic identity that stood firmly against police clearance and evictions in Islamic Cairo, but which nevertheless wholly favored tourism and cooperation with internationals when possible (fig. 3.11). In this way, the movements interrogated the "images of self and other that animate (in)secure identities" (Anthony Burke 2007) and resisted "the dangers of securitizing identity" (Stern 2006, 188).

The CNC activities were not supported by state funds, and were only mentioned briefly in the state-controlled newspaper. But the CNC did manage to evoke a kind of "vernacular cosmopolitan" (Singerman and Amar 2006, 30–33) public sphere by disseminating poetic flyers to local residents and raising banners in English and German in the most touristed areas of Islamic Cairo that read "What happened in Luxor doesn't belong to us. We are totally different"; "All true Egyptians refuse that murder action in Luxor"; "It's not our wrong as kind people"; and "You are among us, True Egyptian People."[12] The collective struggled to meet with and

FIGURE 3.10. "In Egypt you will never be a stranger." Al-Darb al-Ahmar Committee for National Consciousness banner (1997). Photo credit: Paul Amar.

FIGURE 3.11. "What happened in Luxor doesn't belong to Egypt." Al-Darb al-Ahmar Committee for National Consciousness banner (1997). Photo credit: Paul Amar.

reassure the few tourists that trickled through the area. They also established alliances among foreign monument-restoration workers and tourists who would spread news of their efforts abroad.

Interviews I conducted in 1998, during the height of evictions, reveal that community workers and shop owners in the targeted petty-manufacturing, textile, and vending sectors did not perceive a conflict between their modern activities and cultural-heritage tourism. They tended to see the overlap and interpenetration of economy and culture, of modern and medieval heritage, as essential to survival and development, rather than as risks or as polluting the city's identity or environment. As Husni al-Khawanki, a copper-goods manufacturer in the area, stated, "If we leave this area, our work will stop. Since the time of our grandparents, my work and my product has been wholly connected with tourism, but also to the centrality of the area and the proximity of a variety of work-shops. All the raw materials and assembly parts are available in the area; all sales are made in the area. So how could we move elsewhere?"[13] Magdi Hasan, a metal worker in the area, insisted, "The only possible problem I make is perhaps the noise of my hammering as I shape the handcrafted copper and brass. And the tourists like to watch us as we work our craft. We complement the area and it complements us. We, deprived of the services in the area, are like fish out of water. And the area without us has no life or ambience. This is a diverse area. This zone is famous to us locals, not because of the monuments, but because it is a complete and convenient market. Our customers know they can find everything they need here."[14] The Cairo University architecture professor Abdelhalim Ibrahim Abdelhalim argued, "The medieval city is not medieval. It's a living, vital city, more vital than many other sectors in Cairo. The local community is not squatting or transient. It claims a connection to the process of making and maintaining that city. We're faced with a part of the city that is physically and organizationally valid. At the same time, it is underestimated and under-served" (originally cited in Seymour 1998, 14). Reflecting the high security profile of this heritage project, the Egyptian government banned the sale of the issue of the *Cairo Times* that included the interview with Abdelhalim, conducted by Jenny Seymour.

As the eviction of these workshops at this time demonstrated, the economic-development model of the state saw local manufacturers and labor-intensive craft shops as a drag to growth, not as its engine. The export orientation of the heritage bloc's emphasis on tourism and service-sector growth aligned it with the interests of big national contractors, international agencies, and state policing executives. And this bloc of interests and actors created, in 1998, a new technical authority: the Fatimid Cairo Mechanism for Development, also known as the Fatimid Authority. In one of its first acts, this authority disbanded the local elected municipal councils in the "Fatimid" area. These councils had enjoyed the power to channel community interests and voices, hear local claims, and produce city-scale laws (i.e., regulations and policies). The Fatimid Authority, a parastatal "public-private partnership" body, also shut down local syndicates and commercial collectives and abrogated rent-control agreements in its fiat. President Mubarak nominally chaired the authority, which was situated not in the municipal council or the legislative branch, but within the executive branch in the Ministry of Culture. And the Cairo governor was entrusted with the enforcement, social control, and eviction functions for the Authority.[15] This extraordinary form, blending police-state authority, technocratic urban planning, and museumized cultural governance aimed to create a more rational form of governance for all Egypt and a less violent image of religiosity in the country. In 1998, Culture Minister Farouq Hosni insisted, "This is a national project, the key to our entry into the third millennium. . . . We want in the year 2000 to give the world a new language for talking about Egypt's religious heritage, that we possess the most beautiful place that brings together all religions" (Abu al-Fatah 1998).

Atta's Urbanism

Muhammad Atta's urban-reform plans did not align with the antimarket agenda of the morality bloc, since he did favor the presence of profit-generating tourism businesses in the area. However, his concern for gender "renaturalization," repression of public sexuality, and class segregation did indeed match the attitudes of the more extreme Salafi populists. In addition, Atta did not express sympathy with popular movements or democratic struggles like those of the al-Darb al-Ahmar Committee for National Consciousness. Instead, Atta's writings generate a particular alternative for managing interventions around cultural security, gendered space, and social hierarchy. He articulates a blended technoprofessional and moralistic logic for properly governing globalizing "Islamic" cities. Atta's agenda overlaps with the heritage bloc's securitization logic in that it favors the development of businesses and even tourism in the area, but sees these as strictly cordoned off and secured in controlled, masculine spaces, safely away from those zones identified with piety, femininity, and values. His concern for culture and morality also resonates strongly with the morality bloc's logic of securitization. But Atta's thesis sees the state as a privatized entity, with power delegated not to the business sector but to a moral oligarchy of religiously pure families, a kind of cultural emergency committee that would supervise and privilege the cultivation of a particular kind of "humanity" (that is, the proper gendered behavior and moral values) in the quarter. Atta's vision does not reject roles for transnational capital or the objective of wealth creation. But that wealth would be produced primarily by these elite cadres of religiously "rehumanized" residents of Islamic Cairo, seen not as communities or individuals but as a particular set of nuclear families and domestic norms. These families would mark their privilege through the devoted performance of gender and moral propriety, as well as by embodying conservative notions of cultural security, instead of through the manipulation of market processes.

At first glance, the urban-planning thesis of the so-called mastermind of the 9/11 attacks, Muhammad El-Amir Atta, seems remarkable for its technical and scientific character (McDermott 2002). Here, his is the voice of a very serious draftsman, civil engineer, and urbanist. Atta's thesis, researched and drafted in German at the Technical University of Hamburg in 1998 and 1999, after research trips to Cairo and Aleppo (Syria), assesses economic, environmental, and cultural threats to Islamic monuments. He advocates the active participation of local people in urban planning and development, but asserts that only a particular set of families within the citizenry have the capacity to represent their own culture and oversee policymaking. In Atta's plans, working-class residents are securitized as objects of protection, often explicitly feminized, under a new technical-oligarchical authority designed to police infrastructures of cultural authenticity. This group resembles the heritage bloc's Fatimid Authority, but with very important gender, "family-value," and urban-spatial prerogatives.

Atta's writings tell us much more about the contradictions of neoliberal urbanism and its evolution into a militant cultural-security regime than it does about Islamic radicalism, although his assumptions about gender, culture, and the state do reveal the influence of the rising waves in Egypt and Germany of Salafi sentiment in the 1990s. In 1995 in Hamburg, Atta met a Salafi Moroccan preacher and moved in with a group of militant, purist young men, which was a turning point in his politicization (Moghadam 2008, 90–96). Although his thesis was drafted after four years of living with this group, Atta's writings are not works of Islamic moralism, ideology, or jurisprudence. Atta's prescriptions for cultural and behavioral purification and gender segregation resonate with the discourse of Salafi preaching in Egypt and Europe during this time; but his plans also reflect a high degree of identification with the technical-professional values of urban planning and architecture, and distinctly neoliberal prerogatives aiming to develop heritage and urban spaces as globally marketable commodities. In this context, he lays out a highly technical project for shepherding populations and managing the rescue of culture. He advocates the establishment of a technocratic, culturally pure elite who would oversee a particular blend of modernization and marketization of Islamic Arab cities.

For the most part, journalistic and popular representations of Muhammad Atta spotlighted his "troubled" masculinity, with his gender identity trapped between oedipal complexes and orientalist contradictions. Atta was depicted both as queerly effeminate and as monstrously hypermasculine. As a youth he was "soft and extremely attached to his mother," "tender and sensitive," longing "to be famous," and alienated from his cold and rigid father. But he was also too male—deeply misogynistic, incredibly disciplined, but uncreative as a worker, uninterested in fashion or movies, and incapable of washing dishes or cooking his own food (McDermott 2002).

Jasbir Puar has critically analyzed the discourse of "global masculinity crisis" that took up the figure of Muhammad Atta after 9/11. This crisis language positioned Atta as both a victim of globalization and as a man whose terroristic violence emanated from an intense self-loathing. "Masculinity experts" traced Atta's self-loathing to his inability to achieve proper status as a middle-class professional or as a heterosexual family man or head of household. Puar cites the preeminent figure of mainstream masculinity studies, Michael Kimmel, who claimed that "what is relevant is not the possible fact of . . . Atta's gayness, but the shame and fear that surround homosexuality in societies that refuse to acknowledge sexual diversity. . . . Central to [militant Islamists'] political ideology is the recovery of manhood from the emasculating politics of globalization. . . . The terrors of emasculation experienced by lower-middle-class men all over the world will no doubt continue, as they struggle to make a place for themselves in shrinking economies and inevitably shifting cultures" (Kimmel 2002, B12, cited in Puar 2007, 58). Puar also points to how Barbara Ehrenreich during this period highlighted Atta's preoccupation with avoiding contact with women, and how his fundamentalist misogyny drove his obsession with gender segregation in urban space (Ehrenreich 2001, 12, cited in Puar 2007, 59). Puar evaluates how such representations of fundamentalist misogyny and crisis masculinity essentialize a "global heteromasculine identity" (2007, 58) and ignore the legacies of feminist scholarship that have offered more nuanced accounts of the distinct notions of power, subjectivity, and piety that are attached to some forms of gender segregation and self-discipline in the Arab world, such as the works of Lila Abu-Lughod (2000) and Saba Mahmood (2005).

Reinforcing Puar's critique, Atta's thesis does not give any evidence to support any quasi-psychoanalytical hypothesis that he is grappling with a "sexual-orientation crisis" or "failed masculinity." Such hypotheses would reinforce the idea that terrorism emanates automatically from the clash between "Islam" and "globalization" due to the latter's traumatization of Third World, lower-middle-class men and their honor. Instead of grappling explicitly with questions of honor and manhood, Atta's thesis grapples more specifically with how global markets, gender and class segregation, and morality politics must be articulated through cultural-security governance and urban tourism development. The thesis suggests that Atta generated these architectural, social, and cultural propositions at the contentious intersection of the heritage bloc and morality bloc, not as an atavistic spasm of rage against the "global" or against his inner gayness, nor as an "honor vendetta" against women or Westerners.

Although his thesis' primary object of investigation is the old city of Aleppo in Syria, Atta's research also draws on his own personal experiences as an Egyptian growing up in Cairo. In subsequent interviews, his German student colleagues indicated that as Atta was writing his thesis he often visited Cairo in attempts to secure a job working for international heritage-preservation agencies in Egypt. In many ways, Atta's thesis reflects a sophisticated advocacy of a form of second-wave neoliberalism, or what Jamie Peck and Adam Tickell refer to as "roll-out neoliberalism" (2002, 387–90). In the 1980s, the "roll-*back* neoliberalism" of Thatcher, Reagan, and the IMF focused on slashing state expenditures, deregulating business and finance, crushing unions, and dismantling Keynesian policy frameworks. But in the 1990s, as forms of violent social marginalization, civil conflict, and resistance emerged among populations rendered "redundant" by roll-back austerity policies, a new roll-out neoliberalism emerged: "No longer concerned narrowly with the mobilization and extension of markets (and market logics), neoliberalism is increasingly associated with the political foregrounding of new modes of 'social' and penal policy-making, concerned specifically with the aggressive reregulation, disciplining, and containment of those marginalized or dispossessed by the neoliberalization of the 1980s" (Peck and Tickell 2002, 389).

The concept of roll-out neoliberalism helps us identify major shifts in neoliberalism and opens up space for the analysis of local variation in processes of neoliberalization. However, this framework can reinscribe a monolithic timeline and reestablish a top-down, North-over-South trajectory of analysis. Coercive and regulatory formations, as well as processes of securitization and race, class, moral, and sexual humanization, are reduced to reactive or secondary phenomena; they become mechanisms for blocking resistance, rather than processes for producing new forms of power and subjects of governmentality. Furthermore, the accompanying notion of "local neoliberalizations" can atomize the productivity of governance models emerging in the Global South and ignore the epochal shift around "security" and the human or humanitarian that emerged here during this period.

Most of Atta's thesis locates him securely within the camp of roll-out neoliberals, or as I would identify him, as a kind of human-security fundamentalist. His work demonstrates the transcendence of neoliberalism by a concern for cultural security and gendered moral control. Gendered securitization mechanisms, aiming to assure social discipline and wealth creation—defined as rent-seeking, not entrepreneurialism, by developmentalist elites—had displaced the market. In his thesis, Atta looks back critically at the individualist economism of first-wave neoliberalism, and then looks even farther back, to the horrors of "urban-renewal" modernism that preceded it in the 1960s.

Against the population-as-pollution discourses of the more secular-leaning heritage bloc, Atta saw local petty trades and informal-sector workshops as tremendous resources for development. Atta asserts, "It provides many jobs in the area and serves as a dynamic link between the subsistence economy and the small and medium industries . . . oriented toward export. It also produces for local needs and its simple methods of production keep the costs of the process low, which is suitable to the low purchasing power in the area. . . . In this way, the inhabitants of the old city can actively participate in the realization of the development strategy as a multitudinous and almost gratis form of manpower" (1999, 103, 113).

In this voice, Atta speaks as a socially conscious roll-out neoliberal and as a moral-security humanitarian interventionist. He depicts the working classes as creative and their economic informality as an easily exploitable form of low-cost entrepreneurship. In his view, the working classes may need a bit of state help to access technology and seed capital, but they will otherwise flourish if they are left alone and if the perpetual-motion machine of the market is unleashed. Atta, however, does not just idealize the bootstrapping capacity of the poor and champion a minimalist state; he also embraces the cultural-rescue agenda of second-wave neoliberalism. And then he goes further, articulating a romantic, not (yet) explicitly violent mission for a new kind of humanized security state managed by a vanguard of religiously conservative families drawn from the more devout members of the technoprofessional class. In his vision, national culture is to be protected; however, culture is not found in the stone of monuments or the creativity of citizens, but in the "organic" integrity of traditional values located in the domestic realm of the ideal nuclear family, where roles and hierarchy are strictly gendered and policed. Monument restoration, economic globalization, and even tourism promotion can be implemented simultaneously according to Atta, if these processes are all orchestrated in a way that preserves and enhances "traditional Islamic values" in Islam's essential "family form." But this plan requires a very different kind of security-and-development agency, one run by a "managerial state . . . an entrepreneurial team of planners, architects, technicians, sociologists and experienced bureaucrats" (Atta 1999, 139). Atta advocates a form of technoprofessional guardianship constituted by these visionary entrepreneurial managers, and by "well-off conservative [Muslim] families who are following a new trend to return to the old city due to their conservative religious values. [They] are particularly conducive to restoration projects, as it is only they who are able to give voice to the concerns of all inhabitants of the quarter and who have the material resources to invest in the restoration of the houses" (1999, 71–72). Those who "participate in urban development" orbit around the figure of the visionary planner and cultural rescuer. These groups, emanating from "well-off conservative families," articulate the voice of the nation; pious, moral, upper-middle-class professionals stand in for and "give voice" to the general category of "human being."

In Atta's vision, the planner is an unelected, but technically distinguished representative of "humanity," understood as a purist guardian of cultural and moral security. Atta is passionate on this point: "The planner must never forget that he is a human being who primarily represents the interests of other human beings that are affected, and not the interests of groups external to the planning process or even the government. . . . If we think about the maintenance of urban heritage, then this is a maintenance of the good values of the former generations for the benefit of today's and future generations. The objective can never be to turn the old city, which is a place of life, into an 'open museum'" (1999, 108–9).

Atta's blend of technoprofessional authority and deeply moralizing paternalism consistently locates "human beings" and "life" at the center of his analysis, but not as rights-bearing subjects, but as what I call para-human subjects of rescue. As Faisal Devji has written in his book *The Terrorist in Search of Humanity*, "The search for humanity in its modern form defines much of Islamic militancy today; indeed the violence of militant Islam cannot be understood without this quest. . . . [This] is startling because humanity seemed to have replaced properly theological identifications like . . . Islam or even religion in general. . . . In this form it announces a universal community founded upon the principle of humanitarianism" (2008, 28). In Atta's particular variation on humanitarian securitization, projects will rescue humanity by securing a new spatial infrastructure of "values" and "culture"; these infrastructures will supplant the vibrantly popular but perversely "dehumanized" (and religiously aberrant) reality of the working-class social world. In this shift, Atta's humanitarianism is at least partially consonant with the turn toward more rigid human-security governance and revanchist cultural authenticism that marked governmentality at the beginning of the twenty-first century in Egypt. As Atta proclaims, "Here in the Orient, another understanding of 'heritage conservation' needs to be established, as this term cannot be utilized for the maintenance of large-scale vital old city quarters. In its place I will suggest the term 'value protection'" (1999, 110).

This value-protection agenda aims to rescue certain populations from themselves. Atta advocates the erection of urban borders to separate traditional families from modern developments. Modern and Western-built forms and cultural-economic institutions are not seen as a problem, until they violate these spatial borders and threaten timeless values. Atta argues, "A lot of care must be taken when planning and introducing such schemes, in order not to create social and familial conflicts by disturbing the established gender roles in the family and society. The design of these models must never stir up any emancipatory thoughts, as these are out of place in Islamic societies anyway" (Atta 1999, 130). Atta's urbanism—a militant intensification of elements within human-security logic—directs morally and professionally superior custodians to demolish built forms that "compete with traditional architecture" and threaten eternal cultural values. These policy proposals resonated with the intensifying Salafi critiques and their occasional outright attacks during this period on Sufi shrines, mawlid festivals, and women-led forms of working-class popular religiosity. In Atta's urbanism, women figure as cultural protectors and income generators who work from home in strictly residential areas that ensure privacy (1999, 126). In Atta's plan, the male-identified managerial state would set up commercial collectives that would market women-produced goods so they would not have to leave home. In the geography of cultural security, women are spatially identified with quasi-private "cul-de-sacs." In orientalist urban discourse, these meandering alleyways have been stereotyped as the essence of Eastern urbanism, or even as a map of the feminized, irrational "Arab mind." Since the nineteenth century, global-colonial urban-planning discourse identified "the mob" as hyper-masculine, but portrayed the alleyways of popular quarters as embodying particularly feminine (and orientalized) kinds of danger. As Elizabeth Wilson has vividly described, "At the heart of the urban labyrinth lurked not the Minotaur, a bull-like male monster, but the female Sphinx, the 'strangling one,' who was so called because she strangled all those who could not answer her riddle: female sexuality, womanhood out of control, lost nature, loss of identity . . . normalizing the carnavalesque aspects of life. . . . The city is 'masculine' in its triumphal scale, its towers and vistas and arid industrial regions; it is 'feminine' in its enclosing embrace, in its indeterminacy and labyrinthine uncenteredness" (1992, 7).

As analyzed by Farha Ghannam, the dominant orientalist-modernist discourse of the Islamic city (as generated by Arab urbanists as well as colonial planners) portrayed

> a clear dichotomy between the private world of the woman and the public world of the man, such that men, seen as dominant and powerful, monopolize the public domain, while women, viewed as subordinate and powerless, are secluded and confined to the private sphere. Women's segregation has often been seen as central to men's sense of honor, and seclusion has been analyzed as a mechanism to control women's sexuality, which is perceived by the society as potentially destructive. . . . To cross the boundaries that separate the public from the private, women need to protect themselves and prevent any potential social disorder or *fitna* [social-sexual chaos or disruption of natural hierarchies]. . . . [However,] by assuming a rigid dichotomy and fixity in the separation between the "world of men" (always equated with the public) and the "world of women" (always equated with the private), the analysis fails to account for the continuous struggle to define the boundaries between the private and the public. (2002, 90–91)

Revealing the profound degree to which his thinking was structured by the classically gendered binarisms of modern urbanism and orientalist planning discourse, Atta identifies urban cul-de-sacs as the feminine, cultural core of the Islamic city, to be managed, protected, and controlled by the entrepreneurial, visionary planner. Meanwhile, he identifies phallic, high-rise corporate office towers as perversely hypermasculine; they are described as generating their own kind of "male *fitna*" (meaning strife stimulated by sexual or ethnic difference) that perverts the urban fabric and threatens the family values incubated in the woman's world of cul-de-sacs and alleyways. Atta identifies figures of contamination and perversion with tall modern towers, especially when they overlook protected, feminized community spaces of "traditional" Islamic urbanism. As Atta himself wrote in the précis of his thesis, when lamenting the presence of sixteen-story office buildings in Aleppo, "The old city was downright damaged or destroyed in a number of parts. Quarters that had formerly been predominantly accessible by cul-de-sacs leading from the main streets were disjointed and cut off from their original access ways because of this. The 'margins' were then partially newly covered with high-rise buildings, which brought about many new problems in turn" (1999, 2).

Atta's work includes moments in which he angrily disparages tall office towers built in the middle of traditional quarters, which he sees as bringing chaos to the spatial ordering of gender and class, public and private, global economy and Islamic culture. His thesis also reveals his intense concern for the restoration of the honor of displaced Arab commercial and civic elites from a dense kind of urban fabric in which gender, culture, class, and national-identity distinctions could be properly managed through "value protection." In consideration of his concerns, a reader could be led to wonder whether Atta, when doing ethnographic interviews with Syrian merchants evicted from old Aleppo for the erection of high-rises there, also spoke to the descendants of those who lived and owned shops in the cul-de-sacs and bazaars of Little Syria in New York City in the late nineteenth century and early twentieth. This area in Lower Manhattan was "home to countless immigrants from Syria and Lebanon. . . . They were bankers and publishers as well as manufacturers and importers of lace, linen, embroideries and lingerie," but mostly they were "a multitude of transient and resident peddlers crowding the streets" (Naff 2002, 7).[16] This was a mixed community of Christians and Muslims, with a preponderance of the former. Some prospered and moved to Brooklyn Heights and Atlantic Avenue, switching from peddling to wholesaling (Hitti 1924). But many others were removed forcibly when Lower Manhattan was targeted as "urban blight" and cleared for the construction of the Brooklyn Battery Tunnel in the 1940s and the World Trade Center between the late 1960s and early 1970s; some of these displaced Syrio-Lebanese immigrants then returned to Beirut, Aleppo, and Damascus. Was the World Trade Center targeted, in part, because it represented, for Atta, a monumental modernist urban offense to the cultural and family values of an Arab urbanism that once thrived in that part of Lower Manhattan?

In 2010, nine years after the attacks on the World Trade Center, a very different kind of urbanism—an ecumenical cosmopolitan one—was evoked as the vanished legacy of Lower Manhattan's Little Syria. This time, urban memory of Middle Eastern peoples and cultures in the area was resurrected by a very different kind of pious Egyptian, an Egyptian-American Sufi Muslim imam, Feisal Abdul Rauf, who had raised funds and generated plans for a proposed Cordoba Islamic Cultural Center in Lower Manhattan. This center would celebrate cross-cultural exchange and interfaith dialogue along the model of the Andalusian scholars of medieval Cordoba, often commemorated by Arab historians as the Golden Age of Islamic culture, when it was at its most open, creative, and inventive. But the project was slandered by the vitriol of US conservative demagogues who labeled it the "Ground Zero Mosque." Newt Gingrich proclaimed it an "Islamist offensive to undermine and destroy our civilization," and Pamela Geller at the *New York Post* declared it a "Monster Mosque" (cited in Dimock 2011, 3). As analyzed by Wai Chee Dimock, this attack on the "Ground Zero Mosque" ended up redoubling violence against Sufi attempts to produce cross-cultural dialogue and to counter the purism of militant practices and doctrines—Muslim, secular, and Christian. Ironically, as they posed as crusaders against radical "Islamism," Gingrich and the US media were taking up and propelling forward Atta's Salafi agenda, culturally resegregating city spaces and demonizing as apostasy alternative community-based and Sufi-inspired urban visions.

Atta probably would have known the history of the eradication of Little Syria and of cosmopolitan forms of syncretic Arab identity, as he had performed extensive urban fieldwork in Aleppo among return migrants from New York and displaced urban populations there in contemporary Syria. Given this, could one hypothesize that Atta's participation in the attack on the Twin Towers enacted, in part, a radical inversion of the modernist violence of urban renewal? One can do no more than speculate. But what is clear from this analysis is that Atta, for much of his career, was driven not solely by a radical branch of Islamist millenarianism, but rather by a romantic version of the dominant trends and clashing preoccupations within modern urbanism, humanitarian security, and gendered cultural-rescue politics.

Returning from New York to Islamic Cairo, and to the fraught logics of human-security governance, it is important to underline that tensions and contradictions between the blocs of actors and logics of securitization clustered around heritage and moral protectionism opened space not just for Atta's brand of violence, purism, and militant urban renewal, but also for more vernacular, participatory, syncretic forms of resistance of the kind that would stream into Tahrir Square in January 2011. Community movements among working-class groups in the old city of Cairo, like the Committee for National Consciousness, did not embody any of the agendas of Atta's urbanism. They did not want to be protected, corralled into cul-de-sacs, or turned into low-cost subcontractors. They did not want to eliminate the nearby "incongruous" modern towers where they could sell their wares or place their family members in office and service jobs. They did not want to submit to being civilized by a few well-off, devout families. They struggled to deconstruct the fetish binary of culture versus security, and to articulate their lives and livelihoods with state resources, global commerce and tourism, and a diversity of public spaces and cultures.

Conclusion

I have mapped here the terrain of conflicts between blocs of actors that aimed to create infrastructure for national markets, securitize subjects of culture, and protect gendered, classed, and sexualized notions of humanity through projects to "rescue" Islamic Cairo. This case study has provided an alternative lens, a new kind of human-security theory, through which to apprehend how social histories of urban neoliberalization intersect with "war on terror" militancy. I have demonstrated the sets of discourses and interests that defined distinct groups of state, community, and transnational actors; and I have identified fields of security practice that brought them into convergence. Additionally, the findings I have presented here have illuminated divergences around the status of the market, the human, the global, and the moral that brought these blocs into radical conflict, opening spaces of resistance.

In the next chapter I return to Rio de Janeiro in order to analyze another set of uprisings that identified themselves with the 9/11 attacks, and to explore a parallel set of state and transnational projects that aimed to rescue urban heritage and re-infrastructure marketable spaces of national value in the midst of radical forms of racialized and sexualized public violence in working-class communities. By bringing these parallel cases together, I demonstrate the simultaneity of and resemblance between emergent projects of human-security governance supported by cosmopolitan elites, Global South–based security industries, and international development agencies. But more than this, the juxtaposition of these studies underlines patterns of contradiction and countermobilization that take shape in these generative Global South sites and that challenge the securitization logics of "cultural rescue" in an age of "terror." So now we travel from an embattled capital of orientalist fantasy to an epicenter of tropicalist sensuality, from a human-security revival of the City of the Arabian Nights to the restoration of the Cradle of Samba.

4

SAVING THE CRADLE OF SAMBA IN RIO DE JANEIRO

Shadow-State Uprisings, Urban Infranationalisms,
and the Racial Politics of Human Security

Since the 1990s, a new progressive coalition bringing together a contradictory assemblage has emerged in Brazil as a bold force that is both distinct from the global "New Left" of the 1960s and 1970s and much stronger than almost any comparable political left in the Global North. As one of the success stories of what Sonia Alvarez (1999) has called the Latin American "NGO boom," today's Brazilian Left has been strengthened by struggles against military dictatorship (in the 1970s); reaffirmed by impeaching a corrupt president (in 1992); revitalized by feminist, ecological, black, and lesbian-gay-bisexual-transgender social movements; pushed by mass movements against landlessness and homelessness; enhanced by leftist factions of religious groups that would be politically conservative in other countries; driven by movements against both police and drug-trafficker violence; and inspired by regional political mobilizations against neoliberalism, privatization, and US hegemony.

In the 1990s and until recently, Brazil's postdictatorship Left was sandwiched between two racialized justice agendas: one exclusively concerned with security questions, the other focusing on the power of black culture to redeem and integrate. Would activists and policymakers "rescue" black communities by advocating police action to crush trafficker organizations, punish and incarcerate criminals, and secure favelas so that the poor could be integrated into state services and economic developments? Or would they ignore violence, be "soft on crime," and celebrate the contributions of Afro-Brazilians to national heritage by offering cultural and music training to slum residents and marketing racially identified communities and commodities to global tourists?

The political anthropologist and prominent policymaker Luiz Eduardo Soares has long critiqued how the Brazilian Left, particularly in the 1980s and 1990s, ignored issues of security, policing, and public safety. Since the Left argued that issues of policing, law, and security were either obsessions of the right wing or fetish issues of the dictatorship, progressives tended to ignore the issue, letting corruption and police and trafficker brutalities accumulate. Or when the Left did intervene, they did so clumsily, as during the first term of Leonel Brizola, a leftist who served as governor of the state of Rio de Janeiro from 1983–87, during which police were simply removed from favelas and from poor communities in order to "liberate them from oppression," allowing organized crime to move in and thoroughly take over as a kind of "shadow state." Critiquing the Left from within, and offering a radical human-security-type revision in a speech to the World Social Forum on 29 January 2001, Soares stated,

> So when I insist on the need for the political left to embrace the question of security and formulate specific policies, this is not to deny the value of our traditional sensitivity to socio-economic causes of many of the most serious problems that manifest themselves as crime. We do not need to pretend to be naive and deny that the police have acted as guardians of the interests of the ruling classes. But I mean that our social sensitivity on the left has blinded us to the forms of power . . . whose effects are devastating and require us to confront them specifically. The Left needs a security policy, and for this policy to commit to the oppressed and to those who suffer discrimination and to commit to radical democracy, transparency and participation. This combination alone will unite efficiency with respect to human rights, and drive major changes so urgently required in this sector in Brazil. (Soares 2001)

In the first decade of the 2000s, certain black community and state-level leaders of Brazil's political left grew increasingly tired of choosing between agendas of security or samba. They knew the limitations of these hegemonic forms. *Security politics* claimed to ignore race while turning black communities into zones of unending police and trafficker warfare, racketeering, and impunity. As analyzed by Denise Ferreira da Silva, the Brazilian state's "arsenal of raciality . . . justifies the deployment of a security architecture that is becoming the primary mode through which it engages its economically dispossessed black and brown populations. . . . The [security state's] decision to kill certain persons . . . [does] not unleash an ethical crisis because these persons' bodies and the territories they inhabit always-already signify violence" (2009, 213). On the other hand, *samba politics*, once the hallmark of the authoritarian Estado Novo (New State) of the 1930s and favored by some NGOs and left-liberal policymakers in the 1980s and 1990s, tended to celebrate race while favoring small-scale entrepreneurship and photo opportunities rather than any structural changes in the economic, state, or legal spheres. Black movement leaders understood that both sets of policy options reproduced the myths of the racial nature of historical and social inequality, providing "cover stories" for state violence and continuing processes of social and political disenfranchisement.

In this chapter I analyze the police/security and samba/tourism projects that defined the parameters of progressive governance in the early-twenty-first century and reconfigured the racial formations of Brazil's unique modernity. I analyze the discourse of the projects of state and international financial institutions and present a political ethnography of efforts by state, police, World Bank, and racialized residents to remake and market an urban slum referred to as Rio's "cradle of samba." I begin by taking the reader to the state of Rio de Janeiro in September 2002, a unique moment when Rio was governed for the first time by a black woman, Benedita da Silva, born and politically forged in a local favela (fig. 4.1). Da Silva, whose political career embodied the contradictory assemblage of evangelical and socialist formations, as well as corrupt ties and emancipatory practices, that converge in the contemporary Brazilian state, headed a government of visionary new leftists, Pentecostals, and community-movement leaders who wanted to free politics from the security-or-samba trap. I trace how a much-misinterpreted trafficker rebellion, perceived as a "shadow-state uprising," crippled this innovative government, forcing policymakers to return to a repressive kind of human-security agenda defined by a mix of police militarization and samba-celebration projects intersecting in the racialization of violence and the fetishization of national history in urban heritage spaces. With Benedita da Silva's electoral defeat in October 2002 and with the death threats against and harassment of Security Secretary Luiz Eduardo Soares, more innovative projects that had unlocked the radical potential of human-security state governance dynamics in the interests of racial justice were remarginalized, though not forgotten.

Here I examine human-security politics as an intersection of urban-utopian replanning projects and militarized, humanitarian heritage protections, which I refer to collectively as "infranationalisms." I also continue

FIGURE 4.1. Benedita da Silva campaigns for governor (2002). Photo credit: Gabriel de Paiva / Agência O Globo.

to analyze the politics of sexuality, but not in terms of identity movements, orientation issues, or reproductive rights. Instead, I examine how the politics of sexuality are embedded in the naturalization of racialized danger and desire, in relation to militarized and racialized masculinities as well as moral-protective femininities. These subjectivities, in turn, become situated at the center of controversies that pit vulgarity against respectability. I therefore explore sexuality politics in terms of the political productivity of discourses of eroticized black cordiality; of the violent hypermasculinity of traffickers which comes to "justify" the extralegal brutality of the Militarized Police, the *Polícia Militar* (PM); of the sexualized allure and apostasy of popular Afro-Brazilian religious practices; of the sublimated, disciplined sexuality of evangelical women favela leaders; and of Governor da Silva herself, who, as a committed Pentecostal Christian, militated against samba sensuality and overt eroticism in order to base citizenship on a politics of gendered respectability. As both a conservative evangelical and a community-organizing socialist, Benedita's plans for security-sector reform struggled to reconcile moralistic and workerist securitization logics with enforcement and entitlement governance agendas.[1] At the intersection of hypervisible, globalizing imaginaries of race, sex, violence, and tropical urbanism, the projects I analyze here can be seen as a rehearsal for many of the race, class, sexuality, and spatial struggles that marked the launching of planning efforts, security campaigns, and image makeovers as Rio de Janeiro prepared to host the World Cup in 2014 and the Olympics in 2016.

Another September 11

On 11 September 2002, trafficker organizations and prisoner networks, referred to popularly as the "parallel power" or "shadow state," initiated a set of uprisings in the state of Rio de Janeiro.[2] In coordination with corrupt prison guards and Militarized Police officers, inmates in Bangu Penitentiaries I and III burst through doors that their allied guards had left open. Inmates wreaked havoc on their facilities and hung sheets painted with slogans demanding full human rights and better prison conditions (Lemgruber 2003, 71). Claiming to stand in solidarity with the disenfranchised working classes of Brazil, the Comando Vermelho (Red Command), one of the orchestrating trafficker organizations, issued a manifesto protesting "the arbitrary treatment suffered by the prisoners of Bangu I at the hands of the Shock Battalions [Brazil's SWAT teams] and the whole state. . . . They do not enjoy even the minimum of human and legal rights" (Garcia 2002a, 23).[3] The rebels proclaimed sympathy with the actions of the militant group al-Qaeda, interpreting the attack on the World Trade Center in New York City exactly one year earlier as a strike against a repressive world system.

But less radical motives also drove the rebellion. Da Silva's progressive government had launched a campaign against corruption in the police and prison system and had begun shuffling inmate trafficker leaders and corrupt guards and policemen between prisons, in order to break their networks and protection rackets (fig. 4.2). During the previous month, an exposé had revealed that the Militarized Police (PM) in Bangu prison had actually printed up and distributed a price list specifying how much (R$200–$400) a prisoner would be charged if he needed to secure a gun, cell phone, or temporary release, or wished to have the guards organize a catered birthday party for him. Entrepreneurial guards and cops had developed a crafty practice of counting bodies in cells, rather than verifying prisoner identities and presence. Guards could say they were "doing their jobs" while allowing children, women, and homeless people to be substituted in the cells so inmates could "run errands," attend meetings or soccer matches, or access money or drugs on the outside (Araujo 2002b, 30).

FIGURE 4.2. Comando Vermelho leader Fernandinho Beira-Mar is shuffled between prisons (2002). Photo credit: Jorge William / Agência O Globo.

Although prison uprisings with Attica-like political declarations are regular occurrences in Brazil, this one was unique in its ability to coordinate cells of violence throughout Greater Rio and draw on national-scale cartel support. This uprising triggered tactical collaboration among gangs (the militarized, urban narco-transshipment organizations and protection rackets known in Brazilian Portuguese as *comandos*). Each comando usually regards other trafficker organizations as blood rivals. But this uprising brought together comando groups including the Red Command, the Friends of Friends, the Third Command, and even São Paulo's First Command of the Capital. (The prison rebellion and street war in São Paulo that would fascinate the international media four years later, in May 2006, was led by the First Command of the Capital and replayed many of the themes and tactics of Rio's Bangu rebellion.)

Rio's 2002 Bangu rebellion spread to other prisons, then to urban favela neighborhoods as comando gangs mobilized their neighborhood enforcers. Then the uprising spread to the state, too, as prison-guard unions, which had gone on strike just four months before, threatened to strike again (Garcia 2002b, 16). In a show of force, on 30 September, the comandos sent messages to the press and media that Rio's business leaders and government would need to recognize and negotiate with them. To flex their muscle they demanded that all businesses in the beach zones and international tourism meccas of Copacabana and Ipanema must close. The comandos' orders were obeyed. On what came to be called Black Monday, stores, shops, and restaurants barricaded themselves. And although no mass violence took place, residents and tourists locked themselves in, terrorized by this dramatic display of the power of organized crime (Penglase 2005). With this incident, the public was reminded that criminal protection rackets provided "governance" in much of the city and could, at will, suspend the rule of law in even its most privileged quarters. The final blow to the government of Benedita da Silva came when the federal government sent in the national military against her wishes on the eve of the October elections to occupy the city with more than forty thousand troops, more than those deployed during the UN Earth Summit of 1992 or even during the military coup in the 1960s. The armed forces claimed that the actions of organized crime had necessitated this move in order to "restore the principal of authority" (Daflon 2002, 24).

Did this revolt represent an uprising of the wretched of the Earth mobilizing as a popular front for emancipation? On the contrary, evidence suggests that this politically timed violence represented a show of force by a parastatal order that emerged at the end of the dictatorship and has since only flourished and expanded in the climate of privatization, impunity, and deregulation. In this regard, I follow the argument of Alba Zaluar, who stated, "The illegal drug trade is integral to the character of Brazilian democracy, as much as threatened by it" (2005, 338).[4] Corrupt police, comando leaders, and paramilitary vigilantes did not want to submit to the reformist justice and security agenda launched by those spheres of the state that were securely in the hands of Benedita's progressive coalition.

Racialized sexuality framed the processes of militarized and "humanitarian" urban-planning interventions in the wake of these uprisings. An "infranationalist" agenda asserted itself, demanding extraordinary state (and police) interventions in order to preserve the "cordiality" of black culture practitioners and remake the infrastructures of those Afro-descendant communities who generate wealth for the nation. These enforcement practices that targeted intersections of eroticized tourism and cultural heritage preservation dovetailed uncomfortably with criminological legacies that reproduced the figure of the hypersexualized black or mixed-race trafficker *Dono* (Boss) and paramilitary cultures, in which police identified their own masculinity with territorial mastery over black spaces. Moreover, at these fraught intersections in the last two decades, an evangelical and Pentecostal grammar of moral security emerged that rejected what it saw as the vulgarity and sensualism of "samba citizenship" and sought instead to promote more "respectable" forms of business and entrepreneurialism among Afro-Brazilian communities.

Reform in Question

For decades, Brazil's prisons have served as the command centers of narco-traffic comando organizations. Low-paid, entrepreneurial prison guards working in overpopulated and understaffed facilities have often given in to the temptation to profit from rather than repress criminal entrepre-neurs. Prison employees, such as Bangu's notoriously flamboyant guard Marcus Gaviao, nicknamed "Playboy," worked to coordinate communica-tions, smuggle cell phones and arms, and maintain links between arrested leaders confined in different prisons.[5] During the 1980s and 1990s, the neoliberal state exacerbated problems of social exclusion from schools, hospitals, and job-creation programs. In the place of such public ser-vices, illiberal institutions of the prisons and jails, not the "free market," emerged as regulatory apparatuses for much of society. Prisons became the universities of the criminal economy, the command centers of social militarization, and nodal points where police, prison-guard, and gang rivalries and relations were worked out (Leeds 1996). These functions be-came so normalized and institutionalized that it hardly made sense to call them "corruption," although their norms and agendas stood diamet-rically opposed to the projects of legality, citizenship, and development that concerned the more visible spheres of the elected and policymaking state. Enrique Desmond Arias has provided a sophisticated network analy-sis of how state, civic, and criminal actors shared information, planned ac-tivities, and minimized danger by mobilizing proxies and flexible modes of mediation that minimized visibility while maximizing collaboration and impunity (2006, 47–51). Paradoxically, from the standpoint of these powerful paragovernmental networks, it was the statist, public agenda of the new progressive coalition and its emphasis on making visible the link-ages between state and crime that seemed "perverse" or "corrupt."

A Radical Challenge

At the start of September 2002, with national and local elections less than a month away, and with a complex assemblage of bold leftists, evangelicals, and reformists in power in the state of Rio de Janeiro, narcotrafficker organizations as well as corrupt and militarized factions within the state were feeling nervous. Luiz Inácio Lula da Silva was seemingly unstoppable as the center-left candidate for president (and he did go on to win a sweeping victory at the end of 2002). Although his power base was among the trade unions in large cities and among working-class communities in Brazil's northeast, Lula did not oppose free-market ideologies and had earned some acceptance among national and international financial elites. But Rio's brand of leftism was distinct from São Paulo's. Rio's progressive politics involves the constant struggle to unite community organizations, the Black Movement, evangelical churches, antineoliberal forces, unions, Communist Party elements, bohemians, and social movements—a coalition built through fighting dictatorship and corruption. This alliance was in some ways more threatening to the status quo and to both the "shadow state" and the police-security state than Lula's syndicate-based nationalism, which would take a few more years to sort out how it would articulate coherent racial, religious, security, and social-justice policies (Soares 2006).

By 2002, Rio's state government was no longer willing to accept the violent sociopolitical order that orbited around prisons. It did not want to continue the game in which the poor, nonwhite areas of the megacity were left to be controlled by armed rivalries between commando units and PM battalions. They refused to accept the continued use of working-class communities as staging grounds for transshipments of cocaine and arms (as analyzed by Procópio 1999 and Zaluar 1996, 112–13). Rio's government wanted to bring the state back in, extend the rule of law and the rights of the citizen, and sever the links between comandos and corrupt police (Amar 2003, 37–39). But their breed of reform proved hard to articulate in national and international public discourse. "Reform" had become such a confusing proposition. On one side, when investors cried for reform, they meant a push for more privatization. On another, when the press called for reform, they usually meant getting tough on crime, advocating more hardline police tactics, surveillance of public space, and restriction of liberties in the war on crime. But an alternative coalition of community and progressive leaders had promised to take Rio on a path to a different kind of reform.

Benedita da Silva, elected vice governor in 1998, ascended to the governor's office in 2001 when Governor Anthony Garotinho resigned to run unsuccessfully for president of the republic. By 2002, Benedita, then the head official representing leftist and progressive parties in a tense coalition with Pentecostal political organizations, dared to face down massive police corruption and brutality while simultaneously going after the comandos' stranglehold on black favelas. Even more daringly, she and her public-security chiefs, Luiz Eduardo Soares and, subsequently, Roberto Aguiar, had for the past four years developed policies that sought to reign in the protection racketeers, elite development speculators, machine politicians, and absentee landowners, all of whom fed off the power of both corrupt police and traffickers (Soares 2006; Soares, Bill, and Athayde 2005). As Mercedes Hinton asks, "If elected officials often got away with stealing millions, what was to deter a police officer earning a pittance from income supplementing through whatever means were available" (2006, 181). From the start, Soares's policies met with opposition from the comandos as well as the security establishment. Just a few months before the prison uprising, inmate comando leaders had ordered the assassination of Rio's secretary of human rights. The targeting was designed as a protest against the new government's policies for ridding prison cells of communications paraphernalia (often sold to inmates by police and guards) that allowed inmates to network with each other and control organized crime from inside. Traffickers proclaimed this cleanup a human-rights abuse (Amora and Garcia 2002, 17).

Between 1998 and 2002, with Garotinho and then Benedita as governors, a new generation of public-security policymakers, working in consultation with a new set of police and security-focused NGOs, had begun to shift the terms of the racialized discourse of human security and crime fighting. This team had refused to rely on the racist language and militarized discourses that had proclaimed a need for "war" on slums and delinquent youth in the name of saving Rio's civilization of conviviality, "cordiality" (a term referring to a special deference and friendly politeness identified with black respectability), and supposed racial integration. Instead of pursuing militarism and permitting arms trafficking, protection racketeering, and bribe-trading to cement relationships between some police, traffickers, and local officials, Soares's team had begun the task of making the nation's metadiscourses of racial historiography and urban social conflict speak to each other; that is, during Benedita's administration, Soares's team started making policies based on an analysis of racial exclusion that linked it to problems of corruption and militarization in the criminal justice sector and the privatized state. They refused the tradition of linking crime and violence to the degraded moral-cultural character or marginal socioeconomic status of black Brazilians (Heringer and Pinho 2011; Soares 2000).

The Federal Police had belatedly opened an investigation into possible political machinations behind the timing of the prison revolts and comando threats, and Benedita da Silva launched the last-minute R$130 million Integrated Security-Commercial network to protect local businesses and public spaces. But by late September 2002, it was too late.[6] The trafficker revolt and the powerlessness or complicity of police and prison guards broke the will of Rio's voters, who on 1 October voted out Benedita and replaced her with a corruption-friendly evangelical conservative populist, Rosinha Matheus Garotinho, the wife of Benedita's former boss, Anthony Garotinho. Although there was much overlap in the personalities and Pentecostalism of both Rosinha and Benedita, the election loss did evict the progressive security team and its new alternative projects from the state. So the loss ended, for the moment, Rio's historic experiment with courageous, progressive reform and antiracism.

With the election of a conservative governor and subsequent reelection of a conservative mayor, Rio de Janeiro's public institutions again focused their energies on enhancing repressive and militarized policing in a constant cycle of escalation. In order to "humanize" this return to a more purely enforcement-centered rather than redistribution-focused security agenda, the city and state invested in urban infrastructures and cultural-protection projects that again evoked and celebrated Brazil's history as a heritage of racialized culture and interracial conviviality. This cultural-rescue, militarized-humanitarian set of infranationalist initiatives ended up resecuring the urban borders that segregated predominantly black and mixed-race areas from upper-middle-class settlements, and, for the time being, it ended efforts to root out police impunity and government complicity with traffickers.

The shadow-state uprising of 2002 reflected the stakes and strategies of a crucial battle over the deconstitution or reconstitution of the human-security state and its hegemonic organizing ideologies. However, the spectacle also exposed strange forms of complicity among the organizers of state and nonstate violence, and triggered resistance from broad sectors of elites, comandos, police, and the public. In order to explore these developments, I leave the scene of the 2002 events and analyze the racializing cultural-security and humanitarian-development projects in a more geographically marginal favela, Serrinha, where in the 1990s the state launched a highly visible model project called Favela-Bairro that liberated markets and opened spaces for cultural-economic development and the promotion of tourism. Serrinha also served as a space where the racial and militarized agendas of the police war on narcotraffic were tested and deployed in the most deadly of patterns.

Rescuing Samba

The Favela-Bairro project was developed by Brazilian policymakers and launched by the Inter-American Development Bank (IDB, the Latin American branch of the World Bank) in the early and mid-1990s in co-operation with Brazilian sociologists and municipal leaders interested in rationalizing Rio's slums and making them accessible to development (Magalhães 1997, 5). The project aimed to restore municipal security by rescuing national history, particularly through its model project, "Saving the Cradle of Samba" in Serrinha, one of Rio's most black-identified, culturally rich shantytowns (fig. 4.3). Serrinha was, not coincidentally, a crucial police-trafficker battleground and a strategic node of political-party clientelism and vote-buying in the working-class quarters of Rio. Crystallizing the dominant mode of governance in Brazil, which until recently avoided facing the realities of spatial resegregation and violent corruption by pushing projects that celebrated, moralized, and racialized national history in order to sell it through the global tourism economy, Serrinha's Favela-Bairro project is a useful site for interrogating "business as usual" in 1990s Brazil.

Serrinha is located in northwest Rio de Janeiro, in the borough of Madureira. This vast zone of slums and lower-middle-class suburbs serves Rio as a secondary node of commerce, a center for Afro-Brazilian cultural production, a hub for retail shopping, and a sprawling zone of residential settlement (Lindgren 1975; Ribeiro 1993). The favela of Serrinha is a small but nationally renowned and culturally significant settlement that occupies a hillside on the north of the main thoroughfare of Madureira. Serrinha appears in the mappings of the public imagination for many reasons. It is where the first modern government-backed samba school, Imperio Serrano, was founded in the 1930s during the populist modernizing regime of Getulio Vargas. Serrinha was also the historic home of many black leaders of the port-workers union that, given their strategic

FIGURE 4.3. Photo opportunity for favela children wearing Favela-Bairro T-shirts (1999). Source: Municipal Government of Rio de Janeiro.

position on the docks from which Brazil accessed the world economy, successfully fought for labor rights and against racial discrimination during the first half of the twentieth century (Meade 1986). Serrinha is also where many traditional Bantu religious and cultural practices (such as Umbanda and Jôngo) have survived in a supposedly pure form. From the 1920s to the 1940s, Serrinha was a focal point of Madureira's internal tourism and Afro-cultural "parallel economy," serving as a pilgrimage site for white Brazilians and international devotees of Afro-Brazilian spirituality, dance, and culture (Gandra 1995). According to the old guard of Imperio Serrano, Serrinha was the place where white Portuguese immigrant Carmen Miranda came to learn how to samba, before she became a Hollywood star.

But between the 1980s and the 1990s, Serrinha had become a node in another set of racialized, transnational economic and cultural formations: cocaine transshipment. The wider zone of Madureira became Rio's most violent borough and a nexus of transnational crime networks and elite-favoring money-laundering circuits. In this contemporary context the Brazilian and IDB Favela-Bairro project aimed to take Serrinha back to its "golden age" to show how an Afro-Brazilian shantytown could be integrated into the municipal fabric. Serrinha would become a model for racializing urban infrastructure and rescuing cultural heritage, as well as for redeeming the global-city image of Rio itself. The project for Serrinha was built on an entrepreneurial model for improving infrastructure, marketing racial-cultural heritage, and reinstating the image of "racial democracy" and black cordiality—Rio's unique model of racial and global integration. Favela-Bairro aimed to roll back the forces that during the past three decades had dismantled the favela's previous integrative and cultural functions.

During the 1970s and 1980s, two shifts eradicated the viability of favela integration into public life in Serrinha and in similar settlements: first, the spread of drug and arms trafficking among the dispossessed sectors in an age of economic austerity; and, second, the police's turn from battling dissent against the dictatorship to battling illicit activities in the favelas (Pedrosa 1990). Since the eighteenth century, Brazil has served as a central intersection of commerce, labor migration, and cultural flows between Africa, Andean South America, and North America, and until recently Rio had functioned as one of South America's largest ports and entrepôts, where different classes, economies, and races of the region mingled. Since the 1970s, the same intersectionality that had promoted an idealized image of Rio as a model of racial and global integration began to make it attractive for those who wanted to integrate and protect illegal trade networks. Rio became a hub for traffickers in cannabis from Brazil's north and in coca from Andean countries, as well as for organized rackets and gun smugglers from Florida, Colombia, Europe, and everywhere else.

Favela spaces became attractive to traffickers because of the density, informality, and impenetrability of their streets, cul-de-sacs, and public spaces. Paradoxically, these are the same factors that had given the favela its reputation for conviviality, intimacy, and cultural and social richness. The same dense spaces and fuzzy boundaries that had nurtured creativity, cultural vitality, political innovation, and labor militancy were transformed into spatial liabilities and criminogenic attributes starting gradually in the 1960s. Spaces of favela intersectionality became reidentified as miasmas of danger as the military-authoritarian junta began to categorize all sites of social conflict and to identify social mobilization within the black-majority favelas, in particular, as threats to national security and as incompatible with urban modernity and national futurity (Zaluar 1996).

Thus Serrinha was violently transformed by the arrival of the 1990s. Military struggles between gangs, police, and comandos (beginning in the 1970s and increasing during the 1980s) effectively shut down vending and production stalls, often run by women or the elderly, thus remasculinizing economic power and public visibility in these areas. Also gone were the spaces for outsiders to play, visit Afro-religious shrines, and spend their money in the area. Women lost opportunities to work in the community, not just as vendors and shop owners but also as spiritual guides and musical performers for tourists. Many had to commute out to white areas to serve as domestic labor, working for others instead of themselves, or to enter the touristic, service, or sex-work economies outside the shelter of their community context. Opportunities to raise children communally vanished, as did the chance to supervise their recreation and encourage them to adopt cultural proficiency and nontrafficker youth collectivities and solidarities (Fraga 2002). But some women became "governance entrepreneurs," taking advantage of the fact that the hypermasculinity of both trafficker and PM organizations would not absorb them. So women, particularly those identified as "mothers of prisoners," started to assume important roles as community organizers, diplomats, and mediators between public resources, political-party machines, police battalions, prison sites, and traffickers' commands (Souza de Almeida 2000, 100–105).

In the context of this crisis, the public role of the municipality overseeing Serrinha also shifted. In the era of the populist Estado Novo in the 1930s, favela development had been funded by channeling government money through the offices of particular political party members, into Carnaval crafts units, trade union concessions, and the Imperio Serrano samba school (Sepúlveda dos Santos 1998, 131). This form of direct patron-client linkages between the state, party bosses, and communities (criticized as vote-buying or clientelism by some) nevertheless distributed resources into the community and integrated the poor within the apparatus of citizenship and state planning. Thus, Imperio Serrano, like other samba "schools," acted as a hierarchical but functional and consensus-building local council and state organ. This clientelist-populist practice of incorporating Serrinha via its cultural institutions was literally called "samba citizenship" by the Vargas regime of the 1930s and 1940s (Sepúlveda dos Santos 1998, 131).

But in the 1970s, Brazil's military dictatorship cut support to the samba schools and unplugged the clientelist networks of participation and redistribution. It also privatized economic and social control organizations in the favelas (Fischer 2008, 44–50). Samba schools officially became the ward of Riotur, a public-private partnership for tourism development. A new guard of Carnaval leaders drew funding from the new favela economy of gambling rings, traffickers, and tourism companies, rather than from the state and local political-party apparatus. The directors of Imperio Serrano even moved their headquarters and dance space out of Serrinha to a more central zone of Madureira. Serrinha still maintained clientelistic relations with city officials and opposition parties, but negotiations for votes and support came to revolve around providing elements of infrastructure such as electricity, sewage, trash collection, and building materials (Ney do Santos Oliveira 1996).

Starting in the mid-1990s, the municipal government of Rio de Janeiro generated a new and ambitious plan to erase this boundary between informal slums and properly registered neighborhoods and to integrate favelas into the urban fabric of Rio. While other urban regimes throughout Latin America still evicted and relocated squats and slums, Rio's plan envisioned the immediate opening of public spaces within shantytowns, the gradual provision of infrastructure and jobs, and the eventual legalization of property claims for the favela settlers. The project, originally called "Favela Is a Neighborhood," became officialized as Favela-Bairro and went into operation in 1996, with US$180 million in funding from the Inter-American Development Bank and US$120 million from the municipality of Rio (Turcheti e Melo 2010, 25) (fig. 4.4). Its first goal was to pave over the rough boundary zones between favelas and bairros, and open up free circulation and access between the two divided sectors of city settlement.

For Serrinha, integration and entrepreneurial development was to draw first and foremost on the heritage of classic forms of *carioca* racial culture.[7] The Favela-Bairro project's public relations brochure, "Serrinha, a Pole of Popular Culture," stated this explicitly.

> The strong points [of Serrinha] are:
> - black culture and northeastern culture vitality
> - emerging manifestations of "youth culture"
> - architectonic, urban and landscape particularities
> - expressive community organizations, based in spatial or cultural interests
> - sophistication and cordiality of its inhabitants
>
> (Inter-American Development Bank 1999, 4)

The discourse of Favela-Bairro depicted Serrinha not as a political subunit of a municipality, or as a set of economic actors or citizen populations, but as a lush landscape of sophisticated, expressive, racialized culture (fig. 4.5). Within the above list of five attributes, the word *culture* appears five times, including in the brochure's title. Serrinha's small size, of about

FIGURE 4.4. An Inter-American Development Bank official meets with representatives of the Rio government to approve a map of Favela-Bairro (1997). Photo credit: Gabriel de Paiva / Agência O Globo.

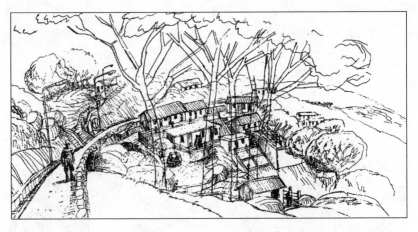

FIGURE 4.5. The future of Serrinha's Favela-Bairro sketched as a timeless, bucolic Afro-Brazilian village of culture, erased of its modern buildings and violent realities. Source: Municipal Government of Rio de Janeiro.

three thousand inhabitants, and its particularly culturalized and racialized profile made it attractive for selection and transformation into the first model of the Favela-Bairro program, which then went on to launch even more ambitious infrastructure, culture, sports, housing, and youth projects in communities such as Mangueira, Vidigal, Rocinha, and Fernão Cardim. The list of "cultural strong points" captures the 1990s "cultural-rescue" revival of the language of the 1930s "racial democracy" idealism, which had equated social expressivity with the sensuality of the tropical landscape and articulated the supposedly deferential and cordial attitude of Afro-Brazilians with respect to white visitors in their communities. This cordiality was a trait that the 1930s Brazilian state imagined as conducive to interracial relations and the production of a uniquely miscegenated, mixed-race future for the country (Hanchard 1998). Serrinha's cultural landscape, as a zone of "racial democracy" heritage, thus remained attractive to Rio's progressive elites, who saw their nostalgic image of Rio reflected in the blackness of the inhabitants. In 1999, a Favela-Bairro official confided to me, "These are 'good' blacks, pure blacks, blue blacks. They are cultural aristocrats of the old regime."[8] The brochure's delineation of Serrinha's strong points strived to reanimate the place of racial democracy's culture of interracial cordiality that marked Serrinha's "golden age." But Black Movement activists and theorists of racial politics, in the preceding two decades, had launched an intensive critique of the "cordiality doctrine." France Winddance Twine (1998) and Edward Telles (2004) have demonstrated that high rates of interracial marriage, often cited as proof of a culture of cordiality, conceal the ways marriage markets reaffirm class and race hierarchies, limiting middle-class interaction to whites and light-skinned, mixed-race people, while dark-skinned women are locked in poverty. Donna Goldstein (2003), Brian Owensby (2005), Marcelo Paixão (2005), and I (Amar 2005) have emphasized how notions of normative cordiality act as the practice of refusing recognition of race, or "racial blindness." Cordialism euphemizes racial hegemony and systematic violence, rendering racialization invisible and displacing blame for "aggression" or for virtually any form of criminal or structural violence on the figure of noncordial blacks. Cordiality also implies sexual accessibility or complicity in self-eroticization. This doctrine underlined the symbolic value of sexualized cordiality in both the national imaginary and the global tourism market. With urban-planning and tourism projects, cordiality was euphemized again, not through interracial marriage but through built spaces and nationalistic infrastructure projects that would sew the urban family together.

The explicit goal of the Favela-Bairro initiative was to stimulate an "urban renaissance in Rio" (City of Rio de Janeiro 1999). The 1999 Strategic Plan for the City of Rio de Janeiro highlighted Favela-Bairro as one of its six major long-term projects. The plan described the goal of the project as "to integrate favelas into the urban fabric that surrounds them, making the physical and social conditions that can segregate them from the city or set them apart disappear" (fig. 4.6). These measures included "open squares for sports, like basketball and soccer, for the use of residents as well as the population. The favela will be illuminated at night and the lengthened roads will provide access to trash collection trucks. At the gateway to various favelas, landscaped parks with benches and kiosks will be installed to smooth the visual shock of transition between the favela and the better neighborhoods, and attract the residents from both sides" (City of Rio de Janeiro 1999).

Whose Urban Renaissance?

The common theme of the project, articulated in its explicit "integrative" discourse, was to open public areas, attract people to cross borders of fear and degradation, and re-invoke a "historic" national spirit of racial mixing, a safe, respectable, heritage version of erotic contact, securitized and

A renascença urbana do Rio

Acabar com as favelas, transformando-as

Como se fossem painéis anunciando a pobreza, elas pontilham a paisagem da que seria a cosmopolita "cidade maravilhosa": as favelas do Rio de Janeiro, as mais famosas da América Latina.

Abrigando quase um milhão de pessoas — um em cada seis habitantes do Rio —, as favelas são há muito tempo uma vergonha para as autoridades cariocas e um peso na consciência da cidade. Situam-se num limbo: são parte da cidade, mas ao mesmo tempo estão isoladas. Para os seus moradores, não existem serviços de água, esgoto, drenagem e remoção de lixo. Até mesmo o correio passa ao largo, porque as ruas não têm nome, as casas não têm número e os "proprietários" não têm escrituras.

"Todo cidadão tem o direito inalienável de viver numa rua com nome e numa casa com número", diz *O Globo*, o principal jornal do Rio.

FIGURE 4.6. Cement poured over favela frontiers produces "urban renaissance."
Source: Municipal Government of Rio de Janeiro.

prioritized in this nexus of humanitarian intervention and economic development aid. City officials proclaimed, "It is important to provide public spaces where people can come together to talk and to converse" (City of Rio de Janeiro 1999). Here is where the racial-culturalist agenda of promoting cordiality was articulated with the securitization objective of creating spaces for the orderly gathering of individuals and the free operation of market forces. The mayor's strategic plan narrated a story about national history and racial heritage that gave meaning and legitimacy to efforts to plow open and exercise surveillance over community spaces. In these areas, residents were to "preserve and purify" the legacy of "samba blackness," thus enhancing their cultural capital. In this framework, the state would create infrastructure, then pull back; community residents were to establish themselves as cultural entrepreneurs and market the innate heritage value of Serrinha. This entrepreneurial cover story permitted the state to push in aggressively, but in ways that made these moves seem to be responses to or restorations of "market-reformed" versions of the samba narrative. Instead, what it really represented was a new initiative that promoted a police-centered form of human-security governance and did nothing to interrupt the impunity of the paragovernmental sectors of the security state.

The strict racialisms hiding behind these technoscientific state discourses of surveillance, markets, and culture revealed themselves when contrasted with an alternative favela project in Rio's settlement of Jacarezinho. As analyzed by João Vargas (2006), this community decided in 2001–2 to install its own high-tech security cameras and community gates to control drug trafficking and keep an eye on police abuses. Although gated communities, closed condominiums, and private security cameras had become nearly universal in white middle-class Brazilian neighborhoods, the idea that working-class blacks would install such protective mechanisms was regarded as ludicrous, intolerable, and an act of criminal aggression. In response, the state banned private security technologies in favelas. Apparently, while the state saw privately deployed security agencies and technologies as its natural supplement in white communities, black communities would remain the objects, not the agents, of security.

Through the imposition of the cultural and spatial infrastructures of Favela-Bairro, rather than through autonomously deployed community-security technologies, the state could re-embed a progressive symbolic imaginary of racial and spatial mixing, transnationally securitized and also imbued with global market value. In Serrinha, Favela-Bairro aimed to open a classic bourgeois public sphere of dialogic exchange, while also stimulating the development of a touristic, culturalized public landscape in line with Serrinha's historical advantages and with Rio's identity as a capital of hospitality, racialized culture, and creativity. Favela-Bairro articulated classical principles of individualist liberalism with contemporary notions of cultural marketing. In 2000, Rio had planned to attract two million foreign tourists and five million Brazilian visitors, according to its 1999 Plano Maravilha (City of Rio de Janeiro 1999). In line with this goal, the mayor's brochure portrays one of its strategic objectives for Serrinha as "to attract consumers of Serrinha's goods and services in the milieu of culture, leisure and in activities related to samba and civil infrastructure" (Campaign Committee of Luis Paulo Conde 2000, 2). In the newspapers, the city made itself clearer: "Serrinha will become a tourism magnet" (Renato 1996).

Favela-Bairro's strategic focus on replacing violent, degraded urban barriers with open spaces of dialogue, tourism, and amusement reflected the good intentions of progressive urbanism based on liberal conceptions of public life and public space, nostalgia for the cultural politics of "racial democracy" (da Silva 2003, 110–11), the marketing of samba culture, and the insistent blindness of municipal authorities to the policing and trafficking that fractured the favela. In the 1990s, as remarked by Frederick Moehn, "individuals approaching debates over citizenship, development, civil society and problems of violence in Brazil evoke music as a kind of audiotopia . . . or a sonic space of an imagined country where inequalities are leveled out" (2007, 181).

Drawing on a parallel symbolic imaginary of samba utopianism, the Favela-Bairro project leveled cement over the militarized front lines of police-trafficker wars and declared the area a playground for free commerce and an "open museum" of racial democracy, always animated by the eroticized subtexts of racial mixing, musical pleasure, and cultural enrichment. But did this set of heritage and space projects resolve the conflicts that produced the violence, and did it face down those who profited from segregation? Urban boundaries in Rio de Janeiro were produced by antagonistic clusters of social protagonists whose "public" manifestations may only be made more dangerous by the unilateral bulldozing of frontiers. Thus, the spectacular visibility of police violence and the structural violence of accords between police and comandos were rendered invisible, or more unaccountable and incomprehensible, by the overwhelming focus on race-heritage projects and samba narratives.

Police and Trafficker Projects

In 1997, the popular newspaper *Jornal do Brasil* published an article headlined "Police Violence Scars Favela Model: On Serrinha hill, the display window of the Favela-Bairro project, it's best not to look, hear, or speak about police atrocities" (Ventura 1997, 8). The article went on to describe the ways in which police act with impunity as they occupy public spaces and trafficked areas:

> A thirty-seven-year-old vendor was among those who felt on their skin the reality of police violence, which came in the form of a punch resulting in a fracture below the right eye. His crime was to witness the beating of a suspected trafficker, known as The German, on the 20th of February [1997] at 1:25 AM. The vendor was having a beer with a couple of friends when, according to him, he saw the police of the 9th Battalion stuffing a boy's head in a plastic bag and punching him repeatedly in the stomach. The torture happened on the most public and busiest point in this favela in Madureira, but according to the vendor, one of the PMs did not like being observed and punched him. Immediately, the officer began beating on his own chest and bellowing, "I am Officer Paulo Roberto." All while the police captain was observing him. (Ventura 1997, 8)

Reports of police abuse in Serrinha had begun to increase around 1996, not necessarily caused by, but certainly coinciding with, the implementation of Favela-Bairro. In order to conform to the "quality of life" norms of Favela-Bairro, public bars at the busy border of the favela, such as the one frequented by the man whose face and skull were fractured, had to begin closing at 10 PM, instead of staying open all night. Police began to increase the force and disruptiveness of their blitz into the favela. In Serrinha, the PM had appropriated the newly redesigned Favela-Bairro public spaces as surveillance and access corridors. Favela-Bairro's elimination of shacks, shadows, and liminal spaces at the border between slum and "asphalt," and the shuttering of businesses at night, had only increased the urban border-zone's dangers and created a space for easy incursion by both cops and comandos. Those found loitering or observing police activities in this public zone, supposedly designed to cultivate free exchange and attract tourism and investment, could find themselves interrogated, arrested, or beaten. The Favela-Bairro project's human-security discourse of opening dialogic public space had ignored or displaced questions of how police interpreted public visibility and interaction as they monitored streets, coerced informants, and staged blitzes of drug-identified communities. The community's claims to civil rights were understood by police as threats to their security imperatives, their prerogative power, and their privilege to control visibility, exposure, and openness, as well as invisibility and impunity, in appropriating the favela's public space and resources.

The security mindset of the PM has deep historic roots. In 1969, Rio's local PM battalions were commandeered by the national armed forces in the creation of the security state that followed the coup. Subsequently, with the beginning of the democratic transition in the early 1980s, the state maintained its militarized police force and a policy of security totalization, which merges internal security with national security, eliminating the distinction between a citizen suspected of a crime and an "alien" threat to national security (Huggins, Haritos-Fatouros, and Zimbardo 2002). Thus, despite the stabilization of electoral democracy, the sociopolitical legacy of authoritarianism only extended and aggravated its hold on society. In the current era of more open democracy, why until recently did Brazilian politics avoid facing the authoritarian legacy of the PM? Here we must turn to the postabolition historiography of race and its important role in substituting legends of cultural mixing for the realities of corruption, segregation, and police-comando regimes.

In a clause held over from the era of military dictatorship, Brazil's constitution gave the Militarized Police independence from federal control and maintained their separation from the Civil Police, which is the agency that investigates crimes, interrogates arrestees, and holds them for court. The PM thus retained its autonomous identity, battalion by battalion, under the often tenuous command of state governors. And PM battalions thus maintained, in practice, the capacity to extort, torture, and set up protection rackets (Bayley 1990; Tilly 1985, 173). Paul Chevigny (1998) argues that the militarized and autonomous structure of these police forces, grounded in a history of racist practices, accounted for the PM's unrestrained use of deadly force, torture, and house invasions during their occupations of favelas. According to Jacqueline Muniz (1999), police were also driven by their own masculinist traditions of asserting dominance over certain strategic territories. She quotes an experienced PM officer: "The street criminal says that he gets his crime diploma from prison. For the police, the diploma is in the street. The street is the school of the police. All that you want to see is there, you just have to look. I learned to have a specialist's eye for the street. What I've seen there I could never tell you about" (Muniz 1999, 15).

In the eyes of the police, the visual profile of the street was often a euphemism for the racial profile of Afro-Brazilians. And in the paramilitary securitization logic of the Militarized Police, the mastery of territory and its masculine prerogatives dictate the terms of social-racial enforcement. In the favelas, the displacement of the language of race into metaphors of "the street" depoliticizes crime issues and masks questions of state, parastatal, and police responsibility for generating forms of structural and social violence. The high visibility of the Afro-Brazilian communities and their purported association with crime drew attention away from how police militarism, shadow-state outlaw organizations, and state privatization and deregulation policies shaped the perpetuation of crime-related violence. Police masculinist identity and its practices of racial targeting fused in an obsession with controlling territory and mastering the street (Cecchetto 2004, 117). For the PM, the street was a battlefield, not a space of commerce and citizenship, where encounters are negotiated and social conflicts mediated. It was the PM's task to master the art of distinguishing the properly educated elites or *doutores* (PhDs), who must be defended, from the enemies of national and public security. In Copacabana or downtown, Rio's Militarized Police saw their job as eliminating *marginais* (marginals, hoodlums) from among the doutores. But the police treated the streets of the favelas as wholly behind enemy lines and assumed that most male civilians there were "suspect elements." In addition, the trafficker *donos* (owners, chiefs) themselves cultivated representations of favela territory as a battlefield.

Community Projects: Alternatives to Favela-Bairro

Serrinha's residents association developed alternatives to the comandos' and the police's paramilitarized security doctrines and the IDB's "humanized" cultural-heritage projects, which romanticized and eroticized black cordiality. Community movements in Serrinha mobilized black agency, samba heritage, and urban reintegration efforts to push for reforming the police and criminal-justice systems, to promote citizen enfranchisement over militarized securitization, and to replace petty clientelisms with a new apparatus of integrated state social-welfare organisms. Dovetailing with the reform agenda of Luiz Eduardo Soares and Governor Benedita, Serrinha's projects everted, or turned inside out, the human-security racial politics, rendering them tools not of market liberalization, but of working-class empowerment and political accountability. These projects served as vehicles for building claims against errant organs of the state as well as against violent organized crime.

Serrinha's residents association and its organizational efforts did not limit themselves to the Favela-Bairro project's purist narrative of racial heritage, but drew instead on several notions of racial identity, even conflicting notions that may have seemed to be imported (fig. 4.7). Community tourism and cultural entrepreneurs sought to detour around police degradation and violence by advocating pride in atypical forms of Afro-Brazilian heritage. Black cultural innovators sought to culturally reidentify, distinguish, and domesticate their own contested public spaces and border zones as sites where tourists, Brazilian visitors, and community residents could translate negative social capital into positive cultural capital that could leverage citizenship, demilitarize public life, and bring the state back in on the community's terms, in part.

In community plans, the border of the favela would become an economically lucrative, culturally empowering black-heritage trail, rather than a stigmatizing rift though the city. Between 1997 and 2002, Serrinha's residents association elaborated several tourism development plans and cultivated Afro-Brazilian dance, music, athletics, and Carnaval costume-making workshops.[9] Serrinha's entrepreneurs did not fit easily into dominant accounts of identity politics. Their street politics of appropriating racial identities to lure tourists and create a noncriminalized public sphere through culture did draw on the narratives and achievements of identitarian social movements, nonessentialist versions of racial democracy miscegenation discourse, and even nostalgic myths about the black "cordials." But these efforts sought a spatially defined community solidarity that had the potential to generate a basis for security and citizenship for community residents, regardless of their racial appearance or identity, taking on a form of pragmatic racial action that Osmundo Pinho identifies as "insurgent consciousness" in the context of touristic "reAfricanization" (2010, 407–16).

Favela Tourism

While small-scale community projects struggled for visibility, funding, and markets, more mainstream state and IDB favela tourism projects simplified or ignored the alternatives launched by communities like Serrinha. Mainstream favela tourism, like the Favela-Bairro project, worked to liberate and integrate the favela into the globalizing urban economy of

FIGURE 4.7. The Serrinha cultural-justice activist Ademir dos Santos presents his "Sexta Negra" project, an alternative to the tourism framework of Favela-Bairro (1999). Photo credit: Paul Amar.

Rio, all while portraying the favela as an alluring externality, as the sexy savage that adds tropical appeal to the modern city. As an entrepreneurial human-security project, favela tourism thus brought the global economy into the urban margins, while rendering invisible state interests and militarized accords. However, these projects continued to flourish under the cover of a discourse that produced the favela, paradoxically, as both a national essence in the cultural-security imaginary of the nation and a zone of extranational territoriality within the paramilitary logic of policing interventions.

Paradoxically, this new kind of favela tourism emerged as an international niche market only after white Brazilian visitors stopped coming to favelas. Throughout the twentieth century, white Brazilians had come to the shantytowns of Rio in order to partake of their reputed musical, religious, and sexual vitality. Only when favelas had become occupied by the police-trafficker war did the landscape become reimagined as terrifying and impenetrable. In this context, internationalized and culturally "enlightening" favela tourism emerged, fusing the exploitation of racialized cultural allure with the potential to discover the sociological and cultural realities lurking inside the realm of narcotraffic power. Several internationally popular films and media representations helped associate this criminal activity with spectacular forms of erotic, criminogenic blackness. These films include *Boca* (1994), in which Rae Dawn Chong takes on Rio's drug lords; *Orfeu* (1999), a remake of the 1959 classic *Black Orpheus*, but with the hero's descent to hell reframed as a battle with narcowarriors; and the beautiful, controversial *City of God* (2003). In 2006, csi: *Miami* taped a season of the television series in Rio de Janeiro, recognizing the city as the new world capital of both glamour and vice crime, and the film *Turistas* plunged buff white Americans into Brazil's jungles, infested with human-organs traffickers. And the two highest grossing films in the United States in the first five months of 2011 were both set in Rio de Janeiro. In *Fast and Furious Five: Rio Heist*, fugitive convict Vin Diesel unites with a Rio drug lord to steal cars from trains. And in the animated film *Rio*, black youth drug smugglers and pickpockets are rendered as cartoon marmosets who help smuggle samba-dancing parrots.

Feeding into this renaissance of film and media interest since the 1990s in the cultural and touristic appeal of Rio (and particularly of its racialized, culturally saturated, and animated crime-scapes), favela tourism reemerged in new state-promoted and mainstream forms. To a much greater extent than in Serrinha back in the "classic period" of samba pilgrimages in the 1930s, or in its new Favela-Bairro attractions of today, favela tourism has flourished in Rio's largest favela, Rocinha. This huge, long-settled community of about 300,000 residents borders the exclusive beach zones of Rio's Zona Sul (Freire-Medeiros 2009) and has served as a front line and laboratory for police corruption, vigilante militia formation, and clientelist mobilization by the state (Alvez and Evanson 2011, 92–95). In the 1990s and 2000s, favela tours here took on a mission of education and community service that aimed at demonstrating the "reality" of the favela and countering the prejudice of the media. "A visit to the favela can assist the effort of forming frameworks," proclaimed one French visitor in a newspaper interview. "It is a rapid sociological incursion, it could be better than reading about this reality in a book or newspaper" (Stycer 1996). Enterprises such as Jeep Tours and Favela Reality Tours emphasized and idealized the safety and diversity within favelas. The guide Camilo Ramirez insisted that Rocinha was "the safest place in the city. Here no one steals; it is the law of the favela. Ninety-seven percent of those who work here are honest workers" (Stycer 1996). The typical favela tour, like the Favela-Bairro project itself, worked to erase the boundaries between the elite visitor and the shantytown resident by insisting on the sameness of lifestyle (fig. 4.8). In the sociological narrative of the progressive tours, favelados were hardworking, television watching, morally upright citizens who aspired to and often achieved the dream of middle-class status. But this sameness was performed in a realm that was externalized from the normal city by the militarization of the comandos' regime, the voyeuristic sexualization of trafficker masculinities, and the racialization of the favela as a whole.

Tours represent the presence of both PM and narco-comandos as external to or as outside adversaries of the "favela community residents." Tours tend to portray the favela community as untainted, occupied by, and disidentifying with these paramilitary organizations. Of course, paradoxically, it was precisely the violence of the police-narcotraffic war and its impact on racialized public spaces and erotic culture that drew the tourists. Moreover, the vehicles that tourists took into the community theatricalized the dynamics of militarization and racialization. Foreign or elite Brazilian guests on favela tours were confined to large military jeeps, a spectacle resembling the entry of military vehicles into a bombed city at the end of the Second World War, or the journey of green safari cruisers into the jungles of Jurassic Park. Favela tours insisted that borders and differences between the favelados and the "normal" population could and must

FIGURE 4.8. Military jeeps bring tourists into the favela (2002). Photo credit: Simone Marinho / Agência O Globo.

be overcome, but the drama of the tour itself restaged and spotlighted the fear and exhilaration of crossing a taboo frontier and entering an outlaw zone, all the while highlighting the dangerous nativeness of the local versus the detached immunity of the international observer. "Gringo!! Gringo!! Gringo!!," the guides would shout continuously from the jeep, to signal to the community and the comandos that these passengers are of international status; they are not plain-clothes police officers making a military raid. This hailing process and the confinement of the tourists to the jeep belied the guides' claims that favelas were "the safest place in the city." The shantytown territory was reinstated as radically "other," appealingly threatening. Favela tours limited the contact of tourists with favela residents and businesses, preselecting a nice shop, a deserted panorama viewpoint, or a children's crafts center in order to provide photo opportunities and a bit of souvenir shopping. Although perhaps sincerely dedicated to overcoming the borders between favela and city, these tour guides, as border entrepreneurs, ended up policing and restricting contact between tourists and locals.

Local residents and entrepreneurs developed other forms of tourism and visitation that were less sociologically enlightening and more blatantly exploitative of the cultural, racial, and pleasurable attributes of favelas. Promoters in the favela of Rocinha have developed a tourist map of their community entitled "Rocinha Tour 2000" (Núcleo de Turismo 2000). Significantly, this map was geared toward local Brazilians who come on their own as consumers, shoppers, or casual tourists, not in an organized tour group. The idea behind this kind of tourism was to stimulate an appreciation of the shows, dance clubs, ice-cream stands, clothing stores, cafés, samba venues, bars, and even clinics and schools in Rocinha. The fact that this marketing strategy, run by a new agency called Nucleus for Tourism Development, was considered "tourism," like a visit "abroad" to an exotic locale, even when sold to white Brazilians residents of the same city, seems to indicate that for Brazilians as well as foreigners, the favela was another country.

While the jeep-based favela tours insisted on the immateriality of favela borders and differences, all the while underlining the militarized threat, the locally produced Rocinha marketing schemes presented the experience of crossing the border of the favela as a gateway to positive difference. These tours attempted to revive the advantageous image of the shantytown as a place of warm interaction, good eating, and great dancing. The favela became a space endowed with a specifically racialized, spatialized cultural heritage that made it not just another safe zone of hardworking middle-class folk, but something better: an unusually creative zone for diverse, unbounded interactions. The efforts of tourism innovators in Serrinha paralleled the development of the much larger Rocinha, but with an overwhelming emphasis on its racial heritage and less attention to the military aspects of invading a parallel world. As George Yúdice writes, "Racialized youth [channeled] violence and pleasure into what these groups call cultural citizenship . . . practices of public participation otherwise left unverbalized" (2003, 133). Claudio Renato, after conducting an interview with the director of the Favela-Bairro project, Maria Lúcia Petterson, reported that Serrinha was selected as a model recipient of development aid because "it is one of the few places in Brazil that maintains century-old cultural traditions and is where jôngo, a black slave dance ancestor of samba, is still cultivated . . . [and because the community] lives surrounded by three samba schools, Imperio Serrano, Portela, and Tradição [and thus] will become known by Brazilian and foreign tourists already tired of the artificial mulatta shows prepared for them" (Renato 1996). Renato went on to report that Serrinha would also draw visitors to its samba crafts production enterprises, its unique children's samba school, and its eight *terreiros de umbanda* (sites of syncretic Bantu-Yoruba Afro-Brazilian cults) dedicated to the patron *orixá* (deity) of war and fertility, Xangó.

The Favela-Bairro project administrators described Serrinha's heritage using a language that designates the favela as an authentic place of origin for Brazil's narrative of "racial democracy," or "samba nationalism." This is echoed in press accounts of Serrinha's efforts to cultivate tourism through cultural development. The language of racial democracy, the nation's collective identity, is a positive tropicalist blend of white rationalism and black musical and spiritual vitality. As drawn from the work of the anthropologist Gilberto Freyre (1963), this national myth posited the blending of these two essential counterparts that first took place on the plantation in the zone of encounter between the master's house and the slave quarters, and continued more recently with the crossing of the boundary between the favela and the properly paved city. But as mass-marketing of Carnaval and the "mulatta shows," the canned, topless Carnaval reviews staged for tourists in burlesques and cabarets have commodified the trope of racial blending within the schemes of a mass-tourism industry, and as racial identity politics have grown more vocally critical of the idealizations of miscegenation and how the concept romanticizes interracial encounter on the plantation, the sanctity and authenticity of this foundational myth has crumbled.

In Serrinha, the municipality of Rio had found a rare example of a so-called pure black community, one that had maintained its plantation music, dance, and religious traditions, and had founded the first modern samba school. Without the preservation and visitation of heritage sites such as Serrinha, the founding "racial democracy" myth could have lost its territorial claims to Rio, the cultural and tourism capital of Brazil, as well as its "empirical" claims to historical truth. Favela-Bairro and favela tourism erased the boundary between Serrinha and the wider city, designating slum borders as spaces of encounter and cultural exchange. These projects contended for globalizing spaces and imaginaries of Rio as they implemented law enforcement, modernization, integration, and security goals. These efforts also drew from and intervened in national racial politics, regrounding through heritage-tourism development the contested myth of the plantation encounter as the cradle of Brazilian collective identity and national uniqueness.

Conclusion

In this chapter I have highlighted the historical, cultural, and political contingency of state and elite-driven urbanization projects and their racializing re-narrations of national samba history and Afro-Brazilian identity. The entrepreneurial Favela-Bairro project drew on nostalgic Brazilian racial ideologies while refusing to push police reform. The project did not challenge, and may in fact have masked and thus indirectly facilitated, the power relations that link narcotraffic comandos and the parastatal or "shadow state" of alliances between prison guards, corrupt police, and incarcerated trafficker leaders. Historically, police projects originated in a twentieth-century context of national-security management and militarization that drove the escalation of violence and celebrated cultures of masculinist mastery over black-identified streets and populations. The research I have explored leads away from romanticized notions of the cultural purity of black samba entrepreneurs and instead traces links between the militarization of the security sector in Brazil and its shaping of international bank-funded police strategies and touristic appropriations.

While many powerful state, international, and community actors all identify Serrinha as the "Cradle of Samba," community actors contested what this meant in terms of the racialization and nationalization of local culture, the hypersexualization of popular religiosity and of trafficker and police masculinities, and the deployment of culture in the service of the emergent prerogatives of the human-security state. Community dissent around race-culture projects resonated with and generated support for the bold agendas of leftist leaders like Luiz Eduardo Soares and complex figures like Governor Benedita da Silva. This daring alternative may have been blocked by the Bangu rebellion and middle-class panics of 2002, but still survives in the social movements, community efforts, and cultural critiques of Rio's uniquely mobilized progressive coalition. And these securitized forms of culturally elaborated and globally imbricated interventions around black cordiality, trafficker masculinity, and police mastery—choreographed around the cultivation of eroticized contact between "slum" and "civilization"—promise to intensify as the World Cup and Olympic preparations unfold.

5

OPERATION PRINCESS IN RIO DE JANEIRO

Rescuing Sex Slaves, Challenging the Labor-Evangelical
Alliance, and Defining the Sexuality Politics of
an Emerging Human-Security Superpower

In this chapter I explore a set of police, legal, religious, and labor-movement interventions deployed around the issues of transnational sex trafficking and child "sex slavery" in Rio de Janeiro between 2003 and 2006. Through this case study, I offer an analysis of framing processes and subversion mechanisms, and trace their impact on social-movement mobilizations and state discourses. My aim is to explain the rise and fall of a repressive human-security model that temporarily united discredited militarized police squads with the interests of ascendant workers' movement actors and evangelical Christian militants. This alliance revolved around a series of rescue campaigns, including one of the most visible, Operation Princess, which consisted of militarized raids on private homes, sex-commerce venues, and tourist sites in the beachside district of Copacabana in Rio, aiming to save underage girls from globalizing prostitution and trafficking networks. The deployment of Operation Princess played out in ways that reflected the contentious politics of security in the country, and brought to the surface the contradictions that riddled Brazil's claim to be an emergent global "human-security superpower" for the twenty-first century.

This set of campaigns against sex trafficking served as a laboratory for state attempts to reconcile and mobilize four contradictory logics—juridical-legal, moralistic, paramilitary, and workerist. Two of these logics of rule—a legalistic, court-based juridical mode of human-rights intervention and a moralistic mode of intervention embedded in evangelical missionary tactics—clashed profoundly, to the point where eventually it became impossible to reconcile them. The state found it difficult to extend legal rights and participatory agency in the sexual public sphere, while also declaring a virtual state of emergency that suspended rights and launched moralistic humanitarian policing operations in the sex-work sector.

To overcome this impasse, local Militarized Police, the Federal Police, and their INTERPOL allies were pushed by the Palermo Protocol process to focus specifically on the trafficking of *children* into prostitution and international sex commerce.[1] By focusing on children, the operations could avoid the considerable controversy around whether adult sex workers were consenting agents who could claim workers' rights or coerced victims whose status as workers with labor rights was irrelevant. So the first operations came to focus on minors, who are by definition not endowed with adult agency or the capacity to consent. The resurgent syndicalist Left, evangelical Pentecostal populists, and humanitarian movements of globalizing civil society came together around the provisional "child-rescue" consensus. But the moralistic mission to rescue child "slaves" combined quite uncomfortably with the newly dominant Workers' Party (Partido dos Trabalhadores, PT) agenda for empowering adults as workers and as participatory political agents (Hirst 2008). How would two other logics of intervention—"workerist" forms that sought to regularize prostitution as labor, and "paramilitary" logics of unregulated police domination and racketeering—reconcile themselves in and around this bold and internationally visible project of human-security intervention (fig. 5.1)?

In May 2003, the Militarized Police of Rio de Janeiro and the Civil Police launched in unison their contribution to the INTERPOL and Brazilian Federal Police initiative against sex trafficking.[2] Operation Princess and its sister campaigns unfolded in seeming disregard for the fact that prostitution is legal in Brazil.[3] The Pentecostal evangelical leaders of Rio gave biblical legitimacy to the campaign, brushing aside questions of legality or the sex workers' resistance to being rescued.

During this phase, the state government of Rio de Janeiro also rededicated two special Civil Police stations and a Militarized Police battalion to the task of rescuing Brazilian women and children from international sex traffickers. On the occasion, the charismatic, evangelical-Christian security secretary and former governor Anthony Garotinho proclaimed proudly that he would purge corruption and promote moral rectitude in the police and the general public by bringing back the spirit of the Vice Police Stations (Delegacias de Jogos e Costumes). These stations had been

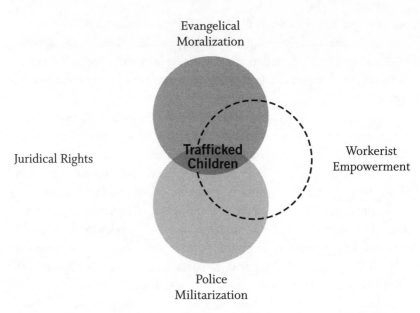

FIGURE 5.1. Operation Princess's human-security field: before subversion. The Workers' Party tries to articulate a common security agenda between Evangelicals and Militarized Police forces. In this early articulation, juridical notions of sexual rights are marginalized.

closed, for the most part, in the 1940s, when prostitution was legalized, and the last remaining stations closed with the end of the dictatorship in the 1980s.[4] Simultaneously, President Lula declared a nationwide war against sex trafficking, designating the campaign a top priority for his new administration.

Contested Logics of Human Security

The Brazilian government's campaigns to stop human trafficking, particularly forced prostitution and the sexual exploitation of children, figured prominently in the early months of the administration of President Luiz Inácio Lula da Silva ("Lula"), who was inaugurated in January 2003. These internationally visible campaigns served to anchor efforts to promote Brazil on the world stage as a new kind of global commercial and humanitarian power. On the home front, they were meant to resolve contradictions within lawmaking coalitions and governance agendas that the new government had inherited. Lula's party and allies had taken over a state that had already woven itself into a set of international obligations and policing frameworks, setting the country on course to frame and target the issue of child prostitution and sex trafficking. These international obligations included the United Nations "Palermo Protocol to Prevent, Suppress and Punish Trafficking in Persons, especially Women and Children," signed by the previous president, Fernando Henrique Cardoso, in 2000 and ratified in 2004 (Pimenta, Corrêa, Maksud, Deminicis, and Olivar 2010, 16). Shifts in internationally linked and state-favored feminist organizations also laid the groundwork for these mobilizations. As Adriana Piscitelli has argued,

> Towards the end of the 1990s . . . in an environment of greater connections with transnational feminism, Brazilian feminists began to become increasingly concerned with sexual tourism and the trafficking of women. This concern was particularly palpable in the discourses of certain non-governmental organizations which dealt with women's issues. . . . However, as the turn of the century approached, the main groups connected to the trafficking of persons issue were movements which fought for children's rights. In 2002, the *Pesquisa nacional sobre o tráfico de mulheres, crianças e adolescentes para fins de exploração sexual comercial* (National Research into the Trafficking of Women, Children and Adolescents for the Purposes of Sexual Exploitation — PESTRAF) was initiated, supported by international funding agencies. This study was to be considered a major reference point for policies directed against trafficking of persons in Brazil. (Piscitelli 2008)

Recognizing the importance of these international dimensions and shifts in logics of security and sexuality, I explore the dynamics of contestation around "sex trafficking" and "child sexual exploitation" in the globally visible and symbolically saturated landscape of urban Rio de Janeiro, the country's security laboratory and "shop window" to the world. From this, I illustrate the contours of conflict that forced certain subjects of race, gender, and moral insecurity into the spotlight. These meaning systems and institutional structural relationships explain the constant crisis of Brazil's security sector and the crossed motivations of its major policy-making social movements, while they also highlight the uniquely dynamic and contradictory character of how Brazil mobilizes for sexual rights. This analysis aims to open up new possibilities for developing movements for equality and entitlement; police and security policies grounded in gender, sexual, and racial justice; and a politics of rights that goes beyond the limits imposed by moralization and securitization. As I have been arguing throughout this book, this conjuncture of securitization logics and militarized humanitarian practices comprises "human-security governance" or the governmentality of a human-security state. It is important to reemphasize that I use the term "human security" as a heuristic device, to highlight epistemic and historical continuities among these formations of power. These projects and operations are not necessarily explicitly referred to as human-security projects in their original context or by their own practitioners. These agendas and practices are described in a variety of ways, as "public security," "citizen security," "women's protection," "child rescue," "human development," "human rights," "ethics reform," and so on.

The human-security model of governance represents a particular conjunction of the four securitization logics that I have consistently identified, each comprising a distinct grammar through which a particular sphere of the state and cooperating parastatals constitute subjects of enforcement or entitlement. Each logic enables the cooperation of international and national agents of governance that share notions and practices within the model's parameters, and that deploy collective and concerted actions in the space of the globalizing city. The first of the four relatively autonomous logics with which I grapple here is *moralistic securitization*. In the case of this set of contests, this logic refers to processes favored by evangelical and piety movements that have incorporated aspects of the state and focus on gendered moral discipline and on the "rescue" of the family and the child. Moralistic securitization favors dependency-producing notions of charity and protection, rather than empowering notions of redistribution or entitlement. The second logic is *juridical-personal securitization*, a human-rights and court-based logic grounded in the classical principles of liberalism. It secures the rights of the individual and protections against discrimination, but also tends to reinscribe a monolithic notion of the state, to locate the individual in the private sphere rather than as a public subject or as a worker, and has little regard for the collective nature of social life. *Workerist securitization*, the third logic, particularly strong and relevant in Lula's Brazil (and which also returned to the fore in Egypt during the uprisings in 2011, analyzed in chapter 6 and in the concluding chapter), aims for collective social security and entitlement through public mechanisms and redistribution efforts. Finally, *paramilitary securitization* enforces territorially anchored and highly masculinist notions of security that proliferate in the context of deregulated, privatized, or entrepreneurial coercive interventions.

In this chapter I provide a political-process model (McAdam 1999) that highlights the mutability and contested, internally contradictory character of human-security governmentality. The political-process model relies on the notion that a social movement is a continuous phenomenon (Bostic n.d.) that thrives on the interplay of four factors: the emergence of broad socioeconomic processes that expand the capacity for more political opportunities over an extended period of time; the "readiness" of dissident organizations—armed with alternative frames, discourse, and mobilizing capacity—to assert themselves when political opportunities become available; the emergence of a collective consciousness among the challenging groups that encourages the belief that the movement is leading in a successful direction; and the ability to win the support of external groups in order to broaden the opposition against the conservative political structure (McAdam 1982, 40). This model underlines the capacity for social movements to disrupt these four hegemonic securitization logics; they do this through intentional collective action as well as by taking advantage of the fortuitous breaches triggered by accidental, external, or unintended events. Through the interaction of specific subversion mechanisms, these movements can *evert* (turn inside out) repressive human-security dynamics and unleash emancipatory projects. To illustrate this subversion process, I identify certain mechanisms or structured actions that came together to break these four logics of securitization and rearticulate them in a more empowering way. Through the processes of reframing and subversion, the model of securitized governance associated with police raids and moral purification (drawing on a discourse that became mockingly termed "genital xenophobia") fell apart, and activists were able to articulate and empower an agenda that brought together movement logics that centered on gender and race consciousness, worker empowerment, and globalist sexual rights.

When I identify securitization logics, I do not use the word *logic* in the structuralist sense, as in the overdetermining logic of late capitalism, although in other parts of this book I do show how these types of security projects resonate with and draw power from massive class disparities and are conditioned by the inequalities of consumerism and tourism, as well as by informal-sector and criminalized social dynamics. Nor do I use the term *logic* in the rationalist sense, as the strategic expression of an interest group. Instead, I employ the term more dynamically, informed by Foucault's notion of discursive power that can circulate and reconfigure spaces of the state (1990 [1979]), and by Ernesto Laclau's analysis of logics that enable the coherence of hegemonic blocs but that can be subversively undermined and rearticulated by counterhegemonic alliances (1997). One could also term these blocs "prerogatives" or "imperatives," informed by Wendy Brown's gendered conception of state governance that captures and interrogates the state's power to rescue and police (1995). As theorized by Jason Glynos and David Howarth,

> If naturalists offer the prospect of a causal explanation by subsuming the phenomena under universal laws or general mechanisms, and if hermeneuticists explain via the use of particular contextualized interpretations, our approach conceives of explanation in terms of a critical and articulated assemblage of logics. . . . [These logics] focus our attention on the rules or grammar that enable[s] us to characterize and even criticize a phenomenon, but they also allow us to disclose the structures and conditions that make these rules possible . . . [and focus] attention on the way their "ignoble origins" are generally forgotten or covered over as the practices and their self-understanding are then lived out. (2007, 164)

By analytically linking together and denaturalizing a plurality of logics, I aim to serve transformative semiotic and political ends, because the identity and significance of the elements studied are "modified as a result of the articulatory practice" (Laclau and Mouffe 1985, 105).

The process model that I present here explains the shift from a repressive to a more empowering articulation of securitization logics by tracing the interaction, first, of *three framing mechanisms* that sustained the appeal and legitimacy of the moralistic-repressive campaign: (1) representation of racialized abolitionism; (2) moralization or ethical upgrading of the role of police paramilitarism; and (3) mobilization of "genital xenophobia" by evangelical antitrafficking groups. Then I trace the cultural-political process by which *three subversion mechanisms* undermined and provisionally rewired the matrix of subjects and relations between these logics: (1) surveillance of police racketeering by tabloid media; (2) mobilization of worker-empowerment projects by the state and sex-worker rights groups; and (3) the revival of a discourse of "erotic nationalism" by the lobbying of the tourism industry as well as the advocacy of organizations promoting sexual rights.

The first mechanism that helped frame the moralistic-repressive consensus was *representations of racialized abolitionism*. The name Operation Princess resonated with the nineteenth-century iconography of missionarism, child rescue, and abolition in Brazil. These representations worked

FIGURE 5.2. The statue of Princess Isabel in Copacabana presides over an anticorruption protest (1 October 2006). She holds the pen with which she signed the Lei Áurea, the Golden Law, which abolished slavery in Brazil in 1888. Photo credit: AP Photo / Andre Luiz Mello.

to displace the more macho depictions of state power centering on the iconic masculinities of militarized enforcers or organized workers. Replacing them was a revived, feminized image of the state as an aristocratic abolitionist and social-purity advocate. These representations drew on Brazil's nineteenth-century history as well as the fact that the gateway to Copacabana's sex-work district ran along an avenue named after a female icon of the abolition era in Brazil. Avenida Princesa Isabel is the grand boulevard that brings travelers from the airport and central Rio to Copacabana Beach, a mixed-class and mixed-race coastal community that also serves as a center of sex tourism, sports and cultural events, and international diplomatic and business conferences. Copacabana was a focal point of the new vice policing operations. The statue of Princess Isabel stands, with her arms outstretched, where the avenue meets the sea (fig. 5.2). The statue holds the feather-pen with which Isabel signed the emancipatory Aurea Law. The figure seems to bless those she liberated and also to offer a gesture of tolerance and welcome to those who pass through this urban gateway to the topless dance clubs and all-night saunas of the Lido of Copacaban. The monarch's signing of the 1888 abolition law (see

Skidmore and Smith 2001) enacted the end of slaveholding in Brazil, but also triggered the downfall of the imperial family and state apparatus. Her proclamation of abolition was, in the end, a self-sacrifice that ignited a republican revolt among the resentful coffee-planter oligarchy, which then overthrew Isabel and her family.

Antiracist historians and the intellectual leaders of the Black Movement in Brazil have identified what they call the "Princess Isabel Syndrome," as they critique the commemoration of this Victorian-era regent—married and forty-two years old when she signed the Aurea Law—as if she were a virginal, saintly child monarch, and how she is honored as the primary agent or hero of abolition (Elisa Nascimento 2007, 231; Hanchard 1999, chap. 2). These scholars assert that the veneration of Isabel takes credit away or renders invisible the centuries of sacrifice and mobilization among Brazil's Afro-descendant population and the impact of their national and transnational civil, legal, and social movements that pushed for abolition. Given the history of hypervisibilizing Isabel and displacing black agency, the princess representation resonates vibrantly with the politics of social "whitening" (embrancamento) and the infantilization of black slave agency (David Theo Goldberg 2011). Operation Princess and its sister interventions thus drew on rich gender and national metaphors of rescued slaves and liberator child-monarchs. These mechanisms of representation focused on identifying victims, rather than on forms of antiracist social movement or collective labor, or on questions of the gendering of work and consumption in the sex and tourism industries. In these ways, these rescue operations conformed to what Elizabeth Bernstein calls the "new abolitionism," an agenda reflecting the evangelical movement's recent adoption of new transnational policing and legal frameworks that designate prostitution and sex trafficking as the "new slavery" (2007, 130).

> For modern-day [evangelical] abolitionists, the dichotomy between slavery and freedom poses a way of addressing the ravages of neoliberalism that effectively locates all social harm *outside* of the institutions of corporate capitalism and the state apparatus. In this way, the masculinist institutions of big business, the state, and the police are reconfigured as allies and saviors, rather than as enemies [of sex workers and unskilled migrant women,] and the responsibility for slavery is shifted from structural factors and dominant institutions onto individual, deviant men . . . as in the White Slave trade of centuries past. . . . What is perhaps most ironic and surprising about

the sexual politics of the "new abolitionism" is that it has emerged not only from the simultaneous rightward migration of feminists and other secular liberals toward the politics of incarceration but also from a *leftward* sweep of some evangelical Christians away from the isolationist issues of abortion and gay marriage and toward a "new internationalist" social justice-oriented theology. (Bernstein 2007, 144)

Since the 1990s, Brazil "has experienced the rapid growth of Protestant evangelical churches, whose members now comprise 26% of respondents self-identified as religious in the 2000 census. While the Catholic and evangelical churches presently compete for the Brazilian spiritual market, dogmatic Catholics and evangelical Protestants converge . . . influencing electoral results through the recruitment of voters and blacklisting based on issues such as abortion, homosexuality, drug use, prostitution and paedofilia" (Corrêa, Maria, Queiroz, Zilli, and Sívori 2011, 30). And as Cristina Pimenta, Sonia Corrêa, Ivia Maksud, Soraya Deminicis, and Jose Miguel Olivar state, "Although it is an exaggeration to say that an [evangelical] abolitionist wave is sweeping the country, there are signs that positions and views radically opposed to the exercise of prostitution as work are gaining space and legitimacy" (2010, 17).

These evangelical antiprostitution representations of "humanitarian rescue" and "new abolition" were not limited to the revival of the figure of Princess Isabel, but also to the reframing of the moral mission of the Brazilian state and its governing Workers' Party itself. In a speech delivered on 27 May 2003 to an assembly of public-sector union leaders in Rio de Janeiro, Lula imagined Brazil's early neoliberal era (1985–2000) as a stationary exercise bicycle pedaling away in a shuttered apartment. This metaphor evoked the white middle classes in Brazil's gated condominium developments, which proliferated in the 1990s (see Caldeira 2000), exercising in their private gyms and fearing racialized crime outside. Lula declared that he wanted to liberate that bicycle and invite Brazil to come outdoors and pedal toward a new horizon of progress, where the national landscape would be cleared of the stigma and injustice of its favelas and exploited children.[5]

"Workerism" as articulated by Brazil's Workers' Party is not antagonistic to human-rights politics but draws on a distinct notion of citizenship and cultivates its own notions of the subjects of politics. Workerism, in Brazilian socialist theory, draws on the Italian philosophy of *operaismo*, emphasizing that the agency of mobilized workers and popular-class communities has always been responsible for pushing the evolution of modes of capitalist production. It also argues that liberalism and modernism misrepresent capitalism's evolution as a monolithic, "top-down" process driven by technological innovation and market forces.[6] According to workerism, workers and popular classes must turn the power of their agency into an advantage and a source for innovation, in order to block efforts to replace them with machines or with flexibilized, racialized low-wage labor. Workerists do this by mastering tactics of self-organization into councils, expanding networks of solidarity, engaging in direct-action politics, and insisting on participatory planning to reallocate property, decision-making power, and resources in ways that reconcile efficiency with justice. As in Italy, workerism in Brazil and throughout Latin America has developed and survived in strong association with Catholic liberation theologies and other movements that value religious faith and community solidarity as core labor-movement values. In Brazil, the center of gravity in workerism since the 1970s has moved from the factory floor toward popular-class communities and a broad range of municipal, rural, and new identity-based groupings. Since the time of Lenin, critiques of workerism have emphasized that its ethical politics can lean toward evocations of romantic or communitarian notions of popular faith and moral solidarity, or narrow populist gestures and assertions of paternalistic traditionalisms rather than more radical, critical policies. And, since the 1970s, liberal-socialist critiques have warned that workerism ignores the rights of minorities and reproduces oppressive faith-based myths about gender and community. Colored by these critiques, the term *trabalhismo* ("workerism" in Portuguese) has begun to have pejorative connotations; in its place, the positive aspects of workerism have been rebranded as *cidadania* (citizenship), *solidariedade* (solidarity), and *participação* (participation).

In today's Brazil, the agenda of participatory empowerment of labor and citizenship remains critical of top-down state power, which includes a critique of the elite orientation of the human-rights framework, with its focus on judges and courts, rather than on social structures. The latter can tend to trap the progressive agent in the position of the victim, individualized and isolated, longing for a court decision or humanitarian agency to come to the rescue. The workerist critiques this process, arguing that it is this positioning of citizens as supplicant victims that reinforces gender, race, and class indignities and the disempowerment of labor. Workerists also argue that court victories can often lead to token symbolic judgments or, worse, provoke protective tutelary responses or "civilizing missions" that do nothing to promote empowering or emancipatory transformations. Of course, as a tool for struggle against tyranny and dictatorship, human-rights politics have served Brazil well. But the era of Lula was marked by the development of a theory of democratic empowerment, which he explicitly identified as postneoliberal, with a profound commitment to the promotion of solidarity, the direct participation of citizens in assuring access to justice, and rebalancing political and individual rights. As stated by Sonia Corrêa, Marina Maria, Jandira Queiroz, Bruno Dallacort Zilli, and Horacio Federico Sívori, "Participatory models, although already existing in various areas, have become the trademark of the Workers' Party administration at municipal and state levels, and were transported to the federal administration during the eight years of the Lula administration" (2011, 24).

Representing a distinct turn in workerist politics, Lula's language as in his "stationary bicycle speech" indicated that the state and its privileged worker protégés were to fulfill roles remarkably similar to that of the late-nineteenth-century bourgeois social reformer. Victorian-era "green city" discourse returned in Lula's projection of the nation as a landscaped park to be traversed by bicycle once it has been cleared of slums and purged of the miasmas emitted by open sewers. The provisional adoption of a nineteenth-century-style missionary reformist discourse by this new Left-leaning government is not surprising in itself. The Left-populist authoritarian regime of Getulio Vargas in the 1930s combined campaigns to enfranchise workers and redistribute income with moral crusades against "white slavery" (prostitution among white European migrants to Brazil) and vigorous slum-clearance campaigns in the inner city (Caulfield 1997). Lula was certainly aware of and influenced by this legacy. But equally significant was the late-twentieth-century rise of evangelical Protestant (primarily Pentecostal) churches in Brazil linked to transnational missionary and humanitarian campaigns, which have gained influence within syndicates and party organizations, and who speak a political language that revives wholesale late-nineteenth-century discourses of salvation and abolition (Corten 1999; Fonseca 2003).

These experiments in transferring Victorian-era moral-evangelical ideas into the contemporary context and articulating them with workerist projects caused considerable friction. This form of rescue politics, which was developed in the nineteenth-century context of imperialism and mass urbanization, infantilized and condescended to its objects by focusing on children first and voiceless female victims second. Set explicitly, then as now, against the "machine politics" of mass mobilization, redistribution, and aggressive, masculinized labor politics, this missionary rescue politics focuses on civilizing, evangelizing, and controlling populations. Lula's deployment of evangelical rescue discourse early in his term reflected the political need to build a supportive coalition between his Workers' Party and Pentecostals, a growing power on both the Right and Left. International factors, such as the established commitments to the Palermo Protocol, and reports by the United Nations Office against Drugs and Organized Crime (UNODC) and PESTRAF also generated significant momentum behind this alliance and its concerted discourse of rescue.[7] Another strong incentive for the adoption of this rescue politics was the state's overarching commitment to improving the image of the country in order to promote Brazil as a leader of the ascendant Global South with sufficient moral authority and political legitimacy to make a claim to a permanent seat on the UN Security Council (Bourantonis 2005; Hirst 2008).

In 2001, the US Department of State and UNODC released reports claiming that Brazil was the worst perpetrator of sex trafficking in the Western Hemisphere.[8] Even before the inauguration of President Lula in January 2003, a massive child-rescue initiative was deemed essential to Brazil's plans to legitimize and empower itself on the world stage, as well as address social-justice concerns at home. For Brazil to assume leadership of the democratic Global South, as the country established the explicit goal of claiming a permanent seat on the UN Security Council (Nieto 2012), the image of Brazilian law enforcement had to change from Death Squad to Rescue Mission, from authoritarian to humanitarian, from national security to human security. For this to happen, the landscape of the global imagination of Brazil had to be cleared of victimized children. This complex assemblage of influences and ambitions came to intersect around these antitrafficking initiatives.

In this context, we can identify the consistent operation of a second framing mechanism, that of the moralization of police paramilitarism. From 2003 to 2004, the "War of Rio"—a violent mix of organized crime, police racketeering, and armed trafficker attacks—escalated, leading to the closure of businesses and the suspension of the rule of law even in the most exclusive neighborhoods and tourist areas.[9] Attempts to reform police and disentangle them from militarized, criminal elements met stiff resistance during this period. Rather than enforce the law and bring trafficker organizations like the Red Command or Third Command to justice, police had formed a rival trafficking and extortion ring, a militia nick-named the Comando Azul (Blue Command).[10] With the police being in-volved in vigilante actions and extrajudicial assassinations, "the image of police [had] never been so negative."[11] Police and prison guards went on strike, and the Brazilian military was sent in to try to bring order to Rio's favelas. The mayor of Rio at the time, Cesar Maia, considered declar-ing an *estado de defesa*, a hybrid of a state of emergency and siege, where slums would be walled off and civil rights suspended.[12] Unable or unwill-ing to demand police reform and accountability during this time, Gover-nor Garotinho instead launched a "moralization" campaign, where police would be encouraged to assume a more ethical role promoting moral rec-titude in the population as well as within their own stations and battal-ions.[13] This initiative sought to encourage men and women police officers to self-identify as paternal and maternal figures. Appropriating and di-verting the progressive gender-empowerment initiative launched by the visionary public-security reformer Luiz Eduardo Soares, nearly three hun-dred women were integrated into the Militarized Police of Rio, but pri-marily into the tourism battalion, which was repurposed to carry out the moral mission of saving trafficked children.[14]

The moralization and sexualization of the campaign against human trafficking drew from both international and particularly Brazilian narra-tives of race, gender, and urban agency. The category of nonwhite women became defined as an intersection of vulnerabilities and dishonors, natu-ralized by skin color or social position, rather than as a category of rights claimants. For example, in a conference at the headquarters of the Rio de Janeiro State Council for Women's Rights, a government spokesperson as-serted that "Afro-descendant women, living in the margins of Rio, [and] economically excluded" were "highly vulnerable" to sex traffickers and thus would find it "difficult to travel internationally with security." At the same panel, a Federal Police officer lamented the passing of the old days of the dictatorship, when "we could just take one look at someone" and tell that "they should not travel" and deny them a passport. At the National Conference to Confront Human Trafficking in October 2008, held in Rio, the Justice Ministry affirmed, "No one will be able to leave Brazil until they can leave with dignity." This championing of dignity had the collat-eral effect of sacrificing women's rights to geographic and economic mo-bility in order to save the status, honor, and moral reputation of the state (Blanchette and da Silva 2008, 22).

The paradox of this moralistic version of abolitionist anti-sex-trafficking politics is that it expresses commitments to peculiar forms of Brazilian nationalism and links itself to the rise of a new wave of US exceptionalism, based in a mix of evangelical neoconservatism and national supremacism. As Michael C. Williams notes, this neoconservatism is driven by moralistic ideologies that idealistically ignore the shifting material bases of security in the world order, and remain hostile to "rule of law" notions of security (2007, 221).

Would the gender-sensitive moralization of the transnationally linked missions of policing affect the structural violence of police corruption and criminality in Brazil? For many years, observers had critiqued the extent to which international and local humanitarians "infantilized" Brazil's social problems (David Theo Goldberg 2011), displacing questions of race and racism, and masking the violence of state institutions and neoliberal policies. Does this evangelical fascination with rescuing miserable or immoral children (almost always represented as of African descent) actually reinforce the infantilization and disenfranchisement of blacks; reproduce stereotypes of atavism, violence, and sexualization; and promote dependence on outside humanitarian and development "experts" (Rahnema and Bawtree 1997; Smillie 2001)? Critics in Brazil have suggested providing jobs, social services, and political voice to these kids' black parents could be more effective in generating social justice and public safety than would giving more jobs and prestige to white, middle-class missionaries who want to capture and reeducate these children (Rosemberg and Feitosa Andrade 1999).

Despite these criticisms, the Brazilian state's need to reform its international image, compose a coalition between evangelicals and Left-progressives, and act aggressively in the public-security sphere led the national government, and the provincial administration in Rio de Janeiro, to launch a major campaign against sex trafficking and child slavery in 2003. Both the legalist logic of empowerment through rights and access to justice and the workerist logic of security through participatory socio-economic citizenship took back seats as the missionary logic of humanitarian moralism defined the terms of action. But the launching of the anti-sex-trafficking campaigns by the new Lula government in 2003 and the evangelical provincial administrations of Anthony Garotinho and Rosinha Matteus in Rio revealed the difficulty of proceeding with ambitious national mobilizations when the state is split between distinct securitization logics, between humanitarian legal movements, morality campaigns, worker-empowerment efforts, and liberal sexual-rights initiatives.

Rescue Operations Mobilized

Operation Princess was the shorthand term for the Rio-based operations of a broader federal and state campaign, launched (and repeatedly re-launched) between 2003 and 2005, that was officially termed "The Plan to Combat Sexual Exploitation of Children and Adolescents" and included many other operations and subplans.[15] The implementation of the overall plan began to gain momentum in early 2004, expanding with a series of media-friendly stings. In February 2004, just before Carnaval season, the chief of Rio's Civil Police announced the launch of the Division of Oversight for Public Amusement. For the first time since the 1940s, a Vice Police station would be opened, now to combat sex tourism and child exploitation in Rio during the high tourist season. Since the Civil Police in Brazil cannot deploy armed operations on the street or make arrests, their station paired its activities with the revitalized Militarized Police Battalion for Tourist Areas (BPTur), which integrated up to a hundred new women officers trained in both military and social tactics for interventions against child and adolescent prostitution.[16] The Public Ministry (similar to the Attorney General's office in the United States) issued the *Manual of Sex Crimes and Child Prostitution* to all Militarized Police Battalions, with seventy-one pages mapping crimes throughout Rio state and instructing police on how to deal with child victims of sexual exploitation.[17] The UN Special Rapporteur for Child Trafficking, Prostitution, and Child Pornography lauded Brazil for asserting itself at the vanguard of Latin America in these issues; and President Lula agreed to submit to international inspectors in its sex-work sector.[18]

Operation Carnaval became the first test of this revived Vice Police campaign.[19] As if to mock the new police operations, "the Lion of Nova Iguaçu" a "Group A" samba school (the massive dance and drum troupes that march and present their elaborate thematic floats at Carnaval), celebrated "Prostitution in Copacabana" as their theme that year. Their four thousand sequined dancers marched through the downtown Sambadrome, singing a samba about the joys of the sex trade.[20] In its debut, the police's anti-sex-trafficking campaign during Carnaval netted a total of one arrest, charging a Brazilian man with pimping. From the start, members of the Workers' Party complained that the campaign would have no real effect, since the pimps and sex traffickers worked under police protection or in rackets run by the Militarized Police themselves. The "cleaner" Federal Police would need to get involved.

As the anti-sex-slavery campaign intensified and multiple policing agencies became involved, the absurdity of having Rio's Militarized Police lead this campaign, even under the supervision of the reformed Federal Police, became apparent. In this context the first subversion mechanism, that of the tabloid crime media's fascination with closed-circuit camera footage, began to make an impact. It captured police involvement in coercing women into protection rackets and constructing rather than busting trafficker networks. In May 2004, Brazil's Federal Police infiltrated a sex-trafficking ring made up of forty-five individuals, all of whom were agents of the state, including Militarized Police officers, Civil Police officers, federal agents, customs agents, and tax collectors.[21] In July, the Civil Police closed down an illegal brothel in the district of Itatiaia in which a fifteen-year-old and a sixteen-year-old, both girls, were working; it turned out that the brothel was owned by a Militarized Police officer from the adjacent battalion.[22] In September, secret video cameras set up by media outlets to apprehend sex traffickers preying on girls instead witnessed the regular visits of eleven Militarized Police officers of the Shock Battalion (a heavily armed "special ops" unit) delivering pizza to young-adult women prostitutes and extorting protection rent from them.[23] In April 2005, a recently retired officer of the Militarized Police of Copacabana (19th Battalion), then working as a pimp, shot a Russian mercenary, Oleg Starykh, during the negotiation of the transfer of an adult sex worker. The Russian was in town for the "International Conference and Exhibit on Helicopter Technology and Operation." The tabloid media began exposing direct links between Militarized Police protection rackets and Eastern European private-sector military.[24] Their cameras exposed sex trafficking and slavery, rather than as being a local matter of the morality and deviance of urban marginals, as a transnational set of coercive relations enabled by police militarism, entrepreneurialism, and impunity, and expanded through global private-sector networking with other shadowy militarized groupings.

In this context, in April 2005 the troubled 19th Battalion of Copacabana along with the Civil Police Station for Protection of Children and Adolescents (DECA) launched the actual sting called Operation Princess.[25] The police coordinated efforts to scour Copacabana for brothels and underage sex workers. According to the testimony of a sixteen-year-old girl's mother, the operation busted a brothel in central Copacabana and arrested a twenty-three-year-old man for putting ads in the paper to recruit young escorts. Although the tabloid media were not explicitly intending to undermine the antitrafficking campaign, their revelations raised new kinds of questions and inserted the campaigns into the public sphere: Were these operations rescuing child slaves from captivity and forced labor, or harassing adults involved in consensual pursuits? Was Operation Princess making serious progress against trafficking networks, or was it breaking up independent, safe businesses, which were often run by women, and thus forcing those women onto the street, where they must submit to police protection rackets and hypermasculine, militarized transnational crime organizations?

By May 2005, a public backlash against the hypocrisies of the vice campaign had gathered steam and began to penetrate the press and public sphere, shedding light on nationalistic antitrafficking narratives and critically rebranding these panic campaigns as "genital xenophobia." Social movements acted to turn this moral-panic politics inside out, reviving a form of sex-friendly nationalism. During Operation Shangrilá the Federal Police raided a showboat in Rio's Guanabara Bay. Forty Brazilian prostitutes and twenty-nine American tourists were arrested for having committed the "crime" of sex tourism. This incident was immediately trumpeted as a major victory in the war against human trafficking. According to the sex-worker-rights NGO Grupo Davida, evangelical and humanitarian antitrafficking sites registered this operation as the capture of twenty-nine traffickers and the rescue of forty child sex slaves. But legal and rights activists, and a growing cohort of supporters in the press, soon revealed a very different reality: no Brazilian law had been violated (Grupo Davida 2005, 158). None of the prostitutes were underage, nor had they violated any pimping or brothel laws. The only way this situation could be imagined as "trafficking" is because the foreign tourists had crossed international frontiers (obviously), although without breaking any laws or violating visa restrictions. Furthermore, "sex tourism" is not against any Brazilian law, unless one assumes that consensual sex tourism is categorically always synonymous with coerced sex trafficking. Soon after Operation Shangrilá, all parties were cleared of charges, and no one was deported or imprisoned. But the police maintained it had been a "model operation," and the evangelical websites continued to trumpet the arrests as a great victory and as proof of the threat of trafficking.

In spite of this cheerleading, public opinion had by this point begun to associate these campaigns not with the polishing of Brazil's national image, but with "imperialist" interference coming from the United States. The antitrafficking campaigns that aimed to rescue the image of the nation and the purity of its children were mocked. Members of the public started to express their frustration with the Workers' Party's collaboration in these "un-Brazilian" vice raids: "In Brazil, contrary to the United States, prostitution is not illegal. So why is a group of Americans arrested in a boat full of women in Guanabara Bay even though everyone is professional and adults? To protect our sexual market? Genital xenophobia? To combat sex tourism? Why combat sex tourism if the visitors' objects of desire are adult men and women that do this by choice?" (Motta 2005, cited in Grupo Davida 2005).

The moralistic-repressive conjuncture of logics that had driven the evangelical character of these rescue campaigns was turned inside out. Rather than draw positive world attention to Brazil's redeemed law enforcement as protecting corrupted children, Operation Princess and its sister campaigns drew renewed attention to the corruption, militarization, and ethically aberrant behavior of the police, and thus of the Brazilian state itself. Instead of rescuing child slaves, these operations had apprehended adult workers. The operations had either criminalized the Brazilian adults or forced them into the street, where police rackets then attempted to capture, degrade, or extort from them. And it certainly had not helped the tourism sector, which is Rio de Janeiro's largest job creator and represents a vast sector of service, industrial, creative, and construction activities much larger than mere "sex commerce."

The focus on child sex slaves, selected as objects of rescue and subjects of securitization because of their lack of agency and rights, proved a precarious way to fuse the prerogatives of the police, evangelicals, and the juridical-legal principles of postdictatorship Brazil. These operations ended up highlighting the conflicts and incompatibilities between the governance projects of police militarism, juridical legalism, and worker nationalism, rather than providing a seamless project through which to reconcile them. In the wake of these tensions and failures, another alternative alliance emerged, reviving worker-empowerment frames in the sex-work sector. During the anti-vice period of 2003–5, Brazil's Ministry of Labor had gone against the trend in other spheres of the state and pushed antimoralistic, pro-labor perspectives, designating prostitutes officially as "tourist accompaniment workers." Meanwhile, the Tourism Ministry had jumped on the Operation Princess bandwagon and deemed prostitutes "trafficked sex slaves."[26] The more internationally linked Tourism Ministry was strongly influenced by both the UNODC/PESTRAF reports and the internationalized evangelical campaigns against sex tourism. Political appointees developing tourism-promotion campaigns were absorbed by the logic of the humanitarian militarist language and pushed a very visible campaign to vigorously police prostitution and demonize sex tourism while promoting Brazil as a destination for fans of baroque architectural heritage and ecotourism. Meanwhile, the Labor Ministry supported sex workers and promoted further regularization of prostitutes as service-workers and as bearers of broader legal status. At first, they did provisionally agree that the child prostitute was an object of "rescue," so police focused on hunting down child sex workers, rather than deploying a larger "blitz" against sexual commerce and sex tourism.

Brazil's Security Dilemmas

Security politics in Brazil in the first decade of the twenty-first century comprised a set of powerful conjunctures and contradictions, rendered visible as the nation began to make a dramatic attempt to leap from being one of the planet's most unjust, unequal societies to being a global role model of social justice, humanity, and safety. As described in its own government reports (Alston 2008; *Anuário dos Trabalhadores* 2007, 2008), Brazil remained one of the most violent and economically unequal countries on the planet. Yet it also stood out as the originator of some of the world's most progressive and admired policy agendas, including its bold commitments to provide universal AIDS care in the context of its integrated Unified Public Health System, or SUS (Berkman, Garcia, Muñoz-Lavoy, Paiva, and Parker 2005); to support affirmative action and racial justice; to achieve energy self-sufficiency; and, in the public-security sector, to promote human rights, police reform, and disarmament. Since 2000, the decentralized SUS program for universal AIDS care, particularly its Esquina da Noite (Night Street Corner) prevention program, aimed to strengthen the National Prostitutes' Network and to work with local sex-worker NGOs and networks to enable them to receive federal funds and provide preventative care and education (Pimenta, Corrêa, Maksud, Deminicis, and Olivar 2010, 19). As these forms of cooperation proceeded, leaders in the sex-worker networks realized that "it was not sufficient to intervene in HIV prevention alone, rather it was necessary to link prevention work with other issues and demands put forward by the prostitutes' movement itself . . . including aspects concerning labor rights" (Pimenta, Corrêa, Maksud, Deminicis, and Olivar 2010, 19).

Would Brazil promote its ascendance on the world stage as an advocate of gendered "human security" by championing free and universal AIDS care, rights for sex workers, and an affirmative, inclusive rights agenda for racial and sexual "minorities"? Or would Brazil define its human-security ambitions according to the terms of moral policing and a particularly paternalistic program of humanitarian rescue by focusing on excluding sex workers from AIDS alleviation programs, repressing all aspects of the sex trade, and enhancing the power of police and churches to define and limit the terms of sexual and gender publics? Or would Brazil find some accommodation that would reconcile aspects of these two alternatives by focusing on interventions that would improve Brazil's moral reputation on the world stage and reduce real, gendered violence and sexual exploitation? This could take place without allowing the agendas of missionaries and puritans to achieve hegemony in national politics in ways that recriminalize and disenfranchise sexual minority and sex-worker groups. Brazil's long history of violence, militarization, repressive securitization, and political polarization informed the high stakes of these interventions and left open the ultimate outcome of these struggles.

Since the military regime transitioned to democracy, in the late 1980s, militarization of the public-security sector in Brazil has tended to increase, not decrease in the process of "liberalization" (Huggins 2000; Wacquant 2008). During the military dictatorship that governed Brazil from 1964 to 1985, the junta executed about six thousand individuals over two decades (this number includes only victims of political assassination, not those shot as "criminals"). In the first two decades of democratization (1985–2005) the police in Brazil killed about fifteen hundred people in Rio de Janeiro and about forty thousand nationwide *each year*, according to former National Security Secretary Luiz Eduardo Soares.[27] Indeed, the democratic Brazilian state killed more people in the "urban-security operations" of the 1990s and 2000s than have been killed in any Latin American war since the nineteenth century (Mir 2004).

This grim record has been amplified by the racialization and sexualization of security politics since the 1980s, the mapping of race and sex fears onto urban spaces, and by the moralistic and bellicose character of "crime wars" on trafficking (Vargas and Amparo Alves 2010). Social movements had hoped that the election of leftist-nationalist President Lula, whose term lasted from January 2003 to January 2011, would provide space to critique and expose the causes of security-sector violence and fear politics. At first, Lula seemed to adopt the agenda of the progressive social movements, targeting police corruption and violence as primary causes of insecurity and as priorities of security-sector reform.[28] But countering this trend, new evangelical parties and right-wing morality campaigns found common cause with entrepreneurial elements of the police who were looking for a new mission that could justify their repressive, extralegal tactics, and which would block efforts to deeply reform or even wholly supplant them as the core public-security agency.

This moralistic-repressive coalition demanded broad leeway for police in their campaigns against traffickers and organized crime. The invigorated moral mandate for the Militarized Police came just as racketeering among police, particularly in Rio de Janeiro, had reached stunning new levels. In fact, between 2003 and 2007, several heavily populated working-class areas of the city were invaded and taken over by vigilante *milícias* (militias) calling themselves Autodefesas Comunitárias (Community Self-Defenders), which were in fact made up of rogue active and retired police officers in league with evangelical church operations, and which sometimes routed trafficking cartels, sometimes joined forces with the traffickers to establish absolute, extortive control over the areas (Boueri and Lemle 2006; Lemle 2007).

Bush *Ex Machina*

Brazil's antitrafficking campaigns were driven by an assemblage of contradictory securitization logics and, in part, by President Lula's need to promote the country on the international stage as a model of human security. But under pressure from three subversion mechanisms, the militarized humanitarian campaign against child sex slavery fell apart and backfired politically. These subversions exposed the forms of violence, corruption, and contradiction within the state, and disrupted attempts to promote Brazil as a unique model of security and justice for the Global South through a tense alliance between paramilitary police, labor parties, and evangelical mobilizations. The nineteenth-century missionary character of the rhetoric that surrounded these operations and the language of abolition, slavery, and warfare against crime and trafficking created no room for substantive worker's issues, legal rights strengthening, or pragmatic forms of empowerment. Creating mythic power for rescuers and protectors had ended up empowering the very racketeers that serve as the hubs of the global sex-trafficking industry. But it was when this missionary logic became identified with the military and ideological ambitions of the highly unpopular US president George W. Bush, that Rio de Janeiro's sex workers reclaimed their status as subjects of security and agency, not just as spectacles of enslavement or objects of rescue.

In 2003, just after Brazil launched its sex-rescue project, the Bush administration, via the US Agency for International Development, launched a campaign to cut off American and UN support for Brazil's AIDS program because it empowered prostitutes to serve as health advocates and as legitimate agents of the government's public-health campaign.[29] Already upset by Brazil's insistence on bending international patent protections to produce affordable HIV/AIDS medications, the US government was appalled that Brazil would reject abstinence-based approaches and instead grant commercial sex workers status as safe-sex counselors and public-health providers. Starting in 2003, Pedro Chequer, coordinator of Brazil's program to fight AIDS, rejected US$48 million in USAID/PEPFAR funds because they were tied to the public condemnation of prostitution. Mr. Chequer said, "One of the reasons for the success of the Brazilian program is exactly its realistic acceptance of the existence of prostitution, as well as homosexuality and drug addiction. To close one's eyes to this reality, as the American government wants, would be to condemn to infection not just many prostitutes, but also their clients and the spouses of their clients."[30]

President Bush's and USAID's attack on Brazil's prostitutes and its AIDS-fighting methodology was the final trigger that enabled the three subversion mechanisms—surveillance of police racketeering by tabloid media; mobilizations of worker-empowerment projects by the state and sex-worker rights groups; and the revival of a discourse of "erotic nationalism" by the tourism industry's lobbying as well as by sexual-rights advocates—to produce cumulative and coordinated effects. Public conversations in Rio began to link the internationally supported police campaign against vice and sex trafficking in Rio to the "imperialist" and "fundamentalist" attack on Brazil's sex workers and their participation in AIDS-fighting projects. The United States' attempted coup d'etat against Hugo Chavez in Venezuela in 2002 and its extremely unpopular invasion of Iraq in 2003 generated a huge wave of anti-American venom (fig. 5.3), and Brazilians started wondering: Was the police-based humanitarian intervention against sex trafficking a war of aggression against Brazil's resurgent nationalism? Was the United States or the Washington Consensus threatened by Brazil's project to empower worker agency, in this case,

FIGURE 5.3. A woman protests US president George W. Bush's decision to invade Iraq and to attack Brazilian AIDS policies during his visit to Brazil (8 March 2007). Photo credit: AP Photo / Andre Penner.

sex-worker agency? Was President Lula, the "man of the people," being targeted by Bush?

The consensus around the moralistic-repressive model and its neo-abolitionist approach to sex trafficking had been split by its tensions with other logics of state intervention from the start. But when people began linking this nineteenth-century-type agenda to contemporary US fundamentalist crusades and unpopular wars, the missionary consensus around the armed rescue of child slaves crumbled. Instead, juridical-personal justice linked up with worker-empowerment logics to form a new human-security consensus that switched sex workers from being targets to being agents, and reidentified militarized protectors as targets of reform rather than agents of mercy. A form of humanitarian legalism merged with worker-empowerment projects in the form of mobilizations by prostitutes and the Workers' Party to include sex-worker issues within the framework of state protections for workers' rights, but also, uniquely, to recognize prostitutes as providing services to the nation, leading the struggle against AIDS, and welcoming tourists whose revenues were key to development and employment in many large cities (fig. 5.4). In this sense, Bra-

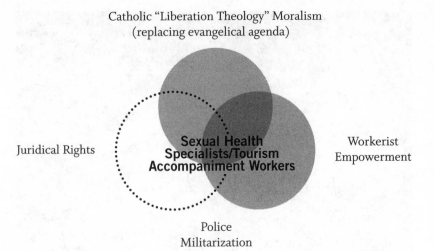

Catholic "Liberation Theology" Moralism
(replacing evangelical agenda)

Juridical Rights

**Sexual Health
Specialists/Tourism
Accompaniment Workers**

Workerist
Empowerment

Police
Militarization

FIGURE 5.4. Operation Princess's human-security field: after rearticulation of component logics. A radically more emancipatory human-security regime emerges as evangelical and police agendas are subverted and a new articulation materializes between workerists, sexual-rights activists, and progressive Catholic feminists. Militarization logics are disarticulated.

zil boldly left the neoliberal fold, along with its typical focus on extending property rights and minimizing worker rights, and its traditional delineation of sexuality as a set of limited rights associated with private expression or identity, rather than with public space and commerce. In August 2003, Justice Minister Thomaz Bastos supported a law, proposed by the Rio de Janeiro national assembly delegate Fernando Gabeira, to regularize prostitution, thus guaranteeing prostitutes' rights as a class of workers (Dantas 2003).

By the end of 2005, the Brazilian federal government and the Rio de Janeiro state police had largely abandoned, for the time, the most corrupt and militarized aspects of Brazil's anti-child-trafficking campaign. Instead, the government began to elaborate an integrated social-empowerment and gender-justice approach that linked problems of trafficking, child victimization, and AIDS to broader Workers' Party efforts to promote adult employment, end hunger, improve youth education, and reduce economic and sociopolitical marginalization. On 29 May 2008, the Brazilian Federal Police issued an arrest warrant for Anthony Garotinho, the country's chief evangelical politician and former governor of Rio de

Janeiro. He had been the key figure in the launching of Operation Princess and the mobilization of the moral crusade in 2003, when he chose to take the moralistic route, rather than purge corruption and militarism from the police. Mr. Garotinho was arrested for forming an armed gang, working with corrupt police to traffic arms and drugs, and erecting protection rackets and money-laundering operations. Evidence against the former governor revealed the great extent to which the militarized morality campaigns around Operation Princess had extended masculinized violence, impunity, and corruption, rather than alleviating the exploitation of children and women. President Lula and his social-movement allies in Rio, meanwhile, moved to expand Brazil's model anti-AIDS program, including the leadership role of sex workers within it. After the suspension of USAID funds, "the *Sem Vergonha* [Without Shame] project was created and funded exclusively by the National HIV/AIDS Program . . . as an umbrella project and focused mainly on capacity building of leaders of the National Prostitutes Network" (Pimenta, Corrêa, Maksud, Deminicis, and Olivar 2010, 23).

In June 2008, Marina Pereira Pires de Oliveira, a prominent Catholic feminist who led the drive in the Ministry of Justice in 2003 to pass new laws against sex trafficking, resigned from government and published scathing articles on how these laws had been misused to promote moralizing agendas and to increase abusive treatment of women by the state and police (de Oliveira 2008). She complained that the state had (mis)used the new laws to push an old-fashioned "normative" campaign that reinforced the perception that adult women in prostitution represented a "moral and ethical perversion" (de Oliveira 2008, 131). Also, the state had utilized the new antitrafficking laws to intensify the repressive victimization of women by increasing the extralegal detention of women, raising their sentences for vice crimes, and harassing single women traveling across borders, while virtually no "real" traffickers were brought to justice. De Oliveira suggests,

> It continues to be difficult to have a prostitute seen as any other citizen, that she can have her rights violated, but also to show that the central element of traffic is not prostitution. Although prostitutes can be victims of this crime, the [crime itself represents] the violations of rights that can be suffered by a domestic worker, a rural worker, or a sex worker. But declarations of this broader type tend not to be well received by the hegemonic morality of society

and do not help to attract allies to our banner. This is one of the traps of this matter. (2008, 133)

In October 2008, Fernando Gabeira, who had pushed for the decriminalization of practices related to prostitution (such as "facilitating" prostitution and brothel owning) and for a wholesale revision of the new laws around human trafficking, missed being elected mayor of Rio de Janeiro by one percentage point, thanks to massive electoral fraud by his opponent's supporters.[31] Gabeira's near victory demonstrated that his politics were not fringe. In December 2008, the president of the National Lawyers Guild of Rio de Janeiro served as the keynote speaker at the fourth annual meeting of the Brazilian Prostitutes Network, saying that "owners of establishments take advantage of illegality to exploit this work. With the regulation of the profession, this work will be reformed and women will receive workers' benefits, including social-security pensions" (Lenz 2008). At the same moment, Margarida Pressburger, a human-rights activist and leader of the Rio Bar Association's Human Rights Commission, inverted the moralist discourse, insisting her group would push strongly for decriminalization legislation in order to promote dignity in Rio and stop violence against women.

But in January 2009, Eduardo Paes, the mayor who had narrowly defeated Gabeira, promised to launch a new round of Operation Princess and other antitrafficking raids. And in the same year, under Law 12015/2009, the Penal Code established "domestic trafficking" as a crime, which means that any movement or "displacement" of sex workers can "be used by police and other institutions as 'proof' that sex workers living outside their places of origin are victims of trafficking" (Pimenta, Corrêa, Maksud, Deminicis, and Olivar 2010, 16–17). Would the sex-worker empowerment model of human-security governmentality survive?

Conclusion

I have explored internationalized local, federal, and transnational experiments in deploying child-rescue and antitrafficking operations, and how conflicts over the roles of worker agency, sexual citizenship, and international control led to the hasty abandonment, at least for a time, of Operation Princess and related rescue campaigns. Clashes between incommensurable logics of governance, and the actors that advocated them, led to a crisis in the security sector and to the unraveling of this platform of consensus among Brazilian evangelicals, worker-empowerment activists, and international humanitarians. Findings presented here on insecurity politics in Brazil enhance the nuance and update the applicability of constructivist political-process models in contemporary social-movement and feminist political-sociology scholarship. The case I have presented also provides resources for sexuality studies, demonstrating how conflicting logics of governance generate shifting notions of the deviant, perverse, queer, and moral not just around questions of sexual orientation, but through security crises that generate panic around the sexual citizenship of children, the rights of racialized victims, and the status of workers in sexual commerce.

The failure, even if conjunctural, of these moralizing, militarized logics of intervention around Operation Princess provide evidence that Brazil's state and civil society are still in flux, as are the articulations of its securitization logics. There are strong indications that the country has the political and discursive resources to promote new kinds of public agency and national identity. It can assert sexual rights while reigning in police militarism under the framework of a mix of humanitarian legalism and worker empowerment. This, in turn, expands the notion of "human security" beyond the militarized urban geopolitics of late-twentieth-century neoliberalism. With the dismantling of Operation Princess, Brazilian activists showed us that, under certain conditions and with certain mechanisms mobilized, they can come together to reconfigure state logics and realize a truly empowering and emancipatory human-security project of governance.

$$
\left[\; 6 \;\right]
$$

FEMINIST INSURRECTIONS AND
THE EGYPTIAN REVOLUTION

Harassing Police, Recognizing Classphobias, and Everting the
Logics of the Human-Security State in Tahrir Square

The security forces appeared from behind and front. We started running, and security police in civilian clothes ("baltagiyya") started grabbing randomly many young men and women. I saw them grab and beat a young innocent man, pushed him to the ground and kept kicking. I protested against the beating up, and kept screaming at them to stop acting like animals. 4 or 5 huge men grabbed me from my hair and said "well join him you bitch" and slapped me on the face and cornered me next to the young man and kept hitting me on my head, arm, shoulder, back, stepping on my head with their shoes until I bled from my mouth and could not speak any more on the ground. . . . They threw us all in the microbus. And while pushing me inside they were trying to pull off my clothes and sexually harassed me, one grabbed my breasts, another held my waist, and another grabbed my bottom. They grabbed the mobile from me, then threw me to the asphalt road. Despite the pain, I will go on protesting. — **Mona Prince**, Egyptian writer and professor, during the "Day of Rage" protests, 25 January 2011

Egyptians! Four people set themselves on fire because they hated the security agencies and did not fear the fire. Four people set themselves on fire in order for you to awaken. We are on fire so that you will take action. . . . I have no intention of destroying myself, but if you police will set me on fire, go ahead! Because I am not leaving Tahrir Square. — **Asmaa Mahfouz**, young woman leader of the 6 April national labor movement, addressing protesters in Tahrir Square on 18 January 2011, video of which "went viral" in Egypt and helped spark mass uprising on 25 January

The uprisings and mass protests that occupied Tahrir Square in central Cairo between 25 January and 15 February 2011 were haunted by the figure of "sexual harassment" or, to put it more accurately, by the sexualized assault and terrorizing of women activists. Gender-sensitive coverage of the revolution by Egyptian, as well as Western, media outlets provided two contrasting frames of representation, constructing two incommensurable sets of metaphors for the gendered security predicament of Tahrir Square. One framing was that of Tahrir Square as a utopian space, forging a new gendered social contract (El-Saadawi 2011) and hosting a new "model for how democracy should be" (Naib 2011). There, Egypt's rich and poor, men and women, people and state, struggled to establish and perform a new concord based on mutual respect and human dignity, with assertive women youth activists as primary articulators of this accord. On the eve of what would become a revolution, Asmaa Mahfouz summoned Egyptians to Tahrir Square. She did not claim the international subject of "woman victim" in order to decry human-rights violations or to plead for police and legal protections. Instead, she described herself metaphorically as an "Egyptian on fire." Explicitly not a suicide bomber, Mahfouz recounted how her fire — her rage and righteousness and political passion — was dismissed as hysteria, madness, and shame by the State Security officers and thugs who attacked her initial, small protests. She presented herself as a fearless, unprotected woman in public channeling the "manhood" (rugula) of Egypt through political action, in order to make legible the violence of the state and to challenge the security state's manipulation of notions of gendered honor. "Show your honor and manhood and come down to Tahrir on 25 January. If not, then you are a traitor to the nation, like the police and the President are traitors" (Mahfouz 2011b) (fig. 6.1).

In a second set of representations wholly incompatible with those above, Tahrir served as the mosh pit for a hypermasculine mob where orientalist tropes of the "Arab street" were concentrated and bottled up. This was a space constantly bursting with predatory sexuality and not disciplined enough to articulate either coherent leadership or policy. These latter, phobic representations in the international media were tempered for a time after plain-clothes police and Mubarak-allied thugs viciously attacked the CNN journalist Anderson Cooper (Hajjar 2011). In the wake of this attack, journalists articulated a tentative new discourse in which brutality in Egypt, including sexualized brutality, was seen as an instrument of state terror that the police state deployed tactically, rather than as a cultural attribute shared by all male Arabs. But just a few days later, when a similar attack was made against the South African CBS correspondent Lara Logan, most of what had been learned during the analysis of the attack on Cooper was suddenly forgotten (Kurtz 2011; Lindsey 2011). Instead, Logan's blondeness and femininity were incessantly underlined, and the discourse of the "frenzied" Arab mob and its uncontrollable sexu-

FIGURE 6.1. The political activist Asmaa Mahfouz in February 2011. Photo credit: Al Masry Al Youm / Mohamed Hesham (http://www.almasry-alyoum.com).

ality returned with a vengeance (Gharavi 2011, 5). Fox News condemned the entire Egyptian people as not yet ready for modernity or democracy, with Glenn Beck insisting that the incident proved his theory that the uprisings were backed by an "Islamofascist" conspiracy (Easley 2011). As the blogger Maya Mikdashi wrote, "The use [by the *New York Post* and Fox News] of the words 'animals' and 'beasts' to describe the male protesters at Tahrir Square, who are all rendered potential rapists within this discourse of the sex crazed Muslim/Arab mob, highlights what is perhaps an uncomfortable truth about political discourse in the United States today. In the contemporary US, it is socially acceptable to vilify Arabs and/or Muslims, just as it is OK to be outspokenly racist against this group of people" (2011).

Media reports did not consider that the harassers could have been plain-clothes paramilitaries or subcontracted thugs sent by State Security to attack internationals, as they had been doing for weeks, or that the attacks could have been stirred up by the incessant government propaganda insisting that "imperialist journalists" should be challenged and humiliated. Instead, the media ignored the issue of the security state and its practices. The predatory culture of Muslim men became the talking point. No reporters followed up on the fact that Logan had been rescued by a group of Egyptian young women political activists and twenty male military officers. Were these subjects not also representative of Egypt, "Muslim culture," and the revolution?

In this chapter I explore the deeper social-historical context and political culture of women's movements around urban public sociability, sexualized state terror, and the policing of what is called "sexual harassment" (*al-taharrush al-jinsi*) in Egypt's public and political spaces. Through this lens, the progressive achievements of the recent Egyptian Revolution can be seen as driven in significant part by the ingenuity of Egyptian feminist activists who have mobilized new kinds of assertive women's subjectivities. They are critiquing the sexual agenda of police-state repression while also deconstructing the class and geopolitical interests behind international and local discourses that portray working-class Arab men and Islamic cultures as inherently predatory. These feminist agendas have been forged at the contentious intersection of United Nations–level, Arab regional, and Egyptian subaltern forms of feminist mobilization.

I also explore how feminist movements in Egypt confronted the gendered governance logics of the human-security state in the lead-up to the mass uprisings of January and February 2011. I analyze, in particular, the processes by which sexual harassment politics in the Global South came to serve as a crucial laboratory for testing and reformulating the mix of emancipatory and repressive securitization practices that constitute contemporary gender-sensitive security states. In Egypt, between 2003 and 2010, internationalist feminist campaigns advocated antiharassment projects that demonized working-class youth masculinities as well as "disreputable" public femininities in an attempt to intensify the policing of the city and discipline public sociability. Through a politics of respectability, a hypervisibilization of working-class "thug" (*baltagi*) masculinities, and "strange bedfellow" processes of NGOization, a set of state-allied, middle-class-linked, and UN-system-recognized feminist organizations generated antiharassment campaigns that demobilized class-conscious movements for democratic change and amplified calls for police to intensify enforcement efforts to ensure the "protective" segregation of class and gender groups. By contrast, a set of alternative and effective working-class-linked Egyptian organizations bent UN gender doctrines and legal mechanisms to their own purposes, mobilizing mass campaigns that critiqued frameworks of police protection and social respectability. They cultivated forms of assertive female agency came to occupy center stage during the Egyptian Revolution that began with the uprisings in January and February 2011. In order to reveal the mechanism that generated change in governance and mobilization practices during this period, I compare these two forms of global/local feminist organizing and assess which mobilizing tactics and frameworks of gendered representation were most (and least) successful for countering the social products of the securitization logic I term "the baltagi effect." In analyzing these forms of state securitization, social movement organization, and media framing, I reveal the queering power of new metaphors of masculinity, class struggle, and global female insecurity. My analysis also helps build a new critical theory of security-state practice that identifies alternative Global South feminisms that contest rather than facilitate securitized and militarized appropriations of internationalist gender and security interventions.

Securing Women

In the year 2000, the UN Security Council passed Resolution 1325 on "Women, Peace, and Security," designed to assure the inclusion of women in military-humanitarian deployments and to legalize international armed interventions in response to rape, femicide, and sexual violence in situa-

FIGURE 6.2. Hillary Clinton promoting US support for coordinating the US action plan and a global approach to the UN Security Council Resolution on "Women, Peace, and Security" (Washington, 19 December 2011). Photo credit: Georgetown University.

tions of armed conflict, as well as in the context of peacekeeping operations (Shepherd 2008). In May 2003, UNSCR 1325 was cited in the preamble to UNSCR 1483, which authorized the US invasion of Iraq. This weaponized the gender/security resolution as "a tool to justify military occupation on behalf of 'liberating' women" (Cohn, Kinsella, and Gibbings 2004, 138). And, by 2009, UNSCR 1325 was being cited in Egypt as a precedent for deploying police and state-of-emergency powers in order to protect women, in the local context, from street harassment (fig. 6.2).

In 2005, the *Arab Human Development Report*—which is published annually by the United Nations Development Program and which, in the past twenty years, has become a controversial forum for liberal-secular-cosmopolitan voices in the Middle East—focused its entire volume on "the rise of women in the Arab world" (Regional Bureau for Arab States, UNDP 2006). The report identified the problems of sexual harassment of women and the discriminatory attitudes of Arab men as priority "human-security" concerns, marking the shift in UN "Women, Peace, and Security" discourse from the ambit of war, genocide, and state terror toward a sphere of morality, personal attitudes, and quotidian class and gender violence. In July 2009, Egyptian First Lady Suzanne Mubarak hosted an extraordinary meeting of the Non-Aligned Movement, in Egypt's heavily militarized Sinai beach resort of Sharm alSheikh. The First Ladies Summit of the Non-Aligned Movement focused its agenda on demands to increase state protection of women and girls through intensified policing of sexual harassment and transnational trafficking (Leila 2009). In July 2010, at the Regional Workshop for Arab Parliaments, women parliamentarians discussing the implementation of the Convention on the Elimination of All Forms of Discrimination against Women (CEDAW) spent much of their time fine-tuning legislative language around sexual harassment and sex trafficking.[1] As Sally Engle Merry analyzed, the CEDAW is "a cultural system whose coin is admission into the international community of human-rights compliant states. At the heart of this legal process of monitoring this international human rights convention is the cultural work of altering the meanings of gender and of state responsibility for gender equality [through which] national and international NGOs . . . shame non-compliant governments [whose] sovereignty [is] increasingly defined as contingent on its human rights performance" (2003, 943).

Despite the fact that they were meeting in Beirut—a city troubled by bursts of renewed sectarian violence and protests led by immigrant women domestic laborers and rebuilding in the wake of Israeli bombing raids—the parliamentarians discussing violence against women ignored the looming questions of war, refugees, and labor migration as women's issues. Instead, the politicians highlighted the cultural problems of Arab men committing sexual harassment in city streets, which they termed a "human-security" priority.

But what does this securitization of feminist humanitarianism and its politics of shame look like on the ground, in the quotidian fabric of class conflict, gender power, and authoritarian politics in the security states of today's Middle East? In the area of providing security for and preventing violence against women, UN policy consensus and the practice of its government and NGO allies have gravitated away from war and macroeconomic development toward daily life and morality. And within this sphere of daily life, policy is shifting away from a private space and cultural backwardness model that had focused on policing domestic violence, protecting individual dignity in the workplace, and reforming aberrant "cultural practices" such as genital mutilation, honor crimes, and misogynist personal status laws. Instead, we have witnessed a move in internationalist feminism toward an emphasis on public morality, that is, toward a social deviance model (or urban vice model) concerned with enforcing access to public space, reforming public masculinities, and moralizing and desexualizing urban quality of life.

Of course, these two models of intervention—culturalist and urbanist—are not mutually exclusive and have overlapping historical and social origins. For example, in the high-colonial period of 1880–1930, transnational temperance and "anti-white slave" campaigns piggybacked on colonial and missionary governance projects that fused feminist internationalism, Protestant moralism, and working-class-phobic policing efforts (Margaret Jacobs 2005). This is not to say that the contemporary re-ascendance of urban-vice forms within international feminist antiviolence politics simply reflects colonial continuity. Instead, the articulation of this politics indicates that coloniality informs broader changes in the nature of security-state governance today. This public space and social deviance model has been taken up by the security state in Egypt, and the figure of sexual harassment has became a nodal controversy for addressing (and deflecting) issues of labor mobility, police brutality, class conflict, youth alienation, and social disintegration in an increasingly polarized polity. It is novel and broadly significant that these urban efforts, which merged juridical and cultural forms of protection, were legitimized by and tied into new international law efforts to regulate warfare and to deploy emergency UN security and humanitarian interventions around the figure of the woman, rescripted and deployed by class actors and security-state operations in Egypt.

To this point, most analyses of the rise of human-rights internationalism have consisted of studies of agents of dissemination and routes of diffusion from north to south. These studies have provided insights into the emergence of the modern form of human-rights internationalism in Europe after the Second World War; the mobilization of coalitions that articulated those norms into codified international doctrines, treaties, and resolutions around the United Nations; and the social movements, cultural discourses, and communicative networks that channeled these norms toward the postcolonial, "nondemocratic" world (Finnemore and Sikkink 1998; Lutz and Sikkink 2000; Sikkink 1993; Steiner and Alston 2008). Studies of diffusion have focused on the achievement of certain "tipping points" where gender and security norms are accepted by a critical mass of relevant government actors, allowing a "norm cascade" to facilitate processes of institutionalization and internalization (Hill 2005, 59). Felicity Hill argues that UNSCR 1325 generated its "tipping point" through NGO-organized public campaigns, report writing, and individual meetings with Security Council members and UN forums (Hill 2005, 59). However, what if the norm cascade occurs when these discourses are appropriated, resignified, and built into subjects of power at various scales, rather than when public campaigns at the top rain enlightenment on backward institutions in the Global South or at the local level?

The dissemination model or globalization-as-enlightenment model, in general, has come under criticism from two sides in the past two decades. One cluster of critical scholarship focuses on the Western colonial character and imperialist imperatives that may be attached to the dissemination of liberal political rights. Human rights are seen as divorced from (or opposed to) global struggles for economic and social rights, and unconscious of (or reproducing) the racial, colonial, religious, and cultural prejudices embedded within Western legalities and identities (Cobbah 1987; Massad 2002; Mohanty 1988; Mutua 2001). Another cluster of scholarship has focused on international human-rights doctrines and resolutions as spheres of contention, sets of signifying practices, and repertoires or "tool boxes" that have neither an ideal form or singular direction of dissemination, nor one meaning or legacy that would maintain them as exclusive property of the West (An-Na'im 1995; An-Na'im 1996; Goodale 2006; Grewal 2008; Grewal and Kaplan 2006; Merry and Goodale 2007; Orford 2003; Slyomovics 2005). These scholars demonstrate that human rights and international law can be reworked and rearticulated by struggles and signifying practices in the Global South that do not set aside or ignore colonial legacies, military imperatives, or the liberal limitations of "disseminated" human-rights internationalism. Instead, they raise consciousness about these legacies or render them politically legible and recognizable. In doing so, they remake human-rights politics by rearticulating it with alternative struggles explicitly linked to class, development, religion, and cultural justice.

In this chapter I build on this latter set of approaches. In so doing, I do not trace the routes of missionaries and disseminators, nor do I spotlight the "Westernness" of human-rights internationalism in a way that reproduces simplistic notions of the unitary power of the West. Instead, as throughout this book, I identify processes of appropriation, resignification, and contradiction in the dense space of social, cultural, and urban-spatial intersections in the Global South. Here I examine the clashing ways that UN resolutions and international feminist human-rights doctrines materialize in the context of class inequalities, institutional conflicts, cultural innovations, and complex matrices of governance. I draw on an "urban geopolitics" approach (Graham 2004) and on the praxis of feminists in Egypt themselves (Mozn Hassan 2011; Ilahi 2010) to develop a political sociology of how states deploy class, youth, and masculinity around the enforced protection of women, and provide a mapping of the securitization of "war on terror"–era feminist internationalisms.[2] I do this by examining lively subaltern political spheres in the megacity of Cairo that gave rise to contradictory deployments of gendered practices of protection and violation during the Egyptian Revolution itself.

Dynamics of Securitization

The term *securitization* emerged in the Copenhagen School for Peace Studies in the late 1990s (Buzan, Waever, and de Wilde 1998) in order to describe how political speech acts or media representations produce subjects of politics that "justify" the transformation of everyday social, economic, and cultural governance into emergency police enforcements and military occupations. I regroup these subjects into the category "parahuman." In relation to the study of colonial or postcolonial governance, the term *parahuman* has been utilized to refer to populations "disabled" by racism or war. Genetic science and sci-fi discourse also use the term parahuman, but to refer to chimeras, mutants, or modified embryos. My use of this term is specific to the sphere of contemporary transnational security practices. I define this term as the semantic child of paramilitarization and humanitarianism; and, in turn, humanitarianism can be defined as securitized parahumanism.

Semiprivatized, but state-serving, parastatal enforcement agencies increasingly deploy humanitarian forms of securitization. These agents include certain police-dependent or military-embedded NGOs. Parahuman subjects are thus hypervisibilized subalterns who become fetishized subjects of politics, while their ability to act in emancipatory ways is buried by multiple intersecting modes of sexual, cultural, moral, and social discipline. These are forms of both racializing and queering power. Notions and categories of racial blackness or sexual orientation are not universal. Nevertheless, security doctrines and governance practices move transnationally to deploy and institute modes of embodiment composed of sexualized and bodily-marked fear and desire (Amar 2010, 1–15). In this light, securitized power is essentially about queering and racing subjects who are segregated by gender and culture. By "queering," I do not mean the policing of lesbian, gay, bisexual, transgender (LGBT), or non-heteronormative populations or even the emancipatory reappropriation of those policed spaces by sexual dissidents. Rather, here I am interrogating "queering" in one of its avatars, as a set of security-state practices that generate sexualized, criminalized, and sanctioned subjects of social and moral panic. These subjectifications naturalize and justify the intensification of enforcement regimes and hierarchies, anchoring the coloniality of securitization. Thus, the intensity of queering is directly proportional to its sexualized coloniality, not to its homosexuality. And progressive queer politics is then identified with performative recognitions and reversals of the processes of sexualized coloniality at the heart of security-state interventions. It may be useful to underline that in this framework there is no "real" nonqueer or nonraced or noncolonial subject underneath the parahuman subjects of security. But this parahuman positionality can also be a nodal site for change. This position becomes an agent if analyses and narratives illuminate state and elite forces of subjectification, rendering queered subjects recognizable, articulate, and legible; that is, if securitization dynamics are turned inside out.

Here, sexuality operates as a power grid of fear and desire engineered by the colonial humanitarianization of modern subjects of governance. In the context of sexualized human-security governance, subjectivity can gain agency by embracing submission to these subjectifying disciplines, where, as Saba Mahmood argues, "submission to forms of (external) authority is a condition for the self to achieve its potentiality" (2005, 149). This trajectory would include the process by which hypervisible subjects assimilate into apolitical invisibility via the practice of respectability. However, alternative feminist projects in Egypt can, and do, challenge the project of cultivating the ethical self or performing respectable sociality. To put this conceptual and theoretical framework into action, I examine the complex politics of harassment, feminist internationalism, and human-security state practice.

As Protests Surged, the Security State Regendered

In the 1990s and 2000s, waves of political protests and strikes surged in Egypt, year by year. Those who followed these labor mobilizations were not surprised by the revolutionary events of 2011. Since the International Monetary Fund restructuring agreement of 1994 and the Asian Financial Crisis of 1997, Egyptian farmers protested at being evicted from their smallholdings by the mechanization of agriculture and by the prerevolutionary landowning classes' reclaiming of estates. Workers' groups reorganized and held nationwide strikes and sit-ins in response to the privatization of factories, the closing of manufacturing collectives (Beinin 2011a), and the liberalization of trade with China, Russia, and the European Union. Social movements, the Muslim Brothers, and judges' syndicates challenged political exclusion and authoritarian rule. And feminist groups—middle-class seculars, Islamic feminists, working-class populists, and others—grew more visible and central to protest movements and as legal, cultural, and political innovators. In these contexts, working-class women were often the most organized and often generated the majority force behind the national strikes and mass protests that led to the January 25 Revolution of 2011 (Amar 2011b).

In the period between 2003 and 2006, levels of mass public protests in Cairo escalated dramatically, driven by the renaissance of an Arab nationalist sentiment and antiwar mobilization caused by outrage at the US invasion of Iraq and the Israeli raid on Lebanon. Both of these actions centered on the bombing of civilian targets and infrastructures, inflicting mass casualties largely ignored and rendered invisible by US and Israeli media coverage, but covered extensively in the Arab media. This period also witnessed the rise of a new assertiveness among political opposition parties and the formation of new fronts and alliances among leftists, liberals, and democratic Islamists in Egypt aiming to end the three-decades-long state of emergency (initiated after the assassination of President Sadat in 1981), to identify alternative presidential candidates to replace President Muhammad Hosni Mubarak, and to block the accession of his son, Gamal.

The security state's initial response to the rising tide of protests during the 1990s was to attempt to delegitimize, intimidate, and blur both the image and message of these movements by infiltrating and surrounding them with plain-clothes thugs, deputized by police and paramilitary security forces. Whereas in the 1990s, *baltagiyya* (the gangs of "thugs" and networks of violent extortion rackets seen as emanating from the informal settlements surrounding downtown Cairo) were identified as terrorist enemies of the security state (Ismail 2006, 145), by the 2000s, the baltagiyya had been appropriated as useful tools of the police. The Interior Ministry recruited these same gangs to flood public spaces during times of protest (Tisdall 2006). They were ordered to mix with protesters and shout extremist slogans in order to make the activists look like "terrorists," or, alternately, to wreak havoc, beating civilians and doing property damage in the area of the protest, while, of course, brutalizing the protesters themselves (El-Nadeem Center 2006). These practices aimed to produce what I call the *baltagi effect*. This effect not only terrorized the protesters but also generated new images for domestic and international media and criminological narratives for international security agencies and local law enforcement. Protesters were resignified as crazed mobs of brutal men, vaguely "Islamist" and fiercely irrational, depicted according to the conventions of nineteenth-century colonial-orientalist figurations of the savage "Arab street" (Bayat 2003; Lynch 2003). And protesters became targeted as assemblages of hypersexualized terrorist masculinities. As analyzed so vividly by Jasbir Puar (2007), these masculinities are configured as the necessary and codependent constituents of twenty-first-century forms of both liberal incorporation and geopolitical domination. In Egypt, the security state thus deployed and revived the Islamophobic, gendered, and working-class-phobic metaphor of the "Arab street," rendering peaceful political movements with overwhelming public support into hypervisible, but utterly unrecognizable, mobs. The production of such hypervisible parahuman subjects is regularized by discourses that cohere around powerful metaphors (Carver and Pikalo 2008). In this case, I focus on the overarching metaphor of the "Arab street," whose meaning is enhanced by a field of other gender and culture metaphors, in particular, the "time bomb," the "predator," and the "slum."

As analyzed by Rabab El-Mahdi, "In the first occasion, those feminist activists defined the enemy as state security, but used a lot of objectification messages related to the 'honor of women' which definitely served the purposes of temporary mobilization but were harmful in the long-term since it prompted the counter call of 'women should preserve their honor by not joining demonstrations'" (2009, 130). In response to such challenges and to the public spectacle of this orchestrated baltagi effect or Arab-street effect in the 2000s, Egyptian feminists generated plans to publicly deploy gender and class-specific protests in order to resist the performative cultivation of terroristic hypermasculinity by the Egyptian security state. Since the staging of "terrorist-mob" performances depended on the powerful colonial metaphors attached to the bodies of brutal working-class men, Egyptian progressive organizations realized that placing "respectable" (i.e., upper-middle-class) women in mass protests could play a crucial symbolic role. This is not because of anything essential to the gender or political subjectivity of this class of women, but because they were deployed in specific strategic relation to the metaphor of the hypermasculine Arab street. Women's intervention in public space became politically powerful because the human-security state had invested so intensively in generating and hypervisibilizing women as subjects of piety, self-policing, moralization, and cultural security. In this context, activists theorized that if women (particularly those visibly marked by class and moral bearing as pious and respectable) were to stand up against the police, rather than collaborate with them,[3] the logic of hypervisibility and misrecognition could be subverted, to some extent (El-Nadeem 2006).

In addition to this gendered security-state dynamic, women political protesters in Egypt draw on a social history of Arab nationalist modernity that has embodied the nation in the figure of the woman (particularly the respectable, literate, middle-class mother) (Baron 2007; El Shakry 2007, 165–96). So when women professors, medical doctors, lawyers, university students, and syndicate leaders began to command the barricades at major political protests, it became difficult for the state to draw on class and geopolitical phobias to portray them as terrorists; the thugification tactic or baltagi effect unraveled. Granted, the international media, and even many Egyptian reporters, could easily believe that crazed thugs could emerge "naturally" from within a group of working-class male leftists and Islamists. However, when middle-class Egyptian women were harassed, terrorized, and brutalized by men during protests, this allowed for a disarticulation of the body politic of the protesters from that of the brutalizers, enabling a recognition that the baltagiyya were cops in plain clothes, not men from within the dissident organizations. This strategic placement of certain classed and gendered bodies at the forefront of protests successfully eroded the "Arab mob" metaphor. The state responded by shifting its aims from using demonized masculinity in order to delegitimize political opposition to using state-imposed sexual aggression in order to undermine class respectability. Women who protested were sexualized and had their respectability wiped out, not just by innuendo and accusation, but literally, by being sexually assaulted in public and getting arrested for prostitution, being registered in court records and press accounts as sex criminals, and then getting raped and sexually tortured in jail (El-Nadeem Center 2004; El-Nadeem Center 2006; Tisdall 2006). The aim was to render impossible the figure of the respectable, pious woman as a legitimate protester against the police, rather than as a victim protected or rescued by the police. Any woman who protested would be juridically categorized as a prostitute, would be given a police file and criminal record, and would have her body and psychological integrity broken (Al-Dawla 2008).[4]

Everting Gendered Security

In this section I identify and map an alternative Egyptian feminist approach to the politics of sexualized violence against women, one generated by Cairo's El-Nadeem Center as it struggled to counter the Egyptian security state's gender logic of repression during this period. Its approach rescripts the roles of women activists in three ways: (1) they are rendered expert disassemblers of respectability discourse, rather than as victims of shame and dishonor; (2) they are interpellated as laborers conscious of the violence of class repression and how those battles take place in public space, rather than as gendered consumers unmarked by class; and (3) they are imagined as physically assertive challengers to the police state who strive to apprehend and illuminate the state's and elites' complicity in generating and exploiting hypervisible subjects of masculinity, femininity, and respectability. This innovative mobilizing framework was confronted by the backlash of internationally linked antiharassment NGOs, which deployed a more standard middle-class, law-enforcement-centered rescue-protection framework. As a primary articulator of this "alternative feminism," the El-Nadeem Center for the Rehabilitation of Victims of Violence in Cairo (or El-Nadeem) led national and international campaigns from 2003 to 2009 to expose the state's efforts to assault the respectability of its most effective dissidents through systematic sexual violence.

El-Nadeem is not a typical NGO in Egypt in that it has systematically resisted trends toward "NGO-ization" (Alvarez 2009, 175–77). It does not seek to "modernize" women or to realize cultural or development projects. Instead, El-Nadeem offers direct psychological and medical aid to victims of police harassment in the streets and to victims of torture in prison, particularly to women or others whose harassment or torture displays a gendered or sexualized dimension (El-Nadeem Center 1998b; El-Nadeem Center 2002). El-Nadeem has never become "NGOized" or appropriated by the state or neoliberal agendas. But the price of this independence has been that it has suffered repeated raids and intimidation (El-Nadeem Center 1998a, 1998b, 2002, 2004). Sabine Lang (1997) defines NGOization as the process by which radical and redistributive movements, including feminism, become contained and reframed so as to service rather than resist neoliberal globalization. Islah Jad, in "The NGOization of Arab Women's Movements," argues that "NGOization has a cultural dimension, spreading values that favor dependency, lack of self reliance, and new modes of consumption" (2007, 175); NGOization leads away from the generation of ideological alternatives, toward ad hoc, project-based development (Morena 2006). Anna Marie Smith, when looking at the "reform" of the welfare state in the United States, has traced an equivalent process whereby states withdraw from redistributive policies and intensify moral policing of class-inflected, racialized, and sexualized gender. The participation of women's NGOs in this project is essential for the ideological construction of this process as "a vehicle for the delivery of therapeutic intervention," when they would otherwise be read as deploying punitive and disempowering mechanisms (Anna Marie Smith 2007, 4–5). According to Kristin Bumiller, when "sexual violence became important to the agenda of the 'therapeutic state' . . . the feminist movement became a partner in the unforeseen growth of a criminalized society, a phenomenon with negative consequences . . . for those women who are subject to scrutiny" (2008, xii). Janet Halley (2006) calls this political project "governance feminism," where certain feminists operate through state projects in alliance with World Bank and police officials, deploying a three-pronged governmentality that she calls the injury triad: female harm (victim subjects), female innocence (class-marked and infantilized subjects), and male immunity (predator subjects). This injury triad "places its feminism in a position to trump all players and all contesting visions. . . . Objectively verified and morally absolute, the Injury Triad comes in as the a priori of politics" (Halley 2006, 338–39).

Seeing through these critical lenses, we can reframe the struggles around the NGOization of the women's antiviolence movement in Egypt as the institutionalization of a class-specific politics of respectability (Balos and Fellows 1999; Stoler 1989; White 2001). Respectability politics does the governance work of queering vulgar subjects of disrespect that are essentially racialized (or embodied as parahuman) and then sexualized as targets for rescue and therapeutic intervention, reviving colonial practices of social control in the guise of emancipatory civil society action. This process makes up what UN doctrine and Egyptian state discourse constitute as "human-security" deployments. As analyzed from two distinct directions by Jacqui Alexander (1994) and Karen Booth (2004), the nationalist politics of respectability among the postcolonial ruling classes in the semiperiphery of the Global South can appropriate a certain feminist politics of gendered respect that reproduces colonial notions of class distinction and generates its own menagerie of queer targets for discipline, spectacle, and punishment.

In much of the critical gender studies scholarship on the politics of rights in the Muslim world, the history and power of "respectability politics" have dropped out of analysis. For example, the groundbreaking work of Saba Mahmood has analyzed women's mosque-based "piety circles" that teach scripture, shape behavior, and moralize social relations in a way "considered germane to the cultivation of the ideal virtuous self" (2005, 2). Mahmood finds these practices that emphasize moral subjects who perfect their own conformity to rules to be radically non-Western and incompatible with international feminist traditions of the liberal subject of rights, autonomy, and self-emancipation. One can complement and extend this argument, reinserting the politics of piety into the long tradition of the state's involvement in disciplining the respectability of the nation's women. After all, the Egyptian state, until 2011, did appoint all imams in Egypt and also carefully controlled mosque sermons. Given this context, perhaps we need to shift the axis of analysis of gender politics away from the frame of "liberal rights versus Islamic virtue" to one of "respectability versus vulgarity." With this shift, the political theory of class, space, and the body asserts itself differently. The West-East and liberal-religious binaries dissolve into more complex matrices of intersections and contradictions, as evidenced in the work of Omnia El Shakry (2007) on the formation of respectable middle-class modernity through the invention of domestic mothering; of Khaled Fahmy (2002) on the "vulgar" protests of women nurses and prostitutes in nineteenth-century Egypt; of Bruce Dunne (1996) on the nationalist cultivation of respectable spaces versus subjects of "debaucherous" sexuality; and of Wilson Jacob (2011) on the urban discipline of street boys and the emergence of middle-class respectability. These scholars open up the conjunctures around and between class, embodiment, propriety, and sexualized morality.

Likewise, El-Nadeem's contemporary campaign around harassment represents a self-conscious effort to engage the complex, intersectional history of piety movements and respectability politics in both internationalist and nationalist gender politics in Egypt. El-Nadeem's campaign against harassment and torture in public space and jails began in the 1990s, but expanded in the 2000s as the baltagi effect began to impact the practices of protest and repression (El-Nadeem Center 1998a; El-Nadeem Center 2004). However, rather than aim to rehabilitate the respectability and piety of the harassed protesters, El-Nadeem kept the light of critique aimed at the state, the practices of the state security services, and police and prison officials. Shame, immorality, and hypocrisy were to be exposed in the security state (not among working-class boys). And middle-class professionals who collaborated with the state—in particular, doctors, social workers, and aid officials—were held responsible for "crimes against humanity" in the El-Nadeem reports. As analyzed by the Egypt-based political scientist Rabab El-Mahdi, El-Nadeem remains conscious of "the dialectical relationship between participants forming this initiative and their organizational structure, the discourse and frames they use, and the broader political context in which they exist" (2010, 384).

El-Nadeem made a bold move: rather than try to rehabilitate the reputation of middle-class political protesters, they insisted that even "real" prostitutes did not deserve disrespect and harsh treatment by the police and state. El-Nadeem made the pioneering move to offer legal aid and psychological treatment, not just to political dissidents abused and branded as prostitutes, but also to actual working-class sex workers. Those who had suffered police harassment and torture were given equal access to El-Nadeem's legal aid, counseling, and social resources. El-Nadeem provided these abjected workers a platform from which to speak, recording their testimonies and stories alongside those of jailed political leaders. Prostitutes were not treated as "trafficking victims" to be forcibly rescued and redeemed, but as workers whose public rights and erotic capital were being violated and extorted by police rackets and state violence. Thoroughly everting (turning inside out) the gendered respectability politics of the security state, El-Nadeem made campaigns against torture in custody and sexual harassment in the street into a political movement against the repressive policing practices of the security state. The logic of hypervisibility and moral panic was rearticulated into a campaign to bring political recognition to a campaign for gendered social justice.

In 2006–7, El-Nadeem and a few other bold groups began to expand the campaign against police sexual harassment and torture of politicized and criminalized groups by filing lawsuits against police and other individuals for having committed al-taharrush al-jinsi (sexual harassment). In this framing, harassment was not a timeless problem linked to masculinity (Amar 2011a). Rather, harassment was defined as the particular perversion practiced by the repressive security state. Everting the essentialist gender politics and respectability project of the UN-linked campaign, El-Nadeem and allied organizations in 2007–8 made another bold move, queering the NGOization framework again by reaching across gender and class divides to report on the state's sexual harassment and abuse of young male prostitutes and youth labor union protesters.

In 2007, police in Cairo rounded up groups of young men whom they identified as homosexual prostitutes; in 2008, unarmed boy factory workers in Mahalla al-Kubra were shot with rubber bullets and arrested. Youths in both cases were harassed, sexually brutalized, and then photographed, bloodied and handcuffed to prison hospital beds, in order to spectacularize their humiliation and intimidate the public (El-Nadeem Center 2008). El-Nadeem revealed the gender-constructive nature of the state's hyper-hetero-masculinity, while refusing the UN trend and NGO-ization process that favored re-essentializing the categories of femininity, heteronormativity, respectability, and victimization by focusing instead on state sexual violence against middle-class women protesters and prostitutes, male hustlers, and workers alike.

NGOization Strikes Back: Policing Time-Bomb Masculinity

In 2006–7, a series of events created opportunities for the human-security state to block the momentum of the El-Nadeem Center's counterhegemonic project, pulling the rug from underneath its radical gender politics. The state reasserted its dominance by fusing police powers, gendered morality politics, and class respectability discourse in a new, internationally articulated, multimedia campaign against sexual harassment. As reported by the magazine *Al Jadid*, "During the downtown celebrations of the holiday of Eid al-Fitr [in 2006], a crowd of hundreds of sexually frenzied young men participated in violent attacks on dozens of women, surrounding them in the streets, groping and even trying to undress them. As police stood by and watched the scene ambivalently, no one, not mothers nor veiled women were safe from the mob" (Atassi 2009).

The Eid al-Fitr holiday is usually a time when Egypt's popular classes — men and women together — enjoy strolling the markets and public squares and shopping in the boulevards of Cairo, a time during which exuberant overcrowding is usually experienced pleasurably in the spirit of festivity and community. However, in 2006, several occurrences of sexualized mobbing of women were reported, with a few incidents being captured on cell-phone video. Significant in each report was the presence of police who permitted, and even encouraged, the attacks. We can recall that the security state in the period between 2003 and 2006 intensified and generalized its practice of targeting publicly and politically active women. The policy was to harass, sexualize, and torture them, to impugn their respectability and undermine their status as political subjects or as citizens, except when they acted in collaboration with state-legitimized morality and policing campaigns.

Meanwhile, security services had been actively involved in cultivating the "thugification" of Egypt's police, retraining them into the equivalent of Italian *camicie nere* (black shirt) or Iranian *basiji* (morality militia) paramilitaries. However, public sphere NGOs and commentators did not connect the dots here. Rather than seeing these sexualized attacks as fully consistent with the security state's policy of assaulting women's respectability (with the aim of replacing political questions with moral ones), outrage was displaced onto working-class masculinity. In this police-centered human-security discourse, "woman" became the middle-class consumer who must be protected, and "man" became the unemployed working-class youth who must be arrested. Working-class women who work on the streets or pass through them to go to work were rendered irrelevant and invisible by the terms of the controversy, as were the women who mixed rage and flirting to project vulgarity and stake claims to public space on their own terms, without calling on the police and the state. Rather than challenge the state's securitization of the politics of respectability, a series of civil society and governmental campaigns erupted that hypervisibilized and intensified classphobic moral panic, focusing on the restoration of respectability and piety.

Rather than critique the role of the security state and police in generating these aggressions against women and working-class male youths, many progressive and feminist social movements mobilized to demand the extension and intensification of security-state powers (fig. 6.3). Concern shifted from the police and security state as agent of sexual harassment and sexualized torture to the libidinal perversions of working-class boys. This shift inscribed the international neocolonial discourse of the Arab street or Islamist mob into the fabric of class politics and police enforcement. On the one hand, leftist or social-progressive commentators in Egypt saw the aggression of the "mobs" as "a clear manifestation of an oppressed society deprived of its right to have a decent life and a lost youth fulfilling suppressed needs." In this narrative, explosive youth had been created by the corruption and ineptitude of a government that "squandered public monies" and failed to exert "serious efforts to ensure citizens a healthy life that meets the basic needs of edible food and clean water, and the basic services of transport and education" (Halawi 2006).

The Egyptian analyst Amr Abdelrahman (2007), in an article cleverly subtitled "What Respectability Veils When It Enters Public Space," adds another important factor: that of the rapidly changing consumer cultures of the middle and upper-middle classes in Egypt. Abdelrahman argues

FIGURE 6.3. Protesters in Cairo demand a new law against sexual harassment (11 September 2006). Photo credit: Al Masry Al Youm / Ahmed Al-Masry (http://www.almasry-alyoum.com).

that upper-middle-class women in Egypt today need to access broad sectors of the city in order to enact new consumer identities and practices. And they are loathe to risk class degradation by mixing with the popular classes that took over the city center after the middle classes moved out to new suburbs and gated cities. Thus, by moralizing and gendering what was essentially a class conflict over the social cleansing of urban consumer spaces, officials and NGOs were able to demonize downtown boulevards with the same discourse that criminalizes "slums." They could thus empower police to launch a "direct attack on the poor" (Abdelrahman 2007). The Egyptian sociologist Mona Abaza's (2011) work on parastatal efforts in Egypt to evict masses of rent-control tenants and popular-class venues from downtown Cairo confirms this internationally financed and legitimized class politics in play.

Nevertheless, in the NGO discourses of harassment, these issues are stripped of class analysis and framed as social problems of boys radiating explosive sexual indiscipline. As the columnist Salama Salama stated, these deprived youth then grow up in "unplanned zones, not to use the word ghetto, where all kinds of pressures are bound to build up. . . . We have failed to give our boys and girls chances to interact in a healthy way in their childhood and puberty, leaving them forever puzzled and a bit immature . . . just roaming the streets — ticking like a time bomb" (2008).

The harassment and sexual brutalization of women, whether working-class women or middle-class political protesters, is matched by the quasi-racialization and parahumanization of working-class male youth in urban Egypt. Deployed by the Egyptian state and the upper classes themselves, this process of policing masculinity shares many of the same tropes with the wave of Islamophobic racism in Europe and extremist militarism in Israel. "Masculinity studies" and NGO projects to contain, detain, and retrain youth have proliferated in recent years (Amar 2011a). This process of managing class inequality through racialized gender and criminalized sexuality has left behind the economistic discourse of the 1980s and 1990s (when providing jobs and microcredit were the solutions for youth frustration). Today, the project has become securitized and de-economized, reframed as a "human-security" project saturated with the metaphors of the war on terrorism. Today's assemblage metaphor of "time-bomb masculinity" has at least two contemporary origins: one in contemporary urban law enforcement, the other in international security terrorology, with these formations overlapping.

In the late 1980s and 1990s, feminist and LGBT activist scholarship began expanding the notion of fighting hate crimes into a broad politics of confronting sexual harassment in public. They called this a war on what they labeled "sexual terrorism," usually waged against ethnic minority young men in the urban context (Kissling 1991). This dovetailed with police development of gang injunctions in North America, originally called "street terrorism" laws (Astvasadoorian 1998), which emerged in dialogue with simultaneous attempts to police and reform gang masculinities in the informal urban settlements of Cairo. Of course, "time-bomb masculinity" is also just a dumbed-down or depoliticized version of the "suicide bomber" trope, which has become the justification for ratcheting up surveillance and undercutting civil liberties in the Middle East, as well as in European cities. In this sense, it represents the ultimate militarization of the respectability discourse of urban modernity. As discussed by Jasbir Puar (2007), the production of the respectable subject of certain kinds of liberal, Western LGBT and feminist politics depends on the production of the constituent "other" in the form of the terrorist subject, overwhelmed by orientalist sexual excess.

In a more provocative move, the conclusion to Puar's *Terrorist Assemblages* (2007, 220–23), and also Gayatri Spivak's noteworthy "Terror: A

Speech after 9–11" (2004), revives a bit of the Fanonian romance of the suicide bomber, who is saturated with the erotic power of youth, ballistically projecting a speech act that is phallically and erotically invoked as a "boy's thing," even when the proliferation of female suicide bombers would imply that the practice was not necessarily a gendered phenomenon. In this vein, Gayatri Spivak wrote, "Suicide bombing . . . is a purposive self-annihilation, a confrontation between oneself and oneself—the extreme end of autoeroticism, killing oneself as other, in the process killing others. . . . Suicidal resistance is a message inscribed in the body when no other means will get through. . . . It is only the young whose desires can be so drastically rearranged" (2004, 96). In formulations such as those of Puar and Spivak, there are moments in which time-bomb eroticism stands as a spectral subject imbued with a kind of queer possibility, whose shockwave exposes and illuminates the necropolitical security state or imperialist war machine. However, in security-state practice, the romance of the suicide bomber is not an erotic narrative that can bear its own message. Instead, the time-bomb subject as it operates here serves a blank slate of ultimate hypervisibility that provides for the endless inscriptions of securitizing speech acts, a radical parahuman. The bomber is utterly subjectified by the security state. The youth, sexuality, and queer/femininity of bombers only render such subjects more useful for inscription and securitization as the distilled quintessence of the "Arab street" and "sexual terrorism" metaphors.

Herein lies the genius of the Tunisian self-immolators and Asmaa Mahfouz's metaphorical "woman on fire," who erupted into history as explicitly nonbomber, nonterrorist reconfigurations of parahumanity. The real or metaphorical flames of these self-immolators ritually reestablished popular sovereignty for the Arab Spring and illuminated the terror practices of security states, rather than militarily relegitimizing them as bombers have done. In the discourse of the Egyptian state and its associated NGOs around 2008–9, as they appropriated sexual harassment and UN antiviolence politics to securitize youth as a threat to the public, youth without education or available housing were seen as unemployable and, thus, unmarriageable, leaving them unmoored and sexually undisciplined.

Another factor driving this youth security crisis was the sellout of the country's economy to China. In only a few years, Egypt has become flooded with Chinese vendors selling cheap products made in Asia, continuing the process of colonizing local markets that was started by the United States and Europe during the "Open Door" period launched by Egyptian President Anwar Sadat in 1973. What was left of Egypt's job base and manu-facturing economy after decades of gradual neoliberalization was being crushed by unfettered competition from China, without any attempt by the Egyptian government to assure that Chinese investment in Egypt's economy paid local dividends. Paradoxically, this mainstream sociologi-cal narrative, which offers structural interpretations of the causes behind youth sexual aggression, demands a solution based on heavy-handed secu-rity and police interventions. Fahmi Howeidi stated, "What is taking place in Egypt now resembles a threat to our national security," and Sherine Abul-Naga demanded that the security services intervene more vigor-ously: "In such events, their absence is inexcusable" (Halawi 2006).

Another set of responses came to similar conclusions, although this time focused on issues of respectability and moral self-comportment. One set of moralistic responses took advantage of the attacks in order to blame the women victims and to insist that women wear more modest hi-jabs. These groups distributed posters and e-mailed images (Atassi 2009). "One of them juxtaposes a veiled woman and a wrapped piece of candy, depicting her 'purity.' The other piece of candy is unwrapped with an un-veiled woman in the background, her long hair flying in the wind. . . . The uncovered candy is covered with flies. 'A veil to protect or eyes will mo-lest,' reads the accompanying slogan" (Sandels 2008). These campaigns, generated by Salafi organizations, came close to renaturalizing the tactic of the security state to threaten public women with molestation.

At the same time, other groups, such as the liberal organization behind the youth empowerment magazine *Kelmetna* and the Egyptian Center for Women's Rights (ECWR), shifted attention back onto the immorality of young men. The ECWR released a detailed study, describing the issue of sexual harassment as a "cancer-like problem" infecting the national body and also as "clouds in Egypt's sky" overshadowing the nation's reputation. The study found that "83 per cent of Egyptian women and 98 per cent of foreign women said they had experienced sexual harassment. More than half of the Egyptian men questioned for the survey, 62 per cent, admitted to having harassed women, 53 per cent of them blamed the women for 'bringing it on'" (Sandels 2008). In the ECWR perspective, dressing mod-estly or religiously conservative makes no difference in terms of harass-ment. All focus must be on policing and rectifying the deviant behavior of youthful, working-class men. In the posters and Internet campaigns of *Kelmetna* and the ECWR, the visual icons capture the profiles of fash-ionable, unveiled, upper-middle-class Egyptians and the campaigns are stamped with the logos of international organizations and donors. Their discourse focuses on respectability and security: "Respect yourself" and "Make the street secure for everyone," for example. Although neutral or general in their phrasing, their graphic representations on the Web-ads and posters identify the respectable nation with its internationally linked upper middle classes, and point the finger at out-of-control youth of the popular classes.

International Gender Enforcement

The ECWR and *Kelmetna* represent the organizations that drew most directly on UN gender doctrines and CEDAW institutions, funds, discourses, and legal-juridical mobilizing strategies. The sociologists Helen Rizzo, Anne M. Price, and Katherine Meyer clarified the status of the organization: "Globally, ECWR was part of several transnational networks for human rights and women's rights and received support for its projects from international donor agencies including international NGOs. It had a long-standing relationship with The Global Fund for Women. . . . It also received support from the World Bank Small Grants program and was recognized for its advocacy work at the grassroots level by being named Winner of the World Bank's 2000 Development Marketplace" (2012). Thus, the ECWR and *Kelmetna* were protest movements of a particular sort, which political science does not usually study. These were "protests" that mobilized to demand that an authoritarian state expand its policing powers. These NGOized movements aimed neither for redistribution or justice (as in the era of "social security") nor for consumer power and cultural rights (as in the neoliberal era), but to enforce particular gendered and moralized doctrines of the "human-security" era. In the context of human-security governance, NGOized civil actions tended to move in constant cycles to demand more police protection of gendered and culturalized subjects.

Ahmed Salah, director of a *Kelmetna* group of volunteers, claimed that we needed to get back to the time when "men were more gallant and protective," when Egypt had "real men" (fig. 6.4). We must "arrest the harasser and punish him by shaving his head" (Sandels 2008). When the sexual harassment controversy heated up, Minister of the Interior Habib el-Adly, who was in charge of the police (and later, after the 2011 uprisings, arrested for crimes against people and for systematic sexual harassment), first proclaimed that "sexual harassment does not exist" (Muftah 2007).

FIGURE 6.4. Male "guardians" protect women from street harassment as part of the
Kelmetna campaign (September 2006). Photo credit: Al Masry Al Youm / Hazem Gouda
(http://www.almasry-alyoum.com).

In full defensive mode against the accusations of El-Nadeem and other groups since the 1990s, the police had assumed that they were being accused of being responsible for the harassment of women in public. However, once it became apparent that civil society organizations were ignoring the role of the police and the security state in the generation of sexualized violence, the Interior Ministry and security establishments jumped on board and embraced the antiharassment campaign enthusiastically. They sensed the chance as "gallant, protective real men" to utilize the sexual harassment campaign, extending their prerogative power to "protectively" detain women in public and to round up working-class boys in ways that would degrade and depoliticize their collective aspirations. For example, in the second week of November 2008, the police arrested more than *four hundred* boys between the ages of fifteen and seventeen after they were caught "flirting with girls." As the press reported, "Cairo police director Faruq Lashin confirmed the boys had been arrested for flirting offenses. . . . The arrests will be seen as a major victory for women's groups who have long complained that police ignore sexual harassment claims. Police have been involved in a string of arrests and prosecutions across the country. A teenager was sentenced to two years in prison for sexually assaulting two women this week while a 17-year-old man is on trial for the same offense."[5] The sexual harassment controversy that had begun as a thorough critique of repressive policing and the torture of dissident women and youth had been appropriated by the security state and NGO establishment as justification for extending police brutality, mass arrests, social cleansing of the city, and the necessity of renewing the emergency decree.

Alternative Harassment Feminism

To subvert this well-rehearsed subjectification and securitized inscription of the voice of the subalternized male working-class "time bomb" subject, Egyptian activists mobilized between 2008 and 2010 around the performance of "vulgar" gender-queer forms of street occupation.[6] On 25 June 2008, the truck driver Sherif Gommaa pulled over, got out, and grabbed the breasts of the twenty-seven-year-old filmmaker Nuha Rushdi. She responded by overpowering him and dragging him to the police station.[7] For the first time in Egyptian legal history, a case of sexual harassment was taken to court (fig. 6.5). In October 2008, the court found Gommaa guilty, sentenced him to three years in prison, and imposed a fine of $970,

FIGURE 6.5. Nuha Rushdi in court, bringing a sexual harassment suit
(21 October 2008). Photo credit: Al Masry Al Youm / Mohamed Hossam Eddin
(http://www.almasry-alyoum.com).

equivalent to between five and six months' average salary (UNICEF 2010).
This set a landmark precedent, defining al-taharrush al-jinsi (sexual harassment) in the law and distinguishing it from rape or debauchery. In
February 2010, Gommaa's attempt to appeal the verdict was rejected. Although Nuha Rushdi's campaign began by calling on the police and demanding the extension of enforcement powers, it shifted toward a more
subversive challenge, queering the power of morality politics and the class
and spatial politics of gendered ethics and respectability, not as a liberal-
individualist "women can take care of themselves" project, but as a different articulation of stateness that displaced police and security institutions
and class governance norms, and instead brought together judicial, syndicate, and social-services branches of the state in more empowering ways.

As Rushdi's struggle dragged on, she was labeled a lesbian, a Zionist
conspirator, and almost a mannish thug. Rushdi refused respectable embodiment by physically subduing the truck driver, by performing a citizen's arrest rather than calling the police, and by not resorting to the class-
based respectability politics offered by the NGO mobilizing framework.
Rushdi's campaign gravitated toward congruence with the strategies of
the type advocated by the El-Nadeem Center. These efforts found it dif-

ficult to articulate themselves through the screen of middle-class feminist ideologies. Instead, they drew support from reemergent leftist newspapers (advocating a redistributive workerist or "social security" paradigm for class-conscious gender rights) and alternative Islamic feminist voices (working to repoliticize a politics of piety and intensifying its focus on issues of inequality, criminalization, and sexualization). Two divergent sets of responses stemmed from Nuha Rushdi's eventual legal victory. One, when her legal precedent was taken up by the UN-sponsored NGOs, was to enhance the security and punishment powers of the state.

However, another set of responses put those same powers into question. The ECWR followed the former trajectory by demanding the passage of new laws that mandated much higher sentences—up to ten years—and higher fines for sexual harassment. The conviction would also be a crime that would appear on the permanent record, even that of a youth or minor. Furthermore, these new laws not only encouraged, but also mandated police intervention in this area. This might sound like a feminist victory, but not if one recalls the historic tendency of police to take advantage of mandates in order to extend their racketeering and extortionary social power. When drafting the law, little thought was given to the ease with which the police, military, and security services could misuse it to justify mass arrests of working-class boys engaged in any kind of flirting in any mixed-gender, mixed-class public area. Police used such codes to extort bribes from the boys (even if no evidence was presented, even if no charges were ever filed by women victims). Boys and their families then faced high fines they could not pay, life-destroying criminal records, and long sentences in Egypt's monstrous prison system. One result of this "securitization" of sexual harassment in the law and its mandated extension of enforcement could be the legitimization of the police orchestration of wholesale gender segregation in, and working-class eviction from, public spaces.

Aware of this possibility, Nuha Rushdi herself, the Egyptian Initiative for Personal Rights, and the El-Nadeem Center mobilized a distinct framing for the antiharassment campaign, focusing on the masculinist prerogative power of the security state and critiquing its repressive moralization project and the brutality of its policing apparatus. Through this lens, and in light of these alternative feminist reframings of sexuality, police governance, and class struggle, the attack on Lara Logan and the resurgence of "Arab mob" tropes of predator masculinity during the 2011 demonstrations can be seen from a new perspective.

International Women's Day

On 8 March 2011, two sets of massive demonstrations were organized in Cairo, aiming to extend and deepen the achievements of the revolution that had begun only six weeks before. One set of demonstrations involved many tens of thousands of university students, led by young women in leftist and labor movements in coalition with the men and women of the youth branch of the Muslim Brothers that had become increasingly independent of the conservative Old Guard of the movement. They demanded the abolition of the hated State Security institution and a fresh election for all student governments and administrative committees (and they eventually achieved their demands). A second set of mass protests was led by an interfaith union of Coptic Christian and Muslim anti-police-brutality groups who aimed to expose the complicity of Egyptian security and police forces and military special-operations brigades in attacks on Christians in Alexandria and in Upper Egypt in the previous months. These two demonstrations had been organized on the day that was also designated by the United Nations to be International Women's Day.

Many young women committed to the student, labor, and anti-police movements, as well as many local Egyptian feminist organizations, wanted to support one of these large preorganized demonstrations, but the internationally linked feminist NGOs and UN agencies insisted on a distinct march for Women's Day. Egypt is not and never has been simply an endpoint for vectors of the "dissemination" of internationalist feminism; to the contrary, Egypt has been an originator and disseminator of modern internationalist feminism, of both "maternal" and radical varieties. Egyptian feminists founded one of the first international humanitarian feminist antitrafficking organizations in 1859. Internationally linked Egyptian liberal suffragette movements and militant women's factory-worker organizers were central to the Nationalist Revolution in 1919. Egyptian feminists reinvented both leftist and conservative versions of international Islamic feminism in the 1960s–1980s. And Cairo hosted the United Nations Conference on Population and Development, 5–13 September 1994, which evolved into a dynamic, contentious forum on women's sexuality and citizenship, featuring the diplomatic and mobilizing skills of Egyptian feminists from all sides of the political spectrum. But due to the circumstances and geography of revolutionary protest activities on 8 March 2011, the Women's Day March seemed to evacuate this complex history and imply that one could separate out an "international" level of feminism from the national. And as the protests played out, this distinction seemed to be projected onto the binary of elitist versus popular, as if gender concerns needed to be elevated so that they stood apart from the antisectarian and anti-police issues identified by the broader revolutionary leadership (including by its young women militants, like Asmaa Mahfouz).

Thus on 8 March 2011, a much-reduced group of a few hundred women and UN-agency representatives entered the streets of busy, postrevolutionary downtown Cairo (Chick 2011) for what was originally planned as a "Million Woman March." They were faced with resentment from supporters of the student, worker, and antisectarian movements, from which they had set themselves apart. And, of course, they faced the masculinized class tensions that were still the legacy of the security state's baltagi effect. Disappointingly, these confrontations and tensions materialized in the form of several incidents of sexual assault and harassment of the marchers, as the Women's Day demonstration proceeded. Unfazed, a Women's Day March participant Mozn Hassan (a young Egyptian woman activist, lawyer, political organizer, and director of Cairo's Nazra for Feminist Studies) stated: "It was a good thing for this class of feminists to finally get out of its hotel conference rooms and well-guarded foundation offices and try to take back the streets. But why did they then act enraged and terrified when working-class Cairenes dared to approach them or shout questions or tease them? Why must this kind of feminist mobilization see the Revolution only from the perspective of experiencing, and demanding protection from, sexual harassment? We must fight back for the streets and the state, not sit back in fear demanding that the street and state shower us with privilege and respect."[8]

Inspired and informed by perspectives such as Hassan's, I have followed the struggles around articulating internationalist laws and policies to protect women from violence. Research has demonstrated how this process has been reframed as an intersectional feminist struggle concerned with refashioning subjects of class, respectability, and state security, as well as rendering legible the masculine and feminine parahuman subjects of human-security governance. I have examined the military-humanitarian doctrine and the human-rights legacy of UNSCR 1325 and CEDAW by assessing them in relation to processes of NGOization and the emergence of the human-security state in the Global South. The deconstruction of feminist UN politics I offer here does not aim to render feminism irrelevant, nor does it aim to accuse the international gender movement of being a tool of the West or of dominant classes. Instead, it reveals that there are more productive and emancipatory feminisms emerging on the ground from activists who have learned to evert NGOization and interna-tionalism, to turn their logics inside out. Movements such as El-Nadeem expose and attack the repressive power of the security state, mobilizing class-conscious, pro-worker repertoires. These movements disarticulate the politics of respectability, the enforcement-centrism of UN resolutions, and the quietude or complicity of respectability and piety movements.

As the Cairo-based activist and scholar Nadia Ilahi argues, "Today's Egyptian feminists would help create a safer environment for women spanning diverse class boundaries by focusing on redirecting efforts to encourage alternate forms of masculinity and femininity. Social space as felt in Egypt does convey a different set of experiences for men and women, and further research is needed to illustrate how particular femi-nist notions of reclaiming space are impacted by class divisions. Women in Egypt are reclaiming space, and it is men and women alike who work to challenge the various meanings of these spaces" (2010, 11).

On 1 March 2011, Mozn Hassan, who had been attacked by plain-clothes police and sexually menaced by paramilitary thugs during the revolution, stated, "Women engaged in all revolutionary events knowing there was no chance for protection and they are fully responsible for their bodies, life and security. When the debate on sexual harassment returns, we need to discuss not only the society and cultural issues but also how women see their bodies and how they could work to remake the state, and to gain space and not to lose it" (2011).

Conclusion

In this chapter, I have drawn more specifically on gendered theories of race and coloniality to develop notions of the logic of hypervisibility and to relate it to processes of securitization. These formations give birth to the parahuman subjects that embody the power of the human-security state. Conversations in critical race theory concerned with the logic of hyper-visibility (Reddy 1998; Yancy 2008) focus on processes whereby racial-ized, sexualized subjects, or the marked bodies of subordinate classes, be-come intensely visible as objects of state, police, and media gazes and as targets of fear and desire (fig. 6.6). This is what Frantz Fanon (1988 [1952]) calls phobogenic objectification processes or what Stuart Hall (1996) calls moral panic encoding processes.

Paradoxically, when subjects are hypervisibilized, they remain invisible as social beings: they are not recognizable as complex, legitimate, partici-

FIGURE 6.6. "We revolutionaries are not baltagiyya [thugs]. Why try us in military courts?" (October 2011). Photo credit: Amel Pain / EPA.

patory subjects or citizens. One route by which subjects can escape the logic of hypervisibility is to strive constantly for respectability. This path entails a historically classphobic (demonizing the working class), gender-essentialist moral praxis consisting of self-disciplinary practices that are depoliticizing and aim for assimilation. In the late nineteenth century, this kind of liberal-progressive politics of respectability was called "temperance" and was linked to vice policing and the punitive moral reform of working women and boys. In the late twentieth century, respectability politics was associated with the promotion of values of civility and "gender mainstreaming" in secular "civil society." This dovetailed with the promotion of piety, gendered labor discipline, and moral self-management by Islamic and Christian neoliberal movements. To state it simply, this strategy for moving from hypervisibility into respectability tends to naturalize social hierarchies and modes of governance and make security-state power less visible, accountable, and contestable.

However, other traditions of gender activism have developed more productive options for disarticulating the logic of hypervisibility. These tactics turn the gaze back on the state to reveal the interests, histories, and power relations that generate certain race, sex, and moral subjects and metaphors. This supplants the logic of hypervisibility with a critical project of subversive recognition and embodied occupation that can potentially re-articulate spheres of disciplinary power. This strategy of "critical desecuritization" does not count as a liberal theory of resistance since it does not pretend to predict how parahuman subjects will speak, or which interests will be articulated, once their spectral or shadow characters, these securitized figures of fear and desire, begin to be dispelled. Desecuritization praxis does not guarantee a progressive or liberal sense of telos. Nor, on the other hand, does it cling to the notion that the most authentic or effective resistance will be morally or religiously appropriate for its "cultural context." Through these types of praxis, subversions of power, even mass insurrections within gendered, sexualized, and class-repressive human-security regimes, can surge suddenly onto the stage of history.

THE END OF NEOLIBERALISM?

The neoliberal epoch is over, because this crisis demonstrates that those in the financial sector have to act with serious consideration, they have to be ethical not just economic. It's not just the common citizen that must be ethical. — **Brazilian President Lula**, speaking before the UN General Assembly, 25 September 2008

I guarantee that the Brazilian people are now vaccinated against neoliberalism. But the discourse of anticapitalism is a waste of time. What we need is alternatives! — **Brazilian President Rousseff**, speaking before the organizers of the World Social Forum and the twentieth anniversary meeting of the 1992 Rio Earth Summit, 25 January 2012

The crime of robbing Egypt under the excuse of neoliberal privatization will not slide without prosecution. . . . The Egyptian people are leaders and teachers of revolution . . . opening the door to hope for the future, and we look to those who dream on this same scale . . . most notably to Brazil, where former president Lula da Silva took power through democratic elections when Brazil was almost bankrupt and now has put it in the ranks of the world's top eight economies. — **Campaign statements by Egyptian presidential candidate Hamdeen Sabahy**, who won the popular vote in all major cities in Egypt in the first round of that country's first democratic presidential election, 23–24 May 2012

In this book I have offered a new perspective on "human security," utilizing the term as a heuristic device for analyzing a set of new, intersecting urban-based political movements, globalist utopian assertions, militarized national governance experiments, and transnational flows of security-industry expertise and legal discourse. I have also identified the particular sociopolitical actors, cultural formations, political-economic processes, and spatial "hotspots" that shape the emergence of human-security logics of rescue and protection that circulate between particularly visible laboratories of policing and planning in the Global South. These securitization regimes, sexuality subjects, and humanization processes have taken form during the period that many critical scholars tend to identify with the rise of neoliberalism. However, the specificity of the data and case studies presented here could not have been adequately captured if I had remained faithful to the analytical narrative of liberalization or neoliberalism (or even more specific notions such as "authoritarian marketization"). Certain qualities of power, lines of conflict, bodies of resistance, and operative formations of pleasure and danger would have remained immaterial or unrecognizable from those perspectives.

Thus, in order to more accurately capture the dynamics of struggle and technologies of control that emerged, were tested, and then circulated between the archipelago of governance laboratories during this period, I have substituted the story of neoliberalism's evolution for a new metanarrative, that of the rise of "human-security states." Using my "archipelago method" for researching these processes, I worked to go beyond tracing NGOs and social movement mobilizations, comparing regime types, following liberalization timelines, or tracking patterns of globalizing governance regimes. Instead, through this method I identified new forms of human-security politics that have materialized from the contradictions of global neoliberalism as played out through contentions around morality regimes, social-control practices, and spatial infrastructures in particularly visible and generative sites that act as transfer hubs. Through the models proposed here, we can begin to see new actors and orderings, and thereby imagine the "end of neoliberalism" in at least two ways. First, we can envision an end to the term *neoliberalism* as an overburdened and overextended interpretive lens for scholars; and second, we can conceive of the demise, in certain locations and circuits, of a hegemonic set of market-identified subjects, locations, and ideologies of politics. It is important to underline that these case studies have demonstrated that any shift beyond the politics of neoliberalism does not mean either the exhaustion of capitalism, or the reversal of class polarizations on global and local scales, or the overthrow of powerful liberal cultural notions of sexuality, humanity, or morality. These large-scale formations, of course, persist. However, as I have demonstrated, the contradictions within dynamics of securitization, innovations in forms of militarization specific to the Global South, and shifts in sexuality politics catalyzed by human-security rule provide opportunities for radical change, and even for revolution.

My final task is to articulate specific qualities of the "end of neoliberalism" and its implications. I will suggest that neoliberalism's ending is comprised of three shifts, operating in both the world of globalizing governance practices as well as in the world of ideas. I identify these three transitions as: (1) the shift in dominant policymaking and social-control discourses *from liberalization to securitization*; (2) the shift in political-economic narratives from *renderings of entrepreneurialism and consumerism* (that is, the "culture of neoliberalism") to *narratives of work* that are often explicitly illiberal or antiliberal; and (3) the shift *from Global North "imperial" or regional geography of the "bloc"* to a *transregional, Global South geography of the archipelago*, where new forms of securitized power emerge in particularly contentious enclaves or hotspots where struggles to make territory and to revalue or visibilize certain bodies take on great importance.

The Cyclical Endings of Neoliberalism

The end of neoliberalism has been declared again and again over the course of a generation. In the 1990s, those on the political Left have signaled its passing as they have celebrated the mass mobilization of "anti-globalization" and "alterglobalization" (alternative globalization) movements transnationally, or in the 2000s, with the spread of revolutionary or leftist-populist regimes in Latin America. Neoliberalism's end has been declared, too, by those on the Right and in the political center who hope to brush neoliberalism's sins under the rug or to deny responsibility for the devastating social impact of hasty privatization, wholesale deregulation, or "shock-treatment" policies.

FROM LIBERALIZATION TO SECURITIZATION

In the 1990s, even the World Bank itself declared an end to one kind of neoliberalism and launched a new beginning. Under the tenure of Chief Economist Joseph Stiglitz (1997–99), the World Bank released a series of reports exposing the fallacies of notions of market efficiency and self-regulating economic rationality. In a dramatic turnaround, the World Bank announced that under conditions of "highly imperfect information" — that is, the real-world "irrationalities" of violence, corruption, and social injustice — liberalization processes would unleash "perverse" effects. In this light, Stiglitz advocated state action, particularly to strengthen regulatory apparatuses and launch an ambitious wave of employment and "human-capital development" projects (2003, 220–23). Similarly, "New Labour" in Britain and the Clinton Administration in the United States advocated a "Third Way" (Giddens 1998), between shock treatment and social democracy. In this context, Alain Touraine declared neoliberalism finished. In its place, movements among "underprivileged" groups demanding "cultural rights" would produce a more innovative conception of market-friendly but culturally nuanced social governance for the future (Touraine 2001, 100–104).

Critical scholars insisted that celebrations of neoliberalism's demise in the Global North were either delusional or mendacious. Wendy Larner and David Craig (2005), Doug Porter and David Craig (2004), and John Gledhill (2001) argued that the Third Way's humanization of neoliberalism—its embrace of diversity, the realm of culture, and the active state—reflected not an end, but a redoubling of neoliberalism. The Third Way, for these scholars, represented an intensification of neoliberalism's commitment to financialization and deregulation, extending these processes over and through the cultivation of identities, bodies, and populations—what Foucault (2008) terms the realm of the "biopolitical." And as David Harvey (2005) noted, during this humanization phase or Third Way era, the precariousness of jobs and communities continued to increase. Further, as Ruth Wilson Gilmore (2007) and Neil Smith (2002) proved, the Third Way's commitment to re-enhancing state power in the Global North centered on intensifying urban policing, detention practices, and prison industries. These increasingly profitable, privatized, and thoroughly racialized industries mined disenfranchised and brutalized forms of "human capital" and intensified the militarization of social space.

Another way of describing the "end of neoliberalism" during this Third Way era has been articulated by studies focusing on political elites' re-embracing of strong roles for the public sector and the state. This process has been described by Bob Jessop (2002b) and Jamie Peck and Adam Tickell (2002) as a shift from "roll-back" to "roll-out" or "roll-forward" neoliberalism. During the initial roll-back phase of structural adjustment and shock-treatment privatization, the overwhelming aim of neoliberal policy was to force the state to retreat from economic management, to gut social-welfare expenditures, and to favor wealth concentration over the redistribution of income or opportunities. But in later phases, as neoliberal policy doctrines faced increasing resistance on all levels that threatened to topple client regimes and shred agreements with international financial institutions, revisionists moved away from roll-back policies and instead focused on rolling out the state. They advocated enhanced deployments of the state to mop up some of the social damage produced by mass redundancies, to promote "micro credit" that spread debt and capitalist values without promoting significant redistribution, and to deploy new mechanisms of policing, coercion, and discipline. This return of the state or roll-out phase is not described as marking the end of neoliberalism per se. But when social discipline, policing, and militarized "protection," rather than market promotion and consumerism, became the key terms of political-economic domination, the "liberal" façade that is essential to the epistemology of neoliberalism began to crumble.

As critiqued by John Gledhill, the concept of the Third Way, as articulated by Anthony Giddens or the roll-out advocates, highlights "the individual and 'life politics' in a way that strips 'the poor' of their social personalities while reifying 'society' and evading or misconstruing key issues in the analysis of contemporary patterns of inequality in the north or south. . . . The result is a strongly normalizing and moralizing set of proposals" (Gledhill 2001, 123). To phrase it in another way, resurgence of the state took place through a highly coercive form of "humanization." As this process proceeded, modes of securitization became the primary concern of states and social elites, and human objects of security became the primary units of governance. Military intervention regimes pioneered experiments in deploying new forms of rule for new kinds of intensified policing in the Global South. Of course, this process in the Global North was accelerated by the dramatically securitizing responses to the 9/11 attacks, which produced repressive militarization practices and national-security cultures that seemed anachronistic to Latin American polities that had just emerged from twenty years of struggle against national-security regimes, and even to political cultures in the Middle East, whose populations had grown profoundly frustrated by antiterror discourse generated by decrepit security-state regimes.

During this phase, as the studies presented here have demonstrated, liberalization was gradually replaced by securitization as the hegemonic project of global governance and of state administration. This transition was appropriated, pushed, and globalized first and most vividly in the most contentious quarters of the semiperiphery. Of course, repressive security-state deployments were always part and parcel of the earliest deployments of "liberalization" and "shock treatment." But when projects of securitization came to be deployed as ends in themselves, as foundations of novel, deliberalized notions of the human or parahuman without reference to markets or liberal idioms, as it was in these sites in the South, this marked an epochal shift. Whereas in much of the United States and Europe neoconservative populists eventually embraced securitization as a protective and patriotic process, elsewhere, particularly in the Latin American and Mideast semiperipheries, it faced mass social re-

sistance and populist political opposition that had accumulated over decades of struggle against security-state and militarized forms of rule. In
this context, "human-security" governance, as articulated in the Global
South, blended an apprehension of this shift from neoliberalism to securitization with a set of embedded struggles and resistances already seeth-
ing within these regimes of coercive rule. From the perspective of many
social-democratic and politically liberal actors in the Global North, the
end of neoliberalism had been achieved with the turn toward the Third
Way and the roll-out state. But what may have been more telling was how
discourses of the worker regained prominence, particularly in the populist politics of these Global South hotspots. The "worker" was now identified with protective, humanitarian, moral labors, and reemerged in some
spheres to displace the neoliberal figures of the consumer, entrepreneur,
and debtor.

FROM NARRATIVES OF CONSUMPTION TO WORK, FROM
NEOLIBERAL CULTURE TO ILLIBERAL MISSIONS

In the early 2000s, as leftist and populist governments won elected power
in South America and as the state-planning-centered capitalism of the
Beijing Consensus began to replace the private-sector-centered Washington Consensus as the dominant mode of world political-economic governance, neoliberalism's end was again proclaimed. In December 2001,
Argentina defaulted on $145 billion in debt to the IMF, and workers began
what may be seen as the first wave of what we now call the global "Occupy
movement" by moving in and taking over their own factories. And after
2002, Brazil set up a myriad of massive social programs, reversed some
privatizations, encouraged the spread of its plantation-occupying Land-
less Movement, and partially nationalized its oil. In *Latin America after
Neoliberalism*, Eric Hershberg and Fred Rosen state, "From Argentina and
Uruguay to Bolivia and Venezuela, some have begun to contemplate a
reversal of controversial privatizations and a partial restoration of barriers to US-dominated integration that had been torn down in the 1980s
and 1990s" (2006, 13–14). And Laura Macdonald and Arne Rückert in
Post-Neoliberalism in the Americas identify six elements shared by "postneoliberal" regimes among the New Left in Latin America: "Willingness to
use state power to stimulate the economy and correct widespread market
failures; to substantially deepen democracy by engaging citizens more directly; to use state institutions to reduce social inequalities through redistributive measures; to renationalize some parts of the economy, especially

in the energy and minerals sector; . . . to enact South-South trade agreements . . . based on an anti-neoliberal and anti-imperialist logic; . . . and to launch a Latin American development bank to free financially dependent countries in the hemisphere from the shackles of the international financial institutions" (2009, 7).

But certain critical scholars and analysts during this period insisted, again, that this seeming end of neoliberalism was an illusion. South American leftists and Chinese state capitalists may have reasserted the role of the planner, reempowered certain collective social actors, and disciplined the power of international financial institutions and investors in their home regions. Yet it was the pressure of Chinese workers themselves, laboring under highly repressive conditions that drove global working conditions down, enabling the "competitive" power of neoliberal globalization to persist and the gross surpluses of investment banking to pile up, even as consumer power and middle-class lifestyles retracted (Li 2009, 70–4). Leong Liew in "China's Engagement with Neo-liberalism" argues that "China has not embraced the IMF and World Bank neoliberal model and the state continues to mediate reform. . . . As a monopolistic party in a market economy, where financial power has a huge bearing on political power, the CCP [ruling Communist Party] has to retain dominant financial power and keep within the fold, or at least on their side, others who have financial power . . . ensur[ing] that China's engagement with economic liberalism will not conform to the neoliberal model and will remain a loose hug rather than an intimate embrace" (2005, 333–34).

Moreover, even if the market economics and antistatism of "classical" neoliberalism had been partially displaced in the era of the South American Pink Tide or New Left and the Beijing Consensus, the global discourse on the "culture of neoliberalism" survived and expanded its hegemony. Critical scholars argued that perhaps neoliberalism could no longer be defined by simple antinomies between market rationalities and state logics; instead, it should be identified with a set of cultural tropes that structure subjectivities. Thus scholars during this period came to focus on neoliberal culture, drawing on Stuart Hall's prescient work on "neoliberal common sense" (1996, 25–46). Individualistic, desiring, self-centered consumers and competitive, self-disciplining, market-oriented behavior became the central units of analysis for critical scholars. They examined how these subjectivities undermined social solidarities and possibilities for structural resistance or deep change, but also recognized how these cultural forms did generate novel kinds of self-realization and actualized alternative life-worlds. Jean and John Comaroff argued that "[neoliberalism] is a culture that . . . re-visions persons not as producers from a particular community, but as consumers in a planetary marketplace: persons as ensembles of identity that owe less to history or society than to organically conceived human qualities" (2001, 13). Ara Wilson (2004) captured these dynamics of neoliberal culture operating at the intersection of gender and class subjectivity and political-economic restructuring in Thailand, and Lisa Rofel (2007) mapped the fabric of neoliberal culture, desire, and selfhood in China.

Perhaps one can say that the culture of neoliberalism ends when the consumer exits the center stage of political culture. Of course, the exit of the consumer does not mean the departure of corporate domination or global capitalism. In fact, it seems the departure of the consumer could mark a turn for the worse, as the consumer at least embodied a lingering claim for a "democratic face" for capitalism. In the United States during the decade of the 2000s, book and record stores closed; purchases concentrated in featureless big-box outlets and discount stores, eliminating small businesses and commercial variety; and television advertisements became dominated by pharmaceutical ads, car insurance commercials, and corporate-sponsored electoral campaigns. Whereas the mid-twentieth-century landscape of consumer cultures and identities had come to embody a multicultural universe of taste and styles, in the twenty-first century this consumer world was supplanted by a landscape of medicated, indebted, and propagandized publics. In this context, new media corporations insisted that social-networking sites and digital downloads could sustain and even outperform the twentieth-century world of consumer multiculturalism; but the Occupy movement on the Left and the Tea Party on the Right in the United States rejected technological utopianism and, each in radically different ways, insisted on *working*, collectively, to manufacture physical spaces, repossess social territories, and labor for popular sovereignty.

Seen from a global perspective, and particularly a Global South optic, the recurring crisis of the "culture of neoliberalism" is configured in particular ways. The exit of the consumer as the center of political gravity has marked the return of the worker, although this worker now represents contradictory and ambivalent kinds of productive, moralistic, and social labor. As Laura Macdonald and Arne Rückert state, "In contrast with the Keynesian welfare era, these post-neoliberal interventions attempt to produce 'active' (labor market participating) rather than 'passive' welfare-dependent citizens. . . . [And] social investments are generally highly targeted (toward the poor) rather than universalistic, as in the case of a model based on social citizenship" (2009, 8). This is no longer the worker as a secular, exclusively class-identified subject. Nor is the worker necessarily masculinized or feminized in the same ways or identified primarily with the manufacturing industry. Work is production, yes, but not just of commodities and structures. This postneoliberal work centers more on the fashioning of moralization, care, humanization, viable sexualities, and territories that can be occupied. And the worker can see production as the collective work of vigilance and purification, which all too often is embedded through paramilitarization and enforcement practices. As these studies have demonstrated, new mobilizations of "workerism" have served as crucial wedge-actors in these human-security regimes, sometimes aligning with, at other times radically challenging the moral and cultural security doctrines of evangelical Christians and Islamist neoconservatives. Nevertheless, since these new postneoliberal workerisms offer complex and contradictory assertions, they can often break open the repressive logics of human-security governance and unleash startlingly emancipatory potentialities.

FROM THE "RESISTANT LOCAL" TO THE CONSTITUTIVE ARCHIPELAGO

Another way to analyze where neoliberalism may meet its end has been through studies of local resistance to the global, or through the analysis of emergent transnational solidarities or geopolitical blocs that weave local models into large-scale alternative regimes of governance. Does neoliberalism end when "the local" resists it? Here I will revive the unit of analysis of the semiperiphery and clarify how my proposed archipelago method can reconfigure these notions of locality and resistance.

In most conventional narratives of forms of resistance that are spread globally, Global South actors are positioned as "the local," within mappings of power where "the global" stands for a set of abstracted processes operating on a scale above—a spatial metaphor that often slips into a Mercator projection of a monolithic "North" or "West." In this imagination of scales, globalization is most often identified with Americanization or with the imperialistic spread of Western subjectivities and liberal epistemologies. Of course, there remains an urgent need to extend the political and cultural analysis of North/West agency as we remain attentive to the perpetuation of war; the command of military occupations; the deployment of counterinsurgency and intelligence networks; the cradling of banking, corporate, and investors' powers; the degradation of natural and social environments; and the cultural and governance legacies of colonialism. However, these kinds of studies can also tend to reduce and fragment Global South agency, portraying it through infantilizing and romanticizing lenses, as local ("low scale"), and as a victim of the global scale that is only capable of "resistance" rather than constituting large-scale formations and alternatives on its own distinct terms.

The more interesting studies of the "end of neoliberalism" that focus on local resistance include those that have tried to capture the plurality or multiplicity of modernities, some of which have proven particularly antagonistic to neoliberalism (Gibson-Graham 2002). Some have highlighted the incongruity of local or regional forms of subjectivity or logics of identity that are opaque to the incitements of liberalism and neoliberalism. Other studies have focused on radical transnational solidarities propelled by millenarian, violent forms of moral and cultural critique emanating from the Global South (Devji 2005; Juergensmeyer 2000). While still others have focused on explicitly nonviolent forms of secular, revolutionary globalist solidarity, analyzing, for example, the socialistic-cosmopolitan alternatives articulated by World Social Forums and pushed by alter-globalization protest movements.

As evidenced in the case studies presented in this book, the Global South is not merely a source of resistant forms of localism; it is also a factory for globalizing forms of moralization, militarization, and control. Nevertheless, the fact that many of these forms of control portray themselves as militantly resisting Americanization, liberalism, or neoliberal financialization does not mean they are necessarily leading the way toward anything that might look like regimes of radical social justice. Nor are these forms of emergent power just the same old neoliberalism with a Latin or an Arab face. It is in the complex ambiguities of these securitizing formations, their mixing of resistance and domination, appropriation and subversion that makes these forms of Global South–originating human-security power so interesting, and so politically dynamic.

But what spatial and geopolitical vocabulary can we use to locate these newly emerging orderings? Some have suggested that one way to get beyond the limiting imagination of global-versus-local is to utilize the neologism of "the glocal" or "glocalization" (Swyngedouw 2004). This can be very useful. But instead I would like to explore the advantages of reviving, with some significant updating, the highly productive notion of the semiperiphery. Buried under the ubiquitous but analytically weak terms like "middle powers," "emergent countries," or, simply, "the BRICS,"[1] lies this largely forgotten notion of the semiperiphery:

> The term semiperiphery emerged from ideas developed by dependency theorists in the 1960s. They argued that the development and economic autonomy of rich Western countries was not reproducible elsewhere and that the very advances and power of the West held back development in the periphery and locked the latter into subordinate roles. Because their surpluses were drawn off to the rich countries, periphery countries became perpetual sources of raw materials and cheap labor, unless they partially delinked from Western capitalism and transformed themselves through "inwardly directed development" and "import substitution industrialization." (Cohen and Clarkson 2004, xii)

Distinct from both the core (the "North/West") and the periphery, the semiperiphery is the zone in which ambiguities and contradictions in the world system manifest. It is in these zones where pockets of the most privileged core social actors and interests constantly confront enclaves of the most coerced and marginalized. Some identify a state as semiperipheral because it may lie in the middle of the global income scale, or because it features a mix of productive industries and (neo)colonial-type extractive economies, or because it is nearing some arbitrary "take-off" stage (Rostow 1960). But I find it is more useful to define the semiperiphery in relation to its contentious political and sociocultural character, to highlight these regions because they serve as laboratories of contradiction and subversion. This approach spotlights the semiperiphery's generative capacity to produce novel alternatives, as well as deploy creative violence and forms of repression. As Janine Brodie suggests, "Semiperipheries exist both inside and outside the global economy, exploit and are exploited, and mediate, both nationally and internationally, between the few winners and many losers created by the contemporary global economy. Yet perhaps it is precisely this contradictory location that lends itself to a revived moral imagination and to struggles for more socially sustainable alternatives to neoliberal globalism" (2004, 28).

The chain of enclaves, pockets, or islands—this "archipelago" nature of the distribution of class power and governance formations—that characterized the semiperiphery during the early postcolonial era is no longer limited to any world region. As Saskia Sassen (2004) has demonstrated, this geography of interwoven enclaves constitutes a complex terrain, today enabling the wealth-generating power of world cities of the North as well as megacities in the former Third World. New forms of power arise at the intersections of clustered elite and subaltern enclaves in global cities, and particularly in certain pivotal, heavily militarized postcolonial nation-states. These intersections render the notion of the semiperiphery powerfully relevant today. Global political economy models and World Systems theories have long underlined the importance of semiperipheral states as agents for global change and innovation. Andre Gunder Frank (1966) pointed to their role in ensuring the "development of underdevelopment." Immanuel Wallerstein (1976) underlined the pivotal role of the semiperiphery in the struggles to innovate and enforce certain class and ideological responses to the global economic crisis of the 1970s, responses that would come to be called neoliberalism. Chris Chase-Dunn (1990) highlighted the role of semiperipheral states in mobilizing anti-imperialist modes of governance and alliance. And Ernesto Laclau (1977), whose language has particularly influenced this book, highlighted the complex articulation of contrasting modes of production and logics of social mobilization in the semiperiphery, the seeds of what would become what some call "postneoliberalism." As Owen Worth stated, "Semiperipheral activities remain fraught with instabilities, prompting great avenues of contestation. As a result they often provide us with richer explanations regarding the wider character and stability of the current era of globalization" (2009, 23).

Beyond the End

In contrast with the dynamism and liveliness of the semiperiphery, struggles of neoliberal bodies politic in the Global North since the last financial crisis have taken the form of an unending drama of morbidity and mortification, populated by "dead" agents and ideologies that insist on rising from the grave. After 2008, as the "credit crunch" became the Great Recession, neoliberalism was once again proclaimed dead and the emperor of global finance was revealed to have no clothes. Practices of investment banking, mortgage lending, and derivative trading revealed themselves as having no rational relationship to markets, to supply-and-demand logics, much less to any socially generative logic of "productivity." Financial elites who had claimed to be technical experts capable of mastering market signals and prophesying consumer and investor pref-

erences, were revealed as mere masters of spin and fraud, whose decisions were shaped by predatory herding and hoarding logics (Calhoun
and Derluguian 2011, 15–17). They had practiced coordinated acts of de-
ception to dump their "debt instruments" onto consumers, shareholders,
and investors.

Terms like *plutocracy*, *oligarchy*, and *autarchy* reentered the political
vocabulary of mainstream analysts as they looked to the changes in the
political regimes of the Global North and West (Garfinkle 2011, 4–14).
These seemingly "medieval" or "Third World" terms were redeployed to
describe the electoral political systems of the Global North. The favorite neoliberal term of the 1990s, *market democracy*, had rather abruptly
lost its euphemistic power. "Market" governments could no longer be
described accurately as "liberal" states (neither "neo" liberal nor paleo-
liberal), so they were recharacterized as illiberal regimes of, by, and for
the ultrarich. During this financial crisis, many observers—both on the
populist Right and on the activist Left—were able to confirm their view
of neoliberal finance as an insular and self-serving set of class-distinction
and caste-preservation mechanisms, concentrated in the impermeable,
immensely powerful circuits of global banking. They were monopolistic,
rent-seeking, and racketeering in nature, rather than competitive, entrepreneurial, or productive. This global class formation could no longer
draw on (or no longer bothered to refer to) the market mythologies of
neoliberalism. So as the financial crisis in the Global North progressed,
and as the power of corporate and finance capitalism survived and intensified, it did so without bothering with the cloaking ideology of neoliberalism. The mask of economic rationality was removed. Alan Greenspan,
former chairman of the US Federal Reserve and high priest of privatization, declared that his "fundamental assumptions about economics were
flawed" (quoted in Woodruff 2008). Taking advantage of this window in
discourse, and the opportunity provided by the crisis, social democrats
and more radical actors reasserted themselves.

In the 2008–9 period, it seemed that Left and social-democratic governments would increase their room for maneuver, as the red lines of neoliberalism faded and its ideological power was shaken and partially dispelled.
Banks in Britain were taken over by the state and the term *bank nationalization* was even debated seriously on the floor of the US Congress (Roubini 2009). It seemed that the entire edifice of neoliberalism was crumbling, as some of the key terms of neoliberal hegemony were stolen back
and resignified by social-democratic leaders and the Left. For example,

one of neoliberalism's key framing terms, "investment," was taken back for a moment by the state. In the 1980s, neoliberal ideology had identified the term *investment* with practices of corporate takeovers and liquidation of jobs. And by contrast, public support for human capital, infrastructure, industrial development, or social spending was stigmatized as profligate "spending." This term, *spending*, like the word *welfare*, became (racially, sexually) signified as waste or theft; as an unjust extraction from productive, successful, and hardworking (white) people; or as a dumping of resources on the poor and the public in ways that would only corrupt and spoil them. However, for a time after 2008, the term *spending* was replaced by the Keynesian reappropriation of the term *investment* (Jeffrey 2010). Global North leaders, including US President Barack Obama, renationalized the term *investment*, using it to mean the reassertion of state commitment to planning a productive, inclusive future for a national community.

But soon it became apparent that in the Global North, particularly in the United States and the European Union, the return of state spending and the nationalization or renationalization of parts of the financial sector or the industrial "heights of the economy" would not ensure a return to social-democratic models, New Deal or Marshall Plan initiatives, or a shift in the Global North toward a Beijing Consensus model. Instead, new fiscal regimes would unleash a kind of upside-down Keynesianism, as Kean Birch and Vlad Mykhnenko (2010, 14–16) have described it. That is, predatory and unproductive banks would be bailed out by hundreds of billions of dollars in taxpayer revenue or absorbed into the deep well of public debt. Corporate and bank losses would be socialized (i.e., their losses passed on to the public), while their profits, more than ever, would be privatized (i.e., channeled into the hands of a small class of CEOs and shareholders). Now stripped of any veneer of economic rationality or productive market logic, the institutions identified most with neoliberalism had become, rather explicitly, a massive network of parasitical racketeering operations. Credit-rating agencies, international financial institutions, and investment banks began using the full brunt of their coercive reputational power to force state agencies and governments in the United States and the European Union to squeeze public purses (excluding the military, of course) without bothering anymore to promise that this austerity would produce "growth" or trickle down to eventually enhance middle-class consumer lifestyles. The "culture of neoliberalism," as an array of hegemonic consumerist and entrepreneurial subjectivities and economistic discourses of expertise, had become meaningless but refused to quit the Global North. And a profligate, elitist, racially coded hoarding culture of revanchist postneoliberalism, a post-economistic logic of austerity, reasserted itself in the United States and European Union zones.

Cadaverous Returns

As this post-2008 phase of the "the end of neoliberalism" gathered momentum in the Global North, it was not only political-economy theorists or policy interpreters who began to appreciate the morbidity of this governance regime and the global order it undergirded. Popular cultural imaginaries also wrestled with it. A set of spectacular necromancy metaphors and vivid gothic narratives began circulating transnationally. The popular imagination came to characterize large investment financial institutions (that channeled public bailout money all while emptied of real asset value or depositor confidence) as "zombie banks." As the economist Tyler Cowen stated, "If enough depositors fear frozen accounts, the banks will be emptied out, and they also will require additional government bailouts, on top of the bailouts for the bad real estate loans. The banks come to resemble empty shells, conduits for public aid but shrinking and unprofitable as businesses—and, to a large extent, that is already the case in Ireland. Portugal is moving in this same direction, toward being a land inhabited by zombie banks. It's the zombie banks that doom the current European bailout plans" (2011). From another perspective, the more apt undead metaphor became that of the vampire. Dracula comparisons seemed vividly appropriate to describe the large predatory financial firms that brought themselves back from the dead during the crisis by channeling taxpayers' bailout funds into record profits, thus feeding off the life-blood of the publicly stimulated economy, hoarding this wealth and burying it, deadening economic growth for the economy as a whole and creating few jobs.

In terms of the political instruments of neoliberalism, these, too, appeared to embrace a certain mortality. The press proclaimed a "death of politics" (Marder 2011). Neoliberalism's liberal political façade was suspended, as support for liberal political parties plummeted in Germany, the United Kingdom, and Canada, while the liberal branch of the Republican Party in the United States dissolved. Highly repressive "technocratic" governments were installed in Greece and Italy in 2011, where German bankers and IMF officials selected new prime ministers, Lucas Papademos and Mario Monti, detouring, at first, around democratic processes. These new postpolitical leaders would preside over new bank-pleasing austerity regimes that aimed to terminate not just the norms and redistribution mechanisms of the European welfare state, but also bury the idea of promoting "economic growth" as the driving aim of governance. In the austerity regimes of the Global North, austerity would persist in its most pure form, exorcized of its living political spirit and without the soul of its animating "pro-growth" ideologies and justifications. In this form it would rack up a series of cadaverous triumphs in the postcrisis Global North. As the Nobel laureate economist Paul Krugman summed it up on 19 December 2010, in the *New York Times* opinion piece entitled "When Zombies Win," "When historians look back at 2008–2010, what will puzzle them most, I believe, is the strange triumph of failed ideas. Free-market fundamentalists have been wrong about everything—yet they now dominate the political scene more than ever. . . . We all understand the need to deal with one's political enemies. But it's one thing to make deals to advance your goals; it's another to open the door to zombie ideas. When you do that, the zombies end up eating your brain—and quite possibly your economy too."

The missionaries of shock treatment, fiscal austerity, and roll-out neoliberalism who had spread from Chicago and Washington into the Third World in the 1970s and 1980s were now being forcibly evicted from the Global South and ordered to march back northward. Policy consultants, austerity proponents, and deregulation advocates staggered back onto the shores of Europe and North America, turning their hunger for profits on the pension funds, middle-class mortgages, and the social-security wealth accumulated in public purses in the North. During the 2008–2012 crisis, the same zombie neoliberals banished from the South surged northward to occupy, colonize, and drain the public resources and participatory political structures of the United States and the European Union. Marking this tidal shift, the IMF, now flush with funds from China, Russia, and Brazil, and largely evicted from much of the semiperiphery, came to concern itself primarily with draining economic growth and welfare resources from the EU zone. In the new austerity regimes of the North, the kind of humanity that zombie neoliberalism saw as its object was not "securitized" in the human-security sense; instead, its subjects were utterly abjected, animalized, and intensely racialized. Mediterranean countries with strong pension and welfare systems were called PIIGS, and anti-austerity protesters were sprayed with poison gas, brutalized by police, and branded "scum," "bums," and "dirt."[2]

These shifts confirmed a new global balance of power. The Global South started dictating certain terms of "rescue," with the IMF virtually begging the transitional military government in Cairo to take cheap loans from it in order to help the international institution retain a toehold of influence in the region during the Arab Spring. And Brazil stepped in with China to bail out the euro. While neoliberalism was revived in an undead, vengeful form in the North, policy talk seemed to go in the opposite direction in the surging semiperiphery. On 22 October 2011, Hassan al-Boraei, Egypt's labor minister, proclaimed that "A Marshall Plan." He said, "I am afraid that the Arab Spring could turn into an autumn if the issue of social justice is not achieved" (Oweis 2011). The Arab League secretary general, Nabil Elaraby, in a similar vein, stated, "If the Arab Spring hopes to achieve anything it is to attain good governance. This does not necessitate only democracy and freedom but social justice, meaning economic policies that meet popular aspirations" (Oweis 2011).

Samir Amin, the Egyptian pioneer of "dependency theory," who in 2011 was still at the cutting edge of the analysis of shifts in world ordering, spoke at the World Social Forum, in February 2011 in Dakar, Senegal, after spending a week in Tahrir Square:

> Egypt is a cornerstone of the US plan to control the planet. . . . Neoliberal capitalist integration into the global system is at the root of all these social devastations. . . . What Obama means by "smooth transition" [after Mubarak's downfall] is a transition that would lead to no change, only some minor concessions. . . . The system is strong—nobody can get rid of the system in five minutes. It will be a long process. Nobody in Egypt is antistatist. They feel the state is responsible for the economy. The blah-blah of the market solving problems, nobody buys. The state must take up the responsibilities, subsidies, control, nationalizations, etc. . . . We need a strong, popular, democratic state to restrict capital and to fight imperialism. . . . Egypt is a country of long revolutions. The people are accustomed to it. . . . Everybody knows that in Egypt we shall continue the process of struggle until we have won. (Hui, Tiejun, and Chi 2012, 168–205)

And in the context of a world split between the zombie neoliberalism of the Global North and new kinds of southern restiveness and animation, President Dilma Rousseff offered to take leadership of recapitalizing the IMF so it could manage the Eurozone restructuring and the capping of growth in Europe (Vieira 2012) with the understanding that, in exchange, the IMF would allow Global South powers increased voting rights in international financial institutions to reflect the shift in the world balance of power.[3] Indeed the tables had turned. Yet European and US conservatives within the IMF remained in denial. They rejected Brazil's offer and chose to stand against the tide. When Dominique Strauss-Khan was forced to resign for allegedly raping a hotel maid, the IMF nominated a French fiscal conservative, Christine Lagarde, rather than Mohammed El-Erian, the dynamic Egyptian investment banker who supports public-sector "stimulus" and pro-growth policies (Steven Goldberg 2010), and who had been brought forward as a favorite of Global South–origin IMF officials (dos Santos 2011).

Zombie Neoliberals versus Securitized Parahumans

Although the shifting balance of power away from the Global North was highlighted by the crisis around the euro and the redirection of the IMF, I have not focused in this book on this realm of international institutions and banking politics. Instead, I have worked to underline another landscape of shifts, institutions, actors, origin-points, and processes that came to crystallize a new global ordering during the lead-up to this crisis period. I have illuminated subjects, spaces, and new kinds of governance logics, responding to the need to develop framings for what security means and how it is practiced, and to map how logics of securitization take up and enable new kinds of human subjects. Human-security states emerge through these subjects. Their powers are woven of the contradictory logics of religious moralization, police paramilitarization, and juridical individualism, as well as from insurgent forms of worker ideology and labor politics.

These distinct but intersecting logics of securitizing governance do not converge around any ideal type, and cannot forsake the militaristic, dispossessive, and (neo)colonial relations of power that nurtured them in the semiperipheral context. But these are not forms of zombie neoliberalism or cadaverous imperial continuity either. These forms of securitized humanity and the human-security regimes that constitute them are animated, internally contradictory, and restive. They are propelling our planet boldly toward new futures.

Notes

INTRODUCTION

1. "Triumph as Mubarak Quits," *Al Jazeera*, 11 February 2011, http://www.aljazeera
.com.

2. "Text of Communique No. 4 from Egypt's Supreme Council of the Armed
Forces," *McClatchy*, 12 February 2011, http://www.mcclatchydc.com.

3. "Hosni Mubarak Resigns as President," *Al Jazeera*, 11 February 2011, http://www
.aljazeera.com.

4. "Egyptian Female Protesters Forced to Take 'Virginity Tests': Report," *Huffington
Post*, 31 May 2011, http://www.huffingtonpost.com.

5. "Fact Box: Charges against Mubarak," *Al Jazeera*, 3 August 2011, http://www
.aljazeera.com.

6. "'Agora é presidente Lula,' afirma FHC," *Folha de S. Paulo*, 30 October 2011,
http://www.Folha.com.

7. *Polícia Militar* may be translated directly as "Military Police," which can cause
confusion given that in English it suggests law-enforcement units within the armed
forces. Following other Brazilianists, I translate the term as "Militarized Police,"
underlining that they are independent from and often rivals of the Brazilian military.

8. Ministério da Defesa, Assessoria de Comunicação Social, "Força de Pacificação
do Exército permanecerá nos complexos do Alemão e da Penha até junho," 26 January
2012, *Notícias Militares* (blog), http://noticiasmilitares.blogspot.de/2012/01/forca-de
-pacificacao-do-exercito.html.

9. "Mutirão de Limpeza no Morro da Formiga Perguntas mais frecuentes," http://
www.icoscidadania.org.br/wp-content/uploads/2012/06/Formiga_FAQ.pdf.

10. "Dilma quer Comissão da Verdade neste ano," *Estadão*, 28 February 2011, http://
www.estadao.com.

[1]
MOORING A NEW GLOBAL ORDER

1. "The Earth Summit: A Deficit of $2 Million Imperils Global Forum," *New York
Times*, 5 June 1992.

2. "Earthquake in Egypt Kills 370 and Injures 3,300," *New York Times*, 13 October
1992.

3. "Acrimony Surrounds Racism Summit," BBC *News*, 31 August 2001.

4. "Brasil culpou EUA e Israel por guerra de Gaza em 2008," *Folha de São Paulo*,
6 February 2011; "Brazil Recognises Palestine," *Al Jazeera English*, 5 December 2010.

5. "Brazil's Lula da Silva Named 'Most Influential World Leader' by Time Magazine," *MercoPress*, 30 April 2010.

6. "Brazil President Blames 'White People' for Crisis," CNBC, 27 March 2009, http://www.CNBC.com.

[2]
POLICING THE PERVERSIONS OF GLOBALIZATION

1. "Secretário é favorável ao cadastramento de travestis," *O Globo*, 17 August 1990. *Travesti* literally means cross-dressed, not "trans" or "transsexual," and it seems *travesti* is the only term this group agrees on. Until recently, very few identified as transgendered or as transwomen, and they resisted identification with gay men, too (Kulick 1997, 224). Nor have travesti organizations come to a consensus on how to identify themselves in relation to gender categories or sexual orientation (Ramos and Carrara 2006, 187–88).

2. The Associação das Travestis e Liberados (ASTRAL) can be translated as the Association of Travestis and Liberated People. See Monteiro 1992 on ASTRAL's creation.

3. Murders of travestis increased from the mid-1980s through the 1990s, during which time the courts actually decreased the penalty for brutalizing this sexual minority. In one representative case, a Militarized Police officer who murdered several travesti prostitutes was absolved because the judge argued that travestis in general were "high risk" and a threat to public safety (Godoy 1994).

4. The term *blitz* in Brazilian Portuguese denotes Militarized Police actions and blockades that target internal enemies.

5. "Operação Pudor começa a tirar travestis das ruas," *O Globo*, 29 August 1986; "Risco de prisão cresce no centro," *Folha de São Paulo*, 24 March 1993; "Operação não tira travestis do Centro," *O Dia*, 19 October 1991; "Blitz da polícia tira os travestis," *O Globo*, 12 January 1986.

6. As Don Kulick has pointed out, "Whenever travestis do appear in the news [or in police reports the news draws on], they are featured there as dangerous criminals . . . or as corpses (often photographed in lurid close-up). . . . Whenever they are accused of committing violence, this is always clearly spelled out in headlines. . . . In stark contrast to this, reports of violence against travestis are either without agents, or the agentive, subject position of the sentence is filled with an instrument—a knife, or a gun, or a blow—not a person" (1996, 5).

7. "Conviviality" has reappeared in analyses of the production of social subjectivities because of the term's spatial resonance, its public contingent character, and its resistance to the essentialisms that can adhere to "identity." See Gilroy 2005, Illich 1973, Lash and Featherstone 2002, and Singerman and Amar 2006 for conviviality in relation to migration, racial complexity or mixing, vernacular cosmopolitanism, popular-class agency and creativity, critical multiculturalism, and antifascism.

8. See Kempadoo 2004 on the relationship between globalization, tourism, and gendered sex work in the postcolonial setting. My analysis of sex work has also been shaped by Kempadoo and Doezema 1998; and Kempadoo, Sanghera, and Pattanaik 2005.

9. For analyses of the history and politics of gender and sexual categorization at the

intersections of Marxism, orientalism, colonialism, and Islamic reform, see AbuKhalil 1997, and Hammami and Rieker 1988.

10. Charges continued to merge accusations of prostitution with terrorism, drawing on article 9, law 10 of the 1961 code on the Combat of Prostitution (penalty of prison from three months to three years), and the more recent article 98 of the Egyptian Penal Code, which prohibits offending religion and mandates imprisonment for up to five years.

11. Barbara Limanowska and Ann Janette Rosga (2004) discuss the legal and institutional norms and police practices that frame trafficked women as non-agentic objects.

12. *Cadernos do Patrimonio Cultural* 1 (1991): 27.

13. "Governo lança campanha de combate a turismo sexual," *Folha de São Paulo*, 6 February 1997.

14. "Saiba o que diz o código penal," *O Globo*, 29 July 2000.

15. "Malahi Shari' al-Haram ta'arradat li-l-takhrib," *Al-Ahram*, 20 January 1977; "La budra wa-la mawad hariqa fi-l-takhrib Shari' al-Haram," *Akhir Sa'a*, 9 April 1986.

16. For fascinating case studies of inverted orientalism, see Hirakawa 1998 and Zine 2006.

17. "Izalat mabani kazinu bi-Shari' al-Haram," *Al-Ahram*, 16 March 1980.

18. "Sukkan al-Haram, madha yaqulun 'an naql al-malahi?!," *Al-Gomhuria*, 16 April 1986.

19. "Dughut li-waqf qarar naql malahi Shari' al-Haram wa-tahwiliha li-mata'im siya-hiyya wa-dur sinima wa-masarih," *Al-Wafd*, 10 October 1986.

20. From 2000 to 2007, the Mubarak government diverted tourist and commuter traffic away from Pyramids Road by opening Ring Road, which brought visitors directly to the Pyramids without passing through the nightclub zone. It remains to be seen if this rerouting of traffic will change the symbolic identity of Pyramids Road as a space of cultural contact and conflict. See 'Aashour 1998.

21. World Tourism Organization, "Report on the Cairo World Tourism Conference," October 1995.

22. "Al-siyaha wa-tijarat al-jins," *Rosal Youssef*, 7 October 1999.

23. US and British racial science analyses of the category mulatto, and specifically of the mixed-race Egyptian, emerged during the mid- and late nineteenth century. In 1843, the American racialist author George Gliddon asserted that pharaonic Egypt was powerful as long as it was ruled by whites and black Africans were kept segregated as slaves. Egypt's contemporary weakness, as Gliddon perceived it, was due to racial mixing and the resultant cultural and political degeneration of Egypt, as Arab rulers encouraged black and white intermingling. Later in the nineteenth century, British Victorians took up this racial science but emphasized the uncontrollable sexuality of mixed-race peoples, and Egyptians in particular, which required and legitimized the intervention of an outside, white civilizing and disciplining force. See Young 1995, 126–36.

24. "Dabt akbar shabaka li-l-da'ara . . . tuqaddim al-fatayat li-rijal al-'a'amal al-'arab," *Al-Ahrar*, 1 October 1997.

25. World Tourism Organization, "Responsible Tourism Requires Local Action,"

1996, accessed January 2004, http://www.world-tourism.org/ows-doc/pressrel
/8-10-96.

26. World Trade Organization, "Travel Industry Targets Sex Tourism," 1995, accessed January 2004, http://www.world-tourism.org/ows-doc/pressrel/travind.htm.

27. See Varma 2004, 67, for a detailed analysis of a globalizing provincialization process.

[3]
MUHAMMAD ATTA'S URBANISM

1. As Jonathan Brown states, Salafi organizations in Egypt, until the Revolution of 2011, focused not on politics but on "purification of belief and daily practice," which would "eventually bring substantive change to society and the state" (2011, 4). Although founded in Egypt in the early twentieth century by Levantine religious scholars, the movement started growing in the 1980s. "Increased contact with Saudi Arabia reinforced and accentuated Salafism in Egypt, through the influence of Saudi scholars as well as through the ideas and lifestyles that expatriate workers returning from Saudi Arabia brought with them, including gender and clothing norms" (4).

2. The theoretical framework of this study draws on critical work on tourism economies, authenticity discourses, and heritage cultures (AlSayyad 2001; Gregory 2001; Kirshenblatt-Gimblett 1998; Mitchell 2002; Caroline Williams 2002); new political anthropology approaches that analyze the formation of Arab state institutions and governance agendas in quotidian contexts and in grounded, complex struggles with local-level collective actors (Elyachar 2005; Ghannam 2002; Harders 2003; Ismail 2006; Singerman 1995); constructivist critical security studies approaches that examine the social production of securitization logics and their cultural and discursive aspects (Higate and Henry 2009; Simon 2007; Stanley 1996); and feminist work on the gendering and sexualization of urban planning and public space under colonial modernity and neoliberalism (Colomina and Bloomer 1992; Massey 1994; Elizabeth Wilson 1992).

3. General Organization for Physical Planning for Greater Cairo 1995.

4. *Zikr* is the chanting of verses, performed while swaying or spinning rhythmically in ecstatic unison with a group of devotees.

5. "Iftitah Zawiyat Abdel Rahman Katkhuda bi-l-Darb al-Ahmar," *al-Ahram*, 21 February 1999.

6. "A Nation Challenged: The Mastermind: A Portrait of the Terrorist," *New York Times*, 10 October 2001.

7. "A Nation Challenged: The Mastermind: A Portrait of the Terrorist," *New York Times*, 10 October 2001.

8. "Absha' madhbaha irhabiyya mundhu 'am 1992," *al-Wafd*, 18 November 1997.

9. "Al-ikhfaq fi al-ta'arruf 'ala hawiyyat murtakibi madhbahat al-Uqsur yakshif fadahat al-taqsir al-sabiq," *al-Shaab*, 2 December 1997; "Mubarak: Al-tahqiq ma'a 6 min rijal al-shurta . . . ," *al-Ahram*, 25 November 1997.

10. "Khubara' amn Sina'a ajnabiyya," *al-Ahrar*, 20 November 1997.

11. From interviews by author in al-Khayyamiyya, with S—— (tentmaker, embroiderer) and A—— (grocery owner), December 1997.

12. Between December 1997 and the summer of 1998, these hand-painted banners in English and German were present over the central workshop and tourist corridor of al-Darb al-Ahmar in Islamic Cairo, on al-Khayyamiyya, the tentmakers' bazaar.

13. Field interviews conducted by author in Bayn al-Qasrayn district, November 1998; also cited in Amar and Ahmed 1999, 12–14.

14. Field interviews conducted by author in Bayn al-Qasrayn district, November 1998; also cited in Amar and Ahmed 1999, 12–14.

15. "Tashkil ajhizat tatwir al-Qahira al-Fatimiyya khilal ayam," *al-Gomhuria*, 9 April 1998.

16. "History of Arab New York," *Gotham Gazette*, http://old.gothamgazette.com /commentary/107.history_arab.shtml.

[4]
SAVING THE CRADLE OF SAMBA

1. Because da Silva is a common surname in Brazil, the governor's first name is often used as an abbreviation for her full name, even in newspapers and campaign propaganda.

2. "O poder paralelo," *O Globo*, 1 October 2002, 23.

3. All translations are my own.

4. This is not unique to the Brazilian state; Jonathan Simon has made a convincing argument about the US state's dependence on drug crime in *Governing through Crime* (2007).

5. "Playboy," also known as Marcus Vinicius Tavares Gaviao, the twenty-seven-year-old prison guard and smuggler-networker, was arrested on 23 September 2002 by DRACO (the police organized-crime investigation squad), as reported by Vera Araujo (2000a, 16).

6. "O poder paralelo," *O Globo*, 1 October 2002, 19.

7. A *carioca* is a person from Rio de Janeiro or a culture identified with Rio.

8. Favela-Bairro official (name withheld), interview by author, 13 October 1999.

9. Interviews by author with Sandrinha Nogueira, president of Serrinha Residents Association (Associação de Moradores do Parque Licurgo), Madureira, 10, 11, and 12 January 2003.

[5]
OPERATION PRINCESS

1. United Nations "Palermo Protocol to Prevent, Suppress and Punish Trafficking in Persons, especially Women and Children," ratified by Brazil in 2004.

2. The Militarized Police and the Civil Police are distinct coercive institutions: the former patrols the streets and makes arrests; the latter investigates crimes and interrogates suspects.

3. Although prostitution has been technically legal or tolerated in Brazil for more than a century, the state has continuously hedged in this legality and, in fact, targeted the sector for constant policing under the guise of controlling syphilis epidemics in the late nineteenth century, "gang" violence in the 1980s, exploitation of children in the 1990s, and antitrafficking in the 2000s. And throughout these periods, the

state has prohibited the "exploitation of prostitution," which has allowed the police and judiciary to constantly intervene in the sector (author conversation with Sonia Corrêa, 10 January 2011).

4. The last Vice Police Stations were closed by President José Sarney in September 1989, as noted by Don Kulick (1998, 242).

5. These well-established informal shantytown communities house about one-quarter of Brazil's urban population and suffer as the target and stage for the great majority of trafficker and police violence.

6. See, for example, the journal *Classe Operararia* (1963–66), founded by Antonio Negri; the "Johnson-Forest Tendency" research on Detroit auto workers' culture in the 1940s and 1950s; and the group Socialisme ou Barbarie in France in the 1960s.

7. "pestraf: Study on Trafficking of Women, Adolescents and Children for Commercial Sexual Exploitation," Brasilia, 2002, http://www.childtrafficking.com/Docs /pestraf_2002__trafficking_i.pdf.

8. "Governo deve concluir em 2004 diagnostico sobre trafico de pessoas," *Folha de Sao Paulo*, 25 December 2003.

9. "A Guerra no Rio: Agora a guerra e politica," *Extra*, 14 April 2004.

10. "O 'Comando Azul' agora esta sentado no banco dos reus," *O Globo*, 10 April 2005.

11. "Crime de farad: Sanear a policia e um processo tao dificil quanto imprescindivel," *O Globo*, 12 April 2005.

12. "A Guerra no Rio: Agora a guerra e politica," *Extra*, 14 April 2004.

13. "Garotinho quer agilizar processo de punicao de policiais corruptos," *Folha de Sao Paulo*, 25 November 2003.

14. "Beleza femenina na policia," *Extra*, 29 May 2004.

15. "Governo lança plano contra exploração," *O Globo*, 23 March 2005.

16. "Ação contra mercadores do sexo: Nova unidade da polícia vai reprimir exploração sexual e acusado e preso na praia," *O Globo*, 9 February 2004.

17. "pms aprenderão a lidar com exploração sexual," *O Globo*, 14 February 2004.

18. "stj deve receber relator da onu para crimes de exploracao infantile," *Folha de Sao Paulo*, 4 November 2003.

19. "Força-tarefa contra prostituição," *O Globo*, 10 February 2004.

20. "Sexo pago será destaque na Sapucaí," *O Globo*, 20 February 2004.

21. "onu firma que trafico de mulheres e pouco investigado," *O Globo*, 20 May 2004.

22. "pm acusado de prostituir duas menores e preso," *O Globo*, 9 July 2004.

23. "Entrega de pizzas leva 11 policias a prisao," *O Globo*, 7 September 2004.

24. "Russo e assassinado a tiro em hotal na Barra," *O Globo*, 16 April 2005.

25. "Dez presos por explorar a prostituição de menores," *O Globo*, 20 April 2005.

26. "Para o Trabalho: Prostitute faz 'companhia a turista,'" *O Globo*, 28 April 2005.

27. Luiz Eduardo Soares, interview by author, University of California Humanities Research Institute, 5 February 2008.

28. "Leia a íntegra da entrevista de Lula as radios," *Folha de Sao Paulo*, 2 October 2003.

29. "New York Times: Prostitutição coloca eua e Brasil em conflito na politica para aids," *O Globo*, 25 July 2005.

30. "Não se pode controlar a Aids partindo de principios 'maniqueistas, teologicos, fundamentalistas e xiitas,'" *O Globo*, 12 May 2005.

31. As elected assembly representative, Gabeira proposed national legislation in 2002 that "provides for the right to demand payment for services of a sexual nature and revokes articles 228, 229 and 231 of the Penal Code" (Educação Pública, http://www.educacaopublica.rj.gov.br/biblioteca/documentos/0017.html).

[6]

FEMINIST INSURRECTIONS AND REVOLUTION

Epigraphs: Mona Prince, "A Personal Testimony on Police Brutality during Protests: January 26, 2011, Downtown Cairo," posted on Facebook, 27 January 2011, http://www.facebook.com/people/Mona-Prince/652613580; Mahfouz 2011a.

1. Regional Workshop for Arab Parliaments on Implementing cedaw and Ending Violence against Women, Beirut, 27–29 July 2010, http://www.ipu.org/splz-e/beirut10.htm.

2. Aida Seif Al-Dawla, interviews by author, Giza, Egypt, 3 and 25 March 2008.

3. Aida Seif Al-Dawla, interviews by author, Giza, Egypt, 3 and 25 March 2008.

4. Aida Seif Al-Dawla, interviews by author, Giza, Egypt, 3 and 25 March 2008.

5. "Hundreds of Egyptian Boys Arrested," *Daily Mail Online*, 21 November 2008, http://www.dailymail.co.uk.

6. Paola Bacchetta (2009) offers a useful schematic analysis of "vulgar" feminist protest strategies deployed by Muslim lesbian groups in France.

7. "Egypt Court Jails Man for Sexual Harassment," *Gulfnews.com*, 22 October 2008, http://gulfnews.com.

8. Mozn Hassan, interview by author, Oakland, California, 20 March 2011.

CONCLUSION

Epigraphs: Luiz Inácio Lula da Silva, 23 September 2008, Speech to General Assembly of the United Nations, Statement summary, http://www.un.org/en/ga/63/generaldebate/pdf/brazil_en.pdf; "Brasileiros estão 'vacinados' contra o neoliberalismo, diz Dilma," *Gazeta do Povo*, 26 January 2012, http://www.gazetadopovo.com.br; cbc interview with Hamdeen Sabahy, 10 May 2012, reported in "Presidential Campaigns on Privatization," *Aswat Masriya*, http://en.aswatmasriya.com/news/view.aspx?id=8ac7083b-3438-4af2-beob-ed9bd8f01f77, and first paragraph of Sabahy's presidential election platform, Hamdeensabahy.com, 23 May 2012.

1. brics is the acronym for Brazil, Russia, India, China, and South Africa, which together have formalized a forum for dialogue and policy coordination.

2. piigs is the acronym for Portugal, Italy, Ireland, Greece, and Spain.

3. "Emerging Powers Committed to imf but Insist on Less European Predominance," MercoPress South Atlantic News Agency, 21 April 2012, http://en.mercopress.com/2012/04/21/emerging-powers-committed-to-imf-but-insist-on-less-european-predominance.

References

'Aashour, Hassan. 1998. "Al-ra'iis yaftatih koubri al-muniib wa al-tariiq al-da'iri." *Al-Ahram*, 25 November.

Abad, Gracia. 2010. "The Beijing Consensus in the Shadow of the Global Financial Crisis." United Nations Discussion Paper, United Nations.

Abaza, Mona. 2011. "Critical Commentary: Cairo's Downtown Imagined: Dubaisation or Nostalgia?" *Urban Studies* 48 (May): 1075–87. doi: 10.1177/0042098011399598.

Abdel-Hadi, Muhammad. 1986. "Milahi wa kaziinohaat al-haram al-abqaa 'aleiha bi-shart taghyeer inshaatiha." *Al-Ahram*, 16 May.

Abdelrahman, Amr. 2007. "Altaharrush aljinsi fil 'Eid: 'Ammaa yuhajibu alsharaf 'an-dema yudalif ila sahat aljadal al'aam." *Al-Badil*, 18 July.

Abers, Rebecca. 1996. "From Ideas to Practice: The Partido dos Trabalhadores and Participatory Governance in Brazil." *Latin American Perspectives* 13 (4): 35–53.

Abou al-Futuh, Hossam. 1998. "Conférence sur PNUD EGY/95/004." *Observatoire Urbain du Caire Contemporain: Lettre d'Informations* 48 (June): 48–56.

Abou Hawaar, Zakariya. 1986. "Naql milahi shaari' al-haram: Li-madha?" *Akher Saa'a*, 16 April.

Abraham, Itty. 2009. "Segurança/Security in Brazil and the United States." *Words in Motion: Toward a Global Lexicon*, ed. Carol Gluck and Anna Lowenhaupt Tsing, 21–39. Durham: Duke University Press.

Abrahamsen, Rita. 2005. "Blair's Africa: The Politics of Securitization and Fear." *Alternatives: Global, Local, Political* 30 (1): 55–80.

Abu Al-Fatah, Ilhaam. 1998. "Al-Qahira al-tarikhiya tastai'd l-a'am 2000." *Al-Akhbar*, 14 April.

AbuKhalil, As'ad. 1997. "Gender Boundaries and Sexual Categories in the Arab World." *Feminist Issues* 15 (1–2): 91–104.

Abu-Lughod, Janet. 1971. *Cairo: 1001 Years of the City Victorious*. Princeton: Princeton University Press.

———. 1987. "The Islamic City: Historic Myth, Islamic Essence, and Contemporary Relevance." *International Journal of Middle East Studies* 19 (2): 155–76.

Abu-Lughod, Lila. 2000. *Veiled Sentiments: Honor and Poetry in a Bedouin Society*. Berkeley: University of California Press.

———. 2008. "Do Muslim Women Really Need Saving? Anthropological Reflections on Cultural Relativism and Its Others." *American Anthropologist* 104 (3): 783–90.

Afshari, Reza. 1994. "An Essay on Islamic Cultural Relativism in the Discourse of Human Rights." *Human Rights Quarterly* 16: 235–76.

Agamben, Giorgio. 1998. *Homo Sacer: Sovereign Power and Bare Life*. Palo Alto: Stanford University Press.

———. 2005. *State of Exception*. Chicago: University of Chicago Press.

Agência Brasil. 2011a. "Manifestação no Rio lembra os 18 anos da chacina da Candelária." *Folha de São Paulo*, 23 July.

———. 2011b. "Polícia Pacificadora do Rio ganha reforço de mais de 300 homens." *Folha de São Paulo*, 20 December.

Agência Estado. 2010. "Exército tem plano de ação para todos os Estados brasileiros." *Folha Vitória*, 6 December.

Agustin, Laura Maria. 2007. *Sex at the Margins: Migration, Labour Markets and the Rescue Industry*. London: Zed Books.

Aidi, Hisham. 2003a. "Let Us Be Moors: Islam, Race and 'Connected Histories.'" *Middle East Report* 229: 42–53.

———. 2003b. "State Withdrawal and Political Change: Corporatism, Capacity and Coalition Politics in Egypt and Mexico." PhD diss., Columbia University.

Al-Askar, Abdel-Maqsoud. 1986. "Milahi shaari' al-haram." *Al-Jumhuria*, 25 July.

Al-Diib, Adel. 1986. "Majlis mahalli al-giza yutlub naql milahi shaari' al-haram." *Al-Ahram*, 16 March.

Alexander, Jacqui. 1994. "Not Just (Any) Body Can Be a Citizen: The Politics of Law, Sexuality and Postcoloniality in Trinidad and Tobago and the Bahamas." *Feminist Review* 48 (autumn): 5–23.

Alexander, Jacqui, and Chandra Talpade Mohanty, eds. 1996. *Feminist Geneaologies, Colonial Legacies, Democratic Futures*. New York: Routledge.

alHussein, 'Aoani. 1998. "Al-Qahira al-Islamiya 'ala qa'imat ihtimamat al-ra'is." *Metr Murabaa* 14.

'Ali, Sayyid. 1998. "In Fatimid Cairo: A New Beginning to Beautiful History." *Al-Ahram*, 19 March.

Alkire, Sabina. 2003. "A Conceptual Framework for Human Security." Working Paper, Queen Elizabeth House, University of Oxford.

AlSayyad, Nezar, ed. 2001. *Consuming Tradition, Manufacturing Heritage: Global Norms and Urban Forms in the Age of Tourism*. Florence: Psychology Press.

AlSayyad, Nezar, Irene Bierman, and Nasser Rabbat, eds. 2005. *Making Cairo Medieval*. Oxford: Lexington Books.

Alston, Philip. 2008. *Promoção e proteção de todos os direitos humanos, civis, políticos, econômicos, sociais e culturais incluindo ao desenvolvimento: Relatório do Relator Especial de execuções extrajudiciais, sumárias ou arbitraries*. New York: United Nations Commission on Human Rights.

Alvarez, Sonia. 1999. "Advocating Feminism: The Latin American Feminist NGO 'Boom.'" *International Feminist Journal of Politics* 1 (2): 181–209.

———. 2009. "Beyond NGO-ization? Reflections from Latin America." *Development* 52 (2): 175–84.

Alvez, Maria Helena Moreira, and Philip Evanson. 2011. *Living in the Crossfire: Favela Residents, Drug Dealers, and Police Violence in Rio de Janeiro*. Philadelphia: Temple University Press.

Al-Zeitouni, Basnt. 1998. "'Aoudat gara'im." *Sabah al-Kheir*, 5 February.

Amar, Paul. 1998a. "Blame It on the Road: The Legend of Pyramids Road." *Cairo Times*, 17–30 September.

———. 1998b. "Bright Lights, Hype City: The Ups and Downs of the Recent Tourism and Shopping Festival in Cairo." *Hospitality Egypt* (October–November): 8.

———. 1998c. "The Business of Culture: Will Turning a Corner of the Citadel into a Marketplace Desecrate the Historic Complex or Save It?" *Cairo Times*, 1 July.

———. 2003. "Reform in Rio: Reconsidering the Myths of Crime and Violence." *NACLA Report on the Americas* 37 (2): 37–42.

———. 2005. "Tácticas e termos da luta contra o racismo institucional nos sectores de polícia e de segurança." *Elemento suspeito: Abordagem policial e discriminação na Cidade do Rio de Janeiro*, ed. Silvia Ramos and Leonarda Musumeci, 229–82. Rio de Janeiro: Civilização Brasileira.

———. 2009. "Operation Princess in Rio de Janeiro: Policing 'Sex Trafficking,' Stengthening Worker Citizenship, and the Urban Geopolitics of Security in Brazil." *Security Dialogue* 40 (4–5): 513–41.

———. 2010. "New Racial Missions of Policing: Comparative Studies of State Authority, Urban Governance, and Security Technology in the Twenty-first Century." *New Racial Missions of Policing: International Perspectives on Evolving Law-Enforcement Politics*, ed. Paul Amar, 1–18. London: Routledge.

———. 2011a. "Middle East Masculinity Studies: Discourses of 'Men in Crisis,' Industries of Gender in Revolution." *Journal of Middle East Women's Studies* 6 (3): 36–70.

———. 2011b. "Why Egypt's Progressives Win." *Jadaliyya*, 8 February. http://www.jadaliyya.com.

———. 2011c. "Why Mubarak Is Out." *Jadaliyya*, 1 February. http://www.jadaliyya.com.

———. 2012a. "Egypt as a Globalist Power: Mapping Military Participation in Decolonizing Internationalism, Repressive Entrepreneurialism, and Humanitarian Globalization between the Revolutions of 1952 and 2011." *Globalizations* 9 (1): 179–94.

———, ed. 2012b. *Global South to the Rescue: Emerging Humanitarian Superpowers and Globalizing Rescue Industries*. London: Routledge.

———, ed. 2013. *The Middle East and Brazil: Forging New South-South Alliances, Reviving Transregional Public Cultures*. Bloomington: Indiana University Press.

Amar, Paul, and Sameh Ahmed. 1999. "A 'Renaissance' for Fatimid Cairo? From Thriving Workshop Zone to Open-Air Museum." *Hospitality Egypt* (January–February): 2.

Amar, Paul, and Cathy Schneider. 2003. "Crime Disorder and Authoritarian Policing." *NACLA Report on the Americas* 37 (2): 37–42.

Amin, Samir. 1973. *Le developpement inegal: Essai sur les formations sociales du capitalisme peripherique*. Paris: Editions de Minuit.

Amora, Dimmi, and Renato Garcia. 2002. "Atentado." *O Globo*, 16 May.

Amorim, Celso. 2005. "Preface." *Diálogo América do Sul: Países Árabes*, ed. Heloisa Vilhena de Araujo, i–ix. Brasília: Fundação Alexandre de Gusmão, Instituto de Pesquisa de Relações Internacionais.

———. 2010. "Brazil and the Middle East." *Cairo Review of Global Affairs*, 17 May.

An-Na'im, A., ed. 1995. *Human Rights and Religious Values: An Uneasy Relationship?* Grand Rapids, Mich.: Eerdmans Press.

———. 1996. "Islamic Foundations of Human Rights." *Religious Human Rights in Global Perspective*, ed. J. Witter and J. Van der Vyver, 337–60. Leiden: Martinus Nijhoff.

Antunes, Ricardo. 2006. *Uma esquerda fora do lugar: O governo Lula e os escaminhos do PT*. Rio de Janeiro: Autores Associados.

Anuário dos Trabalhadores. 2007. São Paulo: Departamento Intersindical de Estatística e Estudos Socieconômicos. http://www.dieese.org.br/anu/anuario2007.pdf.

———. 2008. São Paulo: Departamento Intersindical de Estatística e Estudos Socieconômicos. http://portal.mte.gov.br/data/files/FF8080812BA5F4B7012BAAE BB86E03B5/anuario2007.pdf.

Appadurai, Arjun. 2006. *Fear of Small Numbers: An Essay on the Geography of Anger*. Durham: Duke University Press.

'Aqaari, Khabiir. 1998. "Daruuraat: Istighlaal al-tagamu'aat al'umraaniya al-qariba li-muwaagahat ihtiyagaat tafriigh al-sukkaan wa al-anshita." *Al-Ahram*, 11 May.

Aql, Gamal. 2001. "Perverted Satanists before the Coroner!!" *Al-Gumhuria*, 16 May.

Araujo, Vera. 2002a. "'Playboy' traficante preso." *O Globo*, 24 September.

———. 2002b. "Presidios de papel." *O Globo*, 29 September.

Arias, Enrique Desmond. 2006. *Drugs and Democracy in Rio de Janeiro: Democracy, Social Networks and Public Security*. Chapel Hill: University of North Carolina Press.

Arrighi, Giovanni. 1985. *Semiperipheral Development: The Politics of Southern Europe in the Twentieth Century*. Thousand Oaks, Calif.: Sage Publications.

ASPA. 2005. "Cúpula América do Sul-Países Árabes: Declaração de Brasília." 11 May. http://www2.mre.gov.br/aspa/documentos.html.

———. 2009. "Doha Declaration." 31 March. http://www2.mre.gov.br/aspa /documentos.html.

———. 2010. "Horizontal Matrix of Environmental Cooperation." 5 November. http://www2.mre.gov.br/aspa/.

Astvasadoorian, R. 1998. "California's Two-Prong Attack against Gang Crime and Violence: The Street Terrorism Enforcement and Prevention Act and Anti-Gang Injunctions." *Journal of Juvenile Law* 19: 272.

Atassi, Mohammed Ali. 2009. "Taking on Sexual Harassment, a Social Phenomenon in Egypt." *Al Jadid* 15 (60). http://www.aljadid.com/content/taking-sexual-harassment-social-phenomenon-egypt.

Athanasiou, Athena. 2003. "Technologies of Humanness, Aporias or Biopolitics, and the Cut Body of Humanity." *differences* 14 (1): 125–62.

Atta, Muhammad El-Amir. 1999. "Khareg Bab-en-Nasr: Ein gefahrdeter Altstadtteil in Aleppo: Stadtteilentwicklung in einer islamisch-orientalischen Stadt." Master's thesis, Technical University of Hamburg-Harburg.

Awad, Hoda. 1998. "Azmat Idara fi Qita'a Al-Siyaaha." Conference Paper, 18 March, Cairo University.

Aydinli, Ersel, and James Rosenau, eds. 2005. *Globalization, Security and the Nation State*. Albany: State University of New York Press.

Azimi, Negar. 2006. "Prisoners of Sex." *New York Times*, 3 December.

Azuela de la Cueva, Antonio. 1989. *La ciudad, la propriedad privado, y el derecho.* México, D.F.: El Colegio de México.

Bacchetta, Paola. 2009. "Co-Formations: Des spatialités de résistance décoloniales chez les lesbiennes 'of color' en France." *Genre, séxualité et société* 1 (spring). doi: 10.4000/gss.810.

Bacchetta, Paola, and Margaret Power. 2002. *Right Wing Women: From Conservatives to Extremists around the World.* New York: Routledge.

Bachelet Jeria, Michelle. 2009. "Respuesta progresista para la crisis global." *El País*, 29 March. http://www.elpais.com.

Baher, Kamal. 2009. "Mideast: Building New Bridges to Latin America." *IPS News*, 31 March.

Bahgat, Hossam. 2001. "Morality Police Crackdown." *Cairo Times*, 17–23 May. http://tampabaycoalition.homestead.com/files/01MoralityPolice.htm.

———. 2004. "Egypt's Virtual Protection of Morality." *Middle East Report* 230 (spring): 22–25.

Bahgat, Hossam, and Wesal Afifi. 2007. "Egypt: Sexuality Politics in Egypt." *Sex-Politics: Reports from the Front Lines*, ed. Richard Parker, Rosalind Petchesky, and Robert Sember, 53–89. New York: Sexuality Policy Watch.

Bahreini, Raha. 2008. "From Perversion to Pathology: Discourses and Practices of Gender Policing in the Islamic Republic of Iran." *Muslim World Journal of Human Rights* 5 (1): 1–49.

Bailey, Peter. 2002. "Parasexuality and Glamour: The Victorian Barmaid as Cultural Prototype." *Sexualities in History: A Reader*, ed. Kim Phillips and Barry Reay, 222–46. New York: Routlege.

Baiocchi, Gianpaolo, ed. 2003. *Radicals in Power: The Workers' Party (PT) and Experiments in Urban Democracy in Brazil.* New York: Zed Books.

———. 2005. *Militants and Citizens: The Politics of Participatory Democracy in Porto Alegre.* Palo Alto: Stanford University Press.

Baker, Gideon, and David Chandler. 2005. *Global Civil Society: Contested Futures.* New York: Routledge.

Balibar, Etienne. 2003. "Structuralism: A Destitution of the Subject?" *differences* 14 (1): 1–21.

Balos, B., and M. L. Fellows. 1999. "A Matter of Prostitution: Becoming Respectable." *New York University Law Review* 74: 1220–303.

Barbi, Daniela. 1999. "Cidadania posta em xeque: Grupo homossexual unificado ASTRAL pede fim do voto obrigatorio." *Sui Generis* 5 (49).

Barbosa, Regina Maria, and Richard Parker. 1999. *Sexualidades pelo avesso: Direitos, identidades e poder.* Rio De Janeiro: UERJ Instituto de Medicina Social.

Baron, Beth. 2007. *Egypt as Woman: Nationalism, Gender and Politics.* Berkeley: University of California Press.

Battersby, Paul, and Joseph M. Siracusa. 2009. *Globalization and Human Security.* New York: Rowman and Littlefield.

Bayart, Jean-François, Stephen Ellis, and Beatrice Hibou, eds. 1999. *The Criminalization of the State in Africa.* Bloomington: Indiana University Press.

Bayat, Asef. 1998. "Revolution without Movement, Movement without Revolution: Comparing Islamic Activism in Iran and Egypt." *Comparative Studies in Society and History* 40 (1): 141–42.

———. 2003. "The 'Street' and the Politics of Dissent in the Arab World." *Middle East Report* 226: 10–17.

———. 2009. *Life as Politics: How Ordinary People Change the Middle East.* Palo Alto: Stanford University Press.

Bayley, David. 1990. *Patterns of Policing: A Comparative International Analysis.* New Brunswick: Rutgers University Press.

Bedford, Kate. 2005. "Loving to Straighten Out Development: Sexuality and 'Ethno-development' in the World Bank's Ecuadorian Lending." *Feminist Legal Studies* 13 (3): 295–322.

———. 2009. *Developing Partnerships: Gender, Sexuality and the Reformed World Bank.* Minneapolis: University of Minnesota Press.

Beinin, Joel. 2011a. "Egypt at the Tipping Point?" *Foreign Policy: Middle East Channel,* 31 January. http://mideast.foreignpolicy.com.

———. 2011b. "Egypt's Workers Rise Up." *Nation,* 17 February. http://www .thenation.com.

Bellamy, Alex, and Matt McDonald. 2002. "'The Utility of Human Security': Which Humans? What Security? A Reply to Thomas and Tow." *Security Dialogue* 33 (3): 373–77.

Berkman A, J. Garcia, M. Muñoz-Laboy, V. Paiva, and R. Parker. 2005. "A Critical Analysis of the Brazilian Response to HIV/AIDS: Lessons Learned for Controlling and Mitigating the Epidemic in Developing Countries." *American Journal of Public Health* 95 (7): 1162–72.

Bernstein, Elizabeth. 2007. "The Sexual Politics of the 'New Abolitionism.'" *differences* 18 (5): 128–51.

Bernstein, Elizabeth, and Laurie Schaffer, eds. 2005. *Regulating Sex: The Politics of Intimacy and Identity.* New York: Routledge.

Biehl, João. 2004. "The Activist State: Global Pharmaceuticals, AIDS and Citizenship in Brazil." *Social Text* 22 (3): 105.

Biehl, João, and Torben Eskerod. 2007. *Will to Live: AIDS Therapies and the Politics of Survival.* Princeton: Princeton University Press.

Birch, Kean, and Vlad Mykhnenko. 2010. *The Rise and Fall of Neoliberalism: The Collapse of an Economic Order?* London: Zed Books.

Bislev, Sven, Dorte Salskov-Iversen, and Hans Frause Hansen. 2001. "Globalization, Governance and Security Management." *IKL Department of Intercultural Communication and Management, Working Paper 43.* Copenhagen: Copenhagen Business School.

Bittar, Jorge. 1992. *O Modo petista de governar.* Brasilia: Teoria and Debate Press.

Blanchette, Thaddeus Gregory, and Ana Paula da Silva. 2008. "Mulheres vulneraveis e meninas mas: Uma analise antropologica de narrativas hegemonicas sobre trafico das pessoas no Brasil." Paper presented at the ANPOCS National Social Science Congress, Caixambu, Brasil.

———. 2010. "Mulheres vulneráveis e meninas más: Uma análise antropológica de narrativas hegemônicas sobre o tráfico de pessoas." *A experiência migrante: Entre deslocamentos e reconstruções*, ed. Ferreira et al., 325–60. Rio de Janeiro: Gartamond.

Bockman, Johanna. 2011. *Markets in the Name of Socialism: The Left-Wing Origins of Neoliberalism*. Palo Alto: Stanford University Press.

Boellstorff, Tom. 2005. *The Gay Archipelago: Sexuality and Nation in Indonesia*. Princeton: Princeton University Press.

Bógus, Lucia Maria Machado, and Maria Silvia Bassanezi. 1998. "Do Brasil para a Europa: Imigrantes Brasileiros na Península Itálica neste final de Século." *O fenómeno migratorio no limiar do 3º milenio: Desafios pastorais*, 68–92. Rio de Janeiro: Vozes.

Booth, Karen. 2004. *Local Women, Global Science: Fighting AIDS in Kenya*. Bloomington: Indiana University Press.

Booth, Ken, ed. 2005. *Critical Security Studies and World Politics*. Boulder: Lynne Rienner Books.

Bostic, Philip J. n.d. "Social Movement." Learning to Give. http://learningtogive.org /papers/paper59.html.

Boueri, Aline Gatto, and Marine Lemle. 2006. "O Rio entre traficantes e milícias." 8 December. http://www.comunidadesegura.org/pt-br/node/31173.

Bourantonis, Dimitris. 2005. *The History and Politics of UN Security Council Reform: The Case for Adjustment in the Post-Cold War Era*. New York: Routlege.

Bowers, Kate J., Shane D. Johnson, and Ken Pease. 2004. "Prospective Hot-Spotting: The Future of Crime Mapping?" *British Journal of Criminology* 44 (5): 641–58.

"Brasilia Declaration." 2005. Summit of South American-Arab Countries, 10–11 May. http://www.scribd.com/doc/51312638/DECLARACAO-DE-BRASILIA-ASPA.

Braveboy-Wagner, J. 2003. *The Foreign Policies of the Global South: Rethinking Conceptual Frameworks*. Boulder: Lynne-Rienner.

———. 2009. *Institutions of the Global South*. New York: Routledge.

Brenner, Neil, and Nik Theodore. 2002. "Cities and the Geographies of 'Actually Existing Neoliberalism.'" *Antipode* 34 (3): 349–79.

Brodie, Janine. 2004. "Globalization and the Social Question." *Governing Under Stress: Middle Powers and the Challenge of Globalization*, ed. Marjorie Griffin Cohen and Stephen Clarkson, 12–32. London: Zed Books.

Brook, Daniel. 2009. "The Architect of 9/11." *Slate*, 8 September. http://www.slate.com.

Brooks, Bradley. 2010. "Dilma Rousseff Elected Brazil's President." *Huffington Post*, 31 October. http://www.huffingtonpost.com.

Brown, Jonathan. 2011. "Sufis and Salafis in Egypt." *Carnegie Papers* (December): 1–19. Washington: Carnegie Endowment.

Brown, Wendy. 1995. *States of Injury*. Princeton: Princeton University Press.

Bubant, Nils. 2005. "Vernacular Security: The Politics of Feeling Safe in Global, National and Local Worlds." *Security Dialogue* 36 (3): 275–96.

Buck-Morss, Susan. 2003. *Thinking Past Terror: Islamism and Critical Theory on the Left*. London: Verso.

———. 2010. "Theorizing Today: The Post-Soviet Condition." http://falcon.arts .cornell.edu/sbm5/thoughts.html.

Bumiller, Kristin. 2008. *In an Abusive State: How Neoliberalism Appropriated the Feminist Movement against Sexual Violence*. Durham: Duke University Press.

Burdick, John. 1996. *Looking for God in Brazil: The Progressive Catholic Church in Urban Brazil's Religious Arena*. Berkeley: University of California Press.

Burke, Anthony. 2007. *Beyond Security, Ethics and Violence: War against the Other*. New York: Routledge.

Burke, Peter, and Maria Lúcia G. Pallares-Burke. 2008. *Gilberto Freyre: Social Theory in the Tropics*. Oxfordshire, UK: Peter Lang.

Buzan, B., O. Wæver, and J. de Wilde. 1998. *Security: A New Framework for Analysis*. Boulder: Lynne Rienner.

Calavita, Kitty. 2005. "Law, Citizenship, and the Construction of (Some) Immigrant Others." *Law and Social Inquiry* 30 (2): 401–20.

Caldeira, Teresa P. R. 2000. *City of Walls: Crime, Segregation and Citizenship in São Paulo*. Berkeley: University of California Press.

Calhoun, Craig. 2010. "The Idea of Emergency." *Contemporary States of Emergency: The Politics of Military and Humanitarian Interventions*, ed. Didier Fassin and Mariella Pandolfi, 29–58. Cambridge: Massachusetts Institute of Technology Press.

Calhoun, Craig, and Georgi Derluguian, eds. 2011. *Business as Usual: The Roots of the Global Financial Meltdown*. New York: New York University Press.

Campaign Committee of Luis Paulo Conde. 2000. *Jornal do Conde* 2 (July): 2–3.

Cano, Ignacio. 1997. *Letalidade da Ação Policial no Rio de Janeiro*. Rio de Janeiro: ISER.

———. 2011. "Rio de Janeiro's Olympic challenge." *Guardian*, 29 November. http://www.guardian.co.uk.

Carapico, Sheila. 2002. "Foreign Aid for Promoting Democracy in the Arab World." *Middle East Journal* 56: 379–95.

Carby, Hazel. 1992. "Policing the Black Woman's Body in the Urban Context." *Critical Inquiry* 18 (summer): 738–55.

Carrara, Sérgio, and Adriana Vianna. 2006. "'Tá lá o corpo estendido no chão . . .': A violência letal contra travestis no Município do Rio de Janeiro." *Physis: Revista do Saúde Coletiva* 16 (2): 233–49.

Carver, T., and J. Pikalo. 2008. *Political Language and Metaphor: Interpreting the Changing World*. London: Routledge.

Castelo, Claudio. 1998. *O modo português de estar no mundo: O luso-tropicalismo e a ideologia colonial portuguesa (1933–1961)*. Porto, Portugal: Afrontamento.

Castrezana, Rodolfo. 2012. "O Rio de Janeiro passa por um Limpeza Social?" *Domínio Público*. 9 November. http://omedi.net/dominio-publico-rio-de-janeiro/.

Castillo, Mariano. 2010. "Troops to Occupy Brazilian Slum through October." CNN *World*, 30 November. http://www.cnn.com.

Caulfield, Sueann. 1994. "In Defense of Honor: The Contested Meaning of Sexual Morality in Law and Courtship, Rio de Janeiro, 1920–1940." PhD diss., New York University.

———. 1997. "The Birth of Mangue: Race, Nation and the Politics of Prostitution in Rio de Janeiro, 1850–1942." *Sex and Sexuality in Latin America*, ed. Daniel Balderston and Donna Guy, 86–100. New York: New York University Press.

Cecchetto, Fátima. 2004. *Violência e estilos de masculinidade*. Rio de Janeiro: Editora FGV.

Chalkley, Brian, and Essex, Stephen. 1999. "Urban Development through Hosting International Events: A History of the Olympic Games." *Planning Perspectives* 14 (4): 369–94.

Chandler, David. 2006. *Empire in Denial: The Politics of State Building*. London: Pluto.

———. 2007. "The Security-Development Nexus and the Rise of 'Anti-Foreign Policy.'" *Journal of International Relations and Development* 10 (4): 362–86.

———. 2008a. "Human Security: The Dog that Didn't Bark." *Security Dialogue* 39 (4): 427–38.

———. 2008b. "Human Security II: Waiting for the Tail to Wag the Dog: A rejoinder to Ambrosetti, Owen and Wibben." *Security Dialogue* 39 (4): 463–69.

Chase-Dunn, Chris. 1990. "Resistance to Imperialism: Semiperipheral Actors." *Review (Fernand Braudel Center)* 13 (1): 1–31.

Chesnut, Andrew. 2003. *Competitive Spirits: Latin America's New Religious Economy*. Oxford: Oxford University Press.

Chevigny, Paul. 1998. *Edge of the Knife: Police Violence in the Americas*. New York: New Press.

Chick, K. 2011. "On International Women's Day, Egyptian Women Demand Revolutionary Role." *Christian Science Monitor*, 8 March.

Chohfi, Osmar. 2000. "Apresentação." *Relações entre o Brasil e o Mundo Arabe: Construção e perspectivas*, ed. Fundação Alexandre de Gusmão, 1–11. Brasilia: Ministério de Relações Exteriores.

City of Rio de Janeiro. 1999. *O plano estratégico da Cidade do Rio de Janeiro*. http://www.rio.rj.gov.br.

Cobbah, Josiah A. M. 1987. "African Values and the Human Rights Debate: An African Perspective." *Human Rights Quarterly* 9 (3): 309–31.

Cohen, Marjorie Griffin, and Stephen Clarkson, eds. 2004. *Governing Under Stress: Middle Powers and the Challenge of Globalization*. London: Zed Books.

Cohen, Stanley. 1973. *Folk Devils and Moral Panics*. St Albans: Paladin.

Cohn, C., H. Kinsella, and S. Gibbings. 2004. "Women, Peace and Security: Resolution 1325." *International Feminist Journal of Politics* 6 (1): 130–40.

Coimbra, Cecilia. 2001. *Operação Rio: O mito das classes perigosas*. Rio de Janeiro: Intertexto.

Collins, Alan, ed. 2007. *Contemporary Security Studies*. Oxford: Oxford University Press.

Colomina, Beatriz, and Jennifer Bloomer. 1992. *Sexuality and Space*. Princeton: Princeton University School of Architecture.

Comaroff, Jean, and John L. Comaroff, ed. 2001. *Millennial Capitalism and the Culture of Neoliberalism*. Durham: Duke University Press.

Cornelissen, Scarlett. 2008. "Scripting the Nation, Sport, Mega-Events, Foreign Policy and State-Building in Post-Apartheid South Africa." *Sport in Society: Cultures, Commerce, Media, Politics* 11: 481–93.

———. 2011. "Mega Event Securitisation in a Third World Setting." *Urban Studies* 48: 10–24.

Cornwall, Andrea, and Vera Schattan P. Coelho. 2007. *Spaces for Change? The Politics of Citizen Participation in New Democratic Arenas*. London: Zed Books.

Corrêa, Sonia, Marina Maria, Jandira Queiroz, Bruno Dallacort Zilli, and Horacio Federico Sívori. 2011. "Internet Regulation and Sexual Politics in Brazil." EROTICS: *Sex, Rights and the Internet*. Association for Progressive Communications. https://www.apc.org/en/pubs/erotics-research.

Corrêa, Sonia, Rosalind P. Petchesky, and Richard Parker. 2008. *Sexuality, Health and Human Rights*. New York: Routledge.

Correas, O., ed. 1991. *Oñati Proceedings 6: Sociología Jurídica en América Latina*. Oñati, Spain: Graficas Santamaria.

Corten, Andre. 1999. *Pentecostalism in Brazil: Emotion of the Poor and Theological Romanticism*. New York: Palgrave Macmillan.

Couri, Norma. 1993. "'Curso de Inglês' é prositução." *Jornal do Brasil*, 3 November.

Couto, Claudio, and Rogerio Arantes. 2008. "Constitution, Government and Democracy in Brazil." *World Political Science Review* 4 (2): 1–33.

Cowen, Tyler. 2011. "Euro vs. Invasion of the Zombie Banks." *New York Times*, 16 April. http://www.nytimes.com.

Daflon, Rogério. 2002. "Eleicoes no Rio." *O Globo*, 6 October.

———. 2011. "Polícia ocupa Complexo de São Carlos para instalação de Unidades de Polícia Pacificadora (UPPS)." *O Globo*, 6 February.

Da Matta, Roberto. 1993. "Os discursos da violência no Brasil." *Conta de mentiroso: Sete ensaios de antropologia brasileira*, ed. Roberto Da Matta. Rio de Janeiro: Editora Rocco.

Daniel, Herbert, and Richard Guy Parker. 1993. *Sexuality, Politics and AIDS in Brazil: In Another World?* New York: Routledge.

Daniszewski, John. 1998. "Cairo Tries to Reclaim Lost Treasure Amid City's Trash." *Los Angeles Times*, 10 July.

Dantas, Iuri. 2003. "Ministro apoia regularizar prostituicao." *Folha de Sao Paulo*, 15 August.

da Silva, Jorge. 2003. *Violência e racismo no Rio de Janeiro*. Niterói, Rio de Janeiro: Editora da Universidade Federal Fluminense.

Day, G., and C. Freeman. 2003. "Policekeeping Is the Key: Rebuilding the Internal Security Architecture of Postwar Iraq." *International Affairs* 79: 299.

de Gennaro, Mara. 2003. "Fighting 'Humanism' on Its Own Terms." *differences* 14 (1): 53–73.

Degg, Martin. 1993. "The 1992 'Cairo Earthquake': Cause, Effect and Response." *Disasters* 17 (3): 226–38.

de Jong, Frederick. 1999. "Opposition to Sufism in Twentieth-Century Egypt (1900–1970): A Preliminary Survey." *Islamic Mysticism Contested*, ed. Frederick de Jong and Bernd Radtke, 310–23. Leiden, Netherlands: Brill.

Denis, Eric. 2006. "Cairo as Neoliberal Capital? From Walled City to Gated Community." *Cairo Cosmopolitan: Politics, Culture, and Urban Space in the New Globalized Middle East*, ed. Diane Singerman and Paul Amar, 47–72. Cairo: American University in Cairo Press.

de Oliveira, Marina Pereira Pires. 2008. "Sobre armadilhas e cascas de banana:

Uma análise crítica da administração de Justiça em temas associados aos Direitos Humanos." *Cadernos Pagu* 31: 126–49.

de Sousa Santos, Boaventura. 2003. "The World Social Forum: Toward a Counter-Hegemonic Globalization." *World Social Forum: Challenging Empires*, ed. Jai Sen, Anita Anand, Arturo Escobar, and Peter Waterman, 336–43. New Delhi: Viveka Foundation.

Devji, Faisal. 2005. *Landscapes of the Jihad: Militancy, Morality, Modernity*. New York: Cornell University Press.

———. 2008. *The Terrorist in Search of Humanity: Militant Islam and Global Politics*. New York: Columbia University Press.

Dimenstein, Gilberto, ed. 1996. *Democracia em pedaços: Direitos humanos no Brasil*. Rio de Janeiro: Companhia de Letras.

Dimock, Wai Chee. 2011. "Many Islams." Unpublished paper, Yale University, March.

Doel, Marcus, and Phil Hubbard. 2002. "Taking World Cities Literally: Marketing the City in a Global Space of Flows." *City: Analysis of Urban Trends, Culture, Theory, Policy, Action* 6 (3): 351–68.

dos Santos, Nina. 2011. "Names in the Frame for Strauss-Kahn's Job." *CNN: Business 360* (blog), 16 May. http://business.blogs.cnn.com.

Dubber, Markus Dirk, and Mariana Valverde. *The New Police Science: The Police Power in Domestic and International Governance*. Palo Alto: Stanford University Press.

Duffield, Mark. 2007. *Development, Security and Unending War: Governing the World of Peoples*. Cambridge: Polity.

———. 2010a. "The Liberal Way of Development and the Development-Security Impasse: Exploring the Global Life-Chance Divide." *Security Dialogue* 40: 53–76.

———. 2010b. "Risk Management and the Fortified Aid Compound: Every-day Life in Post-Interventionary Society." *Journal of Intervention and Statebuilding* 4: 453–74.

Dunn, Christopher. 2001. *Brutality Garden: Tropicalia and the Emergence of a Brazilian Counterculture*. Chapel Hill: University of North Carolina Press.

Dunne, Bruce. 1996. "Sexuality and the 'Civilizing Process' in Modern Egypt." PhD diss., Georgetown University.

Easley, J. 2011. "Glenn Beck Exploits the Rape of Lara Logan to Push His Egypt Conspiracy." *Politicus USA*, 16 February. http://www.politicususa.com.

Edward, Hoda. 1998. "Lecture on the Occasion of the 25th Anniversary of the GOPP." Edited by Omnia Aboukoura. *Lettre d'Informations de l'Observatoire Urbain du Caire Contemporain* 48.

Ehrenreich, Barbara. 2001. "A Mystery of Misogyny." *Progressive* 65 (12): 12–13.

El Gundy, Zeinab. 2011. "New Batch of Arrests in Tahrir Square to Add to the Ones Suffering in Military Jails." *Ahram Online*, 2 August. http://english.ahram.org.eg/NewsContent/1/64/17874/Egypt/Politics-/New-batch-of-arrests-in-Tahrir-Square-to-add-to-th.aspx.

El-Mahdi, Rabab. 2009. "A Feminist Movement in Egypt?" "Political and Social Protest in Egypt," ed. Nicholas S. Hopkins. Special issue, *Cairo Papers in Social Science* 29 (2–3).

———. 2010. "Does Political Islam Impede Gender-Based Mobilization? The Case of Egypt." *Totalitarian Movements and Political Religions* 11 (3–4): 379–96.

El-Nadeem Center. 1998a. "Three Years of El Nadeem." http://alnadeem.org/en.

———. 1998b. "Torture Report: 1993–1996." http://alnadeem.org/en.

———. 2002. "Torture in Egypt: Facts and Testimonies." http://alnadeem.org/en.

———. 2004. "Days of Torture: Women in Police Custody." http://alnadeem.org/en.

———. 2006. "Torture in Egypt: 2003–2006." https://alnadeem.org/files/torture _in_egypt.pdf.

———. 2008. "Open Message to the Egyptian Minister of Health and Chairperson of the Doctor's Syndicate: These Are Patients, Handcuffed in Your Hospitals!" http://alnadeem.org/en.

El Naggar, Miret, trans. 2011. "Text of Egyptian Military Communique No.1." *McClatchy*, 10 February. http://www.mcclatchydc.com.

El-Naggar, Mona, and Michael Slackman. 2011. "Hero of Egypt's Revolution, Military Now Faces Critics." *New York Times*, 9 April, A4.

El-Saadawi, Nawal. 2011. "The Egyptian Revolution Establishes a New Social Contract and Values." *Bikya Masr*, 7 February. http://www.bikyamasr.com/26024 /the-egyptian-revolution-establishes-a-new-social-contract-and-values.

El Shakry, Omnia. 2007. *The Great Social Laboratory: Subjects of Knowledge in Colonial and Postcolonial Egypt*. Palo Alto: Stanford University Press.

Elyachar, Julia. 2005. *Markets of Dispossession: NGOs, Economic Development, and the State in Cairo*. Durham: Duke University Press.

Enloe, Cynthia. 2000. *Bananas, Beaches and Bases: Making Feminist Sense of International Politics*. Berkeley: University of California Press.

———. 2004. *Maneuvers: The International Politics of Militarizing Women's Lives*. Berkeley: University of California Press.

———. 2007. *Globalization and Militarism: Feminists Make the Link*. Berkeley: University of California Press.

Esmeir, Samera. 2012. *Juridical Humanity*. Palo Alto: Stanford University Press.

Ezzat, Dina. 2003. "Latin Leanings." *Al-Ahram Weekly On-line* 669 (18–24 December). http://weekly.ahram.org.eg/2003/669/re2.htm.

Ezzat, Heba Raouf. 2002. "Rethinking Secularism . . . Rethinking Feminism." IslamOnline.net, http://www.arabphilosophers.com/Arabic/adiscourse/aeast-west /asecularism/Rethinking_Secularism_Rethinking_Feminism.htm.

Fahmy, Khaled. 2002. "Prostitution in Egypt in the Nineteenth Century." *Outside In: On the Margins of the Modern Middle East*, ed. E. Rogan, 77–103. New York: I. B. Tauris.

Falcão, Joaquim. 1984. *Conflito de direito de propriedade*. Rio de Janeiro: Editora Forense.

———. 1991. "Patrimônio cultural: Estratégias de atuação." *Cadernos do patrimônio cultural*, 121–35. Rio de Janeiro: Prefeitura do Rio de Janeiro.

Fanon, Frantz. *Black Skin, White Masks*. 1988 [1952]. New York: Grove.

Farid, Sonia. 2011. "Letter from Cairo: Humanizing the Brute." *Al Arabiya News*, 4 July. http://www.alarabiya.net.

Fassin, Didier. 2010. "Heart of Humaneness." *Contemporary States of Emergency: The Politics of Military and Humanitarian Interventions*, ed. Didier Fassin and Mariella Pandolfi, 269–94. Cambridge: Massachusetts Institute of Technology Press.

Fassin, Didier, and Mariella Pandolfi, eds. 2010. *Contemporary States of Emergency: The Politics of Military and Humanitarian Interventions*. Cambridge: Massachusetts Institute of Technology Press.

Ferdinand, Peter. 2007. "Russia and China: Converging Responses to Globalization." *International Affairs* 83: 655–80. doi: 10.1111/j.1468–2346.2007.00646.x.

Ferndandes, Rubem Cesar. 1998. *Novo nascimento: Os evangélicos em casa, na Igreja e na política*. Rio de Janeiro: MAUAD Press. .

Ferreira, Rubens da Silva. 2003. "Travestis em perigo ou o perigo das travestis? Notas sobre a insegurança nos territórios prostitucionais dos transgêneros em Belém (PA)." *Enfoques* 2 (1). Accessed 12 March 2008. http://www.enfoques.ifcs.ufrj.br /julho03/pdfs/julho2003_03.pdf.

Ferreira da Silva, Denise. 2009. "No-bodies: Law, Raciality and Violence." *Griffith Law Review* 18 (2): 212–36.

Ferret, Jerome. 2004. "The State, Policing and 'Old Continental Europe': Managing Local/National Tension." *Policing and Society* 14 (1): 49–65.

Fiell, Rapper. 2011. "UPP e a Paz Armada: Vejo além da UPP." *Viva Favela*, 27 October. http://vivafavela.com.

Figari, Carlos. 2007. *"Outras" cariocas*. Minas Gerais, Brazil: Editora UFMG.

Filho, Valdemar Figueredo. 2005. *Entre o palanque e o púlpito: Mídia, religião e política*. Rio de Janeiro: Annablume Press.

Finnemore, M., and K. Sikkink. 1998. "International Norm Dynamics and Political Change." *International Organization* 52 (4): 887–917.

Fischer, Brodwin. 2008. *A Poverty of Rights: Citizenship and Inequality in Twentieth-Century Rio de Janeiro*. Palo Alto: Stanford University Press.

Flor, Ana. 2011. "Dilma nega faxina e diz que Brasil não é 'Roma antiga.'" *Folha de São Paulo*, 25 August.

Foley, Conor. 2008. *The Thin Blue Line*. New York: Verso.

Fonseca, Alexandre. 2003. *Evangélicos e mídia no Brasil*. Campinas, São Paulo: Editora Universitária São Francisco.

Fouad, Khaled. 1993. "A'amaal gheir ikhlaqi that sitaar al-funuun al-sha'abi." *Al-Ahrar*, 5 July.

Foucault, Michel. 1990 [1979]. *History of Sexuality: Volume 1*. New York: Vintage.

———. 2002 [1966]. *The Order of Things: An Archaeology of the Human Sciences*. London: Routledge.

———. 2007. *Security, Territory, Population*. New York: Palgrave.

———. 2008. *The Birth of Biopolitics: Lectures at the College de France 1978–1979*. New York: Palgrave Macmillan.

Fox, Gregory. 2008. *Humanitarian Occupation*. Cambridge: Cambridge University Press.

Fraga, Paulo Cesar. 2002. "Da Favela ao Sertão." *Jovens em Tempo Real*, ed. Paulo Cesar Fraga and J. A. S. Iulianelli, 82–107. Rio de Janeiro: DP&A Editora. http://seer .ufrgs.br/CienciasSociaiseReligiao/article/viewFile./2249/954.

Frank, Andre Gunder. 1966. "The Development of Underdevelopment in Latin America." *Monthly Review* 18 (4): 17–31.

Franke, Katherine M. 2002. "Illegalized Sexual Dissent: Sexualities and Nationalisms." Columbia Law School, Pub. Law Research Paper No. 02–48. Social Science Research Network. doi: 10.2139/ssrn.346342.

Freire-Medeiros, Bianca. 2009. "The Favela and Its Touristic Transits." *Geoforum* 40 (4): 580–88. http://www.sciencedirect.com/science/journal/00167185/40/4.

Freston, Paul. 2004. *Evangelicals and Politics in Asia, Africa and Latin America.* Cambridge: Cambridge University Press.

Freyre, Gilberto. 1963. *New World in the Tropics: The Culture of Modern Brazil.* New York: Vintage.

Friesendorf, Cornelius. 2007. "Pathologies of Security Governance: Efforts against Human Trafficking in Europe." *Security Dialogue* 38 (3): 379–402.

Furlough, Ellen. 1998. "Making Mass Vacations: Tourism and Consumer Culture in France, 1930s to 1970s." *Comparative Studies in Society and History* 40 (2): 251.

Gandra, Edir. 1995. *Jongo da Serrinha: Do terreiro aos palcos.* Rio de Janeiro: Giorgio Grafica e Editora.

Garcia, Renato. 2002a. "Agentes do Desipe fazem greve de 24 horas." *O Globo*, 29 May.

———. 2002b. "O ordem foi do tráfico." *O Globo*, 2 October.

Gardel, André. 1996. *O encontro entre Bandeira e Sinhô.* Rio de Janeiro: Secretaria Municipal de Cultura.

Garfinkle, Adam. 2011. "Terms of Contention." *American Interest* (January–February). http://www.the-american-interest.com/article.cfm?piece=904.

General Organization for Physical Planning for Greater Cairo. 1995. *Al Hussein Area Revitalization: Planning Report.* Cairo: GOPP / Government of Egypt.

Ghannam, Farha. 2002. *Remaking the Modern: Space, Relocation and the Politics of Identity in Global Cairo.* Berkeley: University of California Press.

Gharavi, Maryam Monalisa. 2011. "Roger Ebert's 'Sad Focus.'" *South/South*, 18 February. http://southissouth.wordpress.com/2011/02/18/roger-eberts-sad-focus.

Gibson-Graham, J. K. 2002. "Beyond Global vs. Local: Economic Politics outside the Binary Frame." *Geographies of Power: Placing Scale*, ed. A. Herod and M. Wright, 25–60. Oxford: Blackwell.

Giddens, Anthony. 1998. *The Third Way: The Renewal of Social Democracy.* Cambridge: Polity.

Gill, Peter, Stephen Marrin, and Mark Phythian, eds. 2009. *Intelligence Theory.* New York: Routledge.

Gilmore, Ruth Wilson. 2007. *Golden Gulag: Prisons, Surplus, Crisis, and Opposition in Globalizing California.* Berkeley: University of California Press.

Gilroy, Paul. 2000. *Against Race: Imagining Political Culture Beyond the Color Line.* Cambridge: Harvard University Press.

———. 2005. *Postcolonial Melancholia.* New York: Columbia University Press.

Girard, Francoise. 2007. "Negotiating Sexual Rights and Sexual Orientation at the UN." *SexPolitics: Reports from the Front Lines*, ed. Richard Parker, Rosalind Petchesky, and Robert Sember, 311–58. New York: Sexuality Policy Watch.

Giulianotti, Richard, and Francisco Klauser. 2010. "Security Governance and Sport Mega-Events: Toward an Interdisciplinary Research Agenda." *Journal of Sport and Social Issues* 34: 49–61.

Glasius, Marlies. 2008. "Human Security from Paradigm Shift to Operationalization: Job Description for a Human Security Worker." *Security Dialogue* 39 (1): 31–54.

Gledhill, John. 2001. "'Disappearing the Poor?': A Critique of the New Wisdoms of Social Democracy in an Age of Globalization." *Urban Anthropology and Studies of Cultural Systems and World Economic Development* 30 (2–3): 123–56.

Glynos, Jason, and David Howarth. 2007. *Logics of Critical Explanation in Social and Political Theory.* Oxon, UK: Routledge.

Godoy, Marcelo. 1994. "Jutiça reduz pena de matador de travesti." *Folha de São Paulo,* 9 October.

Gold, John R., and Margaret M. Gold. 2008. "Olympic Cities: Regeneration, City Re-branding and Changing Urban Agendas." *Geography Compass* 2 (1): 300–18.

Goldberg, David Theo. 2011. *The Threat of Race.* Hoboken: John Wiley and Sons.

Goldberg, Steven. 2010. "Investing in the New Normal." *Kiplinger,* 19 October. http://www.kiplinger.com.

Goldstein, Donna. 2003. *Laughter Out of Place: Race, Class, Violence, and Sexuality in a Rio Shantytown.* Berkeley: University of California Press.

González, Roberto J. 2010. *Militarizing Culture: Essays on the Warfare State.* Walnut Creek: Left Coast Press.

Goodale, Mark, ed. 2006. *Human Rights: An Anthropological Reader.* London: Wiley-Blackwell.

Gordon, Avery. 1996. *Ghostly Matters: Haunting and the Sociological Imagination.* Minneapolis: University of Minnesota Press.

Graham, Stephen. 2004. *Cities, War and Terrorism: Towards an Urban Geopolitics.* London: Blackwell.

———. 2007. "Demodernizing by Design: Everyday Infrastructure and Political Violence." *Violent Geographies: Fear, Terror and Political Violence,* ed. Derek Gregory and Allan Pred, 309–28. New York: Routledge.

Green, James. 2001. *Beyond Carnival: Male Homosexuality in Twentieth-Century Brazil.* Chicago: University of Chicago Press.

Gregório, José Carlos. 2003. "A lógica do bandido." *Paraíso Armado: Interpretações da violência no Rio de Janeiro,* ed. Aziz Filho and Francisco Alves Filho, 77–87. São Paulo: Editora Garçoni.

Gregory, Derek. 2001. "Colonial Nostalgia and Cultures of Travel: Spaces of Contested Visibility in Egypt." *Consuming Tradition, Manufacturing Heritage: Global Norms and Urban Forms in the Age of Tourism,* ed. Nezar AlSayyad, 111–51. Florence, Ky.: Psychology Press.

———. 2005. "Performing Cairo: Orientalism and the City of the Arabian Nights." *Making Cairo Medieval,* ed. AlSayyad Nezar, Irene Bierman, and Nasser Rabbat, 69–94. Oxford: Lexington Books.

———. 2007. *Orientalism Abroad: Culture Encounter and Political Violence.* New York: Routledge.

Gregory, Derek, and Alan Pred, eds. 2007. *Violent Geographies: Fear, Terror and Political Violence.* New York: Routledge.

Grewal, Inderpal. 2005. *Transnational America: Feminisms, Diasporas, Neoliberalisms.* Durham: Duke University Press.

———. 2008. "Postcoloniality, Globalization and Feminist Critique." *American Anthropologist* 110 (4): 517–20.

Grewal, Inderpal, and Caren Kaplan. 2006. *An Introduction to Women's Studies: Gender in a Transnational World*. New York: McGraw-Hill Higher Education.

Grudgings, Stuart. 2011. "Notorious Rio de Janeiro Slum Taken Over by Brazilian Troops." *National Post*, 13 November. http://www.news.nationalpost.com.

Grupo Davida. 2005. "Prostitutas, 'traficadas,' e panicos morais: Uma analise da producao de fatos em pesquisas sobre o 'trafico de seres humanos.'" *Cadernos Pagu* 25: 153–84.

Guha, Ranajit. 1997. *A Subaltern Studies Reader, 1986–1995*. Minneapolis: University of Minnesota Press.

Guzzini, Stefano, and Dietrich Jung. 2004. *Contemporary Security Analysis and Copenhagen Peace Research*. New York: Routledge.

Haggerty, Kevin D. 2011. "Civil Cities and Urban Governance: Regulating Disorder for the Vancouver Winter Olympics." *Urban Studies* 48: 3185–201.

Hajjar, Lisa. 2011. "The Anderson Cooper Effect on American TV Reporting from Cairo." *Jadaliyya*, 3 February. http://www.jadaliyya.com.

Halawi, Jailan. 2006. "Whatever Happened to Egyptians?" *Al-Ahram Weekly Online*, 1–7 November. http://weekly.ahram.org.eg/2006/818/pr1.htm.

Halberstam, Judith. 1995. *Skin Shows: Gothic Horror and the Technology of Monsters*. Durham: Duke University Press.

Hall, Stuart. 1996. "The Problem of Ideology: Marxism without Guarantees." *Stuart Hall: Critical Dialogues in Cultural Studies*, ed. D. Morley and K. H. Chen, 25–46. London: Routledge.

Hall, Stuart, Chas Critcher, Tony Jefferson, John N. Clarke, and Brian Roberts. 1978. *Policing the Crisis: Mugging, the State and Law and Order*. London: Macmillan.

Hall, Stuart, and Tony Jefferson, eds. 1976. *Resistance through Rituals: Youth Subcultures in Post-War Britain*. University of Birmingham: Centre for Contemporary Cultural Studies.

Halley, Janet. 2006. *Split Decisions: How and Why to Take a Break from Feminism*. Princeton: Princeton University Press.

Halper, Stefan. 2010. *The Beijing Consensus: How China's Authoritarian Model Will Dominate the Twenty-First Century*. New York: Basic Books.

Hammad, Hanan. 2011. "Between Egyptian 'National Purity' and 'Local Flexibility': Prostitution in al-Mahalla al-Kubra in the First Half of the Twentieth Century." *Journal of Social History* 44 (3): 751–83.

Hammami, Reza, and Martina Rieker. 1988. "Feminist Orientalism and Orientalist Marxism." *New Left Review* 1 (170): 93–106.

Hampson, Fen Osler, et al. 2002. *Madness in the Multitude: Human Security and World Disorder*. Ontario: Oxford University Press.

Hanchard, Michael. 1998. *Orpheus and Power: The Movimento Negro of Rio de Janeiro and São Paulo, Brazil, 1945–1988*. Princeton: Princeton University Press.

———, ed. 1999. *Racial Politics in Contemporary Brazil*. Durham: Duke University Press.

Hanieh, Adam. 2011. "Egypt's Uprising: Not Just a Question of 'Transition.'" *Bullet* 462 (14 February). http://www.socialistproject.ca/bullet/462.php.

Harders, Cilja. 2003. "The Informal Social Pact: The State and the Urban Poor in Cairo." *Politics from Above, Politics from Below: The Middle East in the Age of Economic Reform*, ed. E. Kienle, 191–210. London: Saqi Books; Cairo: CEDEJ Press.

Harrington, Carol. 2010. *Politicization of Sexual Violence.* Wellington, New Zealand: Ashgate.

Harvey, David. 1989. "From Managerialism to Entrepreneurialism: The Transformation in Urban Governance in Late Capitalism." *Geografiska Annaler* 71/B: 3–17.

———. 2005. *A Brief History of Neoliberalism.* Oxford: Oxford University Press.

———. 2006. *Spaces of Global Capitalism: A Theory of Uneven Geographical Development.* London: Verso.

Hassan, Fayza. 1999. "Past Glory, New Life." *Al-Ahram Weekly*, 11–17 March.

Hassan, Mozn. 2011. "Discussing a Sensitive Issue in a Critical Moment." Unpublished manuscript.

Herbert, Steve, and Elizabeth Brown. 2006. "Conceptions of Space and Crime in the Punitive Neoliberal City." *Antipode* 38 (4): 755–77.

Heringer, Rosana, and Osmundo Pinho, eds. 2011. *Afro Rio Seculo XXI: Modernidade e relacoes sociais no Rio de Janeiro.* Rio de Janeiro: Editora Garamond.

Herring, Eric. 2007. "Military Security." *Contemporary Security Studies*, ed. Alan Collins, 129–45. Oxford: Oxford University Press.

Hershberg, Eric, and Fred Rosen, eds. 2006. *Latin America after Neoliberalism: Turning the Tide in the Twenty-First Century?* New York: New Press.

Hewison, Kevin, and Richard Robison. 2009. *East Asia and the Trials of Neo-Liberalism.* New York: Routledge.

Hibou, Beatrice, ed. 2004. *Privatising the State.* London: C. Hurst.

Higate, Paul, and Marsha Henry. 2009. *Insecure Spaces: Peacekeeping, Power and Performance in Haiti, Kosovo and Liberia.* London: Zed Books.

Hill, Felicity. 2005. "How and When Has Security Council Resolution 1325 (2000) on Women, Peace and Security Impacted Negotiations outside the Security Council?" Master's thesis, Programme of International Studies, Uppsala University.

Hilmi, Atef. 2001. "Human Rights Activists Respond to Awkward Statement." *Rose al Yusef*, 21 June.

Hinsliff, Gaby. 2009. "Blue-Eyed Bankers Prompt G20 Divide." *Guardian*, 29 March.

Hinton, Mercedes. 2006. *The State on the Streets: Police and Politics in Argentina and Brazil.* Boulder: Lynne Rienner.

Hirakawa, Hiroko. 1998. "Inverted Orientalism and the Discursive Construction of Sexual Harassment in Japan." Master's thesis, Purdue University.

Hirst, Monica. 2008. "Brazil." *From Superpower to Besieged Global Power: Restoring World Order after the Failure of the Bush Doctrine*, ed. Edward Koldziei and Roger Kanet, 280–98. Athens: University of Georgia Press.

Hitti, Philip. 1924. *The Syrians in America.* New York: Gorgias Press.

Hochstetler, Kathryn, and Margaret E. Keck. 2007. *Greening Brazil: Environmental Activism in State and Society.* Durham: Duke University Press.

Holston, James. 1989. *The Modernist City: An Anthropological Critique of Brasilia.* Chicago: University of Chicago Press.

Homem, Renato. 1996. "Intercâmbio pode estar acobertando prostituição." *O Globo*, 29 September.

Hoogensen, Gunhild, and Svein Vigeland Rottem. 2004. "Gender Identity and the Subject of Security." *Security Dialogue* 35 (2): 155–71.

Hoogensen, Gunhild, and Kirsti Stuvoy. 2006. "Gender, Resistance and Human Security." *Security Dialogue* 37 (2): 207–28.

Huang, Yasheng. 2010. "Debating China's Economic Growth: The Beijing Consensus or the Washington Consensus." *Academy of Management Perspectives* 24: 31–47.

Hudson, Heidi. 2005. "'Doing' Security as though Humans Matter: A Feminist Perspective on Gender and the Politics of Human Security." *Security Dialogue* 36 (2): 155–74.

Huggins, Martha. 1991. *Vigilantism and the State in Modern Latin America: Essays on Extralegal Violence.* Westport, Conn.: Praeger.

———. 2000. "Urban Violence and Police Privatization in Brazil: Blended Invisibility." *Social Justice* 27 (2): 113–33.

Huggins, Martha, Mika Haritos-Fatouros, and Philip G. Zimbardo. 2002. *Violence Workers: Police Torturers and Murderers Reconstruct Brazilian Atrocities.* Berkeley: University of California Press.

Hui, Wang, Wen Tiejun, and Lau Kin Chi. 2012. "The Movement in Egypt: A Dialogue with Samir Amin." *boundary 2* 39 (1): 167–206. doi: 10.1215/01903659-1506292.

Human Rights Watch. 2004. *In a Time of Torture: The Assault on Justice in Egypt's Crackdown on Homosexual Conduct.* New York: Human Rights Watch. http://www .hrw.org/sites/default/files/reports/egypt0304_0.pdf.

———. 2011a. "Brazil: Events of 2010." *World Report 2011: Events of 2010.* New York: Human Rights Watch. http://www.hrw.org/world-report-2011/brazil.

———. 2011b. "Egypt: Military Trials Usurp Justice System," 29 April. http://www .hrw.org.

Humphrey, John, and Dirk Messner. 2009. "China and India as Emerging Global Governance Actors: Challenges for Developing and Developed Countries." *IDS Bulletin* 37: 107–14. doi: 10.1111/j.1759-5436.2006.tb00253.x.

Hunter, Wendy. 1997. *Eroding Military Influence in Brazil: Politicians against Soldiers.* Chapel Hill: University of North Carolina Press.

Husain, Saima. 2007. *In War, Those Who Die Are Not Innocent: Human Rights Implementation, Policing and Public Security in Rio de Janeiro, Brazil.* Amsterdam: Rozenberg Publishers.

Ibrahim, Zeinab. 1986. "Milahi shaari' al-haram: Tabqa ao trahil?" *Mayo*, 28 April.

Ilahi, Nadia. 2010. "Gendered Contestations: An Analysis of Street Harassment in Cairo and Its Implications for Women's Access to Public Space." Master's thesis, American University in Cairo.

Illich, Ivan. 1973. *Tools for Conviviality.* New York: Harper and Row.

Inciardi, James A., and Hilary L. Surratt. 1998. "Children in the Streets of Brazil: Drug Use, Crime, Violence, and HIV Risks." *Substance Use and Misuse* 33 (7): 1461–80.

Inter-American Development Bank. 1999. "BID Extra: Renascença urbana: Suplemento do BID." Washington: Inter-American Development Bank.

IPLANRIO. 1995. *Como Recuperar, Reformar, ou Construir Seu Imóvel no Corredor Cultural*. Rio de Janeiro: Rioarte.

Isfahani-Hammond, Alexandra, ed. 2004. *The Masters and the Slaves: Plantation Relations and Mestizaje in American Imaginaries*. New York: Palgrave Macmillan.

———. 2008. *White Negritude: Race, Writing, and Brazilian Cultural Identity*. New York: Palgrave Macmillan.

———. 2011. "Of She-Wolves and Mad Cows: Animality, Anthropophagy and the State of Exception in Claudio Assis's 'Amarelo Manga.'" *Luso-Brazilian Review* 48 (2): 129–49.

———. 2013. "Slave Barracks Aristocrats: Gilberto Freyre in the Intersection between Orientalism and Slavery Studies." *The Middle East and Brazil: Forging New South–South Alliances, Reviving Transregional Public Cultures*, ed. Paul Amar, 113–32. Bloomington: Indiana University Press.

Ismail, Salwa. 2006. *Political Life in Cairo's New Quarters: Encountering the Everyday State*. Minneapolis: University of Minnesota Press.

Jacob, Wilson. 2011. *Working Out Egypt: Effendi Masculinity and Subject Formation in Colonial Modernity, 1870–1940*. Durham: Duke University Press.

Jacobs, Jessica. 2010. *Sex, Tourism, and the Postcolonial Encounter: Landscapes of Longing in Egypt*. Burlington, Vt.: Ashgate.

Jacobs, Margaret. 2005. "Maternal Colonialism: White Women and Indigenous Child Removal in the American West and Australia, 1880–1940." *Western Historical Quarterly* 36 (4): 453–76.

Jad, Islah. 2007. "The NGOization of Arab Women's Movements." *Feminisms in Development: Contradictions, Contestations and Challenges*, ed. A. Cornwall, E. Harrison, and A. Whitehead, 177–90. New York: Zed Books.

Jaeger, Hans-Martin. 2007. "'Global Civil Society' and the Political Depoliticization of Global Governance." *International Political Sociology* 1 (3): 257–77.

Jain, Subhash Chandra. 2006. *Emerging Economies and the Transformation of International Business: Brazil, Russia, India and China (BRICS)*. Cheltenham, UK: Edward Elgar Publishing.

Jamieson, Ruth, and Kieran McEvoy. 2005. "State Crime by Proxy and Juridical Othering." *British Journal of Criminology* 25: 504–27.

Japiassu, Moacir. 1980. "Ó Deus, que vida! O travesti tipo exportação briga e morre em Paris: Aqui, corre da polícia, apanha: Só escapa quem tem beleza de verdade e talento para viver como artista." *Istoé*, 12 November.

Jeffrey, Terence P. 2010. "Obama Used 'Invest,' 'Investing,' or 'Investment' Seven Times in Labor Day Speech to Describe Federal Spending and Special-Interest Tax Loopholes." *CNS News*, 7 September. http://cnsnews.com.

Jessop, Bob. 1995. "The Regulation Approach, Governance, and Post-Fordism: Alternative Perspectives on Economic and Political Change?" *Economy and Society* 24 (3): 307–33.

———. 2002a. *The Future of the Capitalist State*. Cambridge: Polity.

————. 2002b. "Liberalism, Neoliberalism and Urban Governance: A State-Theoretical Perspective." *Antipode* 34 (3): 452–72.

————. 2002c. "Time and Space in the Globalization of Capital and Their Implications for State Power." *Rethinking Marxism* 14 (1): 97–117.

Juergensmeyer, Mark. 2000. *Terror in the Mind of God: The Global Rise of Religious Violence.* Berkeley: University of California Press.

Kahn, Tulio. 2002. *Velha e nova polícia: Polícia e políticas de segurança no Brasil stual.* São Paulo: Sicurezza Editora.

Kaleb, Rodolfo. 2011. "O Estado burguês reorganiza o tráfico de drogas no Rio de Janeiro." *Revolutionary Regroupment*, January. http://regroupment.org/main/page_cl_on_brazilian_trafficking__portugus.html.

Kamal, Islam. 2001. "The Complete Text of the Perverted Organization's Manifesto." *Rose al Youssef*, 17 May.

Kamel, Mahmoud. 1997. "Waahid min kulli 'ashra!!" *Al-Ahram*, 23 November.

Kant de Lima, Roberto. 1994. "Conciliação e julgamento, negotiation e trial: A produção da orden em uma perspective comparada (Brasil/EUA)." *Brasil-EUA: Antigas e novas perspectivas sobre sociedade e cultura*, ed. Guillermo Giucci and M. Dias, 85–108. Rio de Janeiro: Leviatã.

————. 1995. *A polícia na Cidade do Rio de Janeiro: Seus dilemas e paradoxes.* Rio de Janeiro: Editora Forense.

Kapur, Ratna. 2007. "'Faith' and The 'Good' Liberal: The Construction of Female Sexual Subjectivity in Anti-Trafficking Legal Discourse.'" *Sexuality and the Law: Feminist Engagements*, ed. Vanessa Munro and Carl Stychin. New York: Routledge.

Katzenstein, Peter. 1996. *The Culture of National Security: Norms and Identity in World Politics.* New York: Columbia University Press.

Kempadoo, Kamala. 1999. *Sun, Sex and Gold: Tourism and Sex Work in the Caribbean.* Lanham, Md.: Rowman and Littlefield.

————. 2004. *Sexing the Caribbean: Gender, Race and Sexual Labor.* New York: Routledge.

Kempadoo, Kamala, and Jo Doezema, eds. 1998. *Global Sex Workers: Rights, Resistance and Redefinition.* New York: Routledge.

Kempadoo, Kamala, Jyoti Sanghera, and Bandana Pattanaik, eds. 2005. *Trafficking and Prostitution Reconsidered.* New York: Routledge.

Khalil, Nevine. 1997. "Time to Break the Network." *Al-Ahram Weekly*, 27 November–3 December.

Kimmel, Michael. 2002. "Gender, Class and Terrorism." *Chronicle of Higher Education*, 8 February, B11–B12.

King, Leslie, and Judson Ray. 2000. "Developing Transnational Law Enforcement Co-operation." *Journal of Contemporary Criminal Justice* 16 (4): 386–408.

Kingston, Paul, and Ian Spears, eds. 2004. *States within States: Incipient Political Entities in the Post Cold War Era.* New York: Palgrave Macmillan.

Kirschner, Jonathan. 2006. *Globalization and National Security.* New York: Routledge.

Kirshenblatt-Gimblett, Barbara. 1998. *Destination Culture: Tourism, Museums, and Heritage.* Berkeley: University of California Press.

Kissling, E. A. 1991. "Street Harassment: The Language of Sexual Terrorism." *Discourse and Society* 2 (4): 451–60.

Kotiswaran, Prabha. 2008. "Born Unto Brothels: Toward a Legal Ethnography of Sex Work in an Indian Red-Light Area." *Law and Social Inquiry* 33 (3): 579–629.

Krause, Keith, and Michael Williams, eds. 1997. *Critical Security Studies: Concepts and Cases.* New York: Routledge.

Krugman, Paul. 2010. "When Zombies Win." *New York Times*, 19 December. http://www.nytimes.com.

Kulick, Don. 1996. "Causing a Commotion: Public Scandal as Resistance among Brazilian Transgendered Prostitutes." *Anthropology Today* 12 (6): 3–7.

———. 1997. "The Gender of Brazilian Transgendered Prostitutes." *American Anthropologist* 99 (3): 574–85.

———. 1998. *Travesti: Sex, Gender, and Culture among Brazilian Transgendered Prostitutes.* Chicago: University of Chicago Press.

Kulick, Don, and Charles Klein. 2003. "Scandalous Acts: The Politics of Shame among Brazilian Travesti Prostitutes." *Recognition Struggles and Social Movements*, ed. Barbara Hobson, 215–38. Cambridge: Cambridge University Press.

Kurtz, Howard. 2011. "Lara Logan's Egypt Nightmare and Her Recovery." *Daily Beast*, 15 February. http://www.thedailybeast.com.

Laclau, Ernesto. 1977. *Politics and Ideology in Marxist Theory.* London: Verso.

———. 1997. *New Reflections on the Revolution of Our Time.* London: Verso.

Laclau, Ernesto, and Chantal Mouffe. 1985. *Hegemony and Socialist Strategy.* London: Verso.

Lang, Sabine. 1997. "The NGOization of Feminism." *Transitions Environments Translations: Feminisms in International Politics*, ed. Joan Scott, Cora Kaplan, and Debra Keates, 101–20. New York: Routledge.

Larner, Wendy, and David Craig. 2005. "After Neoliberalism? Community Activism and Local Partnerships in Aotearoa New Zealand." *Antipode* 37 (3): 402–24.

Larrinaga, Miguel, and Marc Doucet. 2008. "Sovereign Power and the Biopolitics of Human Security." *Security Dialogue* 39 (5): 517–37.

Lash, Scott, and Mike Featherstone, eds. 2002. *Recognition and Difference: Politics, Identity and Multiculture.* New York: Sage.

Lasswell, Harold D. 1941. "The Garrison State." *American Journal of Sociology* 46 (4): 455–68.

Lauria, Mickey. 1997. *Reconstructing Urban Regime Theory: Regulating Urban Politics in a Global Economy.* Thousand Oaks, Calif.: Sage Publications.

Lecardane, Renzo, and Zhuo Jian. 2003–4. "Great Event, a New Strategic Instrument for Urban Development: On the Impact of World EXPO on City and Society." *Time + Architecture.* http://en.cnki.com.cn/Journal_en/C-C038-SDJZ-2003-04.htm.

Lee, Lynn. 2009. "Soft and Smart Power Combined: Lynn Lee on Hillary Clinton's New Brand of Diplomacy." ST *Blogs*, 19 February. http://www.blogs.straitstimes.com.

Leeds, Elizabeth. 1996. "Cocaine and Parallel Politics in the Brazilian Urban Periphery: Constraints on Local-Level Democratization." *Latin American Research Review* 31: 47–83.

Leila, Reem. 2009. "Uniting under NAM: Reem Leila Attends the First Ladies' Non-Aligned Summit in Sharm El-Sheikh." *Al-Ahram Weekly Online*, 23–29 July. http://weekly.ahram.org.eg.

Leitão, Matheus, and Lucas Ferraz. 2010. "Dilma tinha código de acesso a arsenal usado por guerrilha." *Folha de São Paulo*, 20 November.

Lemgruber, Julita. 2003. "A cadeia: Criando feras." *Paraíso armado: Interpretações da violência no Rio de Janeiro*, ed. Aziz Filho and Francisco Alves Filho, 61–77. São Paulo: Editora Garçoni.

Lemle, Marina. 2007. "Milicias en Rio: Amenaza Paramilitar?" *Comunidad Segura*, 12 March. http://www.comunidadesegura.org/en/node/32392.

Lenz, Flavio. 2008. "Rede divulga Carta de Princípios: Valores do movimento de prostitutas incluem o trabalho sexual como direito sexual e a prostituição como profissão, aliados ao repúdio à exploração e à vitimização." *Beijo da rua*, 12 June. http://www.beijodarua.com.br.

Lezra, Jacques. 2003. "Unrelated Passions." *differences* 14 (1): 74–87.

Li, Minqi. 2009. *The Rise of China and the Demise of the Capitalist World-Economy*. New York: Monthly Review Press.

Liew, Leong. 2005. "China's Engagement with Neo-Liberalism: Path Dependency, Geography and Party Self-Reinvention." *Journal of Development Studies* 41 (2): 331–52. doi: 10.1080/0022038042000309278.

Limanowska, Barbara, and Ann Janette Rosga. 2004. "The Bar Raid as 'Outcome Space' of Anti-Trafficking Initiatives in the Balkans." *Travelling Facts: The Social Construction, Distribution, and Accumulation of Knowledge*, ed. Caroline Baillie, Elizabeth Dunn, and Yi Zheng, 149–70 Frankfurt: Campus Verlag.

Lindgren, C. Ernesto. 1975. *Leituras em organização espacial*. Rio de Janeiro: Editora UFRJ / COPPE / PUR.

Lindsey, U. 2011. "Egypt's Women Rally behind Lara Logan." *Daily Beast*, 16 February. http://www.thedailybeast.com.

Loader, Ian, and Neil Walker. 2007. *Civilizing Security*. Cambridge: Cambridge University Press.

Long, Scott. 2004. "The Trials of Culture: Sex and Security in Egypt." *Middle East Report* 230. http://www.merip.org.

———. 2012. "The State and Your Sex Life." *A Paper Bird: Sex, Rights, and the World* (blog), 4 January. http://paper-bird.net.

Long, William R. 1992a. "Massive Security Forces Readied in Rio Summit: National, Foreign and U.N. Agencies Are Participating in Effort to Protect World Leaders at the Conference." *Los Angeles Times*, 11 June.

———. 1992b. "Rio Hopes Earth Summit Helps to Improve Its Troubled Image." *Los Angeles Times*, 4 June.

Lott, Anthony. 2004. *Creating Insecurity: Constructivism, Realism and US Security Policy*. Burlington, Vt.: Ashgate.

Louzeiro, José. 1993. "Transformistas anunciam revolução." *O Dia*, 25 April.

Lukin, Alexander. 2009. "Russia to Reinforce the Asian Vector: Some Priorities of Russian Foreign Policy after the Crisis." *Russia in Global Affairs* 7 (2): 85–99.

Lutz, E., and K. Sikkink. 2000. "International Human Rights Law and Practice in Latin America." *International Organization* 54 (3): 633–59.

Lynch, M. 2003. "Beyond the Arab Street: Iraq and the Arab Public Sphere." *Politics and Society* 31 (1): 55–91.

Macdonald, Laura, and Arne Rückert. 2009. *Post-Neoliberalism in the Americas.* New York: Palgrave Macmillan.

MacFarlane, Neil S., and Yuen Foong Khong. 2006. *Human Security and the UN: A Critical History.* Bloomington: Indiana University Press.

MacLean, Sandra J., David R. Black, and Timothy M. Shaw, eds. 2006. *A Decade of Human Security: Global Governance and New Multilateralisms.* Hampshire, UK: Ashgate.

Magalhães, Sergio. 1997. "Pobreza urbana, un fenômeno da esclusão: A experiência do Rio de Janeiro com o Programa Favela-Bairro." Presentation to International Forum on Urban Poverty.

Mahfouz, A. 2011a. "Asmaa Mahfouz, Organizer of Egypt Demonstrations, Talks about Her Use of Facebook to Take Action." MEMRI TV, 31 January. http://www.youtube.com/watch?v=2uzdOLXLoes.

———. 2011b. "Meet Asmaa Mahfouz and the Vlog that Helped Spark the Revolution." YouTube, 18 January. http://www.youtube.com/watch?v=SgjIgMdsEuk.

Mahmood, Saba. 2005. *The Politics of Piety: The Islamic Revival and the Feminist Subject.* Princeton: Princeton University Press.

Malz, Bina. 1993. *Antropofagia e tropicalismo.* Porto Alegre, Brazil: Editora da Universidade Federal do Rio Grande do Sul.

Mamdani, Mahmoud. 1996. *Citizen and Subject: Contemporary Africa and the Legacy of Late Colonialism.* Princeton: Princeton University Press.

Marder, Michael. 2011. "The Second Death of Politics." *Al Jazeera,* 23 December. http://www.aljazeera.com.

Martins, Americo. 2000. "Brazil: Country of the Future?" *BBC News,* 21 April.

Massad, Joseph. 2002. "Re-Orienting Desire: The Gay International and the Arab World." *Public Culture* 14 (2): 361–85.

———. 2007. *Desiring Arabs.* Chicago: University of Chicago Press.

Massey, Doreen B. 1994. *Space, Place, and Gender.* Minneapolis: University of Minnesota Press.

Mataawi, Nadia. 1998. "Amraka Al-Athaar Al-Islamiya." *Al-Wafd,* 10 October.

Mayfield, James. 1996. *Local Government in Egypt: Structure, Process, and the Challenges of Reform.* Cairo: American University in Cairo Press.

Mayton, Joseph. 2011. "She Won't Win, but Bothaina Kamel Is Vital to Egypt's Future." *Bikya Masr,* 15 August. http://www.bikyamasr.com.

Mbembe, Achille. 2000. *On Private Indirect Government.* Dakar: Council for the Development of Social Science Research in Africa.

McAdam, Doug. 1982. *Political Process and the Development of Black Insurgency, 1930–1970.* 1st edn. Chicago: University of Chicago Press.

———. 1999. *Political Process and the Development of Black Insurgency, 1930–1970.* 2nd edn. Chicago: University of Chicago Press.

McCann, Michael. 1991. "Legal Mobilization and Social Movements: Notes on Theory and Its Applications." *Studies in Law, Politics, and Society* 11: 225–54.

———, ed. 2006. *Law and Social Movements*. London: Ashgate.

McClintock, Anne, Aamir Mufti, and Ella Shohat, eds. 1997. *Dangerous Liaisons: Gender, Nation and Postcolonial Perspectives*. Minneapolis: University of Minnesota Press.

McDermott, Terry. 2002. "A Perfect Soldier." *Los Angeles Times*, 27 January.

McFalls, Laurence. 2010. "Benevolent Dictatorship." *Contemporary States of Emergency: The Politics of Military and Humanitarian Interventions*, ed. Didier Fassin and Mariella Pandolfi, 317–34. Cambridge: Massachusetts Institute of Technology Press.

McIntosh, Alison, and Jason Finkle. 1995. "The Cairo Conference on Population and Development: A New Paradigm?" *Population and Development Review* 21 (2): 223–60.

McRae, Rob, and Don Hubert, eds. 2001. *Human Security and the New Diplomacy: Protecting People, Promoting Peace*. London: McGill-Queens Press.

McSweeny, Bill. 1999. *Security, Identity and Interests: A Sociology of International Relations*. Cambridge: Cambridge University Press.

Meade, Teresa. 1986. "Civilizing Rio de Janeiro: The Public Health Campaign and the Riot of 1904." *Journal of Social History* 20 (2): 301–22.

———. 1997. *"Civilizing" Rio: Reform and Resistance in a Brazilian City, 1889–1930*. University Park: Pennsylvania State University Press.

Mendes, Cândido. 2006. *Lula, Apesar de Lula*. Rio de Janeiro: Editora Garamond.

Merry, Sally Engle. 2003. "Constructing a Global Law: Violence against Women and the Human Rights System." *Law and Social Inquiry* 28 (4): 941–77.

Merry, Sally Engle, and Mark Goodale. 2007. *The Practice of Human Rights: Tracking Law between the Global and the Local*. Cambridge: Cambridge University Press.

Mesentier, Leonardo Marques de. 1992. "A renovação preservadora: Um estudo sobre a gênese de um modo de urbanização no Centro do Rio de Janeiro, entre 1967 e 1987." Masters thesis, Rio de Janeiro: UFRJ / IPPUR.

Mikdashi, Maya. 2011. "The Marriage of Sexism and Islamophobia: ReMaking the News on Egypt." *Jadaliyya*, 21 February. http://www.jadaliyya.com.

Ministério da Justiça. 2007. *Política nacional de enfrentamento ao tráfico de pessoas*. Rio de Janeiro: Ministério da Justiça.

Mir, Luís. 2004. *Guerra civil: Estado e trauma*. São Paulo: Geração Editorial.

Mitchell, Timothy. 1991a. *Colonising Egypt*. Berkeley: University of California Press.

———. 1991b. "The Limits of the State: Beyond Statist Approaches and Their Critics." *American Political Science Review* 85 (1): 77–96.

———. 2002. *The Rule of Experts: Egypt, Techno-Politics, Modernity*. Berkeley: University of California Press.

Moehn, Frederick. 2007. "Music, Citizenship, and Violence in Postdictatorship Brazil." *Latin American Music Review* 28 (2): 181–219.

Moghadam, Assaf. 2008. *The Globalization of Martyrdom: Al Qaeda, Salafi Jihad, and the Diffusion of Suicide Attacks*. Baltimore: Johns Hopkins University Press.

Mohanty, Chandra Talpade. 1988. "Under Western Eyes: Feminist Scholarship and Colonial Discourses." *Feminist Review* 30 (autumn): 61–88.

———. 2003. *Feminism without Borders: Decolonizing Theory, Practicing Solidarity.* Durham: Duke University Press.

Monteiro, Rosane. 1992. "Gays criam sua associação: A ASTRAL (Associação de Travestis Liberados) vai lutar contra a discriminação e resgatar a dignidade da 'categoria.'" *O Dia*, 28 July.

Moraes, Aparecida Fonseca. 1996. *Mulheres da Vila: Prostituição, identidade social, e movimento asociativo.* Petrópolis, Rio de Janeiro: Editora Vozes.

Morena, E. 2006. "Funding and the Future of the Global Justice Movement." *Development* 49 (2): 29–33.

Motta, Nelson. 2005. "Nacionalismo genital." *Folha de Sao Paulo*, 1 July.

Moustafa, Tamir. 2000. "Conflict and Cooperation between the State and Religious Institutions in Contemporary Egypt." *International Journal of Middle East Studies* 32 (1): 3–22.

Muftah, M. 2007. "Wazir aldakhilia almasriya: Altaharrush aljinsy laisa dhaahira wala yujad ma shii3i." *Moheet Web Magazine.* Accessed 20 October 2009. http://www.moheet.com/newsPrint.aspx?nid=219704.

Muller, Benjamin. 2008. "Securing the Political Imagination: Popular Culture, the Security *Dispositif* and the Biometric State." *Security Dialogue* 39 (2–3): 199–220.

Muniz, Jaqueline. 1999. "'Ser policial é sobretudo, uma razão de ser': Cultura do cotidiano da Policia Militar do Estado do Rio de Janeiro." PhD diss., Instituto Universitário de Pesquisa do Rio de Janeiro.

Muñoz, José. 1999. *Disidentifications: Queers of Color and the Performance of Politics.* Minneapolis: University of Minnesota Press.

Mutua, M. 2001. "Savages, Victims and Saviors: The Metaphor of Human Rights." *Harvard International Law Journal* 42 (1): 201–45.

Naasif, 'Emaad. 1994. "Fatiyaat li-ltasdiir." *Al-Ahraar*, 16 June.

Nacif, Fernanda. 2011. MINIONU *Guia dos Estudos: Cúpula América do Sul—Países Árabes.* Belo Horizonte, Brazil: Editora PUC Minas.

Naff, Alex. 2002. "New York: The Mother Colony." *A Community of Many Worlds: Arab Americans in New York City*, ed. Kathleen Benson and Philip Kayal, 3–10. New York: Museum of the City of New York / Syracuse University Press.

Naib, Fatma. 2011. "Women of the Revolution: Egyptian Women Describe the Spirit of Tahrir and Their Hope that the Equality They Found There Will Live On." *Aljazeera*, 19 February. http://www.aljazeera.com.

Nascimento, Elisa Larkin. 2007. *The Sorcery of Color: Identity, Race, and Gender in Brazil.* Philadelphia: Temple University Press.

Nascimento, Gilberto. 1996. "Prostitutas Made in Brazil." *Istoé*, 6 May.

Netto, Araújo. 1986. "Gladiatoras do Brasil vão à luta na noite romana." *Jornal do Brasil*, 26 October.

Newman, Lucia. 2009. "Arab-Latam Bid for a Diverse World." *Al Jazeera*, 31 March. http://www.aljazeera.com.

Nieto, W. Alejandro Sánchez. 2012. "Brazil's Grand Design for Combining Global South Solidarity and National Interests: A Discussion of Peacekeeping Operations in Haiti and Timor." *Global South to the Rescue: Emerging Humanitarian Superpowers and Globalizing Rescue Industries*, ed. Paul Amar, 161–78. London: Routledge.

Noor, Queen of Jordan. 2008. "Hillary Clinton: A Champion for Human Security." *Huffington Post*, 4 December. http://www.huffingtonpost.com.

Núcleo de Turismo do Fórum de Desenvolvimento Econômico da Roncinha. 2000. "Rocinha Tur 2000." Rio de Janeiro: self-produced booklet.

Nunn, Amy. 2008. *The Politics and History of AIDS Treatment in Brazil*. New York: Springer.

Nye, Joseph S., Jr. 2009. "The U.S. Can Reclaim 'Smart Power.'" *Los Angeles Times*, 29 January. http://www.latimes.com.

Oliveira, Daniela. 2012. "As crianças na era das UPPs." *Infosur Hoy*, 12 April. http://infosurhoy.com.

Oliveira, Ney dos Santos. 1996. "Favelas and Ghettos: Race and Class in Rio de Janeiro and New York City." *Latin American Perspectives* 23 (4): 71–89.

O'Neill, Caitria. 2011. "Birthing a Revolution." *Harvard Political Review*, 12 April.

Orford, Anne. 2003. *Reading Humanitarian Intervention: Human Rights and the Use of Force in International Law*. Cambridge: Cambridge University Press.

Ornat, Marcio José. 2008. "Território e prostituição travesti: Uma proposta de discussão." *TerraPlural, Ponta Grossa* 2 (1): 41–56.

Osborn, Andrew. 2003. "Muslim Alliance Derails UN's Gay Rights Resolution." *Guardian*, 25 April.

Oweis, Khaled Yacoub. 2011. "Mideast Power Brokers Call for 'Marshall Plan' after Unrest." *Al Arabiya News*, 22 October. http://english.alarabiya.net.

Owen, Taylor. 2008. "The Critique that Doesn't Bite: A Response to David Chandler's 'Human Security: The Dog that Didn't Bark.'" *Security Dialogue* 39 (4): 445–53.

Owensby, Brian. 2005. "Toward a History of Brazil's 'Cordial Racism': Race Beyond Liberalism." *Comparative Studies in Society and History* 47: 318–47.

Paixão, Marcelo. 2005. "Anthropofagai e racismo: Uma crítica ao modelo brasileiro de relacões raciais." *Elemento suspeito: Abordagem policial e discriminação na Cidade do Rio de Janeiro*, ed. Silvia Ramos and Leonarda Musumeci. Rio de Janeiro: Civilização Brasileira.

Pandolfi, Mariella. 2010. "From Paradox to Paradigm." *Contemporary States of Emergency: The Politics of Military and Humanitarian Interventions*, ed. Didier Fassin and Mariella Pandolfi, 153–72. Cambridge: Massachusetts Institute of Technology Press.

Parker, Richard. 1998. *Beneath the Equator: Cultures of Desire, Male Homosexuality and Emerging Gay Communities in Brazil*. New York: Routledge.

Parker, Richard, Rosalind Petchesky, and Robert Sember. 2007. *SexPolitics: Reports from the Front Lines*. New York: Sexuality Policy Watch. http://www.sxpolitics.org/frontlines/book/index.php.

Parson, Edward A., Peter M. Haas, and Marc A Levy. 1992. "A Summary of the Major Documents Signed at the Earth Summit and the Global Forum." *Environment: Science and Policy for Sustainable Development* 34: 12–36.

Pazello, Magaly. 2005. "Sexual Rights and Trade." *Peace Review: A Journal of Social Justice* 17: 155–62.

Peck, Jamie, and Adam Tickell. 2002. "Neoliberalizing Space." *Antipode* 24 (3): 380–404.

Pedrosa, Fernanda. 1990. *A Violência que oculta a favela*. Rio de Janeiro: L&PM Editores.

Peluso, Cezar. 2011. "University of Public Security and Social Development." *Supreme Tribunal Federal* (April): 64. http://www.stf.jus.br/arquivo/cms/noticiaNoticiaStf/anexo/univSegPublica.pdf.

Penglase, Ben. 2005. "The Shutdown of Rio de Janeiro: The Poetics of Drug-Trafficker Violence." *Anthropology Today* 21 (5): 3–6.

Peoples, Columba, and Nick Vaughan-Williams. 2010. *Critical Security Studies: An Introduction*. New York: Routledge.

Pereira, Anthony. 2005. *Political (In)Justice: Authoritarianism and the Rule of Law in Brazil, Chile, and Argentina*. Pittsburgh: University of Pittsburgh Press.

Pessoa, Flávio. 2000. "Travestis atacados por lutadores de jiu-jitsu." *O Globo*, 8 February.

Petchesky, Rosalind. 2003. *Global Prescriptions: Gendering Health and Human Rights*. London: Zed Books.

———. 2007. "Sexual Rights Policies across Countries and Cultures: Conceptual Frameworks and Minefields." *SexPolitics: Reports from the Front Lines*, ed. Richard Parker, Rosalind Petchesky, and Robert Sember, 9–25. New York: Sexuality Policy Watch.

Pieterse, Jan Nederveen. 2004. *Globalization or Empire?* New York: Routledge.

———. 2008a. "Globalization the Next Round: Sociological Perspectives." *Futures* 40 (8): 707–20.

———. 2008b. *Is There Hope for Uncle Sam?* London: Zed Books.

———. 2009. *Globalization and Culture: Global Melange*. Lanham, Md.: Rowman and Littlefield.

———. 2011. "Global Rebalancing: Crisis and the East-South Turn." *Development and Change* 42 (1): 22–48.

Pimenta, Cristina, Sonia Corrêa, Ivia Maksud, Soraya Deminicis, and Jose Miguel Olivar. 2010. *Sexuality and Development: Brazilian National Response to HIV/AIDS amongst Sex Workers*. Rio de Janeiro: Associação Brasileira Interdisciplinar de AIDS.

Pinheiro, Paulo Sérgio. 1986. "Temporada da 'caça está aberta no país." *Folha de São Paulo*, 24 May.

———. 1991. "Police and Political Crisis: The Case of the Military Police." *Vigilantism and the State in Modern Latin America*, ed. Martha Huggins, 176–88. Westport, Conn.: Praeger.

———. 1999. "The Rule of Law and the Underprivileged in Latin America." *The (Un)Rule of Law and the Underprivileged in Latin America*, ed. Juan Mendes, Guillermo O'Donnell, and Paulo Sérgio Pinheiro, 1–22. Notre Dame: University of Notre Dame Press.

Pinho, Osmundo. 2010. *"O Mundo Negro": Hermenêutica crítica da reafricanização em Salvador*. Curitiba, Brazil: Editora Progressiva.

Piscitelli, Adriana. 2008. "Between 'Mafias' and 'Help': Building of Knowledge on Human Trafficking." Translated by Thaddeus Gregory Blanchette. *Cadernos Pagu* 1 (se). http://socialsciences.scielo.org/scielo.php?pid=S0104-83332008000100004&script=sci_arttext.

Porter, Doug, and David Craig. 2004. "The Third Way and the Third World: Poverty Reduction and Social Inclusion in the Rise of 'Inclusive' Liberalism." *Review of International Political Economy* 11 (2): 387–423.

Prashad, Vijay. 2007. *The Darker Nations: A People's History of the Third World.* New York: New Press.

Pratt, Nicola. 2007. "The Queen Boat Case in Egypt: Sexuality, National Security and State Sovereignty." *Review of International Studies* 33: 129–44.

Procópio, Argemiro. 1999. *O Brasil no mundo das drogas.* São Paulo: Editora Vozes.

Puar, Jasbir. 2002. "Monster, Terrorist, Fag: The War on Terrorism and the Production of Docile Patriots." *Social Text* 20 (3): 117–48.

———. 2007. *Terrorist Assemblages: Homonationalism in Queer Times.* Durham: Duke University Press.

Rabbani, Mouin. 2011. "The Securitisation of Political Rule: Security Domination of Arab Regimes and the Prospects for Democratisation." *Jadaliyya,* 6 May. http://www.jadaliyya.com.

Rafa'at, Hani. 2000. "Talibaat min kuliat al-siyaaha wa al-a'alaam fi akbar shabka aadaab bi-lumraaniya." *Al-Miidaan,* 26 September.

Rahnema, M., and V. Bawtree, eds. 1997. *The Post-Development Reader.* London: Zed Books.

Ramos, Alicia R. 1998. *Indigenism: Ethnic Politics in Brazil.* Madison: University of Wisconsin Press.

Ramos, Silvia, and Sérgio Carrara. 2006. "A constituição da problemática da violência contra homossexuais." *Physis: Revista do Saude Coletiva* 16 (2): 185–205.

Ramos, Silvia, Leonarda Musumeci, Paul Amar, and Marcelo J. P. Paixão. 2005. *Elemento suspeito: Abordagem policial e discriminação na Cidade do Rio de Janeiro.* Rio de Janeiro, Brazil: Civilização Brasileira.

Redding, Jeffrey. 2006. "Human Rights and Homo-Sectuals: The International Politics of Sexuality, Religion, and Law." *Northwestern Journal of International Human Rights* 4 (3): 436–92.

Reddy, M. 1998. "Invisibility/Hypervisibility: The Paradox of Normative Whiteness." *Transformations* 9 (2): 55–64.

Regional Bureau for Arab States, UNDP. 2006. *Arab Human Development Report 2005: Towards the Rise of Women in the Arab World.* Palo Alto: Stanford University Press.

Renato, Claudio. 1996. "Favela Serrinha vai virar pólo turístico oficial." *O Estado de São Paulo,* 4 August.

Ribeiro, Luiz César de Queiroz. 1993. "The Formation of Development Capital: A Historical Overview of Housing in Rio de Janeiro." *International Journal of Urban and Regional Research* 17 (4): 547–58.

Rieff, David. 2002. *A Bed for the Night: Humanitarianism in Crisis.* New York: Simon and Schuster.

Rigakos, George. 2002. *The New Parapolice: Risk Markets and Commodified Social Control.* Toronto: University of Toronto Press.

Rizzo, Helen, Anne M. Price, and Katherine Meyer. 2012. "The Anti-Sexual Harassment Campaign in Egypt." Draft article for *Mobilization* 17 (4).

Roberts, David. 2006. "Human Security or Human Insecurity? Moving the Debate Forward." *Security Dialogue* 37 (2): 249–61.

———. 2010. *Global Governance and Biopolitics.* New York: Zed Books.

Rochester, Julia. 2008. *The Candelária Massacre.* London: Vision Paperbacks.

Roe, Paul. 2006. "Reconstructing Identities or Managing Minorities? Desecuritizing Minority Rights: A Response to Jutila." *Security Dialogue* 37 (3): 425–38.

Rofel, Lisa. 2007. *Desiring China: Experiments in Neoliberalism, Sexuality, and Public Culture.* Durham: Duke University Press.

Rose, Nikolas, and Peter Miller. 1992. "Political Power beyond the State: Problematics of Government." *British Journal of Sociology* 43 (2): 173–205.

Rosemberg, F., and L. Feitosa Andrade. 1999. "Ruthless Rhetoric: Child and Youth Prostitution in Brazil." *Childhood* 6 (1): 113–31.

Rosga, AnnJanette. 1999. "Policing the State." *Georgetown Journal of Gender and the Law* (summer): 145–71.

Rostow, W. W. 1960. *Stages of Economic Growth.* Cambridge: Cambridge University Press.

Roubini, Nouriel. 2009. "It Is Time to Nationalize Insolvent Banking Systems." *Econo-Monitor,* 10 February. http://www.economonitor.com.

Saadiq, Georgette. 1993. "Akhlaaq al-masriyeen fi al-mizaan." *Al-Watan,* 12 August.

Sadek, Amr. 1999. "Damage Statistics of 12 October 1992, Earthquake in the Greater Cairo Area." *Earthquake Engineering and Structural Dynamics* 26 (5): 529–40.

Sakr, Muhammad. 1999. "Tourism Statistics and Economic Impact Measurement: A Case Study of Egypt." Paper presented at the Tourism and Development in Egypt Conference, Cairo University Faculty of Economics and Political Science, 19 October.

Salama, Salama A. 2008. "Fight Back." *Al-Ahram Weekly,* 30 October–5 November.

Samah, George. 2007. *Privatization of Parastatals: Implications for Socio-Economic Development for Sub-Saharan Africa.* Bloomington, Ind.: Authorhouse.

Sami, Soheir. 1998. "Nagwa Fouad: Hours of Glory." *Al-Ahram Weekly,* 13–19 August.

Sanches, Pedro Alexandre. 2000. *Tropicalismo: Decadencia bonita do samba.* São Paulo: Boitempo Editorial.

Sandels, Alexandra. 2008. "Eye Candy for the Egyptian Man." *Menassat,* 29 August. http://www.menassat.com.

Sassen, Saskia. 2004. "Global Cities and Survival Circuits." *Global Woman: Nannies, Maids, and Sex Workers in the New Economy,* ed. Barabara Ehrenreich and Russell Hochschild, 254–74. New York: Holt Paperbacks.

———. 2006. *Territory, Authority, Rights: From Medieval to Global Assemblages.* Princeton: Princeton University Press.

Schechter, Michael, ed. 2001. *United Nations-Sponsored World Conferences: Focus on Impact and Follow-Up.* New York: United Nations University Press.

Schneider, Howard. 2001. "Cultural Struggle Finds Symbol in Gay Cairo." *Washington Post Foreign Service,* 9 September.

Scott, James. 1998. *Seeing Like a State.* New Haven: Yale University Press.

Seif Al-Nasr, Riad. 1998. "Tatwiir al-qaahira al-fatimiya li-saalih sukkaniha." *Al-Jumhuriya Al-Usbu'iy,* 4 September.

Sepúlveda dos Santos, Myrian. 1998. "Mangueira e império: A carnavalização poder pelas escolas de samba." *Um século de favela*, ed. Alba Maria Zaluar and Marcos Alvito, 115–44. Rio de Janeiro: Fundacao Getulio Vargas Editora.

Seymour, Jenny. 1998. "Fatimidland: Will the Clean-up of Medieval Cairo Steal Its Soul?" *Cairo Times*, 19 March.

Sha'iira, Wafaa, 'Alwaan Magheeb, and Nabil Abu Zeid. 1996. "Sira'aat milaahi shaari' al-haram!" *Rose al-Yusef*, 8 June.

Shepherd, L. 2008. "Power and Authority in the Production of United Nations Security Council Resolution 1325." *International Studies Quarterly* 52: 383–404.

Sheptycki, James. 2009. "Policing, Intelligence Theory and the New Human Security Paradigm: Some Lessons from the Field." *Intelligence Theory: Key Questions and Debates*, ed. P. Gill, S. Marin and M. Phythian, 166–85. London: Routledge.

Sikkink, K. 1993. "Human Rights, Principled Issue-Networks, and Sovereignty in Latin America." *International Organization* 47 (3): 411–41.

Silva, M. M. L. 1994. "Killing of 6,000 Street Kids and the Candelaria Massacre." *C.J. the Americas* 7 (4): 1, 6–8.

Simon, Jonathan. 2007. *Governing through Crime: How the War on Crime Transformed American Democracy and Created a Culture of Fear*. New York: Oxford University Press.

Singerman, Diane. 1995. *Avenues of Participation: Family, Politics, and Networks in Urban Quarters of Cairo*. Princeton: Princeton University Press.

Singerman, Diane, and Paul Amar, eds. 2006. *Cairo Cosmopolitan: Politics, Culture, and Urban Space in the New Globalized Middle East*. Cairo: American University in Cairo Press.

Sinha, Aseema, and Jon P. Dorschner. 2010. "India: Rising Power or a Mere Revolution of Rising Expectations?" *Polity* 42 (1): 74–99.

Skidmore, Thomas. 1983. "Race and Class in Brazil: Historical Perspectives." *Luso-Brazilian Review* 20: 104–18.

Skidmore, Thomas, and Pater Smith. 2001. *Modern Latin America*. New York: Oxford University Press.

Slyomovics, Susan. 2005. *The Performance of Human Rights in Morocco*. Philadelphia: University of Pennsylvania Press.

Smillie, Ian, ed. 2001. *Patronage or Partnership: Local Capacity Building in Humanitarian Crises*. Ottawa: Kumarian Press.

Smith, Anna Marie. 2007. *Welfare Reform and Sexual Regulation*. New York: Cambridge University Press.

Smith, Michael Peter. 2001. *Transnational Urbanism: Locating Globalization*. Oxford: Blackwell.

Smith, Neil. 2002. "New Globalism, New Urbanism: Gentrification as Global Urban Strategy." *Antipode* 34 (3): 427–50.

Soares, Luiz Eduardo. 2000. *Quinhentos dias no front da segurança pública do Rio de Janeiro*. Rio de Janeiro: Companhia das Letras.

———. 2001. "A segurança pública como questão das esquerdas." Paper presented at the World Social Forum, Porto Alegre, Rio Grande do Sul, Brazil, 25–30 January.

———. 2006. *A segurança tem saida*. Rio de Janeiro: Editora Sextante.

Soares, Luiz Eduardo, M. V. Bill, and Celso Athayde. 2005. *Cabeça de porco*. Rio de Janeiro: Editora Objetiva.

Souza de Almeida, Suely. 2000. "Violência Urbana e constituição de sujeitos politicos." *Linguagens da violência*, ed. Carlos A. M. Pereira, Elizabeth Rondelli, Karl Erik Schlhammer, and Micael Herschmann, 97–108. Rio de Janeiro: Editora Rocco.

Spade, Dean. 2009. "Trans Law and Politics on a Neoliberal Landscape." *Temple Political and Civil Rights Law Review* 18: 354–73.

Spearing, Christopher. 2008. "Private, Armed, and Humanitarian? States, NGOs and International Private Security Companies and Shifting Humanitarianism." *Security Dialogue* 39 (4): 363–82.

Spivak, Gayatri. 2004. "Terror: A Speech after 9–11." *boundary 2* 31 (2): 81–111.

Springer de Freitas, Renan. 1984. "Prostitutas, cafetinas e policiais: A dialética das ordens opostas." *Dados: Revista das ciências sociais* 27 (2): 33–54.

Stanley, William. 1996. *The Protection Racket State: Elite Politics, Military Extortion and Civil War in El Salvador*. Philadelphia: Temple University Press.

Steigenga, Timothy. 2003. *The Politics of the Spirit: The Political Implications of Pentecostalized Religion in Costa Rica and Guatemala*. Lanham, Md.: Lexington Books.

Steiner, Henry, and Philip Alston. 2008. *International Human Rights in Context: Law, Politics, Morals*. Oxford: Oxford University Press.

Steiner, Mark Allan. 2006. *The Rhetoric of Operation Rescue: Projecting the Christian Pro-life Message*. London: Continuum International.

Stern, Maria. 2006. "'We' the Subject: The Power and Failure of (In)Security." *Security Dialogue* 37 (2): 187–205.

Stiglitz, Joseph E. 2003. *Globalization and Its Discontents*. New York: W. W. Norton.

Stoler, Ann Laura. 1989. "Making Empire Respectable: The Politics of Race and Sexual Morality in Twentieth-Century Colonial Cultures." *American Ethnologist* 16 (4): 634–60.

Stone, Clarence. 2005. "Looking Back to Look Forward: Reflections on Urban Regime Analysis." *Urban Affairs Review* 40 (3): 309–41.

Strong, Maurice F. 1993. "Beyond Rio: Prospects and Portents." *Colorado Journal of International Environmental Law and Policy* 4: 21–29.

Stycer, Mauricio. 1996. "Europeu faz 'tour sociologico' em favela." *Folha de São Paulo*, 24 March.

Surborg, Björn, Rob VanWynsberghe, and Elvin Wyly. 2008. "Mapping the Olympic Growth Machine: Transnational Urbanism and the Growth Machine Diaspora." *City: Analysis of Urban Trends, Culture, Theory, Policy, Action* 12 (3): 4–12.

Swyngedouw, Erik. 2004. "Globalisation or 'Glocalisation'? Networks, Territories and Rescaling." *Cambridge Review of International Affairs* 17 (1): 25–48.

Tabb, William K. 2003. "After Neoliberalism?" *Monthly Review* 55 (2): 25–33.

Tadjbakhsh, Shahrbanou, and Anuradha M. Chenoy. 2007. *Human Security: Concepts and Implications*. London: Routledge.

Tadros, Mariz. 2011. "The Securitisation of Civil Society: A Case Study of NGOs: State Security Investigations (SSI) Relations in Egypt." *Conflict, Security and Development* 11 (1): 79–102.

Tan, Kenneth Paul. 2003. "Sexing up Singapore." *International Journal of Cultural Studies* 6 (4): 403–23.

Tangri, Roger. 2000. *The Politics of Patronage in Africa: Parastatals, Privatization and Private Enterprise in Africa*. Trenton, N.J.: Africa World Press.

Tarrow, Sidney. 2012. "War, Rights and Contention: Lasswell v Tilly." *Varieties of Sovereignty and Citizenship*, ed. S. Ben-Porath and R. Smith, 35–57. Philadelphia: University of Pennsylvania Press.

Taylor, Laurie. 2005. "No More Mr Nice Guy: Laurie Taylor on Michael Ignatieff." *New Humanist* 120 (5). http://newhumanist.org.uk.

Telles, Edward. 2004. *Race in Another America: The Significance of Skin Color in Brazil*. Princeton: Princeton University Press.

Tilly, Charles. 1985. "War Making and State Making as Organized Crime." *Bringing the State Back In*, ed. Peter Evans, Dietrich Rueschemeyer, and Theda Skocpol, 169–87. Cambridge: Cambridge University Press.

Tisdall, Simon. 2006. "Egypt Finds Democracy Can Wait." *Guardian*, 16 May. http://www.guardian.co.uk.

Touraine, Alain. 2001. *Beyond Neoliberalism*. Cambridge: Polity.

Trinidade, Eliane. 1997a. "Combate à pedofilia: Embratur promove campanha contra os turistas sexuais." *Istoé*, 1 August.

———. 1997b. "Microempresarias do Sexo." *Istoé*, 22 October.

Tsagourias, Nicholas. 2006. "Consent, Neutrality/Impartiality and the Use of Force in Peacekeeping: Their Constitutional Dimension." *Journal of Conflict and Security Law* 11 (3): 465–82.

Turcheti e Melo, Nicole Maria. 2010. "Public Policy for the Favelas in Rio de Janeiro: The Problem (in) Framing." Master's thesis, International Institute of Social Sciences, The Hague.

Twine, France Winddance. 1998. *Racism in a Racial Democracy: The Maintenance of White Supremacy in Brazil*. New Brunswick: Rutgers University Press.

Ungar, Mark. 2002. "State Violence and LGBT rights." *Violence and Politics: Globalization's Paradox*, 48–66. Florence, Ky.: Psychology Press.

———. 2011. *Policing Democracy: Overcoming Obstacles to Citizen Security in Latin America*. Baltimore: Johns Hopkins University Press.

UNICEF. 2010. "Statistics by Country: Egypt." Accessed 7 November 2010. http://www.unicef.org/infobycountry/egypt_statistics.html.

United Nations. 1997. "United Nations Earth Summit Summary." UN Conference on Environment and Development (1992). http://www.un.org/geninfo/bp/enviro.html.

United Nations Development Programme. 1994. *Human Development Report 1994*. Oxford: Oxford University Press.

United Nations Development Programme / Supreme Council of Antiquities, Government of Egypt. 1997. *Final Report: Rehabilitation of Historic Cairo*. Cairo: United Nations Country Office.

Van Nieuwkerk, Karin. 1995. *A Trade Like Any Other: Female Singers and Dancers in Egypt*. Austin: University of Texas Press.

Van Rooy, Alison. 1997. "The Frontiers of Influence: NGO Lobbying at the 1974 World

Food Conference, the 1992 Earth Summit and Beyond." *World Development* 25 (1): 93–114.

Vargas, João H. Costa. 2006. "When a Favela Dared to Become a Gated Condominium." *Latin American Perspectives* 33 (4): 49–81.

————. 2010. "Geographies of Death: An Intersectional Analysis of Police Lethality and the Racialized Regimes of Citizenship in Sao Paulo." *Ethnic and Racial Studies* 33: 611–36.

Vargas, João Costa, and Jaime Amparo Alvez. 2010. "Geographies of Death: An Intersectional Analysis of Police Lethality and the Racialized Regimes of Citizenship in São Paulo." *New Racial Missions of Policing International Perspectives on Evolving Law-Enforcement Politics*, ed. Paul Amar, 37–62. New York: Routledge.

Varma, Rashmi. 2004. "Provincializing the Global City: From Bombay to Mumbai." *Social Text* 22 (4): 65–89.

Vatican. 2004. "Letter to the Bishops of the Catholic Church on the Collaboration of Men and Women in the Church and in the World." http://www.vatican.va /roman_curia/congregations/cfaith/documents/rc_con_cfaith_doc_20040731 _collaboration_en.html.

Vaz, Lilian Fessler, and Carmen Beatriz Silveira. 1999. "Áreas centrais, projetos urbanísticos e vazios urbanos." *Território* 4 (7): 51–66.

Velho, Gilberto. 2002. *Mudança, crise, e violência: Política e cultura no Brasil contemporâneo*. Rio de Janeiro: Civilização Brasileira.

Ventura, Mauro. 1997. "Violência policial cicatriza favela modelo: Em Serrinha, vitrine do projeto Favela-Bairro, é melhor não olhar, ouvir ou falar sobre as atrocidades policiais." *Jornal do Brasil*, 13 April.

Vianna, Adriana R. B., and Sérgio Carrara. 2007. "Brazil: Sexual Politics and Sexual Rights in Brazil: A Case Study." *SexPolitics: Reports from the Front Lines*, ed. Richard Parker, Rosalind Petchesky, and Robert Sember, 27–51. New York: Sexuality Policy Watch.

Vieira, Karina. 2012. "Amid European Crisis, Latin America Wants a Seat at the Table." *Univision News*, 12 March. http://univisionnews.tumblr.com.

Vilhena de Araujo, Heliosa. 2005. *Diálogo América do Sul: Países Árabes*. Brasília: Editora do Instituto de Pesquisa de Relações Internacionais.

Wacquant, Loic. 2008. "Militarization of Urban Marginality: Lessons from the Brazilian Metropolis." *International Political Sociology* 2 (1): 56–74.

————. 2009. "The Body, the Ghetto and the Penal State." *Qualitative Sociology* 39: 101–29.

Wallerstein, Immanuel. 1976. "Semi-peripheral Countries and the Contemporary World Crisis." *Theory and Society* 3 (4): 461–83.

Walsh, John. 2003. "Egypt's Muslim Brotherhood: Understanding Centrist Islam." *Harvard International Review* 24: 32–36.

Warah, Rasna. 2001. "The Emerging Urban Archipelago." *United Nations Chronicle* 38 (1): 30.

Warren, Kay B., and Jean Elizabeth Jackson. 2003. *Indigenous Movements, Self-Representation, and the State in Latin America*. Austin: University of Texas Press.

Weed, Elizabeth, and Ellen Rooney, eds. 2003. "More On Humanism." *differences* 14 (1): 1–17.

Weldes, Jutta, Mark Laffey, Hugh Gusterson, and Raymond Duvall, eds. 1999. *Cultures of Insecurity: States, Communities, and the Production of Danger*. Minneapolis: University of Minnesota Press.

White, E. Frances. 2001. *The Dark Continent of Our Bodies: Black Feminism and the Politics of Respectability*. Philadelphia: Temple University Press.

Wibben, Annick. 2008. "Human Security: Toward an Opening." *Security Dialogue* 39 (4): 455–61.

Wilheim, Jorge. 2002. *Negotiating a New Social Contract in the Urban Archipelago: The Case of São Paulo*. Washington: World Bank.

Wilkinson, Claire. 2007. "The Copenhagen School on Tour in Kyrgyzstan: Is Securitization Theory Useable Outside Europe?" *Security Dialogue* 38 (1): 5–25.

Williams, Caroline. 2002. *Islamic Monuments in Cairo: The Practical Guide*. Cairo: American University in Cairo Press.

Williams, David, ed. 2008. *Security Studies: An Introduction*. New York: Routledge.

Williams, Michael C. 2007. *Realism Reconsidered: The Legacy of Hans Morgenthau in International Relations*. Oxford: Oxford University Press.

Williams, Richard J. 2005. "Modernist Civic Space and the Case of Brasília." *Journal of Urban History* 32 (1): 120–37.

Wilson, Ara. 2004. *The Intimate Economies of Bangkok: Tomboys, Tycoons, and Avon Ladies in the Global City*. Berkeley: University of California Press.

Wilson, Elizabeth. 1992. *The Sphinx in the City: Urban Life, the Control of Disorder, and Women*. Berkeley: University of California Press.

Winter, Brian, and Natuza Nery. 2010. "Special Report: Dilma Rousseff, Brazil's 'Automatic Pilot.'" Reuters, 23 September. http://www.reuters.com.

Wood, Jennifer. 2004. "Cultural Change in the Governance of Security." *Policing and Society* 14 (1): 31–48.

Woodruff, Judy. 2008. "Greenspan Admits 'Flaw' to Congress, Predicts More Economic Problems." *PBS Newshour*, 23 October. http://www.pbs.org/newshour.

Woods, Clyde. 2007. "Sittin' On Top of the World: The Challenges of Blues and Hip Hop Geography." *Black Geographies and the Politics of Place*, ed. Katherine McKittrick and Clyde Woods, 46–81. Cambridge, Mass.: South End Press.

Worcester, Kent, Sally A. Bermanzohn, and Mark Ungar. 2002. *Violence and Politics: Globalization's Paradox*. Florence, Ky.: Psychology Press.

Worth, Owen. 2009. "Whatever Happened to the Semi-Periphery?" *Globalization and the "New" Semi-Peripheries*, ed. Owen Worth and Phoebe Moore, 9–24. New York: Palgrave Macmillan.

Wynn, L. L. 2007. *Pyramids and Nightclubs*. Austin: University of Texas Press.

Xavier, Ismail. 1993. *Alegorias do subdesenvolvimento: Cinema novo, tropicalismo, cinema marginal*. São Paulo: Editora Brasiliense.

Yancy, George. 2008. *Black Bodies, White Gazes: The Continuing Significance of Race*. Boulder: Rowman and Littlefield.

Yaseen, Nevine. 1998. "Athaarna al-islamiya dahiya ehmaal al-mas'uuleen!" *Al-Wafd*, 26 October.

Young, Robert. 1995. *Colonial Desire: Hybridity in Theory, Culture, and Race.* New York: Routledge.

Yu, Ying, Francisco Klauser, and Gerald Chan. 2009. "Governing Security at the 2008 Beijing Olympics." *International Journal of the History of Sport* 26: 309–405.

Yúdice, George. 2003. *The Expediency of Culture: Uses of Culture in the Global Era.* Durham: Duke University Press.

Zaluar, Alba. 1981. *Condomínio do Diabo.* Rio de Janeiro: Editora UFRJ.

———. 1996. *Da revolta ao crime S/A.* São Paulo: Editora Moderna.

———. 2004. *Integração perversa: Pobreza e tráfico de drogas.* Rio de Janeiro: FGV Editora.

———. 2005. "Brazilian Drug Worlds and the Fate of Democracy." *Interventions* 7 (3): 338–41.

Zine, Jasmine. 2006. "Between Orientalism and Fundamentalism: The Politics of Muslim Women's Feminist Engagement." *Muslim World Journal of Human Rights* 3 (1). doi: 10.2202/1554-4419.1080.

Index

Note: page numbers in *italics* refer to illustrations; those followed by "n" indicated endnotes.

alities between, 28; feminist antiviolence politics and, 207; the "Gay International" and, 75; human-rights internationalism and, 208; "parahuman" and, 209; in poststructuralist theory, 25–26; queering and, 210; respectability politics and, 215; tropicalism and orientalism, 21, 28, 58–63, 88–89, 106, 134, 170

Comando Azul (Blue Command), 185

comandos, 144–45, 146, 148, 152–53

Comando Vermelho (Red Command), 143, 144

Comaroff, Jean, 242

Comaroff, John, 242

conferences and summits: ASPA (South American–Arab Countries) Summits, 56–60, 63; Cairo Summit (1994), 42, 51–54, 229; counter summits, 44; dynamics of, 42–43; Earth Summit (Rio de Janeiro, 1992), 42, 43–48; First Ladies Summit of the Non-Aligned Movement, 206; G-20 summit (London, 2009), 61; iron-fist policing, sexualization, and racialization at, 46; as laboratories, 29; Progressive Governance Summit (Chile, 2008), 60–61; Regional Workshop for Arab Parliaments, 206; on sex tourism and trafficking, 92–95; UN cycle of social conferences, 43–44; UN World Conference against Racism (Durban, South Africa, 2001), 54–55; UN World Conference on Women (Beijing, 1995), 54

consumer subjects: consumer literacy identified as queer in Cairo, 76; postneoliberal shift from consumption to work, 240–43; respectability and, 219–20

Convention on the Elimination of All Forms of Discrimination against Women (CEDAW), 206

conviviality: class, 91, 96, 98; cosmopolitan, 72, 90–91; erotic, 31, 70–71, 74, 78, 98; racial, 148, 149, 152; term, use of, 254n7

Cooke, Thomas, 106

Cooper, Anderson, 201

Copacabana, Rio de Janeiro, 179, 188. *See also* Operation Princess

Copenhagen School for Peace Studies, 209

cordiality, black, 145, 148, 156–57, 159

Cordoba Islamic Cultural Center (proposed), 137

Corrêa, Sonia, 43, 181, 183

Cowen, Tyler, 249

Craig, David, 238

critical security studies, 19–21

cultural autonomy movements in Brazil, 47–48

cultural heritage projects. *See* heritage development; tourism and tourist development

cultural purity vs. economic globalization in Rio and Cairo, 70. *See also* religious-moralist movements

cultural rescue. *See* rescue discourses and campaigns

cultural security: Atta on, 32, 128–29, 132, 134; "family values" coalition and, 53, 54, 132–33; favela tourism and, 166; Islamic Cairo heritage bloc, 103–4, 105–12; public space and women as objects of, 213. *See also* samba politics vs. security politics in Rio

culture of neoliberalism, 241–43

Darb al-Ahmar Committee for National Consciousness (CNC or True Egyptian People), 124–26, *125*, 126

da Silva, Benedita, 141, 142, 143, 145, 148–49, 163

Declaration on the Prevention of Sex Tourism (1995), 92

Deminicis, Soraya, 181

de Oliveira, Marina Pereira Pires, 197–98

Devji, Faisal, 133

Dimock, Wai Chee, 137

dissemination model of human rights, 207–8

drug trafficking. *See* narco-trafficking

Dunne, Bruce, 216

earthquake (Cairo, 1992), 51, *52*

Earth Summit (UN Conference on Environment and Development, Rio de Janeiro 1992), 42, 43–48

ECWR (Egyptian Center for Women's Rights), 223–24, 228

Egypt: Brazil as analogous to, 27–29; China, economic sellout to, 222–23; Law of Local Administration (1994), 107; Luxor Massacre (1997), 123; Vice Police vs. State Security, 74. *See also* Cairo; *specific organizations, people, and topics*

Egyptian Center for Women's Rights (ECWR), 223–24, 228

Militarized Police (*continued*)
moralization campaign, 185; masculinism and, 162–63; military vs., 13; prison corruption, 143; represented as external by tourism, 167; Serrinha, abuse and violence in, 161–62; sex trafficking campaigns and, 173–74, 185, 187–90; *travestis* and, 65, 254n3; women in, 185

Millionein Hussein (Two Million March), *114*

Miranda, Carmen, 151

miscegenation: racial democracy narratives, 152, 156–57, 160, 170; tropicalism, orientalism, and, 58–63

Mitchell, Timothy, 25, 69

modernity: Brazil's sexual-orientation resolution and, 63; Moorish miscegenation and, 62; plurality of modernities, 244; sex-nation-modernity realignment in late twentieth century, 67

modernization, inverted, 110

Moehn, Frederick, 160

Monti, Mario, 249

Moorish transnational imaginary, 61–62

moralistic securitization logic: defined, 176; sex trafficking campaigns and, 172–73. *See also* evangelicalism and Pentecostalism in Brazil; religious-moralist movements; rescue discourses and campaigns

moral panics: classphobic, 219; genital xenophobia and, 189; globalization and, 71; Hall on, 17, 231; hotspots and, 15–16; hypervisibilization and, 17, 217; Islamic Cairo and, 101; queer subjects and, 71; security crises and, 199; sex tourism and, 93

Morsy, Mohammad, 6

Moussa, Amr, 55, 56

Moustafa, Tamir, 112

Mubarak, Hosni: al-Azhar and, 115; Fatimid Authority and, 127; Islamic Cairo and, 107, *108*; Luxor Massacre and, 123; resignation of, 1–2; Salafis and, 112; security state identified with, 2–3; trial of, 4

Mubarak, Suzanne, 205–6

Mufti, Hania, 77

mulatto category, 93, 255n23

Muniz, Jacqueline, 162

Muslim Brotherhood, 6, 86, 116

Mykhnenko, Vlad, 248

narco-trafficking: Favela-Bairro project and, 161–62; in film, 166; Lula da Silva and, 147; represented as external by tourism, 167; Serrinha and, 151, 152; shadow-state uprising (Rio, 2002), 143–46

National Conference to Confront Human Trafficking (Rio, 2008), 185

national identity: ASTRAL repudiation of, 66; Darb al-Ahmar Committee for National Consciousness and, 124; municipalization of, in Rio, 80; Rio sex tourism vs. executive identity, 82–86; tropicalist modernism and, 62

nationalism: anti-cabaret movement in Cairo, 86–90; Brasilia Declaration and, 57–58; Egyptian Gay Blitz and, 77; revolutionary Arab nationalism in Cairo, 70; woman figure in Arab nationalism, 213

National Prostitutes Network (Brazil), 191, 198

necropolitics, 21, 222

neoliberalism: Cairo cabaret zones and, 86–92; conceptual tools used to examine, 68–69; consumer literacy identified as queer in Cairo, 76; corrupt police as embodiment of, 13; culture of, 241–43; marginalized or victimized subjects in critiques of, 100; market-state logics, struggling, 14; military-authoritarian period preceding, 78, 79–82; as North-centric, 64; as police practices and racial attitudes rebranded, 63–64; Rio as dystopian theater of, 8–9; roll-back, 131, 238; roll-out, 131–32, 238–39; security-state logic contrasted with human-security logic, 14–15

neoliberalism, end of: balance-of-power shift and, 251–52; consumption vs. work and neoliberal culture vs. illiberal missions, 240–43; Great Recession, Global North, and, 246–49; Lula and Rousseff on, 235; as perspective shift, 36–37; semiperiphery, resistant localism, and the archipelago, 243–46; Third Way era and liberalization vs. securitization, 237–40; zombie metaphors, 249–51

new abolitionism, 180–81

Newman, Lucia, 59

New York City: Cordoba Islamic Cultural Center ("Ground Zero Mosque," proposed), 137; Little Syria, 136; "quality of life" and "broken windows policing" programs, 66; World Trade Center attacks, 136

NGO internationalism: alternative treaties project, 44; Cairo NGO Forum, 52–53; Global Forum (Rio, 1992), 44, 45; Rio summit and, 43–44; World Social Forums, 54, 140, 235, 244, 251. *See also* conferences and summits; *specific cases*

NGOization, 214–15, 217–18, 224

Nile Waterfront district, 86, 90–91

9/11 attacks on the World Trade Center, 136

Non-Aligned Movement, 55, 206

nuclear technology sharing, 59–60

Nucleus for Tourism Development, 169

Obama, Barack, 248

Occupy movement, 240

oil industry in Brazil, 11–12

Olivar, Jose Miguel, 181

operaismo philosophy, 181–82

Operation Carnaval, 187–88

Operation Princess and campaigns against sex trafficking in Rio: Bush and USAID interference, backlash against, 193–95; contested security logics and, 172–73, 174, 174–78; framing and subversion mechanisms, 178; "genital xenophobia" and, 189–90; international obligations and, 174–75; launching of Operation Princess, 188–89; name of, 178–79; Operation Carnaval and attention drawn to police corruption, 187–91; Operation Shangrilá, 189–90; Palermo Protocol, 173, 175, 184; police stations rededicated for, 173–74; political process model and, 176–78; promises for new round of, 198; public opinion on U.S. interference and, 189–90; racialized abolitionism and evangelical rescue narratives, 178–84, 185–86; security politics in Brazil and, 191–93; sex-worker empowerment model, 195–98, *196*; tabloid media subversion, 188–89; War of Rio and moralization of police militarism, 184–85; women's rights and, 185; workerism and, 181–83

Operation Shangrilá, 189–90

orientalism: indigenous elites and, 28; inverted, 88–89; meandering alleyways and,

134; narrativization of Cairo and, 106; tropicalism, cultural miscegenation, and, 58–63

Owensby, Brian, 157

Paes, Eduardo, 198

Paixão, Marcelo, 157

Palermo Protocol, 173, 175, 184

panics. *See* moral panics

Papademos, Lucas, 249

parahuman: defined, 18, 41, 209; securitization, queering, and, 209–10; sexuality and, 17

paramilitary securitization logic: defined, 176; sex trafficking campaigns and, 172–73, 184–85

parastatals: defined, 18; globalizing sexuality subjects and, 75–76; and humanized securitization, emergence of, 7; as human-security phase, 29; nature and function of, 69; sexuality policing and, 68; shadow state, 143–46. *See also specific organizations and cases*

"para" terminology, 17–19

Parker, Richard, 43

peacekeeping vs. peace enforcement models, 35

Peck, Jamie, 131, 238

Peluso, Cezar, 11

"the people," notion of, 104

PESTRAF (*Pesquisa nacional sobre o tráfico*), 175, 184

Petchesky, Rosalind P., 43

phantoms, 18–19

Pieterse, Jan Nederveen, 63

Pillay, Navanethem, 22

Pimenta, Cristina, 181

Pinho, Osmundo, 164

Piscitelli, Adriana, 175

planning and urban renewal: General Organization for Physical Planning for Greater Cairo (GOPP), 109; Plano Maravilha (Rio, 1999), 160; Pyramid Roads and Nile Waterfront cabaret zones, Cairo, 86–92; *rodoviarismo* (highwayism), 79–80; Strategic Plan (Rio, 1999), 157; touristic heritage projects vs. sex workers in Rio and, 79–86. *See also* Favela-Bairro project in Serrinha; Islamic Cairo

Plan to Combat Sexual Exploitation of Children and Adolescents. *See* Operation Princess

police and policing. *See specific organizations, places, and cases*

policekeeping model, 35

Police Pacification Units (UPPS), Brazil, 9, 10, 13

political process model, 176–78

population control, 53

Porter, Doug, 238

postcoloniality. *See* coloniality and postcoloniality

power, hard vs. soft-and-smart, 22–23

preservationism. *See* heritage development

Pressburger, Margardia, 198

Price, Anne M., 224

Prince, Mona, 200

Princess Isabel Syndrome, 180

prison uprisings in Brazil, 143–46

privatizations, reversal of, 240–41

Progressive Governance Summit (Chile, 2008), 60–61

prostitution. *See* sex workers

protection-racket state, 21, 22

Puar, Jasbir, 130, 212, 221–22

public space, securitization of. *See* Favela-Bairro project in Serrinha; Islamic Cairo

public space, sexualized. *See* sexuality politics

Pyramid Roads, Giza, 86, 87–90, 91, 255n20

"quality of life" policing, 66. *See also* sexuality politics

Queen Boat raid, Cairo, 73–74, 76–77, 90–91

queering and queer subjects: Atta, representations of, 129–30; definition of "queering," 209–10; Gay Blitz and securitization of queer globalism (Cairo), 71, 73–78; gender-bending at mawlid, 120; as hyperaggressive agents, 73, 78; hypervisibilization of, 71, 75, 84; Massad on "the Gay International," 75; misrecognition of queer subjects, 76; NGOization, queering of, 217–18; respectability politics and, 215–16; securitization dynamics and, 209–10; time-bomb masculinity and, 222; *travestis* in Rio, 65–67, 84, 254n1, 254n3, 254n6

Queiroz, Jandira, 183

Rabbat, Nasser, 106

racial democracy narratives, 152, 156–57, 160, 170

racialization: Brazilian security politics and, 192; Brazilian sex trafficking campaigns and, 185; *carioca* racialized culture, 154–56; cordialism, 145, 148, 156–57, 159; favela tourism and, 166, 169–70; financial crisis and, 61; Militarized Police and, 162–63; Moorish transnational imaginary, 61–62; mulatto hypersexuality, 93; neoliberalism as rebranding of, 63–64; parahumanization and, 18–19, 209–10; Princess Isabel Syndrome and social whitening (*embrancamento*), 180; sex labor in Rio, gentrification of, 84–85; sex trafficking campaigns and racial infantalization, 186; of "the street," 163; *travestis* in Rio, racist violence against, 65–66. *See also* orientalism; tropicalism

Ramirez, Camilo, 167

Razeq, Gasser Abdel, 77

Regional Workshop for Arab Parliaments, 206

religious-moralist movements: anti-cabaret movement in Cairo, 86–89; coalitions in Brazil, 13; internationalist emergence (1992–1994), 49; Islamic Cairo morality block and Sufi-Salafi conflicts, 112–17; Islamist mission, appropriation of, 54; on sexual rights, 53–54; Victorian, in Brazil, 183–84. *See also* Operation Princess; sexuality politics

Renato, Claudio, 169–70

"Re-orienting Desire" (Massad), 75

rescue discourses and campaigns: Cairo Summit and, 54; cultural autonomy movements in Brazil, 47–48; Egyptian revolution, SCAF, and, 3–4, 4, 5, 5–6; as human-security phase, 29; infranationalism and, 149; new abolitionism (Brazil) and, 180–81; sex trafficking discourses and, 83–84, 93, 186; sexual rights as ally then antagonist to, 48; sex workers and, 78, 86; Victorian, in Brazil, 183–84. *See also* Favela-Bairro project in Serrinha; Islamic Cairo; Operation Princess

resistant localism, 243–46

respectability politics: Benedita da Silva and, 142; consumer culture in Egypt and, 219–20; hijab campaigns, 223; history of, 232;

hypervisibility and, 232; samba citizenship vs., 146; sexual harassment (Egypt) and, 214, 215–17, 223–24; sexual harrassment and, 223–24

Rio de Janeiro: Candelária massacre, 49–51; cultural nationalism vs. economic globalization in, 70; as dystopian theater of neoliberalism, 8–9; Earth Summit (1992), 42, 43–48; favela "pacification" program, 9–10, 13; favela tourism, 164–70, *168*; in films and media, 166; humanitarian "revolution" (2011), 8–14; Jacarenzinho favela and security technologies, 159; Lapa District, 65–67, 79–82, 85–86; leftist alliance and Benedita da Silva reform agenda, 147–49; the Mangue, 81; as narcotrafficking hub, 152; Plano Maravilha (1999), 160; "quality of life" sweeps, 66; security and pacification operation before Earth Summit, 45–46; shadow-state uprising (2002), 143–46, 149; Strategic Plan (1999), 157; touristic heritage projects vs. sex workers in urban spaces, 79–86; *travestis*, 65–67, 84, 254n1, 254n3, 254n6. *See also* Favela-Bairro project in Serrinha; Operation Princess; samba politics vs. security politics in Rio

Rio de Janeiro State Council for Women's Rights, 185

Riotur, 153

Rizzo, Helen, 224

Rocinha favela, Rio de Janeiro, 167–69

rodoviarismo (highwayism), 79–80

Rofel, Lisa, 242

roll-out neoliberalism, 131–32, 238–39

Rosen, Fred, 240

Rousseff, Dilma, 11–12, *12*, 235, 251–52

Rückert, Arne, 240–41, 242–43

Rushdi, Nuha, 224–28, *227*

Ryff, Tito, 82–83

Sabahy, Hamdeen, 235

Sadat, Anwar, 223

Saeed, Khaled, 2

Salafis, 101, 112–17, *114*, 256n1

Salah, Ahmed, 224

Salama, Salama, 220–21

samba politics vs. security politics in Rio: overview, 140–43; Benedita da Silva and state reform efforts, 147–49; Brazilian Left

and, 139–40; cordialism, 145, 148, 156–57, 159; Favela-Bairro project and, 150–52, 153–54, 160, 169–70; favela tourism projects and, 163–69; racial democracy narratives, 152, 156–57, 160, 170; shadow-state uprising (2002) and, 143–46, 149

samba schools, 150, 153–54, 187

Santos, Ademir dos, *165*

Sarney, José, 258n4

Sassen, Saskia, 245–46

SCAF (Supreme Council of the Armed Forces), Egypt, 1

Scott, James, 25

securitization: critical desecuritization, 232–33; defined, 27; evolution from development and liberalization toward, 52; mechanisms of, 67; parahuman positionality, queering, and dynamics of, 209–10; shift from liberalization to, 237–40; subjectivities and, 100. *See also specific cases*

security state, neoliberal: Egyptian revolution and, 3, 5; Mubarak and, 2–3; theories of, 21–22. *See also specific cases*

self-determination, 47–48

self-immolators, 222

semiperiphery: emergence of term, 245; generative nature of linkages between, 41; hotspots and emerging forms in, 15–16; the resistant local and, 243–46; respectability politics and, 215; role of, 245; world-systems theory and, 27–28. *See also* Brazil; Egypt

Sem Vergonha (Without Shame) project, 197

Sen, Amartya, 23

Serrinha, Rio de Janeiro. *See* Favela-Bairro project in Serrinha

sex slavery discourses. *See* Operation Princess

"Sexta Negra" project (dos Santos), *165*

sex tourism: Brazilian feminists and, 175; cabaret zones at Pyramids Road and Nile Waterfront, Cairo, 86–92; Cairo Summit and, 54; conferences and accords on, 92–95; Copacabana and, 179; executive identity vs., in Rio, 82–86; Operation Shangrilá and, 189–91; Vice Police stations in Rio and, 187

sex trafficking: Brazilian feminists and, 175; Brazilian nationalism and, 194–95; CEDAW and, 206; children, focus on, 173, 190;

Starykh, Oleg, 188
Stiglitz, Joseph, 237
Strauss-Kahn, Dominique, 252
Sufism, 112–17, *114*, *119*, *120*
suicide bomber, romance of, 222
summits. *See* conferences and summits
Supreme Council of the Armed Forces
    (SCAF), Egypt, 1

tabloid media, 188–89
Tantawi, Hussein, 1
Tarrow, Sidney, 21–22
technoprofessional class, Atta on, 132–33
Telles, Edward, 157
terrorism and antiterrorist campaigns: Luxor
    Massacre (1997), 123; protesters as hyper-
    sexualized terrorist masculinities, 211–13;
    queer subjects in Cairo and, 74, 255n10;
    Tarrow on, 21; war on "sexual terrorism,"
    221
Third Way, 237–39
Tickell, Adam, 131, 238
Tilly, Charles, 21
time-bomb masculinity, 218–24
Touraine, Alain, 237
tourism and tourist development: Cairo sex
    tourism, 91–92; Egyptian economy, role
    in, 105; Islamic Cairo and, 105–12; Luxor
    Massacre (1997), 123; in Rio favelas, 160,
    164–70, *168*; Rio sex tourism vs. execu-
    tive image, 82–86; Serrinha community
    projects, 164; transnational movement
    against sex tourism and trafficking, 92–95.
    See also heritage development
Tourism Ministry (Brazil), 190
trabalhismo. *See* workerism
trafficking interventions as human-security
    phase, 29. *See also* narco-trafficking;
    Operation Princess; sex trafficking
transregionalism, 55–58
travestis, 65–67, 84, 254n1, 254n3, 254n6
tropicalism: indigenous elites and, 28; ori-
    entalism, cultural miscegenation, and,
    58–63; racial democracy narratives and,
    170
True Egyptian People (Darb al-Ahmar Com-
    mittee for National Consciousness), 124–
    26, *125*, *126*
Twine, France Winddance, 157

UN Conference on Environment and Devel-
    opment (Earth Summit, Rio de Janeiro
    1992), 42, 43–48
UN Conference on Population and Develop-
    ment (Cairo Summit, 1994), 42, 51–54,
    229
UN cycle of social conferences, 43–44
UNESCO, 95
Unified Public Health System (SUS), Brazil,
    191
United Nations, Brazil's sexual-orientation
    resolution at, 63
United Nations Development Programme
    (UNDP), 105, 106, 110
United Nations Office against Drugs and
    Organized Crime (UNODC), 184
United States: Bush and Brazilian sex traffick-
    ing campaigns, 193–94; Iraq, invasion of,
    55, 205; racism against Arabs and Mus-
    lims in, 203; "street terrorism" laws, 221;
    welfare "reform" in, 215. *See also* New York
    City
University of Public Security and Social De-
    velopment (UN), 11
UN Security Council: Brazil campaign for seat
    on, 59, 184; Resolution 1325 on "Women,
    Peace, and Security," 204–5, 207–8
UN Special Rapporteur for Child Trafficking,
    Prostitution, and Child Pornography, 187
UN World Conference against Racism (Dur-
    ban, South Africa, 2001), 54–55
UN World Conference on Women (Beijing,
    1995), 54
UPPS (Police Pacification Units), Brazil, 9,
    10, 13
urban spaces, sexualized. *See* planning and
    urban renewal; sexuality politics
USAID, 194

value protection, Atta's notion of, 134, 136
Vargas, Getulio, 150, 153, 183
Vargas, João, 159
Vice Police Stations (Delegacias de Jogos e
    Costumes), 173–74, 187, 258n4
visibility. *See* hypervisibility
vulgarity: cultural rescue and, 117, 219; femi-
    nist respectability politics and, 142, 215,
    216; mawlids and, 116; as queer politics,
    76, 226; as resistance, 216, 219; Rio's Lapa